Trial By Conspiracy

Jonathan Boyd Hunt

TRIAL
BY
CONSPIRACY

GreeNZone

AUCKLAND   LONDON

A GreeNZone Publication

First published in New Zealand 1998

Copyright © Jonathan Boyd Hunt 1998

The right of Jonathan Boyd Hunt to be identified as author of this work has been asserted in accordance with Sections 77 and 78 of the Copyrights, Designs and Patents Act 1988.

ISBN 0 473 05123 0

Printed and bound in Great Britain by
Caledonian International Book Manufacturing

Typeset in Sabon by Kestrel Data, Exeter

Cover design by Rex Features

GreeNZone Publishing – a division of GreeNZone Ltd

"*Mr Rusbridger is not yet convinced he has made himself safe. In fact, he is worried that the Hamilton affair could yet turn into a Dreyfus case, and that he himself as the main hunter will be hunted himself in turn, and destroyed, as were the others who did down the innocent Jewish captain.*"

Paul Johnson, 15 November 1997

STATEMENT BY IAN GREER

19 Catherine Place
London SW1E

Tel: 0171 630 5651
Fax: 0171 233 7908

On or about 27th October 1997, I received a telephone call from a journalist concerning a planned press conference, at which Mr Jonathan Hunt was due to present the conclusions of his investigation into the so-called cash for questions affair. The report was due to be presented the following day. I was told that The Guardian newspaper were "out to get him." They were, I was told, delving into the past of Mr Hunt and his colleague, Mr Malcolm Keith-Hill. I was informed that the Guardian would be seeking to "rubbish" both men, claiming that their journalistic credentials were dubious and that their business record was questionable. In short, The Guardian would be seeking to destroy the reputation of the two gentlemen and, in so doing, the credibility of their report.

Signed IAN B. GREER   14th November 1997

Acknowledgements

Without Malcolm Keith-Hill, it is doubtful whether this book would have happened. His dedication in unearthing evidence, especially in those darkest of days that followed the publication of the Downey Report, was a source of strength that kept the investigation alive. His contribution was sorely missed when financial circumstances forced him to return home to Brazil in December 1997.

This book would certainly not have happened without the support of my parents, who financed my activities for the best part of eighteen months; and the love and support of Adele Maddock, who worked all hours producing copies of our report as it evolved over the last year. I cannot thank them all enough.

It is a testament to the human spirit that so many people have been disposed to help, for Neil Hamilton was condemned corrupt by a newspaper, then an official Parliamentary Inquiry, and then almost every organisation that makes up the British media. To those journalists with minds of their own who publicised our work, I am especially grateful to the staff and management of BBC TV and BBC GMR Radio, Manchester; in particular Jim Hancock; Liam Fogerty; Robin Crystal; Richard Ewitt and Michelle Daniel. I am indebted to journalist James Heartfield and his editor Mick Hume of *Living Marxism*; Stephen Glover of the *Daily Telegraph* and the *Spectator*; and Frank Johnson and Paul Johnson, also of the *Spectator*. To those who tried but were prevented, my thanks go out to Ambrose Evans-Pritchard of the *Daily Telegraph*; Jane Corbin and Thea

Guest of BBC *Panorama*; and Steve Daly of CNN *Impact*, Washington, USA. For their moral support or counsel my thanks go to Graham Forrester and Ben McCarthy of ITN; Peter Clarke of the Scottish edition of the *Sunday Times*; Eve Kay of RDF Television; and politicians Baroness Turner; Gerald Howarth MP; Nick Winterton MP and Teresa Gorman MP. My apologies go to Steve Boggan and his editor on the *Independent*, whose interest in our work came just after I had entered a contract with my publisher requiring me to lie low until nearer publication date.

For their help in our research, I am indebted to: John Gregson of Great Budworth Post Office; Lorana Sullivan, formerly of the *Observer*; Ian Greer and Andrew Smith, formerly of Ian Greer Associates; Francesca Pollard; Bob Loftus; Eamon Coyle, Clemency Ames; Edward Leigh MP; and the staff of Central Library and Companies House, Manchester. I owe special thanks to Bernard Dillon and his staff at Prontaprint, Northwich.

In May 1997, in the aftermath of the general election, there was little realistic prospect of a book, a TV documentary, or anything else coming to fruition. Yet Neil Hamilton willingly allowed himself to be interrogated day after day, in what, at that time, must have seemed a pointless pursuit during a very low point for him and his wife, Christine. During the months that followed, both their lives were disrupted by my constant telephone calls at all hours of the day and night, and though this must have exacerbated their ordeal, they never complained about my barracking. Over the last fifteen months they have won my immense admiration, respect and thanks.

I save my final thanks for my publisher, for few indeed would entertain a book such as this. With goodwill from decent people it will prevent from ever happening again the possibility that a deranged and powerful man could join forces with a handful of corrupt journalists and, as a consequence, steer an unthinking media and Parliament to lead the national damnation of an innocent man, as happened between 1994 and 1997, in Great Britain.

Foreword

This is a story of dedication and detection.

It is the story of how two men dedicated over a year of their lives to the detection of wrongdoing. How they unearthed a minutiae of evidence to eventually prove that Tory MP and Minister for Trade Neil Hamilton was not guilty of accepting bribes from Mohamed Fayed; in so doing they also proved that Fayed himself was guilty of many nefarious deeds; above all they proved that *The Guardian* newspaper was guilty of publishing gossip as fact and lies as truth, and of vilifying an man whom they knew to be innocent.

1

Damned Without Evidence

THE HAMILTONS WERE PREPARING TO CELEBRATE AND WE WERE preparing to film their joy at being vindicated. We were sitting with Christine Hamilton in her flat in Battersea. It was a modest pied-à-terre on the fifth floor of an unimposing modern block, comfortable but no more. As soon as the good news was announced we would be going to join her husband at a friend's flat in Westminster for a party.

It was 3 July 1997 and for two months my colleague, Malcolm Keith-Hill, and I had been researching for a programme we hoped to make about the Hamilton Affair. We now wanted some exclusive footage of Christine Hamilton's elation at receiving the news over the phone from her husband that his name had been cleared.

Christine was in an ebullient mood as we waited for Neil to ring from a private room in the House of Commons, where he was reading the findings of the Downey Report into the "Cash for Questions" controversy. She damped down her nerves at the long wait by making us endless cups of tea.

Every time the phone rang we started the cameras rolling and proceeded to film her as she picked up the receiver, ready for the spontaneous outburst of relief that was bound to come with the news that their names had been cleared, their nightmare was over and they were free to get on with their lives. Then, as we realised within a few moments that it was not the call we were waiting for, we would switch off the camera and the sound and go back to our tea.

Christine was relentlessly cheerful. When ITN rang asking for an interview, and "Newsnight" wanted Neil to appear in the programme that evening, she told them they would have to pay for interviews now.

'We're out of work, you know,' she said. 'We don't have any income and we have to make our living any way we can. What's the going rate?' The calls kept coming from papers, television and radio companies and she seemed to be enjoying herself as she negotiated with them all.

Then the calls became more intermittent and we began to wonder what was happening. We had expected to hear from Neil within an hour of dropping him off at the House. Eventually the phone fell ominously silent.

'Why doesn't he call?' Christine kept asking to the room at large. 'What can have gone wrong?'

We imagined that the Downey Report would be a hefty document to wade through, but all Neil had to do was read the conclusions in order to know that his name had been cleared once and for all. We had all studied the evidence and submissions a hundred times and almost knew them by heart.

'Perhaps he's gone straight to Razz's flat and he's going to call from there,' I suggested after a couple of hours had gone by.

Christine seemed surprised at the idea. She and Neil were as close as any married couple, who also worked together, could be. She had been his political secretary and neither of them ever seemed to have any secrets from the other. Her fiercely protective attitude to her husband had made her a mockery in the media, who saw her as "a wife from hell" and a "battle-axe". Nevertheless her support had never wavered for a second.

She rang their friend's flat where the celebration was due to take place and we watched her puzzled expression as she tried to get to speak to her husband. Neil was there, but, it seemed, didn't want to come to the phone. She hung up, shaking her head, unable to work out what was happening.

'Jonathan,' she said eventually, 'you ring and talk to him. Find out what's going on.'

I did as she asked and Razz duly brought Neil to the phone.

'Don't let your facial expression betray anything, Jonathan,' Neil warned me and I tried to do as he instructed. 'Downey has found the evidence against me . . . well, the word he used was "compelling." He believes I took the cash on the word of Fayed and his office staff. Don't say anything to Christine, just bring her here to the flat so that I can tell her myself. Okay? Don't let her drive herself. You drive her.'

'Right, Neil.' I spoke as if I were in a trance. I simply couldn't believe what I was hearing. How was it possible that Sir Gordon Downey, the Parliamentary Commissioner for Standards, could have found *compelling* evidence that Neil Hamilton had taken payments from Mohamed Fayed to ask questions in Parliament? We had been given access to the same material as Downey and had been over and over it. We were completely convinced of Neil's innocence. What could we have missed that Downey had found, that had brought him to totally the opposite conclusion?

'What is it, Jonathan?' Christine wanted to know. 'What's happened?'

'Nothing, Christine,' I said, putting on a bright expression. 'Let's all go round to Razz's'.

I tried to bluff my way through it, so that she could hear the news from Neil personally and they could comfort one another. I couldn't have been very convincing because she went through to the bedroom and called the number again, demanding to speak to Neil and to be told what was going on. Minutes passed. We waited, silently in the lounge. Finally, I heard her replace the receiver and I instructed the cameraman to film her coming back into the room. She was nakedly upset and not happy to be filmed.

'Just say something to the camera, Christine,' I coaxed. 'Something for the record. We may need it.'

'Downey's got it wrong,' she said, her voice drained of emotion.

'So what happens now?' I asked.

'Well . . .' She raised her hands. 'We just have to carry on. Life goes on.'

That night our snippet of film appeared on the ITN news and the nation tutted once more over Christine Hamilton's apparent insensitivity. If only they had known what she had been through in the previous few years and what she was going to have to continue going through, people might have seen her in a more sympathetic light.

It was not the first time I had seen the woman who always managed to present such a strong facade to the cameras slide into despair, and it certainly wouldn't be the last. Like her husband, she always seemed to be able to raise her spirits when there were cameras or reporters around, but the downs were just as dramatic as the ups. At that moment, watching her standing in front of us in the flat in Battersea, alone and disliked by almost everyone in the country, I knew that I would not be able to walk away from this story. Not until I had unearthed the truth and forced the British media to face it.

When I had arrived at the flat that morning I had imagined that the exclusive footage of Christine's reaction to the release of the Downey Report would be invaluable when, eventually, our documentary on the "cash for questions" affair was commissioned. It would, I thought, wrap it up ready for someone like "Panorama" to broadcast. Instead, I found that I had entered a tragedy in the making that would consume my every waking hour for over a year, and invade my dreams as well. We were going to have to uncover every possible detail about the affair, correlate every testimony, check and double check every written submission in search of anomalies that might have passed us by in our initial months of research.

The idea of filming the Hamiltons themselves during "Downey Day" had only occurred to me the day before as I drove down to London in my ex-MoD Montego, which is frequently mistaken for a taxi because of the throbbing diesel engine and telephone antennae bristling from the roof. The moment the idea struck me I called Malcolm, who was due to come down later.

'Hire a two man crew,' I said into the hands-free set as I trundled south, 'and have them waiting for me on the doorstep of the Hamiltons' flat first thing in the morning. We'll follow them all day, film them getting in and out of cars, going to the House of Commons and Christine's reaction to the news.' It was going to cost me £700, which was money I could ill spare at that moment, but I was reasonably confident it would be well spent.

The next morning we were ready to film Neil coming out of the flat on his way to breakfast with an accountant at the Hilton Hotel, and then on to a second meeting with somebody who was Somebody in the City. Later that same morning we filmed him going into the Palace of Westminster via the Lords entrance in Abingdon Street, to avoid the media pack waiting at the St Stephen's entrance to the Commons. Only one other crew thought to cover the Lords entrance. They were from the BBC, which meant that all our material was still virtually exclusive. Relieved to see that ITN had missed the opportunity, I dropped a tape into their Millbank studios on the way back to the flat.

After Christine had heard that the inquiry had found against Neil, Malcolm and the film crew climbed into my car while I drove her in the Hamiltons' old Rover. The electric window was jammed half open but neither of us cared. The air was warm and we were both lost in our own thoughts, unable to grasp the enormity of what had happened. Christine still wasn't crying, just sighing in despair and disbelief at the verdict.

When we reached the flat I took her upstairs to the party that had turned into a wake, attended by a few of the Hamiltons' remaining, faithful supporters. As soon as Christine came in Neil embraced her awkwardly, taking her over to a sofa where they sat, silently hugging one another. Rupert Grey, their solicitor, talked in subdued tones to Gerald Howarth MP, one of Neil's staunchest friends and allies. None of us knew what to say or do. Malcolm came up to join us, leaving the camera crew downstairs. An awkward silence hung over the small gathering of people, all of us averting our eyes from the couple whose life together was now officially in ruins. We nibbled self-consciously on the sandwiches and vol-au-vents that were supposed to be for the celebration. None of us could understand how we could all have been so wrong. What could we all have missed in the evidence that Downey had found? Gerald Howarth tried to keep the Hamiltons' spirits up, spouting well-meaning clichés about how we would all have to keep going. They were too shocked to take it in.

Malcolm and I decided to leave them in private and went downstairs to speak to the crew. I would not have let them come up and film the sadness in the flat, even had the Hamiltons agreed to it, but I was more determined than ever to make the film work. Since we had paid for the crew we might as well get some footage of the Downey Report being officially brought out at 4.00pm. For a few moments my confidence had been knocked by the result but the more I thought about it, the more my faith in our research came back. It simply was not possible that both Malcolm and I could have been that wrong.

Howarth had arranged to meet us in the lobby of the House of Commons at four-thirty to hand over two copies of the huge three-volume report. We already knew most of the material in volumes two and three intimately, having had access to many of the submissions and almost all of the transcripts of the oral examinations. It was just Downey's conclusions in the thin volume one that were a mystery.

I took the report and went straight to the green outside to do a 'piece to camera.'

'I've just collected this report,' I said as the camera whirred, 'from inside the members' lobby there, and I don't know what's in it. I don't know what we've missed. How Sir Gordon Downey can have come to his conclusions when our conclusions are completely the opposite is beyond me. So what I'm going to be doing tonight is go through this with a fine tooth comb . . .' But I was so wrought up that every time I tried to finish, the words came out in the wrong order. We did take after take after take as I became more and more frustrated, until eventually I gave up and paid off the camera crew. It had been a long day and I was exhausted.

Malcolm and I went back to our hotel rooms, Malcolm started reading the report's conclusions and I began ringing round the various television and radio news-rooms, the current affairs programmes and political editors of the nationals, trying to lobby people. But I couldn't get anyone to listen. Neil was guilty and that was official.

I decided to go down to the television studios in Millbank to see if I could find someone there to listen to what I had to say. There I found a huge media pack milling around in the corridor outside the Sky TV studio. I soon ascertained that they were there because Neil was giving an interview in the building somewhere. I circulated amongst them without saying anything, listening to what they were saying and trying to assess the mood. There was a balding man of about forty who seemed to be whipping up the crowd with a sort of derogatory monologue on the failings of Neil and Christine, making them laugh like schoolchildren.

'I wonder how much they're being paid for this interview,' he jeered. 'They got seventy five quid for the last one! There's no end to this guy's avarice.'

I felt a rush of protectiveness for the Hamiltons, having seen what they'd been through. I had been present when Christine had negotiated fees for the interviews. At that time she expected to have Neil's name cleared, her spirits were high, and it had not seemed inappropriate to be trying to scrape together some money to pay the mortgage and legal bills.

'Have you got a problem with that, then?' I asked, my voice cutting through the general air of mockery. Every head in the crowd swivelled my way.

The balding man swivelled with the rest. 'Who are you?' he demanded.

'Who the hell are *you*?' I snapped. I could almost hear the bell ringing for the start of the first round.

'John Sweeney,' he said, 'from the *Observer*.'

I recognised his name. I was familiar with some of his work in *The Observer*.

'I'm Jonathan Hunt,' I informed him. 'Freelance journalist. So what's your problem about being paid for interviews? Unless you're against the idea on principle, I don't see what your objection is.'

'But he used to be a Government minister,' Sweeney replied. It was a weak response and he knew it.

'But that's the point. He *used* to be a Government minister and she *used* to work for him. Now neither of them work for anyone, they don't have any income, and they still have a mortgage to pay.'

'Why are you interested in this?' he asked, speaking from the back of a now silent crowd.

'I've been on this case for the last two months,' I said, ' and I don't find any evidence at all that Hamilton took cash for questions and I can't understand why Downey has come to the opposite conclusion. My colleague and I have been through all the evidence and we can't see anything "compelling" about it at all.'

'Who's paying you?'

'No one's paying me.'

'Then why are you doing it?'

'I'm doing it for the same reason you would probably do it. I know I've got a story here that's totally at odds with what everybody else is saying and I'm not going to walk away from that until I've found out what's at the root of it. If you were in my position, I'm sure you'd do the same thing.'

'You don't know about Hamilton,' he protested. 'You don't know about his past.'

'What past? You're not talking about when he went to a Fascist rally when he was a student, are you?'

'Yeah, all that stuff.'

'I don't know about you,' I said, 'but if I was a student on thirty bob a week and somebody offered me an all-expenses paid week in the Adriatic to rip the piss out of a bunch of Italian Fascists I would be on the first plane out.' I was half expecting him to resurrect the old tale about Hamilton larking about on a visit to the Reichstag in 1983, when he gave a comic two-fingered moustache gesture and Hitler salute.

'Look, John,' I said, 'I don't know you from Adam, but isn't it just possible that you have this animosity towards Hamilton because you've been conditioned by what you perceive him to be, rather than what he is?'

He paused. 'It's possible,' he said pensively. I admired him for having the humility to admit that he might be wrong in front of the crowd he had been showing off to a few minutes earlier, especially as I knew of the snide things he had written about Hamilton in *The Observer*. I had a feeling our paths would be crossing again before much longer. He was the sort of person I needed to get on our side.

(Some time later John Sweeney wrote a book about the Tatton election and the demise of Neil Hamilton. At the end, he mentions standing outside the studios that evening, and that it suddenly dawned on him to think, "what are we doing to these people?" Though his book gave a recklessly biased account of the election and the two protagonists, I was still impressed to see that our exchange of words at Millbank had caused him to think that his treatment of the Hamiltons just might be wrong.)

After the Sky TV session Neil and Christine emerged into the pack which reverted to vulture mode, shouting questions. The Hamiltons walked on, heads high, saying nothing.

I popped downstairs to the ITN studios and dropped in the final tape, agreeing a payment of £300 which would help to defray my costs for the day. The film of Christine hearing the news would eventually, with repeat showings, recoup the rest of the cost of the crew but it still wouldn't cover our travel or hotel costs. Lack of money was a constant source of worry.

Later, I returned when Neil and Christine were being interviewed for Channel Four News. When the session got under way, Neil kept trying to put forward his arguments but the interviewer wasn't listening, she just kept on attacking.

'Does he look like a man who's guilty?' I asked ITN producer Adam Barry, standing next to me.

'No,' he admitted. 'He doesn't.'

'He's fighting for his life,' I said, 'because he's innocent.'

On the way out I recognised a chap who had been with a camera crew in among the melee in the corridor outside the Sky studios. 'Hi', I said. 'I don't know what you thought about my little duel with John Sweeney, but I just couldn't just stand there and let him rant on. He's clueless.'

'Graham Forrester,' he said, outstretching his hand, 'who are you again?'

We ended up talking about the case for a good half-hour until he had to leave for the day. 'Here's my card,' he said, handing it to me. My home number's on it, so give me a call when you have time.' The card read *Graham Forrester, Senior Political Producer, ITN.*

'I will,' I said. 'Bye.'

I made my way back to the hotel in Victoria and went up to Malcolm's room to see how he was getting on with his perusal of the Downey Report.

'How's it going? What's in it?' I asked as he let me in.

'There's nothing in it,' he said. 'It's impossible to see how Downey reached his conclusions. It's as if he plucked them out of the air.'

'Thank God for that,' I said, 'I was beginning to think it must be us.'

Before turning in I rang Neil on his mobile phone to check how they were bearing up after such a devastating day. They seemed to have gone back to their defiant "life-goes-on" mode again and Christine told me that they were planning to go on Radio Five Live the next morning.

'Christine,' I said, 'that won't help your case. You've just been branded as corrupt. You need to lie low for a while or people will think you're so thick-skinned you'll lose any residual sympathy that might still be out there for you.'

'We have to keep going onward Jonathan – onward, onward!'

I was not impressed by the battle cry.

'Just have a rest for a week, a period of mourning!'

We must all have be overwrought and over-tired because the argument escalated into a foolish screaming match with both of them.

'Neil,' I pleaded when he took her place on the mobile, 'you've got to think about the Select Committee!' I was referring to the parliamentary committee to which Downey reported. They which had the power to reject his report.

'The Select Committee aren't going to do anything, Jonathan, they're a bunch of plonkers!'

'Yeah, but you can't assume you're not going to have any success with them. Concentrate on your address to them.'

'There's no point, Jonathan.'

'There's every bloody point!'

'What! With people like Dale Campbell-Savours and Alan Williams sitting on it? I have no chance whatsoever!'

It ended with a terse disconnection. Half an hour later I phoned their flat and left a message of apology on their answering machine, to retrieve before they turned in. It wasn't, after all, any of my concern what radio programmes they chose to go on. The following morning Christine rang back, putting the whole thing down to frayed nerves and exhaustion and returning my apology. I had a point, she conceded. Neil shouldn't give up on the Committee but, she explained, they were finished in politics and had no other way of earning a living. They had to keep going as long as the media was interested.

A few weeks later they went on to feature on "Have I Got News for You" and the "Clive Anderson Show," both of which enjoyed a mixed reception. Because they took the teasing so well, some people thought they gave the impression of being thick-skinned and brazen, which did nothing to improve their image. Others thought they came across as jolly good sports. But for sure, the media wasn't going to give them a break they were just going to use them as a vehicle for easy sniggers.

Some time in the future, world historians may look back on the "cash for questions" affair that helped topple the British Conservative Government in 1997, and reopen the case. They may well wonder how Britain's Parliament and press, those two cornerstones of the world's most celebrated democracy, could have allowed themselves to be swept up by their own hysteria into condemning a man who was innocent. They may further speculate how, given that Parliamentary and press condemnation was based exclusively on the testimony of a ruthless, documented liar and his closest staff, such a miscarriage of justice could ever have occurred.

Downey's report could come to be compared with the show trials of Senator McCarthy in America in the early fifties. The historians will probably debate why neither Parliament nor the press questioned Downey's lack of legal training or his suitability for such a task, and how he could have reached the conclusions he did against such overwhelming evidence to the contrary.

Neil's treatment is already being compared with that meted out in France to Alfred Dreyfus in 1894, when the innocent Jewish Captain was accused of passing secrets to the German military. On the back of an outcry of public condemnation Dreyfus was stripped of his honours, tried, sentenced, and exiled. When evidence emerged that another officer, Ferdinand Esterhazy, was the real traitor, the whole of France had so committed itself that, instead of absolving Dreyfus, the French military fabricated new evidence to confirm his guilt. It was not until 1906, four years after his death, that Dreyfus was finally exonerated.

In Britain the injustice against Neil Hamilton was likewise driven by one man – Mohamed Fayed, who found a surprising ally within the British media: a broadsheet newspaper willing to fabricate evidence and lie to support the story they wanted to tell.

The Hamiltons, a pleasant, hardworking couple, have an unfortunate manner in front of the cameras. He appears arrogant, a typical Tory stuffed shirt, while she had the aura of the typical bossy Tory wife who went out of fashion long ago. The media needs heroes and villains and the public was ready to believe the worst of any member of a political party that had been in power since 1979, and whose departure for the Opposition benches was years overdue. The Hamiltons' image fitted the villainous Tory stereotype and they didn't have the presentational skills needed to bring the public round to their side.

The opposition parties saw an opportunity to use the propaganda being levelled at Neil to oust the Tories. In a panic to avoid losing the election, many former friends and colleagues within his own party also turned against their one-time minister, as if trying to exorcise an evil spirit from their midst. No-one seemed interested in whether any of Mohamed Fayed's accusations were true.

The die was cast for the fall of a Government and a huge personal tragedy. The power of the media had proved absolute.

A wholly false story had been manufactured and had become a self-perpetuating prophecy. Once a story is "on the wires," over-worked journalists and reporters, anxious to meet deadlines and fill their pages, often do not bother to check facts themselves; they simply reproduce what has already been said especially if the story has the endorsement of an exalted newspaper.

In the Hamiltons' case, the snowball of misinformation had been set on its course, rolling down the hill, growing in size with every repetition. The public, assuming that the media had checked their facts and that there could not be this much smoke without fire, came to accept that Neil Hamilton was as sleazy as he was painted. So, when a white-clad Sir Galahad appeared to challenge his seat in the Commons, they welcomed him with open arms and Martin Bell was voted into Parliament on the "anti-sleaze ticket". But while the media presented and supported the white-suited man of the people, they avoided publicising the inter-party machinations that went on to make his victory and Hamilton's humiliation on election night a foregone conclusion.

Although the Hamiltons still had a small band of loyal friends and supporters, none of them had the time or the inclination to root out the evidence needed to clear Neil's name and expose the conspiracy that had been perpetrated against him. By the time the Downey report was published the public were heartily sick of the subject anyway, keen to sweep the whole sorry mess under the carpet and start afresh with New Labour. The Hamiltons had become a deeply unfashionable subject and no-one wanted to be associated with them.

Knowing the truth, and being sure that there were sinister forces at work in Neil's downfall, I didn't feel that I could or should abandon them. I had no idea then just how much work it was going to take to unravel the whole conspiracy, or just how much shameful Establishment skulduggery I would uncover, I only knew that I had to do it.

2

Behind The Facade

A YEAR EARLIER, WHEN I FIRST MET NEIL HAMILTON, I WAS vaguely aware that allegations of some sort had been made against him, but I had no idea of the details. The "cash for questions" scandal held no interest for me at all. I had enough cash problems of my own.

I was forty years old and living in a bed-sit in the centre of Manchester, having sunk what little money I had into starting up an independent television and video production company with a business partner. Even though the money wasn't exactly flowing in, prospects looked very promising. I was doing a series of short regional news features for Granada TV called "On the Hunt" in which I would doggedly set out to expose the sort of bureaucrats who make life a misery for the rest of us through their idleness or inefficiency. I was developing a bit of a reputation for myself as an investigative reporter (of sorts) who was willing to ask embarrassing questions of local councillors or police spokesmen, and able to put a humorous spin on the whole thing. People were starting to recognise me in the streets of Manchester, coming up to me and saying, 'Aren't you the guy who was giving that councillor a hard time on the telly last night?'

You could say that I have a somewhat obsessive nature. Once I discovered a good story, whether it was the closure of some much needed public facility or the disgusting state of a beautiful stately home that had been allowed to fall into rack and ruin, I would just keep on digging until I discovered who was responsible. One series of programmes I was particularly involved with was a study of the growing crime problem that was turning a district of East Manchester into an urban wasteland. The series was entitled "The Forgotten People of Openshaw."

As long as I was engrossed in my work I never really noticed my surroundings. My bed-sit in a converted Victorian house was just that – a room with a bed, a chair, and a Baby Belling cooker in the "kitchenette" area. It was clean and comfortable and only cost £45 a week. I was getting used to sharing a bathroom and pumping fifty pence pieces into the hot water meter, content as long as I had a base to operate from.

The Hamiltons' constituency home, of course, was very different from my own modest abode. When, in the summer of 1996, I went over to interview him about why banks were withdrawing from rural communities, we stood on the well-mown lawns outside the sprawling old rectory and he answered my aggressive questions equably and reasonably. He and his wife seemed like a typical Tory couple, not the sort of people I usually became friendly with, but they won my respect. I had known that Neil was a well-thought of local politician, liked by his constituents and nothing he did or said on that pleasant, sunny day, made me doubt that he had worked hard to earn that reputation.

At the end of the afternoon I went away and didn't even use the footage for the programme because I found a Lancaster councillor who had campaigned avidly against bank closures – Geraldine Smith, now MP for Morecambe and Lunesdale. I thought it unlikely the Hamiltons would feature in my life and work ever again.

Beneath that calm and confident facade, however, there must already have been stirrings of the misery to come. Like most of the population I was vaguely aware of the fact that allegations had been made against Neil but my interest in the details was almost non-existent. Even though, as it turned out, it was a story that would have made the best seller lists if written by Jackie Collins – a tale of multi-millionaires and international vendettas, massive business deals and political reputations – it had not caught my attention.

The seeds of the disaster had been sown back in the early seventies, when Lonrho, the multi-national conglomerate, headed by the late Roland 'Tiny' Rowland, came under serious attack from the then Tory Government for its alleged unscrupulous dealings in Africa. The attack culminated in Prime Minister Edward Heath's famous description of the company on 13 May 1973 as "the unacceptable face of capitalism."

The feud between Lonrho and the Tories became even fiercer three years later when the Department of Trade and Industry (DTI), published the findings of a two year investigation into the company. The inspectors' findings were so grave that the City of London Police Fraud Squad were instructed to investigate the allegations of fraud and UN sanctions-busting trading with apartheid Rhodesia. Tiny Rowland came out of it badly.

Ever since that report Rowland had harboured a grudge against the Tories. After acquiring *The Observer* newspaper in 1981, he used its columns to settle old scores, embarking on a number of damaging campaigns against Conservative governments and, in particular, Prime Minister Margaret Thatcher. His campaign made him highly unpopular with many of Thatcher's admirers, of whom the young and ambitious Neil Hamilton was one of the most ardent.

Rowland was perfect casting for a piratical billionaire: suave and ruthless in equal measure and a formidable foe, even for a powerful ruling party, and his swashbuckling exploits in Africa had made him a major player in a number of different businesses. But there was one company above all that he really coveted – the House of Fraser retail group, parent to the world-famous Harrods store in London's Knightsbridge.

Using Lonrho's clout Rowland managed to acquire a 29.9% shareholding in the company, but when Thatcher came to power in 1979 the DTI's investigation into Lonrho was still ringing in the Tories' ears. They had already suffered more than one drubbing from the Labour opposition over Lonrho. Consequently, they felt very jittery about letting Rowland take control of such a high profile company. The Government bought time by referring the matter to the Monopolies and Mergers Commission, whilst hoping that someone else would come along and buy House of Fraser first. They did not realise that there was a shark swimming into the waters who was far more dangerous than Tiny Rowland, and that this was the man who would eventually bring them down.

In the general election of 1983 Thatcher was swept back to power. Neil Hamilton, grandson of two Welsh coal miners and the son of a mining engineer, became MP for the Tatton constituency, one of the safest Tory seats in Britain, right in the heart of leafy rural Cheshire. It wasn't long before Neil's interest in freeing industry from red tape led him to the vice-chairmanship of the Conservative back-bench Trade and Industry Committee. He was a young man with a glittering career ahead of him.

In February 1984, along with other officers of the Committee, Neil attended a lunch with Professor Roland Smith, Chief Executive of House of Fraser, at Harrods. Probably because he was fearful of losing his job, the Professor was fervently opposed to the acquisition of the company by Rowland. The meeting had been arranged by Sir Peter Hordern MP, who was House of Fraser's paid parliamentary consultant. Its purpose was to enable the members of the Committee to learn first-hand how the group was still having to repel Rowland's hostile manoeuvres on the company. These manoeuvres were a challenge to the DTI embargo that frustrated Lonrho's aspiration to acquire absolute control.

On that day Neil went on the record as establishing an interest in the battle for Harrods. It was an interest that seemed perfectly innocent at the time but one that he would come to regret bitterly.

A Government insider then gave Rowland an off-the-record tip.

'All you need to do,' the official told him, 'is get rid of your shares, take the heat out of the situation, and then there's a good chance the DTI embargo on Lonrho will be lifted.'

Rowland decided that this was sound advice. He looked around for someone he could trust with whom to "park" his shares until the time came when he would want them back. His eyes alighted upon one of his fellow directors at Lonrho, Mohamed Fayed.

Born in 1929 in a small Egyptian village in the Nile's western delta, Fayed's childhood had been spent in the poor Gömrök quarter of the port of Alexandria, where his father, a school teacher, had moved his family in his search for a job. Fayed senior worked hard and eventually became a school inspector, but it was clear that, even as a boy, his son Mohamed had powerful ambitions far beyond becoming a humble school teacher.

'When I was eleven years old,' he would later tell journalists, 'I used to stand on the quayside in Alexandria and watch the English ships passing, with the officers on deck in their white uniforms. They were a dream to me. They were men of efficiency and men of honour. I dreamed of being like them.'

And so began his quest to become an Englishman. It was a quest that would grow into a obsession that would possess him so completely that eventually he would be willing to do almost anything in order to achieve a British passport.

After leaving school, (where, significantly, he earned the nick-name "Fayed the liar"), his early career began as a salesman for Singer Sewing Machines and Coca-Cola. One day, while relaxing on the beach, he met a young woman called Samira. Samira's brother was a major businessman with influential contacts. His name was Adnan Khashoggi, a middleman and trader who would later gain the reputation of being one of the world's most controversial arms dealers. Mohamed and Samira married in 1954 and Khashoggi made his new brother-in-law a manager in his business. Mohamed had his foot on the first rung of the ladder.

Four years later Khashoggi sacked Mohamed for doing illicit side-deals. No matter. By then Mohamed had made all the contacts he needed to take him to the court of the world's indisputably richest man, the Sultan of Brunei. By 1975 he was working as a commission agent, handling ever bigger deals, one of which involved a £7-million share swap between construction company Richard Costain Ltd and Lonrho. Acting on behalf of certain unnamed principals, Fayed was in on the deal and met Tiny Rowland for the first time. Within weeks Fayed had worked his way to a seat on the board of Lonrho.

So when Tiny Rowland looked around for someone wealthy enough to buy his shares yet not wealthy enough to do anything with them, Fayed seemed the ideal choice. Most importantly, Rowland needed someone he felt he could trust to stick to an agreement to sell the shares back when he needed them. Conse-quently, on 1 November 1984 Rowland came to an agreement whereby he exchanged his 29.9% shareholding in House of Fraser with Fayed for £138 million. It was probably the single biggest mistake of his chequered career.

Rowland and Lonrho's chairman, Lord Duncan-Sandys, duly gave up their seats on the House of Fraser board on 31 December 1984 and four days later Mohamed and his brother

Ali walked in. They took an instant shine to the place. There is no other store, outside New York, with anything like the international cachet of Harrods. The brothers knew that whoever owns Harrods owns a piece of the British Establishment. They decided they would like to have it for themselves.

Fayed immediately shifted huge sums of money into his Royal Bank of Scotland account from Switzerland and, on 11 March 1985, his merchant bankers, Kleinwort Benson, announced that over 50% of House of Fraser shareholders had accepted Fayed's offer of £4 per share. It came as no consolation to Rowland that Lonrho was released from its DTI block three hours *after* the announcement.

A blinkered Government breathed a sigh of relief that their plan seemed to have worked and Harrods had been rescued from Rowland. No one knew much about the Fayed brothers, they were just thankful to have blocked Rowland.

Rowland was outraged at the betrayal and he could not believe that Fayed had such ready access to the £615 million that had been required to make the purchase. He believed that Fayed had misrepresented his wealth to the DTI and to Kleinwort Benson to facilitate DTI approval, and that he must have been acting as a covert agent for another person or organisation. Rowland immediately ordered investigative journalists Melvyn Marckus, Michael Gillard and Lorana Sullivan from *The Observer* to unearth more about Fayed's background and to uncover the story behind the money that had been used to steal Harrods from under his nose.

Peter Wickman, a freelance journalist commissioned originally by the German magazine *Stern*, joined forces with the trio shortly after and the four set to research a story that would become one of this country's best pieces of investigative journalism of all time. They would uncover evidence which suggested that Fayed had been acting for himself after all, but using wealth he had acquired illicitly from the Sultan of Brunei during a period when he had worked for the Sultan and had enjoyed his power of attorney. But because the *Observer* was owned by Lonrho, the intrepid four never received any press awards for their sensational (and accurate) work.

Less concerned with accolades and more interested in what they found, Rowland collated their findings and, through Lonrho's new chairman, Tory MP Sir Edward du Cann, brought pressure to bear on the Thatcher Government to open an investigation into Fayed's acquisition. But the last thing that the Tories wanted to do, however, was to co-operate with the likes of Tiny Rowland.

Rowland was not a man to give up a fight. His unrelenting lobbying of the Government started to gain momentum and rattle the Fayed brothers. When Mohamed's brother, Ali, met Lord King, Chairman of British Airways, socially, he complained bitterly about Rowland's campaign against him and Mohamed.

'Can you recommend anyone who might be able to help me counter the intense parliamentary pressure Rowland is exerting?' he asked Lord King.

'We have a chap called Ian Greer who lobbies for us,' the BA Chairman replied affably, 'and we're very impressed. Would you like me to arrange a meeting?'

Fayed was as impressed with Ian Greer as Lord King had been and engaged his company, Ian Greer Associates (IGA), for an annual fee of £25,000 to put his case to influential MPs. Neil Hamilton, along with fellow MPs Tim Smith and Michael Grylls, had made no secret of his prior interest in the battle of House of Fraser and looked like a likely conscript to support Fayed's battle against Rowland. IGA's Managing Director, Andrew Smith, contacted all three MPs almost as soon as the ink was dry on his contract with Fayed.

'I listened to Greer's case,' Neil later told me, 'and declared a willingness to help in principle for two reasons. Firstly, I sympathised with Fayed because he seemed to be the underdog suffering Rowland's unjustified onslaught. At the time I was fighting a libel battle of my own against the BBC and could identify with him. Secondly, Rowland had always been very critical of Margaret (Thatcher).' (The libel action was over a "Panorama" programme titled "Maggie's Militant Tendency." Neil won the case, being awarded costs and damages and the BBC was forced to broadcast a humiliating apology.)

Over the next three and a half years Neil attended various meetings with Fayed, either at Fayed's offices at 60 Park Lane or at Harrods. His activity during this period on behalf of Fayed totalled nine written Parliamentary Questions, three parliamentary motions (called Early Day Motions or EDMs), two meetings, and a handful of letters to ministers. In one year (1986) he undertook no activity on Fayed's behalf at all.

In September 1987, although Neil denies that it coloured his support, he also accepted Al Fayed's hospitality, enjoying a private tour of the Duke and Duchess of Windsor's former home outside Paris, on which Fayed had bought the lease. For a few days prior to the tour, he and Christine stayed at Fayed's Ritz Hotel, one of the most expensive and luxurious in Paris.

However, a few months earlier Rowland's barracking of the Government paid off. On 9 April 1987, Michael Howard, Minister for Corporate Affairs at the DTI, appointed two independent inspectors – chartered accountant Hugh Aldous FCA and barrister Phillip Heslop QC – to investigate Fayed's acquisition of House of Fraser. (A month later Heslop resigned after it was suggested that he had links with Rowland; he was replaced by Henry Brooke QC.)

There were signs that Fayed was becoming worried, presumably because he knew that the evidence Rowland had amassed about him would prove to be true, and would completely undo the web of lies he had spun in order to gain control of Harrods. He fought back with desperate attempts to discredit Rowland but nothing deflected the inspectors. It became one of the most extensive and celebrated investigations ever carried out by the British Government. Their enquiries reached around the globe and took a year to complete – at a cost of £1,500,000 to the British taxpayer.

In their report the inspectors concluded that the Fayed brothers had lied in almost every aspect of their representations of their background and the acquisition of their wealth. They further concluded that the funds that had bought Harrods had almost certainly originated from the Sultan of Brunei without his knowledge. They also detailed how Fayed had stolen $100,000 from the Port au Prince Harbour Board in Haiti, had robbed and attempted to bribe his former brother in law, Adnan Khashoggi, and how he ruthlessly attacked and destroyed the characters of those who crossed him. In the years following publication of the report the evidence of just how many lies Fayed had told mounted up until it beggared belief.

The inspectors' conclusions on the deceit practised by the Fayed brothers on the British Establishment were so grave that within a week Nicholas Ridley, the Secretary of State for Trade and Industry, had forwarded them to the Serious Fraud Office and the Office of Fair Trading, delaying publication of the report. Because lying to Government Inspectors did not constitute a criminal offence at the time, however, Fayed got off scot free. As a direct consequence, Parliament's all-party Trade and Industry Select Committee began their own investigation into the powers of Government inspectors to ensure that in future it would be possible to prosecute. The law was subsequently changed and if the same DTI report came out today Fayed would undoubtedly be treated as a criminal.

Within a few months, Fayed's critics in Parliament, such as Labour MP Jeff Rooker and Tory MP Teddy Taylor, were becoming restless and starting to ask awkward questions about the delay of the report's release. Both MPs then received a number of poisonous letters from Fayed in the name of a woman called Francesca Pollard (whom Fayed had tricked into becoming Tiny Rowland's enemy and now used as a mouthpiece) though in fact her letters were mostly composed by Fayed's private detective, Richard New.

Rowland was also becoming impatient while the Government passed the parcel around. Eventually he managed to acquire a copy of the report from a mole within the Fraud Squad. In March 1989, in an audacious move to pressurise the Government into publication, Rowland started up the presses for a special mid-week edition of *The Observer*, blazoning the juiciest extracts from the report about Fayed's scam across the front pages.

A year passed before the SFO completed their investigations and returned the report to the Department of Trade and Industry, which duly published it on 7 March 1990. But apart from causing Fayed and the Government great embarrassment, the exposure of Fayed's character would have one ramification above all others – it shattered his life-long ambition to acquire British citizenship. The prospects of realising his dream of becoming a member of the same society as those naval officers he had seen all those years before from the quayside in Alexandria were more remote than ever. If he wanted to continue his pursuit of a British passport, he had to find a way to have the Report revoked.

So he embarked on legal moves to have the DTI report annulled through the English courts and, when these failed, decided to go all the way to the European Court of Human Rights (ECHR).

But while Fayed overtly used the law to try and achieve his aim, he sometimes resorted to more underhand means.

Fayed exploited Francesca Pollard ruthlessly. Home Secretary Michael Howard, who had appointed the DTI inspectors when Corporate Affairs Minister, had his constituency leafleted with a document Fayed had printed titled "10 things you ought to know about Michael Howard." Members and advisers of the Trade and Industry Committee, who were critical that Fayed had been allowed to get away twice with making bogus representations to the DTI, came under all sorts of attacks, in particular the Committee's Conservative chairman, Ken Warren, who was subjected to scarcely-believable treatment. First of all he started receiving Pollard's (i.e. New's) defamatory letters. Secondly, like Michael Howard, the streets surrounding his home and constituency office were deluged with propaganda. Fayed also wanted Pollard to make similar attacks against other committee members, including fellow Tory Robin Maxwell-Hyslop and Labour members Doug Hoyle and Stan Crowther (more of all this later).

A special adviser to the Committee, Professor Barry Rider, came in for a different treatment that would hallmark all of Fayed's feuds against his enemies thereafter. Rider was an expert on company fraud, who was retained by the Committee in order to study DTI investigations in general, and the House of Fraser case in particular. Previously, he had been head of the Commercial Crime Unit at the Commonwealth Secretariat where, in September 1989, he was accused of fiddling his expenses. The allegations were totally false, and Rider believed they probably originated with any of those who had been incarcerated as a result of his investigations into company fraud. But when Fayed got wind of the allegations he authorised Richard New to leak the news to *Private Eye*, the satirical magazine. And even though the allegations were false, a lot of the mud stuck to Rider, thus doing his reputation immense harm. The result impressed Fayed. He now realised that the media could be a devastating tool in his battles to discredit his enemies.

In April 1992 Neil Hamilton became Minister for Corporate Affairs at the Department of Trade and Industry – the very department that had caused Fayed so much grief. As fate would have it, Neil was charged with responsibility for the same DTI report that Fayed was trying to have quashed in the European

Court. Although the two men had had no contact for two years, Fayed saw an opportunity to wield influence and immediately wrote Neil a fawning letter of congratulation, opening with the words "you can't keep a good man down."

The letter was not presented to Neil until ten days later. He immediately and freely disclosed his former close relationship with Fayed. He was advised by his officials that on no account should he reply, as any official communication from him could be construed as being sympathetic and any sympathy from a Minister at the DTI could be represented as support for Fayed's case before the ECHR against the Government. Neil therefore asked Sir Peter Hordern to pass on his thanks, together with his apologies and explanation that he would not be able to involve himself in issues connected with the Fayeds or House of Fraser, for fear of being accused of partiality in any decision-taking.

Fayed was outraged. He saw Hamilton's lack of a response to his letter as a slap in the face, a betrayal of his friendship and hospitality. Fayed had been preparing for an oral hearing at the Human Rights Commission in Strasbourg to consider the admissibility and merits of his application to the Human Rights Court itself. But instead of a helpful letter from a DTI minister, he received what in his eyes must have seemed a heartless rebuff from a former friend and ally.

Weeks after arriving at the DTI, Neil had made it known to his advisers that he wished to have no further dealings with matters concerning House of Fraser. However, officials advised that, as his support for the company had finished three years before, there was no obligation upon him to delegate matters and that it would be perfectly in order for him to take relevant decisions. Neil, mindful that it would be all too easy to give the wrong impression, still insisted that all matters concerning House of Fraser, Fayed, or Lonrho that came before the Department, should be delegated to another Minister. On June 4 he asked his secretary, Kate Spall, to write to his chief, the President of the Board of Trade, Michael Heseltine, requesting his release from dealing in related matters. From then on another DTI minister, Edward Leigh MP, was charged with all such responsibilities.

Three weeks earlier, however, on May 12, in response to a written question from Alex Carlile addressed to Michael

Heseltine, Neil had signed a standard written answer, prepared for him by DTI officials. Carlile had asked the President of the Board of Trade: '. . . what assessment he has made of the adequacy of the investigations carried out into the take-over of House of Fraser by the Fayed brothers; and if he will make a statement.'

The response, signed by Neil as if it had been written by himself, was formulaic and could hardly have been less helpful to Fayed:

> *The Inspectors' report, which was published on 7 March 1990, reflects a carefully considered and thorough investigation. Copies of the report were disclosed to other regulatory bodies to enable them to consider under their own powers or rules whether any disciplinary or regulatory action was appropriate. The responsibility for deciding whether to take action in such cases rests with the body concerned.*

Fayed was outraged at Neil's seeming endorsement of the DTI report, the timing of which could not have been worse from his point of view. Three days later, on 15 May 1992, the Human Rights Commission considered Fayed's application for the right to appeal to the ECHR. When the Commission granted Fayed his right to put his case before the Court, Fayed must have been pleased that he had overcome the first hurdle even without the help of his erstwhile friend. But, knowing his vindictive nature towards anyone who obstructed him, it is easy to imagine that he felt considerable hostility towards Neil Hamilton. The next logical step was to get even – with the man he now believed not only to have snubbed him, but also to have turned against him.

Having risen to a position of power and influence, Neil could have helped Fayed fulfil his dream of winning a British passport. However, he had amply demonstrated his intention to act with absolute probity. And that was a concept Fayed did not recognise or understand. As is his wont, he set out to wreak a terrible revenge.

None of this background was known to me that summer's day in 1996 as I stood on the lawn in the sunshine and Neil Hamilton fielded my questions about the closure of a local village bank while his wife cheerfully ferried cold drinks from the house. It would never have occurred to me that such a tranquil, prosperous scene in the apparently safe Tory seat of Tatton could have been resting upon such a potentially explosive powder keg of vengeance and political intrigue.

3

Enter The Man In The White Suit

MY PARENTS HAVE LIVED IN THE PICTURESQUE VILLAGE OF GREAT Budworth ever since my father sold up his haulage business and retired. With its leaning, timber-framed cottages, its ancient church, the pub, bowling green and even village stocks, it is everyone's idea of an old English hamlet. A few years ago, after an afternoon pottering in the garden, my mother re-entered the house to be confronted by a group of American tourists, admiring the beams and decor. They had been convinced that the sixteenth century, picture-book cottage was a tourist attraction.

Over the years my parents have become part of the community. My father is sexton at the church and tends the church yard, while Mum sings in the church choir. I would frequently drive out of Manchester, when the four walls of my bed-sit seemed to be closing in on me, in search of a home-cooked meal or two and a cosy bedroom in the peace of the countryside.

The village pub is the *George and Dragon*, where, on April 28, 1997, three days before the general election, I was sitting with my father enjoying a quiet pint when one of his friends came over to pass the time of day.

'What are you doing in here on a Monday?' I asked him, knowing him to be a weekend drinker only.

'That Martin Bell is up giving a talk,' he said, 'so I thought I'd have a listen.'

'Oh, is he?' I said. 'Well, if he comes in here I've got a few questions I'd like to ask him.'

Although I had given no thought to the Hamiltons for some

time, I had become aware of the television coverage they were receiving in the run- up to the May election. In particular I became interested since Martin Bell, the BBC news reporter, had decided to stand against Neil at the forthcoming election on an "anti-corruption" ticket. Because I had met the Hamiltons, and thought they were decent people, my attention had been caught by a news report in which they both confronted Bell during a press conference on Knutsford Heath. They demanded point blank to know if he believed that Neil was guilty of taking money from Fayed to ask questions in the House.

It had struck me as strange that Bell was taking such a stance while the investigation into Fayed's allegations against Neil was still under way. In effect Neil was being judged guilty before the case against him had been heard. I noticed that whenever Neil was interviewed, he was never given a chance to state his case. TV Presenters would just keep firing allegations at him, seemingly intent only on showing their worth as interrogators, rather than giving the man a chance to explain. I knew the technique well, having used it myself on occasion.

'I'll bring Bell over to meet you,' Dad's friend said, and sure enough Bell arrived at our table and made himself comfortable. He was in the company of the American actor, David Soul, the faded star who had played Hutch in the police series "Starsky and Hutch," back in the seventies.

'So, Martin,' I said after the introductions were over, 'why are you standing as an anti-corruption candidate before Downey has given his verdict on Neil Hamilton? There might not be any corruption to be anti about.'

'Well,' he said, obviously still high on the encouragement he had been receiving from his supporters, 'Hamilton's already admitted sufficient wrong-doings.'

'What do you mean?'

'For a start, he didn't declare his income tax or staying at the Ritz. Then he lied to Michael Heseltine. He didn't declare commission payments, he didn't declare his . . .'

'Everybody I know,' I interrupted, 'thinks that you're standing on the "cash for questions" issue. I'm really surprised that someone with your journalistic credentials should be standing for parliament before Downey's report's been published.'

'You don't have to vote for me,' he protested. 'You can vote for Neil Hamilton if you want.'

'I don't live in this constituency,' I replied, 'so that's irrelevant. But the real point is, other people, who don't know anything about these allegations, are going to assume that somebody of your integrity has taken a partisan view because you have satisfied yourself of their validity. Thousands of people are going to vote for you because of who you are and because you say you're against corruption. But how you can take the word of a man like Mohamed Fayed, like a child following the Pied Piper of Hamelin, against the word of a former Minister in her Majesty's Government, is beyond me.'

He looked shifty and unsettled and changed the subject. A minute or so later he made some excuse and headed for the door with Soul, who must have been bemused by it all, in tow.

My father watched them go and took a swallow of beer before speaking. 'You summed that up very nicely,' he said. 'There's not many would stand up for Hamilton against the likes of Martin Bell.'

'I've had enough of all the bullshit,' I grumbled

To be honest I then put the matter out of my mind again. It certainly didn't occur to me that my words might have hit their mark more accurately than I had imagined. Only later did I discover quite how tangled the knot of political intrigue and deal-making that bound Bell had become by the time he reached the George and Dragon in Great Budworth. He may even then have been wondering how he had got himself in so deep.

The roots of Martin Bell's accidental involvement in the conspiracy reach back to his time as a war reporter in Bosnia in the early 1990s. While he was there he struck up close friendships with a number of *Guardian* journalists such as John Mullin, Ed Vulliamy and John Sweeney, and became an admirer of Paddy Ashdown, leader of the Liberal Democrats, for his soldierly stance on the conflict. He also formed a friendship with Tom Stoddart, Tony Blair's official photographer during the 1997 election. Bell became something of a war hero himself in the eyes of the public when a piece of shrapnel got him in the crotch in front of the television cameras.

His friendship with John Sweeney, which started under fire in Sarajevo in the summer of 1992, provided Bell with almost the sum total of his background briefing on Neil. Sweeney had been a scathing critic of Neil's for years, stalking him like Simon Wiesenthal on the trail of some Nazi war criminal.

Bell and his fellow journalists spent many long evenings whiling away the hours at the BBC headquarters in Sarajevo, philosophising about the great issues of life over a bottle of Slivovitz, (described by Sweeney as tasting like a cross between anti-freeze and prune juice). The "cash for questions" affair was a front page story at the time and must have come up for discussion. John Sweeney, however, was not as close to the story as the other journalists. He had been fed a false story by his *Guardian* colleagues David Hencke, David Leigh, Peter Preston and Alan Rusbridger, and, because it fitted his prejudice about Neil, he chose to believe it and pass it on, both verbally and in print.

On his return from Bosnia, Bell became disenchanted with the BBC and criticised the corporation for its fence-sitting coverage of the war. Bell had become a 'journalist of commitment.' He no longer believed that news stories should be covered un- emotionally and objectively. The year of 1996 was a lean one and Bell was given hardly any decent stories to cover. By November he was so unhappy he resigned with effect from 1 January 1997, but a last minute deal was hatched to keep him on.

On Monday, 17 March 1997, John Major prorogued Parliament and announced 1 May as the date of the General Election. A few days later Bell attended the election meeting at the BBC. He must have been disappointed to learn that his role in the election special was to be a minor one – covering the result from Malcolm Rifkind's Pentlands seat in Edinburgh, 400 miles away from the crucible of action in London.

On Thursday, 3 April, at the nadir of his disenchantment, Bell opened an exhibition of Tom Stoddart's photographs from Bosnia, "Edge of Madness", at the Royal Festival Hall in London. The photographs of death and destruction only served to remind Bell of the sterling service he had given the BBC over the years, nearly at the cost of his own life. After the event he joined Stoddart and his friends at the People's Palace restaurant upstairs.

Stoddart sensed his friend's disquiet and mentioned, over the meal, that the Labour Party were looking for someone to stand against Neil as an independent anti-corruption candidate in place of their own, but that they were running out of time.

'You would be perfect for the job,' he is reported to have told Bell.

The suggestion startled Bell, but the more he thought about it the more the idea grew on him. The prospect of playing a part in getting rid of the corrupt politician he had heard so much about appealed to his convictions. He didn't agree to put himself forward for the job there and then, but he didn't dismiss the idea either.

After the meal Stoddart phoned Blair's press secretary, Alastair Campbell, suggesting that Bell would probably agree to stand, providing the Labour and Liberal Democrat candidates stood down. Campbell instantly phoned the Lib Dems and the two opposition parties conspired to withdraw from the fifth-safest Tory seat in order to give Bell the best possible chance of ousting Neil.

The following day Campbell called Bell and passed on the telephone number of the Labour Party in Knutsford. Minutes later Bell received a similar call from the Lib Dem Party and, before the day was out, his old soulmate from Bosnia, Paddy Ashdown, was on the line, offering his full support and urging him to take the plunge. The reasoning within both opposition parties was that Tatton was a safe Tory seat unless they could do something to seriously destabilise it. If neither of them were likely to win it in a traditional contest, they had nothing to lose by "giving it away" to an outsider. Sound, if immoral, reasoning. What they had to gain, on the other hand, was the turning of the national spotlight onto what would otherwise be just a local issue. By bringing in Martin Bell they would put *Sleaze* on the national agenda and implicate the whole Tory party. It ought to be a spectacularly successful publicity stunt.

On Saturday night Bell had dinner at his Hampstead home with Colonel Bob Stewart, Commander of the Cheshire Regiment, another close friend from his Bosnia days. He asked the Colonel what he thought of the idea.

'Do it,' Stewart said promptly, and that, perhaps surprisingly, was enough to make Bell's mind up.

By Sunday morning it was too late for him to have second thoughts. The arrangements were already under way. Senior Lib Dem party worker, Tim Clement-Jones, picked him up and they headed north to Tatton to meet the local party executive at the Wilmslow home of chairman John Talbot. As Clement-Jones went into private session to persuade them to withdraw – a meeting he reportedly described as one of the most difficult of his life – Bell gazed through a rear window at sheep grazing in the field beyond, comparing their simple tranquillity with the racket going on around him as eleven people all shouted to be heard at once. "What am I doing here?" he must have asked himself, but his conviction that Neil was corrupt reassured him, because that justified everything.

The Lib Dems agreed to pull out but only by the narrow margin of six votes to five. The Labour group on the other hand would prove to be much more malleable. Clement-Jones drove Bell to a pre-arranged rendezvous with a Labour activist in a car park. Bell switched vehicles and was taken to another car park where he met Jon Kelly, the Labour candidate, and then on to the White Bear pub in Knutsford for a meeting with the Labour executive. As Kelly joined the discussion upstairs, Bell sipped an orange juice in the bar, signing autographs for the regulars.

'You here on some kind of secret assignment?' one of them asked.

'Actually,' Bell said, with a secretive MI5 smile, 'I am.'

Only one or two people at the meeting dissented and the motion was carried. Bell headed back to Hampstead and his favourite restaurant and home from home, La Gaffe. How apt.

The next morning he awoke feeling, by his own admission, like a fugitive as the enormity of what he was involved in dawned on him. The bandwagon had now picked up far too much speed for him to be able to get off, so he made phone calls to both Labour and the Lib Dems for advice on how to proceed.

'Make it clear,' he was told, 'that you are standing for one term only. The Tory voters who are inclined to suspect that there is no smoke without fire will be far more likely to switch and they might be worth an extra ten thousand votes.'

So, just four days after his intervention had been prompted by Stoddart over a meal, with little or no idea of what the allegations against Neil Hamilton were and no knowledge at all of Neil's side of the story, Bell made his way to the Institute of Civil Engineers in Westminster. The Labour Party had booked a room there for his press conference.

With several dozen cameras staring at him, Bell began to feel slightly nauseous. Just the same, he went stoically ahead to announce to the packed room that he was to stand in the general election as an independent anti-corruption candidate against Neil Hamilton.

'What about the £375 it costs to hire this room?' a voice from the pack enquired. 'I believe it has been paid by the Labour Party.'

Bell was caught off-guard and could only stutter lamely. 'I promise to pay them back.' But this airing of his links with the Labour Party clearly made him feel uncomfortable about the position he now found himself in. If he had known what machinations were going on at *The Guardian*, he would have felt more uncomfortable still.

Alan Rusbridger, *The Guardian's* editor, and his staff knew that neither Bell nor the opposition parties could cite the "cash for questions" allegations in their election battle because Sir Gordon Downey was still considering the evidence. But as *The Guardian* had escaped Hamilton's and Greer's libel actions only by default, the paper continued its campaign against Neil to reinforce the impression of his guilt in the eyes of others. And so Rusbridger and his staff decided to support Bell with some propaganda. Accordingly they set aside a whole page of the next day's issue for a black feature on Neil.

In order to create an impression that Neil had already confessed to serious "wrong-doing," Rusbridger and co. took actual events that Neil had disclosed freely for the earlier libel trial and wilfully twisted and misrepresented them to create a list of misdemeanours. These were then mixed together with other untrue and misleading statements and barefaced lies. In total, thirteen "individual" charges were produced under the headline, "Neil Hamilton: the Evidence." In time it will be seen as one of the most blatant examples of distorted peacetime journalism ever.

As Rusbridger and his staff put the paper to bed, Bell packed his bags and headed back up to Cheshire. There he checked in at the Longview Hotel overlooking Knutsford Heath, where he annexed the basement bar as his temporary campaign headquarters. As Bell settled in, Rusbridger sent the paper down the wire to Trafford Park Printers, Manchester, to be made up for its appearance in Knutsford the following morning. For Bell to gain a full understanding of the case *The Guardian* were trying to make against Neil's "admitted wrong-doings," he only needed to read page 17 over breakfast.

But the next morning, when Bell got up, he was too busy digesting the reaction of the papers to his press conference in

London the day before, and too eager to get out in front of the cameras again, even to think about going through the small print of page 17 of *The Guardian*. It was a major blunder.

After breakfast Bell gave notice of his plan to hold a press conference on Knutsford Heath, unaware that a press pack had assembled outside the Hamiltons' home, fifteen minutes' drive away. Even as he made his dispositions, Christine was venturing out to tell the assembled media for the umpteenth time that neither she nor Neil were going to make a statement and to suggest, perhaps a shade forcibly, that they left them alone.

'We'll all be going soon,' a cameraman assured her. 'We have to cover Martin Bell's press conference at noon on Knutsford Heath.'

Christine went back into the house and passed this titbit of information on to Neil.

'Let's confront him!' he said on impulse, and a few minutes later they were heading towards Knutsford in their battered G-registered Rover 827 which John Sweeney was later to describe mischievously as a "limo." They actually arrived ahead of Bell and were immediately surrounded by news reporters and television crews hungry for sound-bites.

Unaware that he was about to be ambushed, Bell approached from the hotel in the midst of his own media scrum. As they came together the two sides faced up for a kind of medieval joust in front of the entire media. Photographers, perched on aluminium step ladders, shouted the protagonists' names in their attempts to make them turn in their direction as Bell pushed through the crowd and confronted his uninvited guests. Perfunctory handshakes were exchanged and Neil was the first to draw his sword.

'I'd really like to know what act of corruption you think I'm guilty of,' he said politely.

Bell looked flummoxed. 'I'll give you my answer,' he blustered. 'I don't actually intend to talk about you at all, though people are going to ask me about you . . . I want you to run on your record, against your record or whatever it is. I want a . . . I want a clean election. I may talk about trust, I think the issue of trust is important. And if, at the end of the day, the electors of Tatton feel they can trust you more than they can trust me, then, my goodness, they should elect you.'

'Do you accept,' Christine's clear tones rang out across the heath, 'that a man is innocent until proved guilty?'

'Yes, of course I do.' Bell said, almost squirming. He obviously hadn't expected to be attacked by the rival candidate's wife as well.

'So you accept that my husband is innocent?'

'I think there's a lot . . .' Bell was floundering now.

'Do you accept that my husband is innocent?' Christine repeated. She wasn't about to let him off the hook.

'No!' There was panic in Bell's eyes now. 'I'm not going to be facing ambush here . . . let's just . . . let's just see . . . let's just see what I have . . . I don't know! . . . I don't know! . . . I'm standing here because a lot of local people have asked me to stand here . . . and the impetus comes from local people . . . and let them just choose between us.'

'I thought it came from a dinner party in London,' Christine snapped.

'I would just like to know,' Neil cut in, 'that you are prepared to give me the benefit of the doubt on the allegations that have been made against me.'

'Absolutely!' Bell said firmly. 'Absolutely!'

Satisfied that they had obtained the assurance they sought, the Hamiltons left the heath and drove home. Back in charge of his own press conference, Bell turned to the cameras. Bereft of any reason to justify his stance, he said, 'This is not between me and him, it's between him and the voters. This is an election about trust.'

Later that day, Bell received a fax from Alastair Campbell, Tony Blair's Press Secretary, containing a carefully-worded open letter from Bell to Neil Hamilton for Bell to release, as if it were his own composition. Bell read it to the press pack on the steps outside his hotel that evening.

'I am prepared to give you the benefit of the doubt on the unproven allegation which remains outstanding against you. This is that you received cash from Mohamed Al Fayed for asking questions and undertaking other activities in Parliament for him. Mr Al Fayed says he paid you, his employees report preparing envelopes of cash for you, and you dropped a libel action against *The Guardian* which continues to allege that you took the cash. Nevertheless you vigorously deny that you accepted any money. The voters will have to decide who is telling the truth in advance of Sir Gordon Downey's report into the matter . . . I will not be making the charge that you took cash from Mr Al Fayed during this campaign.

'Let me list your alleged wrong-doings,' Bell continued, 'so that issues in this campaign are crystal clear. You accepted gifts, hospitality and payments in kind from Mr Al Fayed, whilst acting on his behalf in Parliament, and in dealing with ministers, thus breaking the rule that MPs should not be for sale. You accepted £10,000 from Ian Greer as a commission for your work in Parliament and in lobbying ministers on behalf of various companies. You failed to register this or tell ministers about it. You took £6,000 from US tobacco, via Ian Greer . . .'

Like almost every interview that Neil had to endure in the weeks and months that followed, Bell's misleading Campbell-prepared statement was based on allegations appearing in that morning's *Guardian,* which Bell had failed to read in time for the confrontation.

Bell's pathetic performance on the heath had caused panic at *The Guardian* as well as at Labour headquarters. The following day Alan Rusbridger despatched northward David Leigh and Bell's old friend, Ed Vulliamy. Their mission was to explain the allegations they had taken so much time concocting, to make sure that from then on Bell was fully briefed for every encounter and would not be caught unprepared again.

That evening, Neil's re-selection vote by the Tatton Tories was being taken at the Dixon Arms in Chelford. Nicholas Jones from BBC News was waiting outside the pub to relay the result to the nation. Bell and his team watched from their basement head-quarters in the Longview Hotel.

'Well,' Jones announced, 'there were 282 party members at this meeting and 182 voted for Neil Hamilton, for his re-selection. He failed to get the support of 100 of the members who were here, and 35 of them actually voted against Mr Hamilton. The other 65 abstained.'

If the abstentions are discounted that equates to 83% of the vote. Even if the abstentions are treated as dissenters Neil had still polled 65% – a remarkable vote of confidence from the people who knew him best.

'So you see,' Jones continued, 'it was a resounding victory for Neil Hamilton.'

'But what do you mean?' Bell exploded at the television set, to the amazement of those present. 'It doesn't sound resounding to me! That's not resounding!'

The following morning Bell went walkabout in nearby Wilmslow, dogged by the television cameras. The great majority of local citizenry he approached wished him well and offered their support. But then a middle-aged man, who had the look of a Tory voter, confronted him.

'Why don't you stick to reporting?' he demanded of Bell. 'You're very good at that. Don't you think you've been set up by the other parties?'

'No,' Bell replied, 'I don't. I felt that there was a demand inside the constituency, otherwise I wouldn't have come.'

'Do you have any fundamental beliefs?' his attacker thundered.

'Yes, I do.'

'What are they?'

'I'm going to talk about other issues after the nomination.'

'Such as?'

'I'm going to talk about education . . .' Bell declared.

'What do you know about education? What experience have you had?'

'Well, what about having two children?'

'Yes, but I mean in terms of being a politician,' the middle-aged man went on relentlessly. 'What experience have you had? I mean, surely the electors of Tatton want a professional politician representing their interests?'

'I think there's an up-side and a down-side,' Bell yammered inanely on.

Back at the hotel at lunch time he had to watch the whole scenario being broadcast to the nation. Furious, he immediately phoned the BBC's One o'clock News in London to complain.

'This is Martin Bell,' he announced. 'This is a call I never thought I was going to make . . .You're bloody right it is. I do my first walkabout in Wilmslow, I have twenty five in favour and three against and you give me just one of the three against! What kind of journalism is that? How can you defend it? . . . Okay, will you send my protests to the non-journalist involved – I'm going to denounce you in 45 minutes. I really am. I'm resigning from the BBC and if that's the BBC journalism well fuck him, you know . . . Bastards! Bastards! Tell them to watch it!'

After a long and distinguished career in journalism Bell had finally found himself on the receiving end of news coverage. He forgot that a confrontation with a "Tory constituent" was a thousand times more newsworthy than any number of casual salutations from passers-by that he, as a media personality, might have expected to receive. That he should allow himself to lose control of his temper before the unforgiving eye of the camera suggested that he was close to the end of his tether and growing aware that he was now way out of his depth.

That evening, outside Wilmslow High School, Martin Bell and his daughter Melissa stood amongst the press pack to hear Tony Blair's deputy, John Prescott, read out a statement.

'The meeting tonight of the Tatton Constituency Labour party overwhelmingly endorsed the withdrawal of Jon Kelly as the Labour candidate, on the condition that the Liberal Democrats confirm their intention to support the candidature of Martin Bell.'

The vote was indeed overwhelming: 144 votes to 11, exactly in line with the executive's pledge to Bell the previous Sunday. As Bell and Melissa walked back to their car, *Guardian* journalist John Sweeney joined them, sitting in the back next to BBC cameraman Peter Sherratt. They could hardly conceal their delight at the result, (although they did manage to conceal that it had all been arranged four days earlier).

'A good result, eh?' Melissa crowed.

'A good result,' her father agreed smugly.

'Wonderful,' Sweeney gushed. 'Well done!'

"What did you reckon to that?" Melissa asked, referring to the announcement.

'Prescott was brilliant tonight,' Bell pronounced.

'He was,' Melissa said.

'He's a star!' Sweeney bleated.

And so on, self-felicitation piled on self-felicitation.

'I need . . .' Bell said. 'I need *minding*. I need people who can get me in and out of cars and so on.'

Meanwhile things were not going so wonderfully at the Lib Dem's re-selection conference where half the members refused point blank to be steamrollered. Disgracefully, Bell's friend, Paddy Ashdown, sent the committee a bullying letter making clear how important it was that they sanction the Lib Dem candidate's withdrawal. That was the clincher. They caved in, naturally keeping Ashdown's interference confidential.

'There is no doubt,' one of the members of the committee told me off the record later, 'that Paddy's intervention was the deciding factor. As far as I was concerned it was Ashdown's status as a Privy Councillor that made me change my mind.'

The vote was announced on April 14 as being unanimous in favour of withdrawing their candidate, Roger Barlow. Barlow, a physics teacher, to his credit, refrained from judging Neil Hamilton and endorsing Bell.

'Standing down was a difficult decision for me and the local party,' he told the *Northwich Chronicle*, surely a monumental understatement.

Aware that Tatton, being in the national spotlight, would keep the sleaze issue uppermost, both Labour and the Lib Dems figured that helping Bell would be an effective use of their own manpower. So they released scores of volunteers from their planned duties and despatched key staff from London to organise them.

Like most of the rest of the population I had, up to that point, assumed that there must have been at least *something* to justify the allegations against Neil, but, also like most of the rest of the population, I was more or less indifferent to the issue. I watched the shenanigans on television, thought there must be more to the whole business than met the eye, and got on with my own life. The whole business seemed too complicated to bother with, just a load of politicians tearing one another to pieces as usual. I had lost track of who was accusing whom of doing what and why.

My career was entering a period of crisis as Granada had decided not to commission any more "On the Hunt" features – it seemed I had got up the nose of Greater Manchester Police and Manchester City Council for the Openshaw series – and I was busy putting the finishing touches to a corporate video I was making for an Australian oil company. I simply didn't have time to give any more thought to Neil Hamilton, Martin Bell or even the General Election. But all that was about to change.

4

Delving a Little Deeper

EVEN THE MOST CYNICAL OF PUNTERS COULDN'T HELP BUT BE impressed by the scale of Labour's victory on 1 May 1997. A sort of blood-lust seemed to grip the nation as we watched one former minister after another sink into obscurity in a matter of hours. Because I had met the Hamiltons and knew a bit about them, I couldn't help but feel sorry for them as I watched their faces that night. I had heard how dedicated Neil was to his work as a constituency MP. It had been his life and it had all evaporated overnight. It was the same for many other displaced MPs of course, but none of them were being accused of corruption. None of them were having to rely on a third party, Sir Gordon Downey, to declare them innocent so that they could continue their lives. I could hardly imagine what a personal strain Neil and Christine must be under.

Martin Bell's election machine had proved ruthlessly efficient once it was in gear. His advisers brought in well over three hundred volunteers to distribute thousands of leaflets and put up hundreds of posters and placards. Neil's own election posters were ruthlessly torn down. Bell and his daughter were popular figures with the media anyway, plus they had the media's national anti-Hamilton campaign behind them, coupled with the withdrawal of the opposition candidates and the support of both their parties. Even this safe Tory seat couldn't help but be rocked by such a concentrated onslaught.

In the last few days before the election, when the prospects for Neil already looked hopeless, an ITN crew caught some candid moments with him when he let his "stuffed shirt" persona slip. In one he was larking about with a group of high-spirited children.

'What do you do?' one of the kids asked.

'What do I do?' Neil thought for a second. 'I behave myself – most of the time!'

The children, delighted by his reply, repeated it in unison, gleefully roaring out the qualification at the end. Neil joined in their laughter, obviously enjoying the irony.

I know now that Christine must have been on the point of tears all the time during that period, but she managed to keep up her "life goes on" facade for the cameras, the defiant "battle-axe," as the media would have it, to the end.

'What will you do if you lose this seat?' Louise Osmond, the ITN programme's producer, asked her.

'If the worst comes to the worst,' she replied cheerily, 'we're reasonably young – just the right side of fifty. We're intelligent, we're not without . . . some sort of minor talent. We're fairly employable and there is life outside politics, which is what a lot of politicians forget. But we're not thinking about that. We'll survive, come what may. We're survivors, Neil and I – you ought to know.'

At the same time Bell was also being filmed, talking to a group of constituents, and was in a more earnest mood.

'We're going to light a beacon, which is going to shed light on some dark corners and illuminate the mother of parliaments itself – but I'm not going to do that, you're going to do that. Let me, before I mix and mingle, quote a couple of lines of Chesterton of which I'm rather fond. It comes from a poem called the Secret People. "Smile at us, pass us – but do not quite forget – that we are the people of England – that have never spoken yet". Well, you're just about to speak and I thank you for it.'

In 1992 Neil Hamilton had a majority of 15,860. When the results were read out that night Martin Bell had polled 29,354 and Hamilton just 18,277. As I watched the screen I saw Bell's supporters erupt into euphoria and the devastation on the Hamiltons' faces. The contrast between them made a deep impression on me. Neil was by no means the only Conservative to lose his living that night, but because I had met him and found him to be a decent man, his loss seemed more real to me and I began to think more seriously about his situation.

It appeared to me that he had been given a particularly rough ride, that everyone had ganged up against him, even before he had been found guilty of whatever he was being accused of. If he really was innocent, I thought, he and Christine must be going through absolute hell.

I had finished my corporate video for the oil company and broken away from my business partner. There were no more commissions coming from Granada and I was looking around for a new project. I wondered if it would be a good idea to make a short film about the Hamiltons. It didn't seem to me that they had been given much of a chance to put their side of the story. I would have to find out exactly what it was he was accused of and by whom, of course, but I thought it would make a compelling human drama. At the time I had no intention of turning it into a huge piece of investigative journalism. The next day I dropped him a line and arranged an interview to hear his side of the controversy.

He remembered the grilling I had given him on the lawn the previous year, but didn't appear to bear any ill feelings as he ushered me into the house.

'I expect you're sick of being interviewed by the media,' I said as we sat down in comfortable sofas in his big, untidy library and Christine brought us tea.

'No.' He shook his head. 'Apart from the local press, no one else has been to talk to me.'

I thought I must have misunderstood. 'What do you mean?'

'Exactly what I say.'

'You mean, in all the time that the "cash for questions" story has been running, and all these allegations have been made against you, not one national newspaper reporter has been to see you to hear your side of the case?'

'No.' He shook his head again. 'None. They've stood around the gate often enough in a pack, demanding denials from me and then not giving me a chance to explain what happened, but no one has actually sat down with me and asked for my version of the events.'

I was stunned. It seemed that I had an exclusive on my hands, something that could be turned into a major documentary feature.

'Listen,' I said. 'If I'm going to be sinking a lot of time and money into this project, I want to be sure that I'm first in the queue. I don't want to spend the next few weeks working with you only to find some big shot from one of the television companies has come along and taken the story.'

'What makes you think anyone from the television companies is going to want to speak to me?' Neil asked.

'Surely they will want to.' I couldn't understand his attitude. 'The man who lost his seat, the pain he went through and so on?'

'If no one's been near me in three and a half years I don't think they'll be round now that there's a new Government to concentrate on. You can have exclusive rights to the story.'

'So can you explain to me exactly what the allegations are?' I asked. I no longer felt foolish for not knowing quite what the facts were. If the media hadn't been talking to Neil, who was at the very centre of the whole affair, it was unlikely that anyone else had a clear picture either.

'Fair enough,' he said, and settled himself more comfortably. 'It started back in 1994, on 20 October to be precise, when *The Guardian* broke a story which said Mohamed Fayed's lobbyist, a chap called Ian Greer, had paid me £2,000 a time to ask questions in Parliament. The article claimed that Greer got his money back from Fayed by invoicing him "£8,000 to £10,000" per month. The paper also printed a non-specific allegation that Fayed had given me free shopping at Harrods.'

'And what was your reaction to that?' I cut in as he paused for breath.

'Well, the whole thing was lies from start to finish.'

'But how did you explain these varying invoices that Greer sent?'

'What invoices? They – *The Guardian* and Fayed, that is – have never produced any.'

'I see,' I said, puzzled as to why a newspaper would print a story that would be easy to substantiate by producing these invoices, yet had not done so.

While I was still figuring this out he went on, 'The following Sunday the *News of the World* ran a new allegation. They claimed Fayed had given me fifteen £1,000 Harrods gift vouchers. There was a big illustration of a £1,000 voucher just to ram home the point. But they said Fayed had given them to me direct, not via Ian Greer.'

'I see,' I said again, not really seeing much at all.

'Four days later the gift voucher allegations were officially communicated to the Select Committee on Members' Interests,' Neil continued, 'from one of Fayed's stooges, Lib Dem MP, Alex Carlile, to the Chairman, Geoffrey Johnson Smith. Now, however, the details had changed and they were accusing me of receiving £6,000 in £100 denominations—'

'Hang on a minute,' I interrupted. 'Let me get this right. The *News of the World* said £15,000 in £1,000 vouchers . . . and the Lib Dem bloke said £6,000 in £100 vouchers . . .'

'Yes, that's right, but I've not finished yet. Let me tell you the rest of the story: at the beginning of December, Fayed's solicitors, D.J. Freeman, wrote a letter, which they claimed was definitive, to Geoffrey Johnson Smith, this time alleging that I had received cash payments direct from their client, not from Ian Greer. They claimed that I was paid in person every time I met Fayed at Harrods and at his offices in 60 Park Lane. A schedule was provided, apparently based arbitrarily on dates he had in his diary when we had met, which listed exactly what I had received, either in cash or in voucher form. In this letter they now claimed I had received a total of £20,000 in eight payments of £2,500 in cash, plus gift vouchers alleged now to total £8,000 in two payments of £1,000 and two payments of £3,000 in £100 denominations.'

'Was that it?' I couldn't believe that anyone could have taken seriously allegations that had varied so frequently within such a short space of time.

'No,' he said, shaking his head. 'Ten days later a supplementary allegation was made in the same vein as the original set – that Ian Greer was a conduit. It was claimed that three cheques had been paid to Greer to enable him to pay me and Tim Smith. One cheque for £6,000 and one for £12,000 paid in May 1987 and a third cheque of £13,333 paid in March 1990. This accusation emerged again later.'

'Was that the lot then?' I asked, by now totally bemused.

'It was for a while.' Neil sipped his tea, apparently pleased to have someone actually showing an interest in the facts of his case at last. 'Then on 27 September 1996 they claimed that as well as the face-to-face payments made to me by Fayed, there were other payments made to me with the involvement of two of his secretaries and a doorman. All three of these people now claimed that they had been party to passing over cash payments in 'brown envelopes,' allegedly left at the door of 60 Park Lane or couriered up here to the house.'

But although his rendition of the changing allegations should have made me more sympathetic to his case, I remember thinking, bizarrely, that he might have just been picking holes wherever he could find them, muddying the waters with technicalities. Though, in hindsight, this was absurd, I did have doubts that he was as innocent as he claimed.

'Do you have an explanation as to why Fayed kept changing the allegations?' I asked.

'Because when the story came out in *The Guardian* Ian Greer and I both commenced libel proceedings immediately – and *The Guardian* couldn't substantiate them with any evidence. That's why.'

'So, just for the record, I'm right in saying that Ian Greer has never given you any money at any time?'

'No, that's wrong. Ian gave me two commission payments when two companies engaged his lobbying firm partly as a result of my recommendation. But you shouldn't read anything into that it's not unusual for companies to give commission payments when they acquire business as a result of a personal recommendation, lots of firms do it across all industries and professions. *The Guardian*, however, have made a real meal of them.'

I sat there wondering what else there was in this story to confuse me. By now I had hoped I would be getting on with questions about Fayed's allegations. What was all this about commission payments? A smoke screen, perhaps, to mask payments from Ian Greer to ask questions?

'I assure you that commission payments are given out by all sorts of companies, not just by Ian Greer,' he repeated, just in case I hadn't heard him the first time. 'And I wasn't motivated in either case by being rewarded. In the first instance, when I recommended a local company to Ian, I didn't even know he gave commissions and anyway I'm pretty certain that I recommended a number of lobbying companies, not just Ian's.'

'Hang on,' I interrupted. 'I thought you were a friend of Ian Greer's.'

'I was. What's your point?'

'Well, if he was your friend, why would you recommend other firms as well as his? And for that matter, why didn't he tell you that he gave commissions?'

'Look, it isn't like what you're implying. Despite what *The Guardian* has cajoled the rest of the Press into believing, Parliament isn't a cess-pit of MPs on the make. On the whole, MPs of all sides act properly, which is all so boring and why the press makes these stories up in the first place. I mean, the very idea of Ian Greer saying to me on the side, "look here, me old mucker, introduce a few clients to me and earn yourself some lovely lucre" just isn't on. Ian certainly never said anything like that to me, anyway. The first I knew about Ian giving commissions was when I received his phone call after this company signed him up.'

I felt as though I was being side-tracked into a whole new issue, rather than cash for questions, which was my real interest. I decided to continue anyway as we were already discussing the subject and I suspected that the matter of Greer's commission payments figured in the story somewhere. But I could not have imagined just how fundamental to the cash for questions affair they were.

'When did you receive it? Your first commission, that is.'

'1987.'

'When did you first enter Parliament?'

'1983.'

I did some quick arithmetic. He had been an MP for four years before he recommended the first company to Greer.

'How long had you known Ian Greer? As a friend, that is?'

'I've known him since 1979, so in 1983 I would have known him for four years. I first got to know Ian because he was a friend of another MP, Sir Michael Grylls, for whom Christine was secretary. In 1979 Ian provided me with some very useful information for a book I was writing on US-UK double taxation. I suppose that's when he and I became friends.'

'How close were you, as friends?'

'Not *that* close we weren't bosom pals but we used to have the occasional lunch together, stuff like that.'

'What about the second commission?'

'I only received that when another MP, Michael Brown, put forward a list of three lobbying companies to a company that we both supported, but who needed more help than we could give. I didn't even put together the list. But when Ian was selected from the three he split the commission between the two of us because I had endorsed the three names Brown put forward and gave him a good write-up.'

'And the commissions had nothing to do with Fayed or House of Fraser?' I asked.

'Nothing. Nothing whatsoever,' he insisted. 'You still don't look convinced,' he said after a moment's pause, correctly reading my body language. But although I had my misgivings, at least I had had personal experience of receiving a commission payment myself twelve years earlier, when I was running my road haulage business. My accountant recommended to me a pensions company with which I took out a policy subsequently. A few months later he told me he had received a commission for the recommendation, which he shared by sending me a cheque for half the amount.

'Look,' Neil said, 'I can go over the commission payments in more detail some time later, but for now the main thing is for you to try and absorb the "cash for questions" allegations. Having said that, there are two points that you should consider. Firstly, in 1990 the Members' Interests Committee investigated Ian's commissions to Sir Michael Grylls, and they found nothing sinister in them at all. Secondly, Ian and I gave full disclosures to *The Guardian* about my two commission payments in our witness statements for the libel trial, over a year before the trial began. Do you honestly think that we would have done so, if there was anything wrong in them?'

What he said seemed logical. 'Okay . . . all right . . .' I said, 'I'll come back to them another time.' I was beginning to feel punch-drunk by this thumbnail sketch of what it was all about. It sounded more like a plot from an Agatha Christie. I tried to clear my mind of the bedlam by getting down to the basic issue. 'So, how many questions did you actually put down that might be termed favourable to Fayed?'

'Nine written questions.'

'Over how long?'

'Three and a half years.'

'And how many oral questions?'

'None. I never spoke once from the floor on the House of Fraser/Lonrho battle – unlike over thirty other MPs, I might add.'

'What sort of questions were you asking?'

'Nothing of any great significance. Such as "when will the DTI investigation into House of Fraser be finished" and things like that. All fairly dull I assure you.'

'And Fayed's suggesting you were paid all this money for putting down just nine questions?'

'Aah.' He sighed and sank back in his seat. '*Now* you're beginning to get a grasp of things!'

'So let's recap: before *The Guardian* printed its story on 20 October 1994, no allegations had been made against you?'

'Well, three months earlier in July Fayed had started ringing round the newspapers making corruption allegations against a number of MPs. Among them was Michael Howard, who by some remarkable coincidence was the former DTI Minister for Corporate Affairs who appointed the inspectors to look into Fayed's past. It is obvious that Fayed was already developing his first thoughts about making allegations against me because I had refused to intervene to reconsider the report when I took over Howard's job. Trevor Kavanagh, chief political correspondent for the *Sun*, phoned me at home and said that he'd heard some vague rumour that I and other ministers had been paid to ask questions when we were back-benchers.'

'What was your reaction to that?'

'I denied that I had ever been involved in such a thing,' Neil told me. 'Initially I thought Tiny Rowland might have started the rumour in his rage against Fayed. The *Sunday Times* had just run a story in which they claimed to have entrapped a couple of Conservative MPs into taking £1,000 to ask questions. This was the first time the phrase "cash for questions" was used. Do you remember the story?' I nodded. 'I thought that it might have triggered Rowland off, because in the 80s I had supported Fayed against him.'

'Did Kavanagh run the story?' I asked.

'No, there was obviously no evidence to back it up. The *Sun* has more integrity than I had previously credited it with.'

'So why do you think *The Guardian* printed it, and why do you think it took the paper three months to get round to it?'

'For one thing, I don't think Fayed told *The Guardian* until three months later, and for another, when he did, it obviously suited their political agenda. *The Guardian* isn't a newspaper worth buying any more it's just a nasty vicious rag run by lunatics, with an over-the-top arts section to draw in all the lefties and luvvies.'

It was Neil's description that seemed over-the-top if anything was, I remember thinking. 'So what do you think triggered Fayed off?'

'Shortly before 21 September that year, Fayed received advance notice that the European Court of Human Rights was going to reject his application to quash the DTI report, a report that condemned him as a liar and a fraud, thus destroying his chance of the British passport he craved. It must have been the last straw for him.

'Just give me a moment, will you?' Neil got up and left the room. A few minutes later he returned with some documents. 'Yes, here it is. In Peter Preston's witness statement for the libel trial, he mentions that he met Fayed on 19 September 1994.' He picked up another document. 'And this is what Preston said when he was asked about this during his oral examination by Sir Gordon Downey: "There was a meeting on 21 September, something like that, in 1994, after a very long break. That is the meeting I describe in my witness statement. Mr Al Fayed was somewhat distressed. I think he had just heard that he was going to lose the European Court submission and he was very upset about that."' He put the document down and looked up at me. 'I'm pretty certain that Fayed told Preston his "cash for questions" allegations against me for the first time at this meeting, although Preston later claimed differently. Preston says that Fayed made his allegations in July 1993, in other words, a year before the European Court of Human Rights' ruling.'

'And did he?'

'No, I'm sure of it.' Neil was emphatic. 'Fayed couldn't have made his allegations at that time.'

'Why not?' I said, becoming genuinely drawn into the story. If there was a motive for Fayed's allegations, as there seemed to be, then perhaps Neil was a victim after all. Perhaps.

'In July 1993,' Neil answered, 'two *Guardian* journalists interviewed me on the Commons Terrace. But they only asked me about lobbying especially my relationship with Ian Greer and about my registered consultancies, but their main interest seemed to be in my stay at the Ritz. I've never made any secret of the fact that Fayed invited us over to see the Duke and Duchess of Windsor's old home, which he had bought and restored, and also put us up at the hotel. But scores of MPs and journalists have visited the Windsors' and stayed at the Ritz. If I had thought it should have been registered I would have registered it. Back in 1987, *no* MPs registered private hospitality, I can assure you. I have most of the Members' Interests Registers and you can go through them yourself. But to return to your question – no, there is no way they asked me about cash for questions.'

'So you deny all these allegations?' I said.

'Apart from the Ritz – and even that was blown out of all proportion – the whole story is a complete fabrication.'

'What evidence can you provide me with? I need everything you've got – the lot. Whether you think it's helpful to you or not.'

He led me into the dining room and showed me a stack of storage boxes containing files galore. He dipped into one of them and extracted a sheaf of folders which he handed to me.

'This is my submission to Sir Gordon Downey – it's as good a place as any to start. And here are the transcripts of Downey's examinations of witnesses. Pay particular attention to the depositions of Fayed and his employees.' He opened another box and passed me an even thicker wad of files. 'That's everything from the libel trial. It'll take you weeks to go through this lot. Are you sure you're up to it?'

'I can't say right now, but if I don't have them I won't be able to even if I wanted to.'

A third batch of files came my way. 'These are accurate notes of all sorts of Government memo's and suchlike that were produced for the libel trial. The originals were returned to the Government when the trial collapsed. You'll find them useful. Don't let any of this out of your sight.'

'Oh, just one thing,' I said. 'How many meetings did you have with Fayed on your own, just you two, during which Fayed said he paid you?'

'Quite a few.' He looked uncomfortable as he thumbed through yet another document. 'Fayed says we had twelve private meetings during every one of which he paid me either cash or gift vouchers.'

'So why did you have twelve meetings with Fayed, if you only put down nine written questions?'

'He was always ringing me up asking me to go round to see him. He used to go on about Tiny Rowland and the injustice of the DTI Inquiry all the time. I think he felt letdown and wanted a shoulder to cry on.'

'Do you always go to see people that ring you up for a shoulder to cry on?'

'Of course not'. He said, looking even more uncomfortable. 'He was a larger than life character who I felt was being badly treated. He could also be very convivial and amusing and charming too. I don't deny it, I enjoyed his company and I was fascinated by his battle with Tiny Rowland.'

'I see.' I said, concealing my scepticism. I felt as if I was the Counsel for both the Prosecution and the Defence at the same time, being swung back and forth by my suspicions about each side's case.

Thus, laden with files of documents and a head full of confusion, I left for home to begin work.

5

Simple Truth and Complex Lies

BACK HOME, I SIFTED THROUGH THE REAMS OF PAPERWORK AND wondered if I would ever be able to get my head round all the various aspects of the story. There seemed to be so many of them. I was tempted to forget the whole thing and find an easier project to work on. But, having spent some time with the Hamiltons, it bothered me that they were completely isolated and alone in their battle. As far as the rest of the world was concerned they were finished. Everyone was now looking to the bright new dawn of New Labour. If I didn't stick with them, who would? And I was beginning to feel there was something genuinely wrong with the whole situation – particularly the role played by *The Guardian*.

That evening I headed out to Great Budworth to visit my friend, John Gregson, who ran the local Post Office. In his office, above the shop, John has a computer linked to the Internet and I wanted to find out exactly how much material existed on the case out there (I had been meaning to link up myself for months but never seemed to get round to it). John took me upstairs and logged on. After a few minutes he discovered that *The Guardian* had its own web-site on the story entitled "Corruption in the Commons," containing scores of articles about the case.

'Down-load that lot for me, will you, John?' I said.

'Why? It's not going anywhere?'

'Download it, please,' I repeated. 'Just in case they wipe it. And can you print out all the articles?'

John looked mildly horrified. 'What – *all* of them?'

'Yes. The whole lot.' He looked at me sideways, incredulously, with an eyebrow raised. 'Please', I said.

It would have been around 11.00pm when I eventually left the Post Office, now armed with two hundred-plus sheets of print-out, and walked back up the street to my parents' cottage. I poured myself a large scotch and settled down in the parlour for another reading session. None of it made much sense, being mostly vague or contradictory. The coverage seemed completely over the top and hysterical, like machine gunning a dead man. It was also impossible to work out quite what the allegations were. I eventually came across a print-out of the article that appeared on page 17 of *The Guardian* on 8 April 1997.

It was the article that Martin Bell ought to have read in preparation for questions on his campaign trail and in his press conferences. Here were the thirteen charges against Neil, actually laid out concisely. It gave me something specific to put to Neil. I would read each charge to him, one at a time, and if I didn't understand his answers I would ask supplementary questions until I was sure I had grasped what was going on.

I noticed that the first twelve allegations all had a sort of uniformity in their style. They were all about his commission payments and Fayed's allegations. The thirteenth one, however, seemed to jar; it was different from the others. This was the charge that he had lied to the Downey Inquiry when he told them that he hadn't been asked about "cash for questions" when interviewed by *Guardian* journalists in 1993.

The question looked out of place, as if it had been stuck on the end to add more weight to the numbers. Why, I asked myself, would *The Guardian's* writers think that the general public would be interested in such a minor detail? They weren't accusing him of lying about taking Fayed's money, they were accusing him of lying about whether he had *been asked* about taking it when they interviewed him a year before they printed their story. It seemed an odd place to put such a trivial accusation. And then I remembered Neil's insistence that Fayed had made his allegations at a time when he had a demonstrable grudge when the European Court of Human Rights rejected Fayed's appeal. Perhaps, I reflected, the people who had compiled the list of accusations – i.e. the *Guardian* journalists – wanted to establish that Neil had lied about this seemingly inconsequential matter in order to disprove that Fayed had made his allegations out of spite. I made a mental note of the anomaly before retiring to bed.

The next day I drove back to Manchester and rang Neil to book a couple of days with him for a week hence. I decided that sitting together in the library had been too cosy and chummy. I needed to make the interrogation more formal. I suggested that for the future we would sit opposite one another at the big mahogany table in their dining room. Possibly to humour me, Neil agreed.

When the day came I was greeted warmly and immediately we got down to business. I laid out a selection from the documents he had given me, alongside everything I had down-loaded from the Internet. And so, using the article that listed the thirteen charges against him as a basis for the interrogation, we started.

All day long, with Christine coming in once an hour with fresh teas, we hammered away at the issues. By the end of the first day we had only covered the first two charges, and already I was satisfied there were substantial grounds to suggest that I should persevere with the investigation.

At the end of that first day I felt that I was beginning to develop an understanding, and I was encouraged that at no time during the interrogation did he become defensive or evasive despite the intensity of my questioning. My earlier scepticism was ebbing away, albeit only a drip at a time.

'We'll have to go on film,' I said at one stage in the session, dreading the prospect of going through the whole thing again for the cameras.

'No,' Neil said. 'I think it would be better if you got the story straight in your head first, then you'll know what questions to ask for the cameras. Otherwise you'll have so much material you won't know what to do with it.' He was right, of course.

When I first developed the idea of making a programme about the Hamilton affair, I wanted to see what sort of response I was likely to get from the television companies. I needed to know what sort of approach they would prefer, and whether they would be willing to commission the piece. In short, I needed to do a bit of networking.

A few weeks earlier, when it had become clear that my series at Granada was not going to continue, I contacted Peter Salmon, Granada's Director of Programmes, now since moved to the BBC to become Controller of BBC1 Television. He had written me a nice letter a short while after my Openshaw programme, praising my work for Granada. I subsequently went to see him and asked him for some ideas on people I should approach in the business, to capitalise on the success of the series and to try to get new projects going. He was generous with his advice and gave me introductions to several independent producers. Now, better informed about the Hamilton affair, I made appointments with these producers and while chatting generally about possible projects, I mentioned to each of them that I had exclusive rights to the Hamiltons' story. I told them that I thought there was more to the story than met the eye and that the man might have been wrongly accused. The reaction of producer Ali Rashid was typical of all of them.

'Oh no, we don't want to do anything on Hamilton. We've got a new Government now, a new optimism. We've got to move forward. No one wants to hear about all that old Tory sleaze.'

'But from what he tells me the guy may not be guilty,' I protested. To no avail.

When I put the idea to another producer the reaction was, 'I think Neil Hamilton has had enough air-time, don't you?'

'Well, as a matter of fact, I don't,' I replied. 'Every time I've seen him on television he's never allowed to get a word in; he spends all his time fielding one allegation after another.'

I came away from each meeting with my resolve newly strengthened. If this was the media's idea of fair play, then there was something seriously wrong with the system. Neil deserved at the very least a decent, impartial hearing. The negative reactions were making me all the more determined to prove that my instincts were right and their prejudices were wrong. I didn't like the way everyone I approached seemed to be sticking together and turning a blind eye to anything that didn't fit in with their bigoted pre-conceptions. If I didn't follow up this story, who else was going to? I no longer felt I had any option. To walk away from the Hamiltons would have been worse than not getting involved in the first place.

Even my father was sceptical about my chances.

'Oh for God's sake, Jonathan,' he said. 'Get yourself a job and stop messing about with this stuff. Even if the man's innocent, you'll never prove it.'

I wasn't about to argue with him there and then. For a start, I was still deeply confused by the huge amounts of data, names

and dates that Neil kept throwing at me, and the many conflicting stories. One thing, however, was clear. The man at the
root of the whole thing was Mohamed Fayed and I needed to
build up a picture of his background and present circumstances.
I phoned Neil.

'What can you tell me about Fayed?' I asked.

'Not a lot,' he said, 'but I can point you in the right direction.
There are two documents that will give you most of what you
need to know: one is the DTI report from 1990 and the other is
a book Tiny Rowland published called "A Hero from Zero".'

I got hold of a copy of the book. In it Rowland had collated
a number of articles from the *Daily Mail, Daily Telegraph,
Financial Times, Sunday Times, Sunday Telegraph, Wall Street
Journal, New York Times* and *Mail on Sunday*. The tone in all of
them was the same – an awed sycophantic acceptance of whatever information Fayed's PR machine put out.

For example: *The billionaire brothers, Mohammed, Ali and
Salah, control more than half the shipping in the Mediterranean,*
the *Daily Mail* gushed in November 1984. Five days later they
went further: *Mohamed and his brothers, Ali and Salah, have
climbed a social Everest since their great grandfather, Ali Ali
Fayed, founded the family fortunes a century ago by growing
cotton on the banks of the Nile and exporting it in his own ships
to the mills of Lancashire . . . Mohamed's tonnage in freighters
plying the Mediterranean makes him an 'Onassis' of Cargo.*

The *Telegraph* was scarcely less fulsome. *The Al-Fayeds –
Mohamed, Ali and Salah – are members of one of Egypt's
most distinguished families, and have had a close association
with Britain. The origins of their wealth go back to 1876 when
their grandfather began business in Egypt, shipping cotton to
Liverpool. The brothers were raised in Alexandria and educated
at British schools.*

Even the exalted *Financial Times* had joined in this festival of
misinformation. *The Al-Fayed brothers – Mohamed, the brains
of the business empire, Ali and Salah – are fourth generation
Egyptian money. Their great grandfather founded the family's
financial dynasty growing cotton on the banks of the Nile and
exporting it in his own ships to the UK.*

A few months after their first story, the *Mail* were ready to
apply a few more admiring daubs to the portrait of a successful
business mogul. *His family fortunes were planted in cotton by*

his great grandfather, who began shipping it in his own freighters from Alexandria to the cotton mills of Lancashire, via Liverpool. He and his brothers left their native Egypt, as the nationalisation of commerce loomed with the abdication of King Farouk.

The brothers delicately pointed out, the *Sunday Times* wrote later in 1985, *that their family lived in some luxury when even the Saudi royal family lived in tents in the desert. The family does not see itself in the Arab tradition at all, but as part of something much older. Egypt, Mohamed pointed out, was the cradle of civilisation. He and his family, he implied, are inheritors of the tradition of the Pharaohs, not that of the desert . . . Already wealthy when they left Egypt, the Al-Fayeds have multiplied their fortune many times since . . . They display a lofty disdain for the nouveaux riches of the Arab world. Their great grandfather, Ali Ali Fayed, began the family fortune growing cotton in the Nile delta. This was shipped to mills in Lancashire and sometimes even ended up as Egyptian sheets, a great luxury at the time, in Harrods.*

The further I got into the pile of articles the more I felt I was in the midst of some giant *Hello* Magazine conspiracy.

Can there be any real doubt about the Al Fayeds or their money or their background? the *Sunday Telegraph* asked rhetorically. *Would top city names like Kleinwort Benson, Warburg and Cazenove have approved this deal without checking them out? Or the canny Professor Roland Smith? To say the very least, I very much doubt it.*

According to Mr Al Fayed, the *Wall Street Journal* reported, *the source of the family's wealth is the Egyptian cotton business. The family traded in cotton and owned several ships, and was able to spirit its money out of the country ahead of the massive nationalisations of Gamel Abdel Nasser in the 1960s.*

Mohamed took the lead in establishing the family outside Egypt, the *Mail on Sunday* agreed, *using the world-wide contacts that came from shipping. 'Our ships go everywhere. You are known and your family is known' he explains.*

Mr Fayed's account of his life is one of honourable enterprise and duty to family, the *New York Times* fawned.

The only doubting voice – paradoxically as it would turn out later – was *The Guardian.*

Kleinwort declines to give specific details of the Al-Fayed shipping interests, it reported in 1985, *but after several conversa-*

tions with John MacArthur, the Kleinwort's director handling the Al-Fayed affairs, he confirmed that the brothers had no fewer than 40 ships. These include liners, a tanker, and cargo vessels operating primarily in the Mediterranean. Asked which company runs the shipping operation, Kleinwort points out that in the shipping industry 'you have one ship holding company for each ship, for taxation purposes. If you have got 40 cargo vessels, you will have 40 companies'. But Kleinwort declined to name either the ships, or the companies which operate the Al-Fayed ships. Further enquiries in shipping circles provide no firm additional evidence about the Al-Fayeds' shipping interests.

But this was *The Guardian's* financial staff writing in 1985. As my inquiry was presently to show, *The Guardian's* political staff of today are not the same beast.

No one else seemed to have picked up on this hint of suspicion. The glamorous, aristocratic Egyptian family was simply too good a story, obviously. Tiny Rowland, the media must have decided, was just bitter about losing Harrods and trying to stir up trouble by his demand for a DTI report.

In 1990, however, the DTI report was published, all 752 damning pages of it, and it made all the press coverage that had come before look like corporate press releases.

I obtained a copy and the further I ploughed through this massive document the more amazed I was that anyone, in the media, in the Government or even in the opposition parties, could ever have given any credence to anything Fayed said after its publication.

Throughout this report, the inspectors announced, *we refer to the brothers by the name 'Fayed'. We explain in appendix 3 of our report how they decided to assume false birth dates and a new name 'Al Fayed' after they left Egypt and how Mohamed has given an explanation of this name which is bogus as far as Egyptian law is concerned . . .*

The report contained one theme in particular, that kept popping up: that of the Fayed brothers' integrity:

As month after month of our investigation went by we uncovered more cases where the Fayeds were plainly telling lies. These discoveries culminated in a two-day questioning session in March 1988 when it became more obvious to us, from the manner and demeanour of both Mohamed and Ali

Fayed, that they were witnesses who were only prepared to assist our inquiry when they believed it suited them to do so. In consequence of watching them give evidence we became reluctant to believe anything they told us unless it was reliably corroborated by independent evidence of a dependable nature . . .

The Fayeds dishonestly misrepresented their origins, their wealth, their business interests and their resources to the Secretary of State, the OFT (Office of Fair Trading), the press, the HoF board and HoF shareholders, and their own advisers . . .

We received evidence from the Fayeds, under solemn affirmation and written memoranda, which was false and which the Fayeds knew to be false. In addition, the Fayeds produced a set of documents they knew to be false. This false evidence related mainly, but not exclusively, to their background, their past business activities and the way in which they came to be in control of enormous funds in the Autumn of 1984 and the Spring of 1985 . . .

The evidence before us, however, indicates that it is highly likely that the Fayeds used their association with the Sultan of Brunei and the opportunities afforded to them by the possession of wide powers of attorney from the Sultan of Brunei to enable them to acquire those funds . . .

The Fayeds' assets were worth a fraction of what they portrayed to the public. They were certainly not worth several billion dollars as a director of Kleinwort Benson said on television on 10 March 1985 . . .

The Fayeds are not 'members of an old established Egyptian family who for more than 100 years were ship-owners, landowners and industrialists in Egypt' as was said of them, with their knowledge, in November 1984 and as was repeated in a draft of their offer document which was provided by Kleinworts on 13 March 1985 to the DTI. After very detailed inquiries which were confirmed by a visit by a member of our staff to Egypt, we concluded that they came from respectable but humble origins and were the sons of a teacher . . .

The Fayeds produced to us birth certificates which were false and which they knew to be false. They repeatedly lied to us about their family background, their early business life and their wealth. Furthermore, in the course of giving their own English solicitor a tour of properties and people during a visit to Egypt in September 1987, the Fayeds either caused him to obtain an incorrect impression of their past or allowed him to develop that impression unchecked. He returned to England and gave his account of what he had seen and heard in good faith. Very little of it stood up to independent inquiry . . .

During the course of our investigations the Fayeds made serious accusations of lack of professional integrity against a responsible freelance journalist who had discovered the true story of their Egyptian past. We inquired into those allegations at great length and we reject them . . .

Certain aspects of press coverage in this case concern us deeply, because the overall impression created by the press in a matter of this complexity is widely accepted . . .

In our judgement, this submission reveals the Fayed's character very vividly. The evidence that they were telling lies to us was quite overwhelming. But they were still determined to counter-attack and try to pretend that they were the innocent victims of some gigantic conspiracy against them . . .

One of the difficulties confronting anyone seeking to test the truth of the Fayeds' account of the generation of their wealth is that the story changes as different parts of it are demolished or discredited . . .

In a situation where more and more of the Fayeds' representations or stories turned out to be untrue or mis-leading, as will be evident from our report, it would have been difficult for anybody in our position not to feel increasingly sceptical about the merits of the new stories which later took their place . . .

Mohamed's skill in exaggerating the truth before an audience whom he believes to be ignorant of the true facts was clearly apparent to us during our two-day questioning session of the Fayeds . . .

In the end the Fayeds relied on a story that they had an immense sum of money available to them in 1978, which grew steadily between 1978 and 1984 and which was supplemented by an additional $400-million from secret oil trading profits. This was not the story which they told in

1984–85 and the Fayeds have not put any supporting evidence of any kind before us to confirm the truth of what they are saying. In the total absence of any such evidence, and in the light of the unreliability of the Fayeds as witnesses of truth in other areas of our investigations, we reject this story more or less completely

The Fayeds' account of the reasons for Lonrho's conduct on and after 2 November 1984 appeared to be wholly unconvincing and as the evidence went on, there appeared more and more pointers that Mr Rowland was telling the truth and the Fayed account was unreliable . . .

We regret that after all the care we had taken to protect ourselves against reliance on evidence from a single source we found (the Fayeds') submission to be both sad and ludicrous. Sad, because it showed how blinkered the Fayeds now are in trying to hold up an entirely untenable and false story about their Egyptian past. Ludicrous, because the sheer scale of the dishonest conspiracy allegedly organised by Dr Marwan (a much-respected former Chief of Staff to President Sadat who knew both Rowland and Fayed) which the Fayeds suggested to us, is utterly preposterous. The evidence that they were telling lies about their past is quite overwhelming . . .

The Fayeds' misconduct was, in our opinion, aggravated by the way in which they completely deceived their own solicitor with the intention that he should, in all innocence, give us evidence which they knew to be false . . .

On almost every page I found material claiming that the Fayeds had lied about many aspects of their lives. What seemed most incredible was that even though this report had now been in the public domain for over six years, the media and people of influence were still willing to believe Fayed's latest proclamations. It seemed to me to be impossible that intelligent journalists and politicians could be so patently gullible the only answer could be that few had actually read it. Either that, or it could be because *The Guardian's* "cash for questions" campaign fitted into some other agenda of their own. An agenda, conceivably, like toppling a Government, or humiliating a man they had a dislike for. But knowing how the media worked, I thought it far more likely that it was simply due to the cash for questions affair being 'such a good story' and nobody actually checked to see if Fayed or *The Guardian* had any evidence to back it up.

The final paragraph of the report was a frightening summary of how Fayed had manipulated the British press:

> *In the present case it appears to us that two processes were at work concurrently. On one hand Mohamed Fayed was telling lies about himself and his family to representatives of the press, and once those stories were on the cuttings file or in a press cuttings library they grew and multiplied without much further inquiry into their accuracy. On the other hand he gave instructions to his very able lawyers to take legal action against any who sought to challenge his claim that discretion was the better part of valour and preferred to write about other things than get involved in an expensive libel action with a rich man. As a result of what happened, the lies of Mohamed Fayed and his success in 'gagging' the press created, as Mr Fisher would put it, new fact: that lies were the truth and that the truth was a lie.*

But despite this most damning of indictments, Fayed, by making substantial donations to the Royals' favourite charities and sponsoring the Royal Windsor Horse Show, had succeeded in courting the Royal Family itself. Even more incredible, if the events of the next few months had taken a different course, the man who had been so roundly damned in this report, and who had contributed to the fall of a democratically elected Government out of plain old-fashioned spite, could conceivably have even ended up as the step-grandfather to the future King of England.

This man, I was coming to realise, was an awesome adversary indeed.

6

A New Partner

AFTER SPLITTING FROM MY BUSINESS PARTNER, I FELT I NEEDED someone else to help me with the evidence that was starting to silt up in the small office I rented. I was trying to balance my growing obsession with rooting out the truth in the Hamilton saga with the constant nagging voice of my conscience that told me that I should be seeking out other projects to keep some cash flowing into the business. So far my father's goodwill had kept me financially afloat, but I couldn't afford to rely on him indefinitely. I was counting on eventually being able to find a buyer for our intended "cash for questions" documentary. And certainly, the more evidence I uncovered, the more optimistic I became that I would be able to make a programme that would appeal to "Panorama" or one of the other major current affairs programmes.

A film editor I had been working with on the oil company video told me about a good cameraman he knew who had also directed documentaries. 'I'll get him to give you a ring if you like,' he said. 'He normally lives in Brazil but he's over here for a few months and he's looking for a project.'

A few days later Malcolm Keith-Hill phoned and we arranged to meet at the Toll Gate pub, just opposite Trafford Bar tram station. He was in his mid-forties and struck me as a mature and sensible man, exactly the extra pair of hands and eyes I needed.

To begin with he was not keen on the idea of working on anything that might help the Hamiltons, being an avid anti-Tory and convinced to boot that Neil was guilty of all he stood accused of. But he was also a keen fan of *The Guardian* and thought its standards had dropped over the years and he was suffering just a bat-squeak of doubt about whether the paper had reported the "cash for questions" story faithfully. I was keen to work with him, feeling that his scepticism would help when it came to assessing the evidence. We decided to join forces and put some serious work into examining the facts, so that we could put together a programme proposal, working title: "From Ritz to Writs" (later, after Downey Day, we revised this to: "A Shred of Evidence").

The first job was a mundane one: making two photocopies of the hundreds of pages of documents that Neil had given us, including all the articles off the Internet, so we each had all the evidence to enable us to research whatever subject took our fancy independently of each other. So, having first equipped myself with around ten large lever-arch files, over the following two weekends the lobby of the business centre where I have my office took on the appearance of a copy-shop, with piles of papers stacked on the floor as the Xerox churned non-stop.

Initially, we ended up with two sets of files containing: articles from *The Guardian*'s Internet web-site and other web-sites; transcriptions of oral evidence given to the Downey inquiry; all the evidence that was submitted to the libel trial by Mohamed Fayed, *The Guardian*, Ian Greer, Neil Hamilton, and other witnesses; and a file each for other documents that didn't fall into those categories. Two single files were made up, which we shared. One contained press cuttings and another containing all the Members Interests Registers from 1983-1996 covering Neil's period in Parliament.

As I already had made arrangements to interrogate Neil, it was agreed that I should continue until I had exhausted *The Guardian's* thirteen charges and established the story's framework and the veracity or otherwise of his answers, while Malcolm acquainted himself with its various aspects by reading through the mountain that I had provided.

'We could spend all year on this,' Malcolm said, little realising that it would actually take longer. 'Well, I don't have a year,' he added. 'Six months at the most and then I'm off back home to sunny Rio.'

Over the following weeks our assembly of evidence, coupled to my question and answer sessions with Neil, helped us get a feel for whether Fayed had indeed made his allegations out of spite in September 1994, as Neil contended. Malcolm and I spent endless days in the office, arguing over the importance or unimportance of every tiny piece of evidence or anomaly that we turned up. We would bat each argument back and forth, sometimes losing our tempers, but eventually paring everything down to facts that both of us found completely acceptable as truth.

Malcolm was the perfect foil to my increasing identification with the Hamiltons' plight. A more sceptical and perceptive person I could not have found, but crucially, as far as the evidence was concerned, he was untainted by prejudice and prepared to look at it on its merits. Nevertheless, in those early days our contrasting standpoints occasionally resulted in arguments between us that became so heated that the girls working in the lobby downstairs would come up and ask us to quieten down. Meanwhile, the piles of documents grew on the shelves around the walls and the computer files expanded and expanded with each new discovery.

The events in the days immediately prior to Fayed's allegations being printed in *The Guardian* began to take shape . . .

On September 22 1994, the very next day following the European Court of Human Rights Ruling, Fayed telephoned Ian Greer, his former lobbyist, and arranged a meeting, during which Greer claimed Fayed was irate and greatly critical of Neil Hamilton.

Greer referred to this in his witness statement: "He said that he had thought that he (Neil), was a friend and someone who, given the opportunity, would help him. He complained that, contrary to these expectations, Mr Hamilton, on being appointed to his ministerial position, had ignored him and not even replied to a letter of congratulations he had sent him on his appointment to the DTI."

Greer went on to say that Fayed also alleged that Margaret Thatcher had been involved in "deal making" during and after her premiership. Fayed suggested this was why Thatcher lived in a £4-million house and went on to claim that no Prime Minister from Edward Heath onwards had been free from bribery and corruption. He also made allegations of corruption against the Home Secretary, Michael Howard MP.

On 25 September Fayed was on the phone again, this time to

Brian Hitchen of the *Sunday Express*. Still agitated, he told Hitchen that Neil had stayed three days at the Paris Ritz and had quaffed bottles of wine costing £200 each; and that Neil had received £50,000 from him via Ian Greer to ask 17 questions on his behalf in the House of Commons.

Five days after receiving the call, Brian Hitchen met Prime Minister John Major. Christopher Meyer (the PM's Press Secretary) and Sir Robin Butler (the Cabinet Secretary) also attended the meeting. Alex Allan (the PM's Private Secretary) took notes. Hitchen related Fayed's allegations and his request that the DTI report should be withdrawn and that Major should see him. He also passed on Fayed's threat that, if he did not get satisfaction, he would go to the leader of the Opposition, Tony Blair, and repeat his allegations. Hitchen said that Fayed was livid that the ECHR had rejected his appeal to quash the report that had crushed his reputation to pulp.

Major told Hitchen to go back to Fayed and tell him in plain English that he would not succumb to blackmail, even if his allegations would ultimately damage the Government. When Hitchen left, Major asked Robin Butler to investigate all Fayed's allegations. Butler set about his inquiry that very evening, nominating Peter Gregson, Permanent Secretary at the DTI, and Gerald Hosker, Treasury Solicitor, to investigate. Their subsequent investigation found nothing to substantiate Fayed's "wild" corruption allegations or to arouse comment on Neil's behaviour.

Three days later Sir Robin met the Prime Minister again at Number Ten to discuss Fayed's threats to destroy the Government with allegations of corruption. Alex Allan suggested that Fayed had made these sorts of allegations against other people before, but had not produced any evidence. He suggested they should not expect any evidence to be produced now against Neil.

'Sir Robin telephoned me here at home on Sunday,' Neil told me, 'and put Fayed's allegations to me. I told him that when I was a back-bencher I had sympathised with Fayed in his battle with Tiny Rowland, and that I had put down a number of questions in support. I admitted the stay at the Ritz but assured him that, although I had enjoyed it, it had never coloured my motivation to support Fayed. I also assured Sir Robin that I had never taken any money for the support I gave. I arranged to meet him at Number Ten about a week later.'

Meanwhile Fayed continued to meet Peter Preston, promising to send *The Guardian* documents that would support his allegations. They did nothing of the sort, consisting largely of copies of letters between Fayed, Neil and Ian Greer. They were not incriminating at all, but a jaundiced spin on them could make them appear so.

The day they arrived at *The Guardian's* offices in Farringdon Road, October 17 1994, Preston went back to their "Egyptian friend," later in the day to obtain a statement confirming that he had paid Neil Hamilton to ask questions, while at Number Ten Downing Street John Major met Robin Butler and Richard Ryder yet again. It was decided that Major would ask Neil for a written assurance that he had not received any payments from Fayed.

The following day, 18 October 1994, David Hencke, the journalist, talked with Fayed for about ten minutes. Fayed told him that Neil had been paid £2,000 per question to put down seventeen questions, (i.e. £34,000 in all). Hencke also claimed that Fayed released a copy of the Ritz bill during this meeting, although we would establish later that the evidence does not support this.

That evening Fayed's emissary, Brian Hitchen from the *Sunday Express*, went to Number Ten for his second meeting with John Major. Christopher Meyer took notes:

> *There could be no question of the Prime Minister seeing Fayed or doing deals with him. Fayed had been making threats, but the PM would not allow himself to be drawn into something which looked like blackmail. Hitchen said that he agreed entirely. Major said that there was no prospect of the DTI investigation being re-opened, or treating Fayed's passport application differently to anyone else's. The PM remarked that Fayed was wrong if he thought that his threats would succeed.*

'Fayed is not very stable,' Hitchen told the meeting. 'He doesn't think like we do. He is very ruthless. If he thought he could bring people down, he would do so. He also claims to have given certain papers and made allegations to Paddy Ashdown because he was fed up and wanted something done about the DTI report and his passport. I can't keep stalling him.'

The same day the Privileges Committee charged with investigating the two Tory MP's, David Treddinick and Graham Riddick, (whom the *Sunday Times* claimed had been entrapped into taking £1,000 each to ask a question), narrowly voted to conduct their inquiry in private session. The Committee split down party lines and the Labour contingent were not happy. And, as if that were not enough, that same day sixty-one Labour MPs signed a Commons motion demanding publication of an investigation by Michael Heseltine into allegations that Tory peer, Lord Archer, had been involved in insider-dealing of shares in Anglia Television.

Peter Preston faxed Fayed a draft outline of a proposed article by David Hencke, based on his allegations against Greer, Hamilton and Smith, for his approval. Despite Hencke's conviction that Fayed's documents meant that Hamilton and Greer were "banged completely to rights," Preston complained in his fax: ". . . *nothing in the paperwork proves that Hamilton was doing this for money.*"

The following day, 19 October 1994, Hencke and Preston put together at least two drafts of Hencke's story about Hamilton's stay at the Ritz, and Greer paying him and Smith to ask questions on Fayed's behalf in the 1980s.

Later that day Neil wrote a letter in long hand to John Major, setting out his response to Fayed's specific allegations, as communicated by Brian Hitchen:

> *I refute the allegations reportedly made against me by Mr Al Fayed that he paid me £50,000 (or any money) via Ian Greer (or anyone else) to ask questions on his behalf in the House of Commons – or to do any other thing on his behalf.*
>
> *I refute also the allegation that I telephoned him following my receipt of a letter from him on my appointment as a DTI minister. I accepted the advice of DTI solicitors that I should not reply and have had no contact with him since I joined the Government in July 1990.*
>
> *As to the allegation of three nights stay at the Ritz, I actually stayed there longer. I cannot remember the nominal cost of a room there but I am absolutely certain that I ordered no wine costing £200 a bottle. As I recall non-vintage champagnes were about £50 each and we had one per night.*

More allegations of sleaze were being piled on the Tories in the form of questions in the house by Labour MPs Tam Dalyell and Jeff Rooker, over allegations that former Prime Minister Margaret Thatcher's son, Mark, had been earning large commissions from arms sales to the Saudi Government. In a separate attack Paddy Ashdown appealed to John Major to introduce a bill to improve the standards of ethics in public life.

As the commotion carried on developing, David Hencke and Peter Preston were putting the finishing touches to an article based wholly on Fayed's wild allegations.

The evening of that day the Privileges Committee investigation into Riddick and Tredinnick broke up in disarray, when all seven Labour MPs walked out in protest at the decision to hold the inquiry in private. Later still, as David Hencke's ill-researched and reckless story rolled off *The Guardian*'s presses, Hencke contacted Labour MP Alan Williams. He got him to persuade Neil's opposite number, Labour MP Stuart Bell, to raise Fayed's allegations contained in his article from the floor of the House of Commons. In this way, Fayed's allegations would benefit from Parliamentary Privilege before his article hit the streets the following day.

The next morning *The Guardian*'s headline screamed, *TORY MPS WERE PAID TO PLANT QUESTIONS SAYS HARRODS CHIEF*, accompanied by a large photograph of Neil. The article stated that between 1987 and 1989, lobbyist Ian Greer had paid Neil Hamilton and Tim Smith £2,000 a time to ask questions in parliament on behalf of Fayed, that Neil and Christine had free shopping at Harrods and a free stay at the Ritz.

By the end of the day Tim Smith's letter of resignation was in John Major's hands, admitting that his actions might damage both himself and the Government. But he resigned not because he had taken any money from Ian Greer, as Hencke's article alleged, but because he had taken money off Fayed directly, an allegation which, at that time, *had not even been made*.

Disastrously for Neil and Ian Greer, Smith didn't clarify this in his resignation letter, thus giving *The Guardian* and the rest of the British media the impression that *The Guardian*'s allegations against Tim Smith were true and that Greer and Hamilton were equally guilty. Smith disappeared into obscurity, allowing the impression to fester and grow.

'Did you think of resigning?' I asked Neil.

'I decided that would compromise my standing. Some of the Cabinet thought I should resign because Tim had, but the Prime Minister argued that it would be against the principle of natural justice to force me to resign when Robin Butler's internal investigation had not found any evidence of improper behaviour. And the PM won the Cabinet round to his view.'

Nevertheless, it was undeniable that Tim Smith's resignation represented a massive breakthrough in Fayed's campaign, while simultaneously damaging Neil's credibility. Fayed did all he could to exploit it. He set his spokesman, Michael Cole, to drip-feeding various newspapers with false exclusive stories relating to Tory sleaze, hooking each one in turn.

Five days after the article had appeared in *The Guardian*, Neil was called into the Chief Whip's office for another meeting with Richard Ryder, this time also attended by Robin Butler and Michael Heseltine, to answer another two allegations. The first was that he had been paid to ask questions by Mobil Oil. The second that he had been financially involved with a company that had links with another company under investigation by the Serious Fraud Office. Neil was able to refute both allegations subsequently, but the simple fact that more allegations had been made was enough to push Heseltine over the edge. Overwhelmed by the media onslaught, later that day he and John Major demanded, and received, Neil's resignation from the DTI.

For Neil and Christine it was the start of a three-year battle – a battle with a powerful newspaper that had printed an entirely false story and wouldn't admit it. That story started a blind rampage amongst the media industry, which trampled everywhere and looked nowhere.

Christine brought another tray of tea into the dining room, placed it on the table with a wan smile, and left. 'Returning to the issue of the commission payments you took from Ian Greer,' I said. 'What were they for?'

Neil explained: In early 1987 he had been approached by National Nuclear Corporation (NNC), of Knutsford who wanted professional parliamentary advice.

'I did not propose myself to them as a consultant because I didn't feel able to represent them as capably as a professional lobbying company. They asked if I could recommend any lobbying companies and I gave them several names. I told them Ian

Greer had done good work for British Airways and that, in my view, he was the best.'

After receiving an endorsement from Lord King of British Airways, NNC appointed Greer's company, IGA, in April 1987. Greer subsequently offered Neil, in accordance with his usual practice, an ex-gratia commission of £4,000 for the introduction, calculated at 10% of the first year's fee of £40,000.

'As I already told you last week, I did not know beforehand that Greer made such payments,' Neil said firmly. 'But I was happy to accept it when it was offered. There was absolutely nothing improper in doing so.'

Six months later, NNC, while expressing no dissatisfaction with IGA, approached Neil again and invited him once more to be their consultant. This time he accepted and was engaged at a fee of £7,500. Neil registered the consultancy as required in the MPs' Register of Members' Interests. But by coming back to him, NNC proved conclusively that they would have hired him as a consultant earlier, if he had been agreeable. So Neil could be seen to have knowingly passed up an opportunity to generate legitimate income very easily. This stopped me in my tracks.

'When did Fayed allege he gave you your first payment?'

'June 1987.'

'That would be two months after you turned down the chance of a consultancy with NNC, is that right?'

'Er, I'm not sure.' He rummaged through some of the documents. 'Yes. That's right. NNC first approached me in April, Fayed alleged his first cash payment of £2,500 was given to me on 2 June.'

So Fayed would have the world believe that in April 1987 Neil Hamilton turned down a legitimate consultancy, but only two months later he corruptly accepted a bribe from him. Did it seem likely, I asked myself? What would be the point? Neil left the room for a moment while I mulled over my interpretation of these events.

'What about the second commission payment?' I asked when he returned.

'In 1986 a BBC "That's Life" programme attacked United States Tobacco (UST) for marketing its oral tobacco product, Skoal Bandits, claiming they were a major cause of mouth cancer. UST contacted me for my advice as they knew I was involved in my own battle with the BBC over the "Panorama" programme, "Maggie's Militant Tendency." They said that the "That's Life" programme was a gross distortion of the truth and that they intended taking the BBC to court.'

'UST showed me research, subsequently confirmed by the Swedish Government's own independent research, which proved that their product was over a hundred times less damaging to health than cigarettes. Two years later, UST also told me that they suspected that the British Government were threatening to ban Skoal Bandits after having been persuaded by the Government with grants to build a new factory in Scotland. I offered them my support from the outset. In my opinion UST were being treated disgracefully, and the fact that they are a tobacco company doesn't make any difference.'

'So how come you earned a commission for supporting them?'

Neil frowned. 'I didn't "earn a commission for supporting them", as you put it, at all. I was not alone in supporting UST. Other MPs, including Eric Forth and Michael Brown, thought the company was getting a raw deal too, and when it became clear that they needed more help than we could give, Brown recommended three lobbying companies to them. Greer was selected from the three, and when he was signed up he granted a commission, which he split between Brown and myself because I endorsed the list Brown put forward. I told you all this last week.'

'Yes, I know. Don't be surprised if I ask you about it again and again, either.' I reflected on Neil's support for a tobacco company and a company that designs nuclear power stations. 'You're not really "Mr Politically-Correct," are you? Are there any other unpopular causes you've championed, such as seal-clubbing, perhaps?'

He was far too civilised to take offence at my baiting. 'Well, there was Associated Octel.' I happened to know the company well. It was the one that made lead additives for petrol.

'What?' I exclaimed. 'When everyone is dead against lead in petrol? Why?'

'Primarily because they were a significant local employer, and they provided me with independent research which showed that lead substitutes polyaromatics and benzines are highly carcinogenic. In the big push for unleaded petrol everyone relied on inconclusive evidence that suggested that lead additives contribute to brain damage in children, but we've had lead in petrol for decades, and nobody has done any research into the effect of millions of cars spewing out benzines. They seemed to have a good case, and as a major local employer, I supported them.'

'You don't half go against the grain, don't you?' I started to count on my fingers. 'I mean, a company designing nuclear power-stations, a company making tobacco products, and to top that, a company making lead additives for petrol!'

'I suppose if anyone wanted a nuclear-powered lead-tipped cigarette designing, I'd be the perfect person to organise it,' he chuckled, and the sheer absurdity of the combination set us both off in a laughing fit that had tears running down my face and face muscles aching. It was no wonder he had got himself into such trouble.

Christine popped her head around the door. 'I thought you two were supposed to be getting down to some serious work?'

'It's just your husband,' I said. 'He's been telling me of all the politically-correct causes he's supported over the years.'

Christine rolled her eyes into her forehead like "Gromit" the ever-suffering dog in Nick Park's famous animation films. 'You can see what I've had to put up with, can't you? More tea?'

'Yes please,' I replied, automatically.

'But to be serious about this' Neil said. 'I'm a constituency MP, or rather, I was, and both NNC and Octel were large local employers. As for UST, I have a brain of my own, thank you very much, and if I think a cause should be supported, I support it. The Commons these days is full of lobby-fodder and there are enough MPs saving whales and hugging trees as it is.'

Any support given to a tobacco company by an MP is invariably slated as inappropriate, yet Neil's actions were entirely in keeping with his own professed beliefs in an individual's right of choice. Unlike many other MPs, he had never been a supporter of politically-correct causes, purely for the reflected kudos to be garnered thereby. As it happens, his support for UST was vindicated when subsequent regulations banning oral tobacco were later quashed by the High Court as "unfair and unlawful." Furthermore, in mid-1998 it was reported that the New Zealand Government was considering putting lead back into petrol on environmental grounds.

Thus far, although Neil had enjoyed two commissions from Greer, totalling £10,000, he did not pursue this easy way of acquiring perfectly legitimate income. He referred no more companies to Greer, despite being perfectly placed to do so in his position as vice chairman of the Conservative back-bench Trade and Industry Committee.

I looked back down to the thirteen charges on the list in front of me. Of all the allegations *The Guardian* made, one of the most striking was the charge that he had accepted "free gifts" from Greer; two tickets to America (purchase price £1,594), a painting (£700) and garden furniture (£959.95) – making a total of £3,253.95.

'Tell me about these free gifts from Ian Greer' I invited.

'I never received any free gifts from Ian Greer. What you're referring to is *The Guardian's* wilful misinterpretation of facts to confuse the media. When Ian told me that he was giving me a commission, I naturally expected to pay income tax. There were a number of things I wanted for the house, and I had plans to visit the States. By getting Ian to provide these and offset them against the commission, I thought that I would be reducing my income tax.'

'Why? What's the difference?'

'Well, the Inland Revenue deems the taxable value of goods to be their market or second-hand value rather than their purchase price, and as the second-hand value of goods is invariably less than their purchase price, you save tax. Companies spend thousands with clever accountants to avoid paying tax legally. I was doing no different. *The Guardian* has really gone to town on these, both in the paper and in their book *Sleaze,* making it look as if Ian was providing freebies willy-nilly. He wasn't. The sums he paid out were deducted from what he had granted me.'

The facts bore out everything Neil said. In July 1989 Greer settled his payment to Neil in full with a cheque for £6,746.05 which, when added to the purchase value of the "free" gifts, makes £10,000 exactly. Neil proved from his bank statements that this cheque had been paid into his bank five years before *The Guardian* printed its allegations. The cheque and the goods were also properly entered into Greer's books, which he would hardly have done if there had been anything to hide. Although Greer had freely surrendered his books to *The Guardian*, the paper, in its article on 8 April 1997, led its readership to the inference that its journalists had discovered, by their own investigations, some new corrupt facet of Neil and Greer's relationship.

For instance:

Hamilton took £10,000 in undeclared sums from Ian Greer in relation to companies he was lobbying for.

And:

Hamilton admitted taking the money.

The paper did not mention that the rules on the registration of commission fees were not clarified until much later; nor did it explain why Neil gave his support to NNC and UST, nor did it mention that he had pro-actively and freely disclosed receiving commission fees from Greer.

Despite having already listed the commission payments as one "charge", *The Guardian* then listed a separate "charge" that Neil took "free gifts" to the value of £3,249.95 and a cheque for £6,746.05, with no mention that the gifts and the cheque were part of the same £10,000 they had already listed, not something additional.

Neil's commission fees were then broken down into their component parts of £4,000, (for Greer's engagement by NNC), and £6,000, (for Greer's engagement by UST), and then repre-sented as two additional and separate charges, leading *The Guardian's* readers to the conclusion that Neil had received even more money from Greer. In the end they listed the commission payments and various goods in kind eight times in eight different contexts in the same article, giving any casual reader the impression that a simply enormous amount of money had changed hands.

'So, why didn't you register these commission payments?' I asked Neil.

'Because the rules which governed registrations at the time only covered payments which might influence a Member's parliamentary behaviour,' he explained, 'like directorships or consultancies. I've already mentioned that two other MPs had received commissions too: Michael Brown and Sir Michael Grylls. And they hadn't registered them either. As I told you last week, in 1990 the Select Committee on Members' Interests investigated the commissions to Grylls. Well, they didn't find anything improper in them at all, and though they recommended that all payments of whatever nature should be registered from that point onwards, the committee agreed that the rules were unclear and that there was no category in which to register them even if someone had wanted to. Check it out for yourself. And, for that matter, check out my behaviour as a back-bench MP and as a Minister to see for yourself if they did influence my behaviour. You'll find that they didn't.'

'Don't worry,' I assured him, 'If I'm putting myself up against a national newspaper I'm going to have to check everything.'

But before I left for the day there was one last charge which I wanted to address. I picked up my list. 'It says here that you didn't declare these payments for tax purposes, but that you did declare them once the libel trial became public.'

'This is one of the best examples of misleading reporting you will find. You should bear it in mind when looking at all the other things *The Guardian* says about me and what I'm supposed to have done. The facts are these. I did "declare" these payments to my accountant, but he told me that ex-gratia payments that bore no contractual obligation did not attract income tax. Therefore, they were not "declared" to the Inland Revenue because there was no point in doing so. You don't declare income that isn't taxable.'

'Then why did you try and reduce your income tax by taking goods in kind from Ian Greer, instead of taking a cheque for the full amount?'

'Because I didn't know at that time that commission payments carried no income tax. If I had, I *would* have taken a cheque for the full amount. Look, the very fact that I sought to reduce my income tax by taking goods surely proves that I intended to declare the payment. If I had intended defrauding the Inland Revenue there would have been absolutely no point in my attempting to reduce what I expected to pay.'

'What do you mean when you say that "payments that carried no contractual obligation were not taxable". I'm not quite sure I understand you.'

'The criterion is whether I could have sued Ian if he didn't pay me. The fact is I wouldn't have had a leg to stand on if he didn't. It was an *ex-gratia* payment.'

'Oh. I see.' But I was not convinced. Who would be? I started to stare into the middle-distance again when the thought again crossed my mind that there might indeed be something fishy in among the red herrings. Neil divined my doubts before I expressed them.

'Look, my accountant is one of the most reputable in London, and has all sorts of MPs as clients. There is no way he would support me and put his reputation at risk for the couple of hundred pounds he bills me each year, unless it was the truth.'

'Did he support you? What did he say?'

'You'll find a letter from him in among the documents I gave you last week. He bears out everything I've told you, and if you read my submission to Downey I quote the case law that proves that my accountant's advice was spot-on.'

I looked back down to the "charge sheet." 'But it says here that you did declare them to the Inland Revenue after the libel trial collapsed. Why did you do that, if they weren't taxable?'

'I didn't "declare them" as *The Guardian* says at all. After they started making these allegations against me I wrote to the Inland Revenue for confirmation that my accountant was right, and that I had acted properly on his advice.'

'What was the reply?'

'So far I haven't heard anything from them, but I would be very surprised if they disputed what he advised.'

There were still a number of allegations that needed addressing, but it was past seven o'clock and I was tired and hungry. As I said my goodbyes and drove back to Manchester, I pondered that I had spent more time investigating *The Guardian's* other allegations against Neil than I had the "cash for questions" affair itself. It was hardly a surprise that nobody in the media had bothered to get involved and examine the evidence for themselves.

Now then, I wondered. Was that *The Guardian's* plan?

And then my thoughts drifted to something that I had meant to broach during the interview: the collapse of his libel action against *The Guardian*. Surely you don't pull out of libel actions unless your case is weak? Unless you were guilty as charged?

His explanation for *that* would make interesting listening.

7

A Disproportionate Risk

WHILST I HAD BEEN INTERROGATING NEIL, BACK AT THE OFFICE Malcolm had been examining just how active Neil had been in his back-bench support for Fayed. Was it as fulsome as *The Guardian* intimated?

Of the three MPs (Labour's Dale Campbell-Savours and Conservatives, Tim Smith and Neil Hamilton) who stood out as championing Fayed's cause in Parliament in his battles against Tiny Rowland, we discovered that Neil was demonstrably the least active. First, we looked at his record of written Parliamentary questions, as they were the focus of *The Guardian's* allegations.

Neil's questions were particularly anodyne, and I reproduce them here:

> Is the Secretary of State for Trade and Industry satisfied that the independent directors appointed to the board of the Observer Ltd, in accordance with the conditions recommended by the Monopolies and Merger Commission in 1981, can effectively exercise the role ascribed to them? (11.11.85)
>
> Is the Secretary of State for Trade and Industry satisfied that all the conditions recommended by the Monopolies and Mergers Commission in 1981 for the transfer of the Observer Ltd to Lonrho are being met in full; and will he make a statement? (11.11.85)
>
> May I ask the Secretary of State for Trade and Industry

(1) when his Department expects to be able to reply to letters from Mr M.J.Palmer dated 30 January and 6 February; and (2) when he expects to be in a position to reply to a letter addressed to him dated 2 February from Mohammed Al Fayed. (24.2.87)

May I ask the Chancellor of the Duchy of Lancaster what is the estimated cost to the public funds so far of the current inquiry into House of Fraser plc? (7.6.88)

May I ask the Chancellor of the Duchy of Lancaster when inspectors were appointed to carry out the current inquiry into House of Fraser plc; and what is the earliest date on which he expects to receive their report? (7.6.88).

May I ask the Secretary of State for Foreign and Commonwealth Affairs whether Dr Ashraf Marwan is an accredited diplomat representing the Arab Republic of Egypt in the United Kingdom? (6.4.89).

May I ask the Secretary of State for Defence what representations he has received on the effects of Lonrho's attempts to frustrate British arms sales to Kenya; and if he will make a statement? (7.4.89)

May I ask the Chancellor of the Duchy of Lancaster what information he has on the volume of arms export business with Libya conducted by Lonrho or its subsidiary company, Tradewinds plc? (10.4.89)

May I ask the Secretary of State for the Home Department whether foreigners holding diplomatic passports, but not accredited in the United Kingdom, are exempt from normal entry procedures when visiting this country? (12.4.89)

Rather than directly supportive of Fayed, most of these questions seemed to be merely designed to make mischief against Tiny Rowland and Lonrho, which was exactly why Neil said he supported Fayed in the first place. And if animosity towards Tiny Rowland made for a corrupt politician, Neil has a great many bedfellows.

When we looked at Fayed's sympathisers' record of oral questions, we thought this was particularly revealing. Unlike Dale Campbell-Savours and Tim Smith, Neil asked *no* oral questions nor did he make any representations from the floor of the House, despite having numerous opportunities to do so.

We also studied the record of Early Day Motions (EDMs) and found that Neil had put down just three:

Harrods agreement with staff: EDM 724 applauding agreement reached on 19 February 1987 and noting withdrawal of proposed motion tabled by Clare Short condemning Harrods treatment of their staff. (10.3.87)

Mr Tiny Rowland: EDM 1358 condemning barrage of propaganda being sent to Hon. Members on behalf of Lonrho plc; demanding that he pursue vendetta against House of Fraser elsewhere, and that DTI should urge completion of their inquiry into House of Fraser without delay. (12.7.88)

EDM 809 That this House notes with concern the close links between Lonrho, its subsidiary Tradewinds, and Dr Ashraf Marwan, a close friend of Colonel Gadaffi and the Libyan regime; takes account of serious security implication; and calls for an immediate investigation into the company's operations. (3.5.89).

Tim Smith had tabled only one EDM, but Dale Campbell-Savours tabled fifty-eight, many of which were drafted by Fayed's legal adviser, Royston Webb. All of them were far longer and more vehement than Neil's, yet, perplexingly, *The Guardian* had never suggested that Campbell-Savours had been paid a penny by Fayed.

Neil's unrecorded performance was equally unimpressive, for he had provided us with *proof* of his refusing to put his name to letters to Ministers on Fayed's behalf. Moreover, he was present at only half as many meetings concerning House of Fraser matters as some of his colleagues from the back-bench Trade and Industry Committee – preferring as often as not to attend to other Parliamentary duties that he could easily have passed up had be wished to do so.

Nothing we found was contradictory of anything that Neil had told me. His record of only nine written questions and three EDMs fell well short of Tim Smith's, who tabled twenty-five written questions, one oral question, put down one EDM and initiated an adjournment debate. However, all of Fayed's Tory sympathisers were dwarfed by Campbell-Savours, who tabled eleven written questions, asked two medleys of oral questions, and put down fifty-eight EDMs, almost all of which attacked Tiny Rowland's ownership of the *Observer* newspaper. But here existed one real contradiction that, at that time, we didn't trouble ourselves to solve.

Curiously, in 1986 Campbell-Savours had put down seven written questions and a medley of four oral questions supporting Lonrho's lobbying of the Government to investigate Fayed. In other words, he used to be *pro*-Lonrho and *anti*-Fayed. Yet three years later he swapped sides to become so ardently pro-Fayed and anti-Tiny Rowland that in less than 2½ years from 30 March 1989 to 11 July 1991, his output eclipsed the collective support of all Fayed's Tory sympathisers over the previous six.

In fact, in one five-day period from 24 July 28 July 1989, Campbell-Savours put down twelve lengthy and passionate EDMs and two written questions, thus exceeding the total parliamentary support Hamilton gave Fayed during 3½ years from his first in November 1985 to his last in April 1989. Curious, no?

Furthermore, Campbell-Savours' earlier support for Lonrho against Fayed was during a period when the general opinion was that Lonrho was the unjustified oppressor and Fayed the Establishment victim. Yet, after extracts from the damning DTI report had been printed in the *Observer* newspaper on March 30 1989, Campbell-Savours instantly became Fayed's most ardent supporter, seemingly, even though he had no prior relationship with him to justify his loyalty.

But to return to the extent of Neil's preoccupation or otherwise with House of Fraser and Lonrho affairs, *vis-à-vis* his other activity, to arrive at a clearer picture we consulted Hansard again and made a table of *all* his questions over the same period. This revealed that he asked a total of two hundred and sixteen questions relating to other matters, outnumbering his House of Fraser related activities 25 to 1. Or to put it another way, House of Fraser matters accounted for just 4% of his total questions – hardly the all-consuming obsession that *The Guardian* had implied in their coverage.

Nothing we had found so far discouraged us. On the contrary, it seemed worth digging around a bit more. We thought about the money. The *final* allegation from Fayed was that Neil took £8,000 in vouchers and £20,000 in cash over three years. Since Christine was his parliamentary secretary that meant, on the face of it, that he would have risked both their careers, and maybe even his marriage, for just £28,000. But everyone with any knowledge of the Hamiltons would agree that the couple's whole raison d'être was Neil's political career.

It seemed even less likely to us that Neil would have taken such a risk, particularly as the relevant sum would have been not £28,000 but only £2,500, which was the first (alleged) payment. The lesser sum *alone* would have been enough to establish a corrupt relationship, as there would have been no way of knowing if any further payments would have ensued. So, if Fayed's version is to be believed, it would appear that Neil was prepared to risk all for a single payment of a mere £2,500!

Of course, Tim Smith, who also had a bright political future, did allow himself to fall into Fayed's snare. But Neil's first (alleged) payment is supposed to have taken place in June 1987, and I had already established that Neil turned down the opportunity to acquire a parliamentary consultancy in April, two months earlier. Presumably *The Guardian* expected us all to believe that, despite having passed up a legitimate consultancy in April that later proved to be worth £7,500 per annum, two months later, in June, he was prepared to risk both his and his wife's careers and reputations for a paltry £2,500. It certainly wasn't *proof*, but by any yardstick it was a strong piece of evidence in support of Neil Hamilton's claim to innocence.

Malcolm and I felt that we were beginning to colour in our initial outlines of the two protagonists. We now knew a great deal about Fayed's murky record and we had yet to catch Neil Hamilton out doing anything that came even close to dubious practices. So we started to look at the relationship between the two.

The way the press reported the visits to the Windsors' home and the Paris Ritz made the Hamiltons look grasping and opportunist, though most of us would accept such an offer, provided no strings were attached. And they never made any secret of the fact that they stayed there, as *The Guardian* implied. A number of MPs from both sides came forward to tell us that Neil had frequently talked about their Ritz holiday.

'Not only did Hamilton tell *me* about his stay at the Ritz,' Labour MP Gwyneth Dunwoody told me in the lobby of the Commons a couple of months later, 'he told *everybody* about it.'

And there is documentary evidence both from Fayed's records

and from one of Neil's diaries to show that, just as Fayed had entertained Neil to lunch at 60 Park Lane, so did Neil return the gesture more than once by inviting Fayed to lunch or dine with him at the Commons, both typical indications of an open friendship. I wondered if anyone, had they been in a corrupt relationship, would have flaunted his or her paymaster at the Commons (despite Fayed's interest in securing support in Parliament, he never took up Neil's invitation).

'The thing is,' I suggested to Malcolm after another long day poring over the files, 'these allegations against Neil have resulted in him being subjected to intense media coverage across the world in one of this country's highest-profile, longest-running news stories – agreed?'

'So what?' Malcolm sipped at his mug of tea and waited for me to go on.

'So this: no one has come forward with similar allegations of corrupt practice, or any other instance where Hamilton suggested or even hinted at a similar corrupt arrangement – agreed?'

'But that doesn't prove anything.'

'No, but why would he act so out of character on this one occasion?'

We both fell into a thoughtful silence for a few minutes. 'I suppose it's a point,' Malcolm piped up eventually. 'Whenever anyone is fingered on "Crimewatch UK," other victims and witnesses always come forward. But the fact that no one has in this case doesn't mean anything. He could have been careful. I know if I wanted to keep quiet about £20,000 it would be the easiest thing in the world.'

'Except that Fayed alleges Hamilton received between £6,000 and £15,000 in Harrods vouchers, which were supposed to be depending on which version you take in either £100 or £1,000 denominations. Well, you can only spend those in Harrods. So how come not one member of Harrods counter staff has come forward to the tabloids claiming that he or she saw the Hamiltons buying stuff with vouchers?'

'If you think I'm going to stick my neck out and say that Hamilton is innocent on the basis that no one from Harrods has been to the tabloids you're wrong. As far as I'm concerned it means nothing. For all I know he could be as bent as Fayed and as far as I'm concerned he still is until we find something to make me change my mind.' Malcolm paused and added: 'Because I've not been Hamiltonised like you have.'

I let his side-swipe pass. 'All right then, will you accept this? For Hamilton to have taken £20,000 in £50 notes and hidden it from the world's gaze, including Downey's forensic accountants who crawled all over his and Christine's financial records, he would have to have been pretty "careful," as you put it. Do you accept that?'

'Yes, of course.'

'Well what was it that Fayed's secretary said, that you read out to me the other day? You know, the bit that you said you thought sounded plausible.'

'It was Iris Bond.' Malcolm picked up his file of oral examinations from the Downey inquiry, whilst I reached back to the window ledge for my similar file.

'I've got it. Page 21, question 316.'

Malcolm started by reading out the question from Nigel Pleming, QC for the Inquiry. ' "Were you present when Mr Hamilton was in the office at all when the transactions took place?" Bond replied: "No, I can honestly say I have no idea in what form Mr Al Fayed gave Mr Hamilton the money and whether Mr Hamilton had to ask for it which I think in some cases would be more than likely because Mr Al Fayed loved to play with him and make him virtually beg for his money . . ." '

I cut in, 'And in her answer to the next question, Bond claimed that Christine and Neil Hamilton would telephone and say "is there an envelope ready?" '

Malcolm looked across at me. 'I'm a long way from saying Hamilton isn't bent, and I don't accept that stuff you came out with about no one coming forward, but I think we're finally making some headway. Why would Hamilton, on one hand, be careful about hiding his money, and then, on the other, be so cavalier that he broadcasts his little arrangement to Fayed's staff, whom he hardly knew? If I was on a nice little earner I would keep it close to my chest. It doesn't add up.'

'None of it adds up, Malcolm, because this same man who is supposed to be so avaricious that he would beg for £2,500, turned down a chance of a Parliamentary Consultancy two months before he supposedly started receiving these payments, and the consultancy turned out to be worth £7,500.'

'I don't say you're wrong, but you're way too keen to prove his innocence. It'll be your undoing,' Malcolm cautioned.

Malcolm's scepticism was, I submit, only slightly greater than my own, and I certainly rejected his suggestion that I had been "Hamiltonised." It's just that I had had the opportunity to interrogate the man and satisfy my doubts, whereas Malcolm had to rely on my interpretation of Hamilton's answers.

There were times in those early days that I thought Malcolm's self-imposed policy of maintaining a strict distance from the Hamiltons was frustrating our progress. Neil Hamilton was, after all, the person who was the subject of our investigation and therefore the person we both had to turn to for answers on this and that. If only Malcolm felt more comfortable about picking up the phone to ask him questions, I would be saved from having to act as his go-between.

However, in retrospect Malcolm's role as devil's advocate suited our joint purposes well, as no evidence was ever interpreted in Hamilton's favour without having been tested by argument and receiving both our stamps of approval. But if only Malcolm could *really* believe in the man's innocence, as much as I did, then I felt certain that he would become even more productive in his unearthing of evidence.

I suppose the turning point came when, one evening, I happened upon an extract from one of the papers that the Government had produced for the libel trial. It was a minute made by Cabinet Secretary Sir Robin Butler of a meeting between the Chief Whip, Richard Ryder, and Neil, held on 19 October 1994 i.e. the day before *The Guardian's* article came out.

Richard Ryder had called Neil to his office to relate to him Fayed's allegations against him, as communicated to Prime Minister John Major by *Sunday Express* editor Brian Hitchen. Ryder warned Neil that Fayed's allegations against Tim Smith might turn out to be true, and that this would put pressure on other ministers who had been subject of Fayed's other allegations. I reproduce the extract in full:

The Chief Whip drew his [Hamilton's] attention to Mr Al Fayed's claim that he had evidence to support his allegations in the form of copies of correspondence, cancelled cheques

84

etc. He added that it must be assumed that Mr Al Fayed may have been trying to "set up" Members of Parliament for some time and that conversations might have been taped. He asked Mr Hamilton whether he was entirely confident that nothing discreditable could be produced against him. Mr Hamilton said that there might be thank-you letters for hospitality, but he was sure that there was nothing genuine more compromising than that. In response to the Chief Whip's question whether he knew of anything else in his record which could turn out to be discreditable to the Government when he was put under scrutiny, as he undoubtedly would be, Mr Hamilton confirmed that he could think of nothing in this category.

Until I found this, I had still harboured some doubts as to what might have gone on between Fayed and Neil behind the closed doors of Fayed's office. Everyone has an imagination and I was no different in picturing in my mind a discreet wad of notes being passed from one to the other. However, after reading Butler's minute, what few doubts I had disappeared: ironically, it was Fayed's known mania for secret recordings that did the trick.

The important feature to me was Ryder's warning that Fayed claimed to have lots of evidence to support his allegations, including, crucially, secret tape recordings. Yet Neil, in spite of these warnings, went ahead with libel proceedings against Fayed and *The Guardian* the very next day when the allegations broke. If Neil had taken money behind closed doors, then audio or video tape recordings would have provided lucid proof. His libel action – an action that was set to cost him a small fortune – would have been torpedoed in the most humiliating fashion imaginable if tapes of the type described were produced half way through the proceedings. There could be only two interpretations: either Neil was reckless to the point of delirium, or he was innocent.

The next morning I had Butler's minute on the desk in front of me when Malcolm breezed in. 'I read Fayed's cross examination again last night,' he said. 'The bloke's an idiot. He contradicted himself that many times I actually started laughing.'

I was glad to hear this, but other matters were uppermost in my thoughts. 'Malcolm, one of the problems about proving

Hamilton's guilt or innocence is that it is all supposed to take place behind closed doors, right?'

'What about the brown envelopes at the door of 60 Park Lane?' He was referring to supposed envelopes of cash left at the door of Fayed's Park Lane apartment block.

'That's an allegation that relies on Fayed's closest employees, and it didn't even surface until two years after the first. So if we leave that aside for a moment, we're still stuck with payments behind closed doors, right?'

'Yes, go on.'

'Put yourself in Hamilton's shoes, and imagine that he, or rather, you, had taken wedges of fifty-pound notes.'

'Okay.'

'Well, if you had, would you have embarked on libel proceedings if tapes of your illicit dealings could be produced half-way through the trial?'

'Perhaps he didn't know that Fayed covertly taped his meetings at that time.'

I threw him Butler's minute. 'Oh yes he did' I said, music-hall-style. I left the office to brew up while Malcolm digested the note. When I re-entered with the tea, he was smiling. I knew that he found it as important as I did, but he didn't say so, reverting instead into devil's advocate-mode. But I knew that he knew that I knew he knew.

'Perhaps he's daft as a brush.'

'Well he might be daft, but he would have to be as daft as a lobotomised goldfish to have run up £150,000 of legal bills with the prospect of tapes being playing in Court of him saying something along the lines of "thanks for the money and the vouchers Mohamed, they'll come in useful during the holiday." '

'I must admit, Fayed has a bit of a reputation. Who's he bugged?' he asked himself, looking up the ceiling. 'He's bugged Christoph Bettermann... he's bugged Tiny Rowland . . .'

'He's bugged Lady Powell . . .' I contributed.

'. . . and half of Harrods' staff. He's a bit of a lad, isn't he?'

'A bit of a lad?' I exclaimed. 'He's a bugger!' We broke into laughter, all the more amplified due to our newly-strengthened belief that we were on the right track all the time.

'But what about the Hamiltons' stay in Dodi Fayed's Paris apartment?' Malcolm said, bringing me back down to earth. 'How do you justify that?'

I pondered this for a second. 'I can only tell you what Hamilton told me. As I understand it, the Hamiltons stayed at the Ritz in 1987. When they were invited to a wedding in Paris in 1990 they thought they would see if they could cajole a couple more nights. Hamilton says he telephoned Fayed to see if that would be possible and a member of Fayed's staff phoned back to say the hotel was full but that Mr Al Fayed would be happy to put Dodi's apartment off the Champs-Elysées at their disposal. So they did.'

I took the opportunity to make a point and continued: 'Later, Fayed claimed that he denied the Hamiltons a second stay at the Ritz because they had abused his hospitality the first time; but an invitation to stay at the apartment doesn't sound much like a snub to me. If Hamilton was as corruptible as Fayed claims, would he have trusted him to stay, unsupervised by any host, in his son's home, where private and confidential papers could have been lying around for anyone to see?'

'But the DTI report had just been published,' Malcolm pounced. 'How come Hamilton was even thinking of asking favours of a man who had been so exposed as a fraud and liar?'

'He says he had only read the Press reports and they seemed totally at odds with his own impressions of Fayed, gained over a number of years of friendship, or rather, what he thought was friendship. He said he thought that the DTI report was a Rowland-inspired stitch-up, just as Fayed always warned it would be. Even though he has long stopped having doubts about the inspectors' findings, not least because his own experiences tally with what they found, Hamilton still says that many of Fayed's complaints regarding the DTI's investigations procedures were justified.'

'Hmm,' Malcolm mused. 'I can't say it does his case much good, wangling favours out of Fayed.'

'Look Malcolm, I'm not Hamilton's apologist, but staying two nights at a private flat in Paris is hardly a big deal, if you accept, and I do accept, that Hamilton considered Fayed to be a friend. Anyway,' I went on, my voice rising, 'what about Tony blinking Blair? What about *his* freebies? You've only got to say the words "Tuscany" and "villa" in the same sentence and Tony's got the car packed with Cherie and the kids, the mother-in-law and the nanny and that's the last you see of him for a fortnight!'

'I'm just keeping you in check, that's all. If I didn't, no one would, and the next thing you'd be telling me he's as innocent as Mother Teresa.'

I smiled in acknowledgement as I prepared to leave for Nether Alderley and another session with Neil.

'What's on the agenda this time?' Malcolm asked, as I packed up my material.

'The collapse of the libel trial. And all these lies that they say he told. There's two articulated in that Internet article with all the charges, and another five listed in *Sleaze*'. I was referring to *The Guardian's* book on the "cash for questions" affair by David Leigh & Ed Vulliamy.

I left Malcolm to his studies and set off for leafy Cheshire.

'Hi Neil' I said, as he opened the door. Christine automatically put the kettle on as we settled down in the dining room across the table. It was becoming a ritual. I opened up my briefcase and pulled out my copy of *Sleaze* plus the Internet article and settled down. A few minutes later Christine brought in a tray with the tea.

One of the most damaging events from Neil's point of view, after the initial allegations, was the collapse of the libel trial against *The Guardian* for its first article, as this confirmed many people's belief that he was guilty as charged.

But the way this came about is illuminating and, as I was soon to find out, reflects not one bit on the strength and justice of Neil's case: despite both Neil's and Greer's actions to prevent it, *The Guardian* had successfully applied to the High Court to have their cases heard together and treated as one (the term used is a "consolidated action"). This meant that *any weakness in either of the two plaintiff's cases would affect the other's,* as they were inseparable. And that was exactly what happened.

'Talk me through the collapse of the libel action, from the very beginning,' I said.

'I know this off by heart, its been etched into my memory forever.' He shuffled in his seat like a pianist about to hit the keys. 'It all began in the evening of 26 September 1996, whilst driving to a speaking engagement. I received a call from my solicitor, Andrew Stephenson of Peter Carter-Ruck and partners: "There's a problem regarding Greer's evidence," he said, "you had better come in and see me tomorrow morning." '

'What was the problem?' I asked.

'It concerned Ian Greer's action, which included a separate claim for "special damages" for loss of business, because clients had gone elsewhere for fear of being tainted by association. To quantify the damages, Greer engaged accountants to examine his books and the evidence was also submitted to *The Guardian's* counsel. The next morning, Andrew Stephenson told me that Greer's books showed that Greer had paid the Conservative MP Sir Michael Grylls six commission payments for introducing clients in the years up to 1990. There would have been no problem about that, except for the fact that, in 1990, Greer told the Select Committee on Members' Interests that he had given only *three* commissions to Grylls during that period.'

'So how did this affect your case?'

'Our legal team advised me that this discrepancy was going to have a devastating effect on Ian's credibility, and that they would have to advise him to drop the case. Can you imagine how we felt? We'd just run up legal bills for God knows how many thousands of pounds, and our co-plaintiff was about to jump ship. It would be bound to affect the perception of my case, detrimentally.'

'So what did you do? Couldn't you carry on?'

'The ridiculous thing is, as things transpired, if I had reacted to the news by grinning and saying something inane like: "Tut, tut. Oh well, never mind", I could have carried on. However, I reacted the same way that anyone would. I exploded and called Ian all the names under the sun for being such a stupid berk and not realising the time-bomb that was ticking away all that time we were preparing our cases.'

'So, why did that cause you to have to pull out?'.

'Well, after I ranted and raged, my legal people blithely informed me that "an irreconcilable conflict of interest between you and your co-plaintiff clearly now exists, and as such we are obliged by the rules of professional conduct to discontinue acting for either client. We therefore have no choice but to withdraw forthwith as your legal representatives. In other words, "you'll find the Yellow Pages on the shelf and our invoice will be in the post." '

Neil had already incurred legal bills of well over £100,000 and was right back at square one. Later the same evening, *The Guardian* announced that they had three new witnesses to corroborate yet another (different) version of Fayed's allegations. The emergence of these witnesses was subsequently and dishonestly quoted by the paper's new editor, Alan Rusbridger, as being one of the reasons for the collapse of Neil's libel case, implying that it wouldn't have stood up in court anyway.

In the minds of the public and the media, none of whom would have known the truth, it furthered the conclusion that Neil and Greer must indeed have been guilty all along. From then on *The Guardian* had carte blanche to write more or less whatever it liked about them, free from any threat of a libel action.

It was this freedom from legal action that allowed *The Guardian* to portray Neil as a consummate liar – one of the paper's most effective devices to distract attention away from an examination of its evidence. It seemed that as long as everyone was convinced that he was not a man to be believed, people would swallow anything that was said about him.

It was time to see if there was any substance in this. I opened up *Sleaze* at page 162 and restarted the interview.

'I've got a list of seven lies *The Guardian* allege you told,' I said to Neil. 'So, in other words, according to *The Guardian* you're a pathological liar. What do you say to that?'

'When the libel trial collapsed, Preston, Rusbridger, Leigh, Hencke and the rest of them ran amok in a vindictive campaign against me. The real lies are their stories of my "lies", but their power and influence is such they've succeeded largely in persuading the indolent media that it's all true. But it's not. Put them to me, one by one.'

I picked up the book. 'In here Leigh and Vulliamy refer to a letter you wrote to Peter Preston in October 1993. Before we address the specifics, why did you write it?'

'Three months earlier in July 1993 I was interviewed by David Hencke and John Mullin. I told you about this during our very first session in the library.' I nodded. 'Well, that was just before the Summer Recess. Three months later I heard from either Greer's Managing Director, Andrew Smith, or Ian himself, I can't remember now but it doesn't matter, anyway, I heard that *The Guardian* were planning a defamatory article against me based on that interview, so I wrote to Peter Preston and warned him that if the paper implied my stay at the Ritz was in any way linked to the support I had given Fayed, he could expect to hear from Peter Carter-Ruck and Partners.' Carter-Ruck are one of the most famous solicitors' firms in England specialising in libel cases.

He continued. 'Anyway, I made a handful of totally innocuous mistakes in my letter to Preston that can be equated to proof errors.'

I started to put each of these allegations to Neil, one by one. 'Leigh and Vulliamy claim you lied when you said that Fayed had told you that private rooms existed at the Ritz in Paris. They say that The Ritz does not have private rooms.'

'I'm not sure Vulliamy claimed anything,' Neil replied, 'Leigh usually gives a by-line to another journalist for his most poisonous work so it doesn't draw attention to him. It gives his stuff credibility Vulliamy was probably just roped in for window-dressing.' I made a mental note as he started to answer the question. 'When we were invited over by Fayed, I politely expressed reservations about accepting, as it might mean that paying guests would be displaced, which would lose the hotel revenue. Fayed assured me that he always maintained private rooms which we could use if the hotel was full, so there would be no question of any paying guests being displaced.'

'Leigh says that there are no private rooms. What do you say to that?'

'Well, I suppose he wouldn't say anything that could be disproved so easily, so I suppose I must accept that it's true. But I'm telling you, I know what Fayed told me and he definitely said that private rooms existed. I'm not a liar and I wouldn't lie to you now.'

I was perplexed. I believed Neil's version of what Fayed said to him, but if private rooms didn't exist, then that was that. 'Okay, I guess we can't go any further on that one. Next one: It says here that you lied when you claimed that you never saw a bill for your stay.'

'I never said there wasn't a bill at all. When I was interviewed about this, almost six years had passed since our stay and I couldn't honestly remember one way or another. Now if I had paid a bill, I would have remembered that, but, as I say, we were Fayed's guests so I wasn't sure whether I had signed a bill or not. Leigh's making something out of nothing. Here, give me the book a minute.' I passed it to him. 'Here, see, Leigh reprints my letter and I specifically allow for the possibility that I was presented with a bill to sign. See.' His finger rested half-way up page 160.

I read the extract from his letter out aloud ' "it is surprising that Mr Hencke claims to have a copy of the bill, which he declines to show me, if there is such a document it can only be a notional transaction for internal accounting purposes as Fayed owns the Hotel." '

I looked up at him.

' "If there is such a document" is what I wrote,' he pointed out. 'I never discounted the possibility that a bill existed. As it turns out, I was right about its purpose too. It was an internal bill for meals and wine and other sundries, which would have cost Fayed a couple of hundred pounds at the most. Despite what *The Guardian* implies, they still haven't produced any bill for the six nights stay.'

'Okay. Next one . . .'

'I hope you've taken that on board, Jonathan. There's a chasm of difference between being guest of the owner of a hotel, and someone paying a hotel bill on your behalf that costs them thousands of pounds of their own money.'

'Don't worry, I get the picture. Oh, before I move on, why didn't you register the stay?' I asked.

'Because the hotel was owned by Fayed, my stay would have had a status akin to staying in a friend's private residence and would therefore not be registrable, or so I thought. The Select Committee investigated this in 1994, and didn't agree with me, but they did say that seven years earlier things were far less clear and strict than after 1993 when the rules were tightened up. It would have been more helpful if they also said that, if I had registered it, it would probably have been the first registration of private hospitality by any MP since records began. But they didn't.'

'Okay. Next one . . .

'Incidentally, Tony Blair and John Prescott both stayed the weekend at Gleneagles hotel, paid for by Conoco Oil in other words, Blair's and Prescott's stays cost Conoco a packet unlike my stay at the Ritz and they didn't register them either.'

'Why didn't the Tories complain?'

'They did, in 1995. The same Members' Interests Committee investigated Blair's and Prescott's failures to register and, as in my case, recommended no action, even though Prescott stayed there in 1994 – *after* the rules were changed, mind you, when there could have been no room for doubt about the matter.'

'So how come I haven't heard about it?'

'Because the media was only interested in its chosen agenda of "Tory sleaze" under an unpopular Government. No one was interested in the Opposition.'

'Yes. Okay. Anyway, we must press on. The next one says that you uttered a "blatant lie" when you claimed that it was untrue that you and Fayed were acquainted before Greer came on the scene. What do you say to that?'

'Leigh playing his poisonous games again. Perhaps he should invent a board game: "Twisted Reporting, a game for all crazed left-wing zealots." It would sell like hot cakes on Farringdon Road market. If they still have one.'

'Seriously, please.'

'If you look at the beginning of my letter I make it clear that I first took an interest in House of Fraser in 1984, nearly two years before Greer came on the scene.'

I read out the relevant section:' "Almost all my time as a back-bencher I was a Trade and Industry Committee officer. Sir Peter Hordern MP was consultant to House of Fraser and in 1984 invited the officers to lunch at Harrods to meet Professor Roland Smith [then chairman] and fellow directors. The main issue was the continuing Lonrho offensive in the wake of the prohibition by the Government of the Lonrho take-over".'

'Pass it to me.' I did as he asked and he began to read out another extract from his letter. 'Here it is: "It seems pretty clear that Mr Hencke is trying to weave a conspiracy along the lines of '*Greer lobbies for Fayed and persuades Hamilton to put down PQs etc. as a backbencher. Hamilton then goes into Government as competition/company investigations minister and uses influence to promote interest of Greer client, Fayed.*' " This falls down as I met Fayed through Sir Peter Hordern before Greer was taken on. My interest in House of Fraser pre-dates Greer's involvement.'

He put the book down. 'The only point I was making is that my interest in House of Fraser pre-dated Fayed engagement of Ian Greer and therefore my interest could not have been influenced by Greer. It's true that I was eventually introduced to Fayed by Greer years later, not by Sir Peter Hordern, as I had thought, but my error of memory is absolutely utterly irrelevant. I could have got the point across just as well if had said for a second time that I was introduced to *House of Fraser* by Sir Peter Hordern, just as I said at the beginning of my letter.'

'So what do you make of it? The charge that you lied?'

'The lie is the charge itself. Leigh's lying when he states that I lied. I can prove that my error is insignificant and obviously not intentional. Leigh, however, would be hard pressed to claim that his tortuous interpretation of facts is anything other than absolutely intentional so that he can label me as a liar!'

'The "fourth lie" it says here, is that you said you did nothing to support Fayed after mid-1988, whereas you "lobbied and pressurised ministers on Fayed's behalf for a much longer period after the DTI report had been published, until December 1989." '

'Well, that's an out-and-out lie.'

'Be specific.' I knew what he was going to say but didn't let on.

'The DTI report wasn't published until March 1990, not 1989 as Leigh states. In other words, I stopped supporting Fayed before it was published. Tiny Rowland, of course, printed extracts in a special mid-week edition of the *Observer*, which he owned at that time, in March 1989, but why should I have taken any notice of that? Dale Campbell-Savours, David Leigh's best mate in Parliament, decried that issue of the *Observer* in Parliament. Wait there, I'll see if I can find it in Hansard.' Neil left the room for five minutes or so.

He came back holding a copy of Hansard. 'Here it is. This is what Campbell-Savours said from the floor of the House on 4 April 1989, regarding that particular issue of the *Observer*, or "DTI report" as Leigh put it.' Neil read out from Hansard: 'This is what he said: "What business was it of the DTI inspectors to examine the family background of the Al-Fayeds? Surely their terms of reference only related to whether they had the money to purchase the store? Is it not true that, despite all the discussion in the Lonrho broadsheet" he means the *Observer* "Mr Tiny Rowland and Mr Donald Trelford have not produced one shred of evidence to date that the money to buy the House of Fraser was not the property of the Al-Fayeds alone? They have not produced that evidence. Indeed, the report that was published equally states that the inspectors were unable to establish what the facts were. Does the Minister not agree that this is the case?" '

I smiled. I enjoyed listening to in full oratory flood.

'So, what's so sinister about me supporting Fayed with a couple of anaemic anti-Lonrho written questions after Rowland published extracts in the *Observer*? What you should be asking yourself, is why Leigh hardly ever mentioned Dale Campbell-Savours' role in *Sleaze,* yet Campbell-Savours only started supporting Fayed in March 1989, just as I was stopping! And he did about ten times as much as me, yet Leigh, Rusbridger and all the rest of them have said nothing about him. Why not? Why not?'

Little did he and I know that it would take another year to unearth the answer to that one. 'Okay' I said, 'I don't have any problem with you supporting Fayed into 1989, but why did you say in your letter that you stopped in 1988?'

'When I wrote that letter, I did so in haste and made an error,' Neil admitted. 'So I'm human. It came about because, when looking in the Hansard index for any questions relating to "Al Fayed" or "House of Fraser," none of the four questions I asked in 1989 showed up because the subjects of the questions were either about a chap close to Tiny Rowland called Dr Ashraf Marwan, or about Lonrho itself, and were recorded under those names. David Hencke and John Mullin both missed those last four questions too in their articles a year later, and they, unlike me, had over a year to do their research. But apart from Hencke and Mullin, on the same day that Mullin's article appeared, John Fraser, who was Ian Greer's Head of Research, he undertook a computer search on the House of Commons database to establish the total number of questions I had asked, and he missed the last four questions as well. When *they* do it, it's a "mistake," when *I* do it, it's a pre-meditated wilful direct "lie".'

I looked at him and realised just how much he must have suffered from the kind of journalism that the facts, not opinion, were exposing. Being called a liar had obviously gone as deep as being called corrupt. 'Who else has asked you about these so-called lies?'

'No one. I told you when you first came to see me. You're the first person to ask me about all this.'

I thought to myself that the Hamiltons must think sometimes that they've woken up in the middle of some dark Orwellian nightmare. I took a break from the interview and asked him about some of the low-points they had endured over the previous three-and-a-half-years. *The Guardian's* original article and his forced resignation from the Government in 1994; the collapse of the libel trial in 1996; the broadcast of a *Guardian* co-produced Despatches documentary and the publication of *Sleaze* earlier that year (1997); Martin Bell turning up to condemn him a few months later in April, all topped-off by losing his seat at the general election the following month. And each of these occasions had been accompanied by an onslaught of condemnatory but incurious media coverage. Christine and Neil and their families had certainly been put through the mill.

I returned to the book. 'Just a few more to go. The last lie in *Sleaze* is your claim that "you removed yourself from dealing with House of Fraser on your own initiative when you became a minister, when in fact you did so only after an unwise letter to the Department from Fayed and "after a considerable delay," to quote the book.'

'Absolute crap! When I became a Minister and Fayed wrote to congratulate me, my officials showed me his letter and advised me not to reply to him as, at that time, he was embroiled in a legal action against the Government in the European Court of Human Rights. But they also advised me I could still take decisions regarding House of Fraser if I chose to, as my back-bench support had ended three years earlier. It was my decision to delegate matters to another minister. *My* decision. I behaved with absolute propriety. Wait a minute.'

He left the room again, obviously to fetch some more documents. From the cursing coming from the library I figured he was having trouble finding what he was looking for. While he was out the effervescent Christine popped her head around the door. 'More tea?'

'Yes please.'

A few minutes later she returned with a tray, followed by Neil with a file. 'It wasn't where it should have been,' he explained. 'I forgot to put it away after you photocopied it, so you have copies of this stuff yourself.' I shrugged apologetically. 'Anyway, as I was saying, I delegated all matters to do with House of Fraser to another minister, Edward Leigh MP.' He held up a couple of sheets of paper and handed me one of them.

It was a minute from June 5 1992, written by Michael Osborne, a senior official at the DTI. It was titled "Quarterly Report to the Minister".

Mr Hamilton did not wish to be involved in decision-making in relation to House of Fraser and the ECHR matter, in view of his previous involvement with a lobby on behalf of the Fayeds. He suggested that Mr Leigh (DTI Minister Edward Leigh) *would deal.*

Subsequently I telephoned Kate Spall (Hamilton's secretary) *who said that she would circulate her minutes of the meeting to PS/President (President of the Board of Trade Michael Heseltine) and PS/Mr Leigh (DTI Minister Edward Leigh) to see if there was any reaction.*

I handed it back to Neil and he passed me the second note, dated 29 June 1992. It had been written by Hamilton's secretary at the DTI, Kate Spall, confirming what had been discussed between Neil and Dr Catherine Bell, a senior DTI official in the Competition Policy Unit at the DTI.

You met Mr Hamilton to discuss possible conflicts of interest on issues involving Lonrho plc, given the Minister's interest in the House of Fraser takeover while he was a back-bencher. Although there are no legal difficulties, Mr Hamilton agreed that in order to prevent any possible presentational problems, he would not take any further part in decisions involving this company.

So Neil had proof that he had not only delegated House of Fraser matters, but Lonrho matters too. Given that he removed himself from decision-taking *despite receiving advice that he need not*, most reasonable observers might feel that he had acted with absolute propriety.

I wondered what Leigh's game was. 'Why would David Leigh go to such lengths to destroy you?'

'Why do people put hamsters in microwaves? I don't know. The very idea that he would attempt to construe my behaviour as a minister, so as to give the opposite impression to the truth, has got to be indicative of some awful dementia or perversion. The only matter I attended to as a minister concerning Fayed before the files were passed on was signing a routine written reply to a question from the LibDem MP Alex Carlile. It was an answer that was prepared for me by DTI officials without any editorial input from me, and it represented the

Government's position which was actually *unhelpful* to Fayed.'

'Right.' I'd heard enough for one day. I looked at my watch. It was gone quarter to five. I had spent nearly two-and-a-half hours going over just five 'lies', what, with all the ferreting for documents and digressing into other related subjects. I guessed that, at that rate of half-an-hour per lie, it would be six o'clock or thereabouts before we finished. 'I'm going to have to deal with the other 'lies' another time, I'm starting to have difficulty absorbing all this, it's becoming tiring taking it all in.'

The session over, I drove back down the A34 through Alderley Edge to Manchester and back to the flat. Once inside, I lay down on the bed and suddenly felt very tired. The work had become all-consuming, stopping me from sleeping, eating or having any sort of social life. My girlfriend, Adele, was complaining that the Hamiltons had completely taken over my life and I had to admit that she had a point. Adele has been a bit of heroine throughout this saga, really. I first met her at my local Prontaprint branch, where she worked, back in 1993, after I quit oil exploration in the Libyan Sahara to restart a career in England before it was too late. During the twelve months' unemployment that followed, I would be down there so often making changes to my C.V. to shoot off to yet another company, that we struck up a relation-ship. Not only had she had to put up with my preoccupation with the Hamilton case, she had also had to put up with the student-style living accommodation of my bed-sit with its single bed and shared bathroom – hardly conducive to romance – and a complete lack of disposable income. At times I sensed that her patience was beginning to wear thin. But I couldn't stop now, or even slow down . . .

As I drifted off to sleep, I reflected on the interview, fully satisfied with the way things went. Though I knew that he was innocent of the corruption charges, I felt more comfortable supporting him now I was satisfied he wasn't a liar either.

8

Witnesses On The Payroll

THE HUNT FOR THE TRUTH WAS BECOMING ALL-CONSUMING FOR both Malcolm and me. The paperwork in the office was mounting up along the shelves, the stacks of lever-arch files threatening to topple every time we tried to extract some vital document from them. We were often up until midnight working at the computers, our eyes propped open by endless cups of tea, as we trawled the thousands of pages of evidence for more information that might help to make the thousand of pieces of the jig-saw fit together. The endless names and dates were head-spinning. Trying to remember who was claiming to have known what and when took all our concentration. We were driving our friends and families mad. But the further we dug, the shakier the evidence against Neil Hamilton seemed to become. In fact much of it ceased to be evidence at all.

Then one morning the phone rang, somewhere under the piles of cuttings and amongst the discarded fast food containers and unwashed mugs. I rummaged for a few minutes before finding it, my mind miles away in whatever it was I had been studying.

'Can I speak to Jonathan Hunt?' a polite female voice enquired.

'This is me,' I confirmed. 'What can I do for you?'

'This is Deborah Turness from Five News at ITN,' the voice informed me. 'You sent your showreel of "On the Hunt" through to Adrian Monck a few months ago.'

'Oh yes.' I remembered. I had almost given up hope of any of my fliers actually eliciting a response.

'We'd like you to come and talk to us about doing some relief reporting over the summer,' she said and I felt my heart sink as I looked around at the chaos of the office. This was just the sort of offer I had been hoping and praying would come in, but not now!

'I'm so sorry,' I said, feeling physically sick at the thought of having to turn down the opportunity to break into national television. 'But I'm right in the middle of a really big story.'

'Oh, that's a shame.' She sounded genuinely disappointed. 'We really liked your work. It was, er, refreshingly different.'

'Could I come and talk to you anyway when I'm next in London, for something in the future?'

'Sure, that would be great, keep in touch,' and that was the end of the conversation. After I hung up, my mixed feelings engrossed me. What if I had just turned down the opportunity of a lifetime? What if we never managed to make sense of the Hamilton affair? What if we couldn't get any television company interested in our programme? What if I was never able to pay my father back the money he was lending me to keep going? Supposing, God forbid, Neil Hamilton turned out to be guilty after all?

But as all these questions spun round in my head, I knew that I couldn't give up now. We had put too much effort into the research. We had put too many backs up. Too many people had told me that I was wasting my time, that Neil was guilty and that even if he wasn't nobody would be interested anyway. What's more, everyone *wanted* him to be guilty. If the previous Tory Government was confirmed as being riddled with sleaze it would make the Labour victory all the sweeter. The Tories themselves wanted to disassociate themselves as quickly as possible from the whole mess so that they could concentrate on regrouping as a credible alternative Government. Above all, no one wanted to sully their hands with someone who had been pronounced corrupt by the all-powerful media.

For media, read Mafia.

I had to keep going until we proved that we were right and they were all wrong. And, apart from everything else, my self-respect wouldn't let me abandon Neil and Christine, and now Malcolm, just because I had received a better offer. Just because it was expedient.

I knew that I had no option but to continue, I was too far in to go back now. Making mugs of tea for myself and Malcolm, who grunted his thanks without taking his eyes of his screen, I sat back down in front of my own computer and returned to work.

'What are you up to?' I asked.

'I'm trying to analyse the roles of the three surprise witnesses whom Fayed had miraculously produced at the eleventh hour. The SMERSH agents,' he grinned, 'Bond Bozek and Bromfield.'

These were Fayed's three office staff who appeared, as if by magic, just before Fayed and *The Guardian* realised that Neil's libel action had been scuppered on the morning of 27 September 1996. Neither Neil nor Greer had made any public announcement that the action was almost certainly going to have to be withdrawn so, as far as Fayed and *The Guardian* were concerned, the case was still due to be heard as scheduled a few days later.

That evening *The Guardian* served three new witness statements at Peter Carter-Ruck's offices. They were from three of Fayed's closest and longest-serving employees, and they detailed a completely new and final set of allegations.

For the first time they were claiming that, as well as the money Fayed allegedly gave Neil in face-to-face meetings – meetings that until then Fayed and *The Guardian* had maintained no-one else was party to – there had been other payments in which other people had been involved. These people were Fayed's former personal assistant, Alison Bozek, his most senior secretary, Iris Bond, and a doorman at Fayed's offices, Philip Bromfield.

In their statements, these three loyal and long-serving employees now claimed that they had processed payments in "brown envelopes" filled with £50-notes and that these envelopes had either been left at the door to the office or couriered to the Hamiltons' home. For good measure, they also alleged that Ian Greer had received £5,000 per quarter, also in bundles of £50-notes stuffed into brown envelopes.

It didn't make sense at all that these allegations surfaced so late in the day – unless of course they were an afterthought, in which case they make all kinds of sense. We already knew that changing his story to suit his purposes was exactly what Fayed had been repeatedly accused of doing by the DTI inspectors. So why, we wondered, was everyone treating these new witnesses, all of whom had been on Fayed's payroll for years, as incorruptible and beyond reproach?

I remembered reading Neil's submission to Downey in which he referred to the story given in *Sleaze* to explain the miraculous discovery of these three surprise witnesses. I pulled out my copy of the book and thumbed through it see what David Leigh had written.

It turned out that Geoffrey Robertson QC was the supposed catalyst. Leigh stated that the barrister was appointed as *The Guardian's* counsel on 7 August 1996, less than two months before the libel trial was scheduled to come to court. One month later, according to the book, Robertson visited *The Guardian's* offices in Farringdon Road and gave them a bleak assessment of their case.

He (Robertson), Leigh wrote, *knew that there were smoking guns somewhere at Harrods – on bits of paper, letters, notes scrawled by secretaries, on message pads . . . "The secretaries,"* Robertson concluded, *"the secretaries must have known."*

I read on a bit further as Leigh described how Robertson then met Fayed's American lawyer, Doug Marvin, who was supposedly visiting England on another matter connected with Harrods. Robertson supposedly beseeched Marvin to overcome Fayed's reluctance to involve his former staff and to obtain statements from them. *"Whether they are helpful to* The Guardian *or not, we must have written and signed accounts by these people of their dealings with Hamilton and Greer,"* allegedly quoth Marvin. *"What did they understand Hamilton to mean when they took down his messages to Fayed about wanting his 'envelope'?"*

It would be strange indeed if Geoffrey Robertson did say such a thing, as no messages were ever logged from Hamilton "wanting his envelope" at all.

Leaving this aside, Leigh went on to describe how Marvin then successfully "persuaded" Fayed to allow him access to his secretary, Iris Bond, who – lo and behold – did indeed "know," just as Marvin had foreseen. Ms Bond told him of her involvement in paying Neil Hamilton and Ian Greer cash in the now infamous brown envelopes. Leigh described how Bond told Marvin that former Fayed PA, Alison Bozek, would also be able to help. Yet another secretary in the know.

Marvin allegedly then spoke to Bozek, who confirmed that she had paid Neil and Greer cash in brown envelopes, which she sometimes left at the door of 60 Park Lane. In *Sleaze* Leigh described how this revelation led Marvin to speak to the third member of the triumvirate – doorman Philip Bromfield, who – predictably – corroborated what Bozek had said.

The more I thought about it, the more Fayed's claim that he wanted to protect his employees and not involve them until he had to didn't ring true. The DTI inspectors, I remembered, had been particularly shocked at the way in which Fayed had been willing to hoodwink his own solicitors and make them tell lies on his behalf unknowingly. Could he have done the same to these people? Or might they have been willing to help him out of nothing more than (a misplaced sense of) loyalty?

Late on a misty, miserable, Manchester Thursday morning Malcolm breezed into the office. 'This story about Fayed being reluctant to involve his staff for two years in pure bollocks,' he announced casually.

'What have you found?' I asked.

'Put the kettle on and I'll tell you.'

A few minutes later I brought in two strong cups of tea. I passed one to Malcolm and, as good as his word, he rattled off his findings.

'After the first article in *The Guardian* in 1994, Alex Carlile wrote a number of letters of complaint to the Members' Interests Committee, articulating Fayed's earliest allegations. The Committee decided to leave the cash and gift voucher allegations until after the libel trial was over, right?' I nodded. 'But they did press ahead with investigating his freebie at the Ritz. Anyway, Carlile's letters of complaint were reprinted in their report.' He opened his briefcase and pulled out the 1994 report. 'This is what Carlile wrote, here it is . . .' He started to read: ' "He (Hamilton) obtained benefits in kind from Mr Al Fayed in the form of Harrods vouchers of the value of £100 each, to a total of about £6,000. Significant circumstantial evidence of these can, I believe, be found in appointment diaries at Mr Al Fayed's office in Harrods, in which Mr Hamilton's visits are diaried, plus direct evidence from Mr Al Fayed and possibly some of his staff." '

He read it a second time, emphasising the last few words.

'So why would Fayed and *The Guardian* not have brought up these accusations of brown envelopes *right at the beginning*?' I wondered aloud. 'If these employees were so willing to talk about them.'

'More correctly, why would Fayed be so "reluctant" to involve them for two years if he was happy to volunteer them right at the beginning to Carlile?'

'As I said, the explanation given in *Sleaze* is pure bollocks from start to finish.'

This was a major discovery. As we learned later, the only real evidence Downey had were these witnesses, and the explanation given for their belated emergence was now shown to be a lie. A real lie, not an error dressed up as one.

Not only was Leigh's explanation for these three employees' sudden appearance now invalidated, their evidence, when put under a microscope, seemed equally bereft of credibility.

Alison Bozek was Fayed's personal secretary, and one of his closest and most trusted employees from 1981 to 30 September 1994 (just before *The Guardian* printed its first set of allegations). She then left to work as an articled clerk at one of Fayed's solicitors, Allen and Overy.

She testified that on Fayed's instruction she packed envelopes with £2,500 in £50 notes, which she sent down to Philip Bromfield at the door for collection by Hamilton. She also testified that on other occasions Fayed gave her white envelopes already full of cash, which she then put into a brown envelope, and sent down to the door for Hamilton to collect.

Bozek gave two different reasons for putting the white envelope into a brown envelope. The first reason was: 'He [Fayed] would scrawl Neil Hamilton's name on it [a white envelope] and as his handwriting is so illegible I would put it into a brown envelope, write Neil Hamilton's name on it clearly so the staff on the security desk could read it'

Later on she gave a different reason for doing this. The second reason was: 'He [Fayed] would open his desk and take out whatever money he wanted to put in the envelope, put into a white envelope, seal it, scrawl Neil Hamilton's name on it and say, "Please leave that at the door for Neil Hamilton." As I say, that is when I would put it in a brown envelope and, because I knew money was inside it and I did not want it to go missing, I would put my initials and seal it with Sellotape, so the recipient would know whether it had been tampered with and there could be no allegations that money had gone astray'.

Bozek's two accounts differ. In the first, she claims to have put the white envelope into a brown one so that she could *write Hamilton's name on it clearly so that the doorman could read it.* In her second account she stated her reason for doing this was so that she could *initial it and seal it with Sellotape, to prevent any tampering with the contents.*

But one facet is constant and Bozek emphasises it conspicuously: that she would always put the white envelope inside a brown envelope. Why would Bozek make such a great point out of doing this? Why was it so important that she always converted the white envelope to a brown one?

It would take months to work that one out.

Bozek claimed that Neil visited 60 Park Lane for meetings with her boss far more frequently than Tim Smith, explaining that not all Neil's visits were logged in Fayed's telephone message book or diary. She stated that Neil met Fayed on average every four to six weeks, except during "busy" periods, when he would visit as often as once a week. But, despite this very high frequency of face-to-face meetings, Bozek claims that on occasion it had still been necessary for her to pack money into an envelope and send it down to the door for Neil to collect.

In stark contrast, although Tim Smith has admitted taking at least £18,000 between May 1987 and February 1989, Bozek claims that she was never required to place any money into envelopes for *him* to collect, notwithstanding that *his* meetings with Fayed were far less frequent than Neil's. In fact, so infrequent that she found it hard to remember whether Smith had visited Park Lane at all.

Smith maintains that he never collected payments from the door of 60 Park Lane, but that he did receive money once or twice by courier, and this is corroborated by Bozek. Bozek also states that she didn't pack any envelopes for Smith. And Bond states that she never packed any envelopes for anyone at all.

So, we wondered, if Bozek had never been required to pack money into envelopes for *Smith* to collect, why would she have been required to do so for Neil, who, she claimed, visited much more frequently and had plenty of chances to collect personally and discreetly from Fayed himself?

Whatever the truth was, it was obvious that Bozek's testimony needed to be scrutinised more closely. As we were to learn later, though, Downey accepted her testimony as it stood. He assessed her credibility on the glowing reference he had received from her employers, solicitors Allen and Overy, who had only employed her for a year at that stage and took her on in the first place because she received a gushing reference from Fayed himself. Her credibility, therefore, ultimately rested on Fayed's word – *a man whom the DTI Inspectors had branded a liar* over and over again in their report. Fayed was also Allen and Overy's client, so they would hardly be likely to say anything to Downey that would undermine their client's, their employee's and their own credibility.

Either Bozek is telling the truth and she did indeed place money into envelopes for Neil and (claiming throughout to being "shocked at the way you could buy an MP") was therefore a willing and knowing party to corruption, or else she lied to Downey as part of a conspiracy to bring about the downfall of an innocent man. Either way she is hardly living up to the glowing reference Downey received from her employers, and either way she is not the sort of witness whose evidence should be accepted as reliable. In a court of law she would have been ripped to shreds.

I rummaged out from my 'bits and pieces' file a *Mail on Sunday* article that Neil had given us. It was dated 23 March 1997 and Bozek was being interviewed about Neil's relationship with Fayed in the 1980s and Neil's refusal to rekindle it after becoming a Minister at the DTI. She was quoted as saying:

We thought he (Hamilton) would be tremendously useful to us. We were very disappointed that he wasn't prepared to help. We expected him to stand by his apparent belief in Mr Al Fayed's cause. He had pursued Mr Al Fayed's cause quite vociferously for a number of years. When he obtained a position that could have been really useful he opted out. He never even replied to Mr Al Fayed's letter of congratulation.

Apart from her description of Neil's support for Fayed, which was far from "vociferous," this was very revealing, for it shows that Fayed was put out by Neil's unwillingness to co-operate once he took on ministerial responsibilities. It also demonstrates how completely Bozek identified with Fayed and her prepared-ness to collude in unethical conduct in his interests a curious attitude for a budding Solicitor of the Supreme Court.

Next we turned our attention to Iris Bond. She has been Fayed's personal secretary for nearly twenty years. In both her oral examination and in her written statement for the libel trial, she revealed the strength and closeness of her relationship with Fayed. She made it clear that she was the most senior of his clerical staff within the offices of 60 Park Lane, enjoying authority over Bozek. Such claims hardly qualify her as the ideal independent witness. She does, however, possess an aura of that middle-England respectability that can be so convincing.

But despite her seniority, and despite a shift system existing between her and Bozek which would have meant, logically, that Bozek would occasionally have been unavailable, nowhere in her testimony does Bond claim to have had any direct involvement in packing envelopes with cash for Neil.

Her evidence, in essence, comprises little more than a recollection of Bozek's and Fayed's alleged utterances relating to their alleged activities, although she did claim to have observed Fayed personally stuffing banknotes into envelopes. In due course she cleverly made the connection between Fayed's envelope-stuffing act and the Hamiltons and Ian Greer and his secretary all supposedly phoning up at various times for their "envelopes".

In her oral examination Bond 'recalled' Fayed saying, "Oh yes, Hamilton is coming up. I must give him some money," and another time, "Oh God! Sometimes he likes the vouchers," and on yet another occasion, "He is coming to Park Lane. Can you see that this is left downstairs for him?" All of it conveniently corroborating the cash payments allegation (which Fayed had maintained for the previous two years could not be corroborated), the gift voucher allegation and the envelopes at the door allegation. None of it sounding very convincing. Not to put too fine a point on it, it sounds more obvious than the script from a 'Carry On' film.

'Mr Greer pops into your life in the 1980's,' Nigel Pleming QC for the Downey Inquiry said to her. 'Did you know him before then?'

'No,' Bond replied.

'And then he pops out again at the end of this period and has disappeared apart from the libel proceedings and the press.'

'Yes.'

'Was he in any way memorable or unusual or why do you recall this particular set of payments?'

'Why do I recall that? Because I think his company had quite a reputation and Mr Greer did appear in various newspapers. I think one was also aware of his closeness to John Major and that also made me think, "Goodness me!"'

Goodness, Ms Bond, had nothing to do with it.

But Greer had told me that in the 1980s, the time that he was alleged to have been taking cash payments from Bond, he had not really been featured in any newspapers. And the first time his friendship with John Major was aired in any newspaper was in the early 1990s, which was *after* the last alleged cash payment from Fayed to Greer.

'Did you know who Mr Hamilton was?' Pleming probed. 'Not after all the publicity, but back in the 1980s?'

'I knew he was a Member of Parliament, yes.'

'Was there anything significant about him, apart from him being a Member of Parliament? You have mentioned a few things already.'

'I think he came across as somebody who, I used to read, said his parents or his grandparents were coal miners.'

When I read that I picked up the phone to Neil and asked him if he could remember any national journal printing anything about his family background prior to his becoming a national news item.

'No, nothing,' he said. 'Why would they? Even political commentators would not have been aware that my grandparents were miners. Why would they be interested? The first time there was any significant airing of my background in the media was in *The Guardian* on 20 October 1994, and in the other papers the following day.'

But that was five years after the last alleged payment was supposed to have been made, so Bond's recollection was false. Again. What is most strange, however, is the fact that, like Bozek, she remembered Greer and Neil being paid, while not knowing that payments had been made to the likes of Tim Smith, who freely admitted that he had been given cash.

Once again, as we were to learn, Downey would not comment on any of these inconsistencies, concluding instead that Iris Bond was a person of good character because he had received a glowing character reference for her from ex-Fayed legal adviser, Royston Webb. But as coincidence would have it, Webb is on an undisclosed retainer from Fayed until September 2001, for no known reason, and Fayed's retainers to his ex-employees are rarely ungenerous.

Finally we come to Philip Bromfield, who has been Fayed's security guard and doorman for fourteen years, and who claims that on two occasions, ten years ago, he remembers clearly Neil collecting an envelope. He further claimed to be ignorant of the contents of these alleged envelopes. But Bozek had admitted in her oral examination that envelopes containing only documents had, on occasion, been prepared for Neil, so Bromfield's testimony is completely worthless (even if it was true) and suggests that he was probably a coerced witness.

'In what form did Neil Hamilton's name appear on the envelopes?' Nigel Pleming asked Bromfield at the inquiry.

'It *would have been a typed name**,' Bromfield replied. 'In this instance "Mr Hamilton" would have been the name on it.' [*My emphasis]

But when Pleming questioned Bozek about the same issue earlier the same day she said *twice* that she *wrote* Neil Hamilton's name on the envelopes, and the first time she even said that she wrote *clearly,* so the staff on the security desk could read it.' [My emphasis.]

Since all typing is by its nature "clear" she is excluding the possibility that she typed the name. They couldn't both be right.

'Do you remember Tim Smith collecting envelopes?' Pleming asked Bromfield.

'I do not remember at this stage,' Bromfield replied, but later in the session he changed his recollection to: 'Yes, they (four people including Tim Smith) have collected envelopes from that address.' Which is not only the opposite of what he said earlier but also at variance with what Bozek claimed.

Most importantly, it is also the opposite of what Tim Smith himself said. It is common ground that Smith never collected envelopes from anyone except Fayed. But if Bromfield's memory is fundamentally faulty in relation to Smith, why would Downey later consider it to be reliable in relation to Hamilton?

Bromfield also changed his recollection about Neil's name being typed. The revised version went: 'No, I think I have put that wrong if I have given that impression. No, it was the name rather than the typing, because most of them are typed.'

Sir Gordon Downey did not comment on any of these

conflicting accounts of what happened. Instead he wrote in his report: *Mr Bromfield impressed me as a reliable witness.*

We wondered what it would take to be considered an *unreliable* witness.

That evening, after telephoning Adele as usual, I settled down to reading the Downey report, also as usual. No matter how many times I digested its contents, each time I would spot something that had passed me by previously.

And then, out of the blue, one of the most bothersome of all the little niggles and conflicts that troubled me was resolved in an instant. The "conundrum of the Ritz's private rooms."

The very first 'lie' that I interviewed Hamilton about that David Leigh in *Sleaze* accused him of, was the 'lie' that Fayed had told him not to worry about displacing paying customers from the Ritz, as he always maintained "private rooms." Leigh said that Hamilton had told a direct lie as the Ritz did not have private rooms. In his report, Downey repeated *The Guardian*'s claim that no such rooms existed. Downey's evidence for this was because it was "a fact confirmed by Mr Al Fayed."

But then I came to Downey's discussion of the Hamiltons' 1990 stay in Dodi Fayed's apartment, which Fayed owned, off the Champs Elysées. Fayed put up Neil and Christine as his guests there when they visited Paris for a friend's wedding, precisely because, Hamilton said, the hotel was full.

Fayed's staff at 60 Park Lane made a note of these later arrangements in their telephone message book, which Downey reprinted.

> "*From: N. Hamilton*
> *Message: Guest Appt (apartment) at Ritz*
> *5 July office*
> *9 July.*"

Then the penny dropped. If Fayed's own employees referred to Dodi's apartment as "guest apartment at Ritz," Hamilton would have assumed that these rooms were within the hotel rather than across the city. Another red herring disposed of.

I looked at my watch. It had just turned 11.00pm. Was it too late to telephone? I decided to risk it and called him at home.

'Neil, hi, sorry to disturb you so late.'

'That's all right.'

'You told me that Fayed assured you that he maintained private rooms where you could stay, whenever the hotel was full.'

'He did tell me that.'

'Is it possible that he told you that he maintained private apartments, instead?'

'I can't remember. Private rooms, private apartments, private suites. What's the difference?'

'It's okay, you've told me what I wanted to know. I'll tell you all about it in the morning. Sorry to disturb you again. Goodnight.'

'Goodnight.'

9

The Missing Witnesses

THE MORNING AFTER "DOWNEY DAY" THE NEWSPAPERS WERE awash with Downey's "compelling evidence" punch-line, and just about every political columnist vented their disgust. Many of the papers carried editorials suggesting that Hamilton should be thrown out of the Conservative Party. These were the same papers that between them had not allocated one dedicated journalist to investigate what they were now crowing about.

After breakfast Malcolm headed back up to Manchester to re-start the research and try to work out what had gone wrong, while I went round to the flat in Battersea to see how Neil and Christine were bearing up.

Not surprisingly there was a small gathering of reporters on the doorstep, waiting for Neil to emerge for his reaction to the calls from the press. The Hamiltons had already done a live radio show in their Mickey Mouse pyjamas and the BBC people were just packing up their equipment as I arrived. I was surprised to find the couple in such an upbeat mood. I suggested that they should give the media mob outside their sound-bites and send them on their way.

'We're not ready yet,' Neil told me. 'The Beeb session was pretty gruelling. We need a few hours to get ourselves together.'

The BBC technicians left and quiet descended on the apartment. The Hamilton's spirits fell as quickly as they had risen for the broadcast. Theirs was truly a roller-coaster ride of ups and downs. Neil was clearly not up to confronting the baying aggression of any reporters.

'All right – why don't I go down there and let them know that you'll talk to them later on?' I suggested, and to this he happily agreed.

There were around four or five of them in total, including two chaps from Sky TV, one from ITN, and a girl from the Press Association called Katherine Road. When I spoke to them they seemed reluctant to believe that I had authority to speak for the Hamiltons. They had been trying to get through to them over the intercom at the front door, without success and had built up a fair old head of frustration.

'You've only got to look at him to see he's guilty,' Road said, with apparent sincerity.

'I think that's your problem, not theirs,' I retorted. 'The prisons are full of working class blacks because white middle-class jurors "think they look guilty." '

She obviously had no knowledge of the background of "cash for questions," but seemed approachable, so I sat down with her on the garden wall and spent an hour explaining to her what our research had uncovered. By the end of it she was still dubious but her tone seemed to have changed a little. But like all reporters with heavy workloads she had only been briefed to extract a quote from Neil, a quick fix. That's all she was there for and that's all she wanted.

'Please,' she implored, as we strolled back to the entrance, 'get Hamilton to say a few words. I've been ordered not to leave here until I have a quote, so the sooner he comes out the sooner we'll all be gone. I need a comment about him and his membership of the Tory party.'

And so I went back inside, back in the lift to the fifth floor and passed this on. Neil agreed to see them around three o'clock. And so back down again and back to Katherine. 'He'll say something for you after three, so you might as well go to the pub for a few hours' I said, pointing to the *Prince Albert* on the corner opposite.

'I'm not leaving the front door,' she said.

'You've nothing to worry about,' I assured her. 'He's promised me he'll talk to you and he will, so you might as well go and have a long lunch. Do you have a mobile?' I swapped mobile phone numbers with her and promised to contact her as soon as Neil felt ready to face their questions. As she and her media colleagues trotted off, I went down the road to buy a newspaper and sat in the car, passing the hours reading and listening to the news bulletins. At around three I buzzed the flat on the intercom.

'I'll be down in a few minutes' Neil said.

The chaps from Sky were sat in a dark blue Volvo estate, but no sign of anyone else. 'Where is everyone?' I asked.

'There's only the girl from the PA still here, and she's just nipped down to the supermarket' said Geoff, sat in the Volvo. Honour bound, I ran down the road to get her.

I spotted her at the back of the shop. 'Katherine,' I shouted. 'Hamilton's about to come down for your interview!' She abandoned her purchases and we raced back to the apartment block. A few minutes later, Neil emerged and Katherine and Geoff put their questions.

'Will you be resigning from the Party?' they asked, as instructed.

'I'm not actually a member,' Neil responded, to their consternation and surprise. 'You don't actually have to join the party in order to become a Conservative MP.'

They continued questioning him for another five or ten minutes or so and then departed satisfied, leaving Neil and Christine in peace to sort out the rest of their lives.

I tried ringing a few more newspapers in the hope of getting someone to question whether it was possible that Downey had got it wrong, but none of them was interested. News was not about rights or wrongs, whys and wherefores. Neil had been pronounced guilty, just as everyone had predicted, and there was no more to be said on the subject, unless the Queen Mother arrived at the Commons on a Norton Commando to say she thought different because that *would* have been news, no doubt. I felt frustrated, unable to understand why not one would even listen to my offers to go through the evidence.

The next day I headed back home, still desperately ringing round the media from my hands-free phone. I remembered having Graham Forester's card, so I called him at home. The conversation became so engrossing I pulled off the motorway into a convenient services area in order to concentrate on the questions he was firing at me.

Graham was receptive to my arguments, but, ultimately, he couldn't go against everything else that was being reported in the media just because I maintained they were all wrong. I could understand that. Although Malcolm and I were able to devote seven days a week to the Hamilton case, for people like Graham it was just one story among hundreds, and there was no prospect of his allocating any resources to an independent investigation. I couldn't blame every editor in the media for the injustice that was being done. It was more to do with the system than the individuals.

I also spent some time talking to the *Daily Mail*, who suggested that I should contact the *Spectator*. I was a bit put out by this suggestion.

'But this is mainstream news,' I seethed, 'not some esoteric theory.' But after I had hung up and was back on the M6 treadmill, I had second thoughts. Perhaps the *Spectator* would be quite a effective medium for getting our point across after all. It was, after all, a serious publication that tended to be read by opinion formers. I made a mental note to get round to it.

On arriving back in Cheshire I contacted Dave Fox of the *Northwich Chronicle*, which is distributed in the Tatton constituency, believing it to be important to get an alternative story into the arena somehow. He ran the story along the lines of "Journalist says Hamilton victim of Establishment stitch-up," but no other paper picked it up. At least it would provide the Hamiltons some small comfort on their return home.

Neil and Christine were keen to get any media exposure they could. Shortly afterwards, the BBC's "Panorama" contacted Neil for a programme they planned at that time on Fayed. They wanted Neil to appear as a witness. For the prosecution, naturally.

'Don't do it,' I cautioned. 'There is no way "Panorama" is going to say you're innocent. So if you're there as a witness it will be as someone whom Fayed succeeded in corrupting, not as someone Fayed had stitched-up.'

'But if it helps to show what Fayed is really like,' Neil argued.

'It will damage you more, Neil,' I insisted. 'Just forget it. If you want me to remain on this I'm going to hold you to that agreement that you gave me. You don't do anything about this affair without my say-so. Let me speak to "Panorama." ' Sometimes it was the only way to speak to Neil so that he got the message. He agreed and I rang the producer, Thea Guest.

'Thea,' I said. 'We've got the rights to Hamilton's story and we're not releasing him to do a programme on Fayed unless you do one on the "cash for questions" affair as well.'

'But we're not doing the "cash for questions" affair,' she protested.

'I know you're not, and we're not interested in doing one on Fayed, but Hamilton can give you more information about that man than you can shake a stick at.'

'What's so interesting about the "cash for questions" affair?' she asked dubiously.

'The interesting thing is that Hamilton has been stitched up and we've got the evidence to prove it. We really want to keep you people on side. There are two programmes here: there's one on Fayed, and one on "cash for questions," which is a far bigger story. If you co-operate with us on one we'll give you our co-operation on the other.'

She came back to me a few days later.

'I'm sorry,' she said, 'but we're not interested.'

'Then neither are we in what you're offering,' I said. 'No deal.'

'Really?'

I don't think she could believe that Neil would turn down the opportunity to be on "Panorama" to put the boot into Fayed.

Two weeks after Downey Day, having spent hours staring at screens and riffling through papers, I decided that Adele was right and I should take a break from the whole thing. So, much in need of some time together, away from files, computer screens and telephones, we flew out of Manchester Airport for a long weekend in Paris. But instead of a nice relaxing break, for three days we seemed to do nothing but walk up and down steps of museums, monuments and churches, and we came back more knackered than when we went. At least we had some time together away from 'the Hamilton Affair we didn't even get around to visiting the Ritz where the whole thing had started. However, I can't say that my mind had ever wandered too far from the case that was fast becoming an obsession. In finding Neil guilty, Downey had proved me wrong in the eyes of the world, and I didn't like that, especially when I was still certain we were right. If the evidence could convince Malcolm, who had started out as an avid sceptic, then surely the rest of the world should be able to see the truth.

As soon as we got back to England I felt myself being drawn back to the office and the research. I knew we weren't wrong. We had enough proof, as far as we were concerned, but there had to be more, somewhere, waiting to be pounced on. The sort of proof that explains how it all happened. I found Malcolm working away at the computer, still building up the chronology of events.

He suggested I look at some of the other players in the drama. The name Royston Webb had come up a few times. He was Fayed's in-house legal adviser at House of Fraser from 1 September 1985 to 30 September 1996 – the day before Neil's libel action was due to start.

Despite having had over two years to make a statement for the libel trial, Webb's testimony against Neil had first seen the light of day in a letter to Downey on 13 February 1997. In that letter he stated that he had known that Neil was being paid cash because he remembered Fayed receiving some House of Commons cufflinks from Neil for Christmas.

'I give him thousands of pounds,' he claims to remember Fayed grumbling to him. 'For what? A cheap pair of cufflinks!'

This recollection of Webb's is very strange and flies in the face of incontrovertible evidence that Hamilton gave me, but of whose existence Webb was blissfully unaware. On October 20, 1994, immediately after the first "cash for questions," allegations against Greer and Neil appeared in *The Guardian*, Greer telephoned Webb, who was in Dubai, and taped the conversation without Webb knowing. Greer told him of Fayed's allegations.

'My only knowledge was of a fixed fee arrangement which was an annual fee agreed and paid monthly,' Webb said. 'I don't know of any variable . . . apart from odd expenses here and there.'

'He (Fayed) is completely dotty,' Greer told him. 'He said that the invoices used to vary on a monthly basis or quarterly basis, dependent upon how many (parliamentary) questions had been asked, which of course is wholly untrue.'

'I have no knowledge of that whatsoever,' Webb replied.

As Webb was Fayed's confidant, his lack of knowledge of any "cash for questions" arrangement would clearly have been very useful to his case, so Neil listed him as a potentially supporting witness. However, after gaining sight of Webb's letter to Downey, Neil naturally challenged Webb's character. Downey, however, did not question the contradiction in Webb's recollections. Instead, he referred to the apparent paradox of Neil originally suggesting Webb as a witness then subsequently challenging his credibility: *Mr Hamilton proposed Mr Webb as a witness to the inquiry but he has since challenged his credibility,* Downey reported. *Although Mr Webb gave his evidence in an apparently straightforward manner, I found it unnecessary to reach a conclusion on this matter since he was not sufficiently close to the alleged events to affect my judgement one way or the other.*

Incredibly, Downey made no mention about Webb's change of testimony and we were both puzzled that he could describe it as "straightforward." Or perhaps not so surprising considering how Downey had evaluated the evidence of other Fayed employees.

Anyone who read Downey's report and hadn't spent months untangling the facts as we had, would infer that Webb was truthful and that this was the reason Neil resiled from using him as a witness. But it is far more likely, however, that Webb told the truth when he spoke to Greer on the phone in 1994, unaware of the tape recorder, than when he testified later in support of Fayed, having had time to be briefed by Fayed and prepare his answers.

Even though Downey stated that Webb was too remote from events to influence his judgement either way, he still cited Webb's testimony over and over again on matters of importance, even to the point of quoting Webb's words directly as a character reference for Bozek and Bond.

'In a decade of dealing with these ladies on an almost daily basis,' Webb was quoted as saying, 'I cannot recall a single instance when I had cause to question their veracity.'

Well, that's it then. Royston Webb vouches for them. In that case, they couldn't possibly be inventing all those stories about Neil Hamilton and brown envelopes, could they?

After leaving Harrods in 1996, Webb was retained for a further five years as Fayed's personal legal adviser (at a fee widely reported to be £1 million), and was therefore as much an employee as Bozek and Bond and Bromfield. Hardly someone with the makings of a reliable, unbiased observer.

On 3 March 1997, Michael Land, a former Lonrho employee, wrote to Downey. Land had previously supplied information to Webb to help Fayed against Tiny Rowland, at a time when Fayed was generally perceived to be a victim of a persecution campaign by Rowland. Although Land was content to be paid for his help, he didn't ask for hard cash, yet over five months he was instructed to collect four payments of £500 in £20 notes from the door of Webb's office. These payments were in envelopes, packed, processed and despatched in exactly the same manner as described by Alison Bozek, Iris Bond and Philip Bromfield in their testimony against Neil. In his letter Land recalled:

During the next four months I had several meetings with Royston Webb. He was the only person I met from the Fayed organisation . . . At the second meeting with Royston Webb I brought up the matter of my fee . . . He said he would not be involved himself, but arrangements were being made in due course. As it transpired a few days after this meeting I was phoned and asked to collect a letter addressed to me at the reception in the South Street offices. I called and was handed an envelope. On opening the envelope I discovered cash totalling £500 in £20-notes.

During the second month of my involvement with Royston Webb he outlined the announcement that the Fayed organisation was about to make. I recall asking how he had acquired what were highly sensitive papers. I was quite taken aback by his reply – which I cannot recall in detail – but it did involve the hiring of private detectives, a break-in to the Luxembourg Bank, and what I consider to be a gross deception perpetrated on the Luxembourg Bank.

In only three or four meetings with Webb over a relatively short space of time I was beginning to doubt whether I should be involved at all with this organisation. During my last meeting with Royston Webb . . . much discussion took place between myself and Mr Webb about the attacks an individual called Ms Pollard (Francesca Pollard) was making against Lonrho, in particular Tiny Rowland . . . I subsequently phoned her and arranged to meet her . . . It was clear to me that she was not acting as a loner – but had funds backing her . . . In other words the Fayeds were backing her campaign against Tiny Rowland.

I felt let down by Royston Webb for not disclosing this. It appeared that I was out of my depth with so many 'minders' about the place, with tales of banks being broken into in Luxembourg etc., copies of illegally obtained documents being shown to me, I felt it was about time to leave.

Downey failed to acknowledge this bleak and independent insight into Webb's character, and also failed to take account of the fact that Land's letter implicates Webb in the highly suspect discharging of payments in cash. Instead, Downey related Webb's rebuttal of Neil's challenge to his character:

> 'Mr Royston Webb vigorously rejected as a slur on his professional standing any imputation by Mr Hamilton that he had been party to any morally questionable practices whilst in Mr Al Fayed's employment and strongly denied that he was under any pressure or inducement from Mr Al Fayed to give evidence in a particular way.'

Well, that's all right then too. Royston Webb says he's a good boy so he couldn't possibly be tarred with the same brush as his employer, could he?

Few attitudes, however, could have been more questionable than Webb's acquiescence in Fayed's enrolment of Francesca Pollard to further his defamatory campaigns to vilify Tiny Rowland, Professor Barry Rider, Jeff Rooker MP, Teddy Taylor MP, Kenneth Warren MP and others. And few practices could be more questionable than the payments of cash in envelopes from his South Street office. Webb is also alleged to have been the person who organised teams of private agents to undertake 24-hour surveillance of Home Secretary Michael Howard as part Fayed's vendetta against him. And as for Webb's claim that he was under no inducement from Fayed, there can be few better inducements to give false witness than being retained for five years, for no apparent reason, at an alleged fee of £1million!

Francesca Pollard's name kept cropping up and we had done some research into her background. The story was that she once stood to inherit £8 million from a business that her grandfather had founded, the Israel British Bank. The bank collapsed in the early 1970s after being subjected to a £30 million fraud that a distant relative, Harry Landy, was convicted of perpetrating. Landy had his conviction quashed on appeal, on a technicality, and later became managing director and deputy chairman of London City and Westcliff Properties Ltd, a company owned by Lonrho.

Coincidentally, Landy was also a distant cousin of Michael Howard, and Fayed later used this tenuous kinship to suggest a link between Howard and Lonrho, and to fuel his false allegations that Howard, (during his tenure as Corporate Affairs Minister at the DTI), had been bribed by Rowland to appoint pro-Lonrho Inspectors to investigate House of Fraser. When Howard later became Home Secretary, Fayed then accused him of blocking his passport application, citing the same reason. In fact, Howard had delegated Fayed's passport application to fellow minister Charles Wardle.

Pollard suspected that Rowland might have been a party to the loss of her inheritance and, after being persuaded by Fayed that Rowland was the root cause of all her troubles, she subsequently allied herself with Fayed against Rowland in a pact to recover her family fortune. So, in exchange for help with her legal battle, for four years her role was to write letters in her own name, under the direction of Fayed's staff, headed by Royston Webb. For that service, as she admitted to me when I interviewed her in Brighton (of which more presently), she was also paid £2,000 a month. This was packed into envelopes that were either given to her personally by Alison Bozek in Fayed's Park Lane office, or left by Bozek at the door for Pollard's common-law husband, Alex Lakhani, to collect.

Pollard's payment arrangements were exactly the same as those that had allegedly applied to Neil. The arrangement with her was more regular, more frequent, more recent and over a longer period of time than the alleged payments to Neil, and Bozek was personally responsible for discharging Pollard's payments. But, despite all this, Downey failed to take any account of Bozek or Bond's denial of processing payments to *anyone except Neil or Ian Greer*. Their memories were clearly selective, and on this count alone should have called into question the veracity of all their evidence about 'brown envelopes.'

Pollard's campaign of letters targeted Fayed's critics such as MPs Jeff Rooker, Teddy Taylor, Sir Peter Tapsell and Sir Edward du Cann (to name but a few), DTI inspectors Hugh Aldous and Henry Brooke and advisers and members of the Trade and Industry Select Committee, including Professor Barry Rider, Kenneth Warren MP and Robin Maxwell-Hyslop MP. Fayed even provided her with a Mazda van, complete with a driver and a posse of bodyguards, for her to distribute his propaganda unhindered.

After four years she withdrew from the campaign as Fayed's

allegations about Rowland became more and more far-fetched. In due course, she became wholly disillusioned with Fayed's ethics and motives. In the end she poured out her heart to Tiny Rowland and denounced her activities and allegations against him in an affidavit. She went on to claim that Alison Bozek lied before the Downey Inquiry and she offered to testify before the Inquiry in support of Neil.

On 10 January 1997 she wrote to Downey saying:

I shall be more than pleased to assist you in any way and shall commence to collate the extensive documentation which may prove useful as evidence, together with my own knowledge of the various facts relating to not only Mr Fayed and Mr Howard but other prominent parties including MPs whose involvement and direct relationships with the above-named have been extensive. I assure you of my co-operation whenever possible.

Downey wrote back:

You mention extensive documentation relating not only to Mr Howard, but also to other MPs. I agree that material relating to other MPs may be relevant to a second (cash for questions) inquiry which I am about to conduct; and I may well come back to you on that.

As promised, on 3 February 1997 Downey wrote to Pollard again:

In your letter of 10 January you indicated that you might have some information to give me of relevance to both of my current enquiries the first into allegations concerning Mr Howard and the second into complaints against Mr Hamilton and other Members.

I am hoping very shortly to bring the inquiry concerning Mr Howard to a conclusion, so I will need to have any statement from you as soon as possible, preferably within the next day or two.

So far as the other inquiry is concerned, could you please indicate whether, as a vehicle for submitting evidence to me, you are content to rely on your affidavit and statement of 28

June 1991, with particular reference to the question of cash payments to you by Mr Fayed and the use for this purpose of envelopes initialled by Alison Bozek. Do you still have the original envelopes? If you do, would you please provide them to me for use in my inquiry (they will of course be returned afterwards). Are you aware of such payments to Mr Hamilton, Mr Smith, Sir Michael Grylls, Sir Andrew Bowden or any other Member? If so, please give details and dates where possible.

An early reply would be appreciated.

Pollard wrote back on 7 March 1997, indicating once again her willingness to testify, reiterating her offer to divulge knowledge about Fayed, his employees, and especially those MPs with whom Fayed had been involved. This was written *after* Fayed's personal assistant, Alison Bozek, was orally examined by the inquiry, during which Bozek disclaimed remembering paying anyone except Neil Hamilton.

On 21 March 1997 Downey replied, but since sending his letter of 3 February (above), and despite Pollard's testimony being crucial in establishing Bozek's credibility, *something in the interim obviously caused Downey's interest in Pollard to disappear*. The full text of Downey's reply was:

Dear Ms Pollard, Thank you for your letter of 7 March, the contents of which have been noted. Yours sincerely, Gordon Downey.

Downey's early extensive collation of evidence from witnesses, whom he then subsequently froze out of his inquiries, without reason, is one of the greatest puzzles of this affair.

After Neil lost his seat, Pollard wrote to him at the House of Commons offering to assist in his defence of Fayed's allegations, but inexplicably her letters were not passed on. Months later, when the Commons debated the Downey Report, Gerald Howarth spoke up in defence of Neil, and his speech was reported in the *Daily Telegraph*. Pollard saw the article and wrote to him, via the paper. Howarth sent Neil a copy of the letter and Neil contacted me. After speaking with Pollard over the telephone I drove down to Brighton to interview her on a crisp, bright 3 December.

'Alison Bozek lied,' she told me, 'in a big way in her testimony before the Inquiry. She couldn't have forgotten about paying me cash. She used to hand £2,000 to me herself most months for four years.'

'I'll tell you something else . . .' She leaned towards me as if to add impact to what she was about to say. 'Not once during the four years that Fayed alleged he was paying Hamilton did he ever mention Neil Hamilton's name. Fayed provided me with a list of sympathetic MPs to whom I should send my propaganda – but Neil Hamilton was not on that list.'

If Neil's name *had* been on the list, there would have been absolutely nothing unusual about that, as he had given Fayed support. But his absence from the list can only mean that Fayed didn't rate him very highly as someone who promoted his cause which flies in the face of the contention that he was worth paying £28,000. Pollard subsequently supplied me with her 150 page affidavit, which she had given to Tiny Rowland. Within its pages, there are all sorts of MPs mentioned, both pro and anti-Fayed, but again not even a *mention* of Neil in any context. Furthermore, she had written this four years before *The Guardian's* article even appeared, so she could not have conditioned it to suit some perverse "I want to help Hamilton" agenda, even if she had one.

'So, what were the sorts of things Fayed asked you to do?'

'All sorts. Mainly writing letters to his enemies and so forth, but the vast majority of the letters that Fayed sent out in my name I didn't even know about. Almost all of them were written by Richard New, Fayed's private detective. He even forged my signature on many of them.'

'What about your harassment of Ken Warren, Robin Maxwell-Hyslop and other Members of the Trade and Industry Committee?' I was referring to the all-party Select Committee on Trade and Industry, not the Tory backbench Committee on which Neil sat.

'I didn't actually harass anyone, although Fayed wanted me to parade in Ken Warren's and other Members' constituencies bearing a placard alleging that they all had been bribed £5 million by Tiny Rowland.' I could hardly believe what I was hearing. 'It's all in my affidavit. The most I did was leaflet Michael Howard's and Ken Warren's constituencies with Fayed's propaganda. I did go down to Devon to do the same in

Maxwell-Hyslop's constituency, but by that time I realised that I was being used, and that Fayed had no intention of helping me with my legal fight for my inheritance.'

'So what did you do in Devon?'

'Nothing. We strolled around Exeter one day and went to the seaside on another. I quit when I came home. Fayed just exploited me.'

'So, who authorised your character blackening campaigns against Fayed's critics?' I asked.

'Royston Webb and he seemed to have a close relationship with Dale Campbell-Savours.'

Campbell-Savours had sat on the Select Committee in judgement of Hamilton, and Webb supplied him with copious information that he used to discredit Tiny Rowland in the Commons. I thought to myself, "What on earth was Campbell-Savours doing on the committee judging Neil with these enormous conflicts of interests?"

I asked Francesca Pollard about the letters she wrote to Downey.

'Not just letters,' she said tartly. 'I phoned his office more than once to offer to testify in support of Hamilton, but I was ignored.'

It has to be admitted that her credibility as a witness would have been undermined by her actions and the way in which her alliances switched back and forth between Fayed and Rowland. But the fact that she had worked for four years at the very heart of Fayed's smear campaigns should have made her evidence worth a hearing. For one thing, she would have had unparalleled information on Fayed, Bozek and Webb, who were Neil's principal accusers. For another, she was also offering information on MPs who had become involved with Fayed, and above all she had gone to Downey voluntarily.

She was just another person whom Fayed had used. And today, after years of promises from two of the most powerful men in Britain, she is still penniless. Used up and spat out. In its own way her untold story is every bit as extraordinary as the "cash for questions" affair itself, and would make a fascinating television programme.

But of even more interest to me, with respect to the Hamilton case, was that Alison Bozek's involvement with Pollard was considered important enough by Nigel Pleming QC to warrant questioning Bozek on the matter and Bozek was the principal witness against Neil.

Pollard wasn't the only prospective (anti-Fayed) witness Downey ignored. Christoph Bettermann was a Fayed executive for seven years, reaching the position of Deputy Chairman of Harrods and Chairman and Director of Harrods Estates. He too offered Downey an insight into Fayed and a lot more besides.

A former barrister and junior judge in Hanover, Bettermann joined a large German industrial group in 1979. In 1981 he was seconded to a subsidiary company, International Marine Services (IMS), a small offshore salvage/support company based in Dubai, becoming President of IMS in late 1982.

In 1984 Fayed acquired IMS, making it a condition that Bettermann stayed on. He agreed and for the following six years worked as Fayed's right hand man in Dubai. In 1988, on IMS's behalf and with Fayed's knowledge, he struck a salvage deal with an oil company, Crescent Petroleum, regarding a tanker that had been crippled by an Iranian gunboat off the coast of Sharjah. The deal was concluded on 11 January 1989 to everyone's satisfaction, including – as far as Bettermann knew – Fayed's.

Bettermann's success in turning IMS into a profitable company did not escape Fayed's notice and he appointed him as Deputy Chairman and Director of Harrods Estates in the summer of 1990, requiring Bettermann to commute between London and the Gulf. But by May 1991 the relationship was under strain, brought about by Fayed's suspicion that Bettermann's bonuses were higher than was healthy for any employee. Although Fayed was assuaged when Bettermann demonstrated how his rising salary was only the result of his bonuses being tied to IMS's escalating profits, Bettermann was disillusioned by Fayed's implied lack of trust in him.

Then, in June 1991, Bettermann discovered that John MacNamara, (Fayed's head of security), had been bugging the private telephone in his apartment at 60 Park Lane. Bettermann was outraged. He immediately resigned and, ignoring Fayed's threats to ruin him if he quit, returned to Dubai.

A few months later, using contacts made in his time with IMS, Bettermann took up a senior post with Crescent Petroleum. Fayed promptly claimed that the salvage deal he made on behalf of IMS with Crescent in 1988 was fraudulent.

Fayed then embarked on a vendetta against Bettermann,

requiring him ultimately to make twenty-five court appearances in Dubai to defend criminal embezzlement charges and a similar civil lawsuit that Fayed lost but which he appealed twice, until the highest court in Dubai finally threw it out for good.

When Fayed wrote a damaging letter to the Ruler of Sharjah about Bettermann, the latter initiated his own libel action against him in London. He won the case and Fayed was forced to admit in a statement in Open Court that all his allegations of embezzlement and fraud were false and invented, and pay damages and costs approaching £1 million.

Like Pollard before him, Bettermann wrote to Downey on 3 January 1997, exposing Fayed's cash payments to his employees and the activities of Royston Webb, Alison Bozek, John MacNamara and Fayed's arch-spokesman, Michael Cole. He enclosed his witness statement from his libel action against Fayed which explained, in detail, the circumstances surrounding the alleged fraud.

Once again, as with other witnesses, Downey followed up Bettermann's offer diligently, replying to his letter, asking him for further information. As a result, Bettermann wrote back on 3 February with clarification of certain points and offered to provide other information about Fayed's attempt to embroil him in a character-blackening campaign against the United Arab Emirates' UK Ambassador. He also offered information on Fayed's damaging false allegations against, and treatment of, Peter Bolliger, a former managing director of Harrods, and Graham Jones, a former finance director of House of Fraser. Further, he warned against taking the word of Fayed's employees as corroboration.

I would be delighted to provide you with whatever details you might require of my case,' Bettermann said, 'which demonstrates Mr Al Fayed's infinite capacity to invent wild allegations calculated to do the utmost damage to the reputation of professional people and to pursue them ruthlessly regardless of expense.

I resigned from Mr Al Fayed's companies in June 1991, after I had discovered that he had secretly intercepted my telephone calls and recorded my private conversations. Mr Fayed thereupon threatened to destroy me which he proceeded to do . . .

> *He, (Fayed), complained in these terms against me (alleging fraud) to the Ruler of Sharjah and, as a consequence of a complaint filed by his lawyer in Dubai, I was summoned and interrogated by the police on 17 December 1991. This began a five year nightmare, which led to me being charged with serious criminal offences and having to stand trial, with a risk of being sentenced to a long term of imprisonment in an Arab jail.*
>
> *There is a simple but very efficient pattern to all Mr Al Fayed's feuds. I am sure that you will be able to discern it in the case you are examining. The scheme he uses is to make serious allegations against individuals to the relevant authorities and then immediately report to the press that the individual is under investigation . . .*
>
> *. . . If I can be of any further assistance to your Inquiry do not hesitate to contact me.*

Downey didn't let go of Bettermann even then, and he wrote back this time requesting more information about an allegation Bettermann made against Alison Bozek, that she had lied to immigration officials to facilitate the illegal entry of a foreign national called Ho Chee Sing, undertaken because Fayed wanted to employ him as a cook.

However, despite Bettermann's three submissions being articulate and detailed, and despite Bettermann specifically contradicting the oral testimony of Alison Bozek, which Downey supplied to him specifically for his comments, something appears to have happened in the first weeks of March 1997 to cause a turnaround in Downey's interest in the man.

In his report, Downey justifies dismissing Bettermann's evidence on the word of Fayed's Chief of Security, John MacNamara, who said that Bettermann had lied or won all his cases on technicalities. This is despite the fact that Bettermann had had his word tested on oath many times in Courts of Law and in spite of the fact that MacNamara's word had been dismissed once before by Downey in the Michael Howard hearing.

Bettermann, a man of unblemished character with unrivalled inside information and a proven track record for exposing the truth, was one of the most important anti-Fayed witnesses whose testimony was never to see the light of day. For reasons to which only Sir Gordon Downey is privy, he was not called to give evidence.

It simply didn't make sense. None of it. The more stones you unturned, the blacker Fayed's character was painted. Yet nothing, beyond Fayed's and his employees' tarnished allegations, had come to light to prove any wrong-doing by Neil. It all seemed so obvious, why was nobody else speaking out? Why was nobody listening?

10

More Missing Witnesses

ALTHOUGH I HAD TURNED DOWN THE PROSPECT OF WORKING
for Channel 5 News to leave me free to finish the Hamilton
story, I thought it would be a good idea to stay in touch. So, on
a trip down to London in August, I went into the news studios to
spend a day getting to know them, in the hope that they would
think of me when I was free to work again.

I shook hands with the people I needed to shake hands
with and then proceeded to get under their feet. They were
very friendly, though looking back I don't think it was a very
productive exercise. Still, it gave me a break from poring over
endless documents, which was therapeutic.

In order to try to clear our thoughts about exactly what had
happened, Malcolm and I agreed we should compile a written
report. We wanted to create something solid that we could show
to television companies when we were pitching the idea of the
documentary and release it to the media as part of our campaign
to bring the truth out. By then the report was only a few dozen
pages long but it was growing daily and I gave a copy to
producer, Adrian Monck, at ITN. He accepted it, but in reality
he was not in a position to use it.

Over the following month I sent copies of the report to
journalists and reporters whom I thought might help, and
still got nowhere. I also sent a copy to Tiny Rowland's home,
asking him to ensure that I had got my facts right in everything to do with him and Lonrho. At that time it was just
fifty-six pages long (the completed work is now over three

hundred and sixty pages long and 173,000 words).

A few evenings later I got a phone call at the office from Tiny Rowland. He was speaking from his yacht in the Mediterranean.

'I've just received the first few pages of your document,' he said. 'My butler faxed them through. I'm so pleased, Mr Hunt. I'm so pleased. This man Fayed is filth. It's marvellous, very good indeed. Though, you know, Neil Hamilton was not very helpful to me. He put down some questions . . .'

'I know, Mr Rowland.'

'He was unhelpful and said some things . . .'

'Perhaps he did so because he believed them to be true.'

'Well, I still think he's been treated terribly by this man Fayed and I would like to help him in any way I can. Please tell him that Tiny has said that he would like to help him, and if I can help you, Mr Hunt, I would like to.'

I'm ashamed to say that my first thought was, "Thank God for that, some money at last." I had no income and no prospects of starting to make inroads on my debt to my father. Neil was in the same position, but for obvious reasons we couldn't let him finance our research even if he was able. We were sinking deeper and deeper into debt every week. So, when Rowland offered to "help" I felt a rush of pecuniary excitement.

'This man Fayed is filth,' he repeated as I imagined what I could do with a bit of financial backing. 'He's a liar and a thief. He's done more harm . . . You must tell me how I can help you.'

Unable to bring myself to ask outright for money, I said: 'Well, perhaps information would be useful.'

'Of course. Any way I can. Do you have a copy of *Hero From Zero*?'

Rowland was referring to his book on how Fayed acquired his riches.

'Yes,' I said. 'It was very interesting.'

'You must come and see me when I'm in London. I will speak to Sir Edward du Cann and ask him to arrange it. Mr Hunt . . .'

'Yes?'

'Would you be so kind as to let Sir Edward have a copy of your report? He's writing a book about Fayed.'

'Of course.' I was always happy to send the report to anyone. Although I had more or less given up hope of getting anyone to commission the project as a documentary just yet, I was bent on getting as many people as possible writing and talking about it.

Rowland and I chatted for a further half-an-hour or so he was obsessed with some emeralds and a letter from the Queen Mother he claimed Fayed had stolen from his Harrods safety-deposit box – but no offers of money were forthcoming. In retrospect it was just as well, as all our findings would have been tainted if anyone had been able to claim that we had been sponsored by an interested party of Rowland's calibre. As it is, whenever I have been asked if anyone has paid me to root out this story, I have been able to look them straight in the eye and say "No." Had Rowland offered at that moment, however, I would probably have snatched his hand off out of desperation. Or do I mean destitution?

The next night he rang again, his butler having managed to get the rest of the pages to the yacht by satellite link. It must have cost a fortune. It was about eight o'clock and I was still working as usual in the office.

'I've read the whole thing, Mr Hunt,' he said. 'I'm so pleased that someone is at last taking an interest in this. Please tell Mr Hamilton that I would really like to help him in any way I can . . .' We talked for at least an hour. It would not be the last time.

I knew that Neil was desperate to start new libel actions against Fayed and *The Guardian* but hadn't the money to fund them. It would have been very useful to him to have someone like Rowland backing him, but again my nerve deserted me. Perhaps that's why people like Fayed and Rowland became multi-millionaires while people like me are forever grubbing for a crust.

The digging (and the grubbing) continued, however, still without the backing of the Rowlands of this world, and the next day it was down to business as usual.

Malcolm breezed in the office with a spring in his step.

'Do you remember David Leigh's explanation for the discovery of the three witnesses in *Sleaze?* Total crap, right?'

I looked up from the screen. 'No, you said pure bollocks, actually. "Total crap" was Gerald Ratner.'

'Eh?'

'The high street jeweller. Sorry, I forgot you normally live in Brazil. Anyway, what have you found this time?'

'It's on page 51, volume two of Downey.'

I reached back to the window ledge and picked it up. The page

Malcolm had directed me to was the transcript of the oral examination of *Guardian* staff Alan Rusbridger, David Hencke, Peter Preston and David Leigh, which all took place during one session on 10 February 1997.

'Hamilton gave us copies of all these transcripts before the Downey report was even published,' I said.

'I know, well, we both missed it. You'll find it halfway down the page in the left-hand column.' I scanned the page. 'Rusbridger refers to the late emergence of the three employees, see?'

I located it and read it out: ' "Our lawyers asked with increasing fervour for evidence from the secretaries, and it is fair to Al Fayed to say that they did form the view that he was genuinely protective and reluctant to involve them in what he perceived to be his own battle." '

'He says exactly the same as David Leigh in *Sleaze,* said Malcolm, 'and we have already established that that is absolute rubbish.'

'So Rusbridger is lying as well.'

'It's more important than that. There was always the chance that Leigh would have tried to explain away the story he gave in *Sleaze* as being due to dramatic licence. Well, now he can't because Rusbridger gives the same explanation for the Downey Inquiry.'

'Excellent stuff. Nice work.'

'I've not finished yet. Have you seen the letter from Doug Marvin in volume two?'

'No.' I'd actually forgotten who Doug Marvin was. 'I've been concentrating on the witnesses who weren't called.'

'Volume two, page 492.'

I picked it up off the desk again and located the page. It contained a reprint of Doug Marvin's letter to Downey dated 22 January 1997. As soon as I started to read it I remembered who Marvin was: he was Fayed's U.S. lawyer who, according to Leigh in *Sleaze,* happened to be in London just days before the libel trial was due to begin. And so Leigh's tale went, the *Guardian*'s Counsel Geoffrey Robertson QC "beseeched" Marvin to persuade Fayed to overcome his reluctance and grant access to the secretaries. I read Marvin's letter silently:

In September 1996, I was in London working on a commercial transaction for Harrods. During the course of that work, I reviewed with Harrods executives the types of legal proceedings that the Company was facing and, in that process, learned that Mr Al Fayed was scheduled to appear as a witness in Mr Hamilton's case against The Guardian. *Mr Stuart Benson and I therefore met with Geraldine Proudler, a partner in Olswangs, and Mr Geoffrey Robertson QC, both of whom who were acting for* The Guardian, *to learn more about the status of the case. Our meeting with Ms Proudler and Mr Robertson occurred about ten days before the Hamilton case was scheduled to commence.*

During the course of the meeting with Ms Proudler and Mr Robertson, Ms Proudler told Mr Benson and me about certain diary entries that had been produced to The Guardian *lawyers by Mr Al Fayed, one of which referred to a woman named Iris and indicated that Ian Greer had called asking for a sum of £5,000 that was supposedly due.* **I told Ms Proudler that the name Iris probably referred to one of the secretaries in Mr Al Fayed's Park Lane office** *and, as I was staying in a flat adjacent to the Park Lane offices, I would ask Iris about it.*

Subsequently, I met with Iris Bond. I asked her about the entry and about her knowledge of Mr Hamilton and Mr Greer in general. It became obvious that Ms Bond was aware of facts that were very relevant to the Hamilton case . . .

I reported to Ms Proudler what I had learned from Ms Bond and told her that there might be other witnesses with relevant information.

'Not only did Marvin make no mention of Fayed's allegedly firm reluctance to give access to his secretaries,' Malcolm exclaimed. 'He states that he informed *The Guardian*'s lawyers of the secretaries' involvement for the first time just days before the libel trial was due to start. That doesn't square up at all with what Leigh says in *Sleaze*, nor for that matter does it square with what Alan Rusbridger said.'

I read Marvin's letter again. 'And where's the mention that Marvin was "beseeched" by Geoffrey Robertson? It's a totally different version!'

In summary, we were expected to believe that Robertson

(according to *The Guardian*'s version), or Marvin (according to his own version), had "discovered" the involvement of Bozek, Bond and Bromfield in barely a day or two, when Preston, Hencke, Mullin, Rusbridger, Vulliamy and Leigh, all highly experienced journalists, did not discover their involvement at any stage in the two years after Neil issued his libel writ in October 1994.

This supposed failure to identify key witnesses beggars belief considering that *The Guardian* was then on the receiving end of Greer's £10 million libel action, which, if successful, would have wiped out up to a year's profits for the entire Guardian Media Group global empire. We were also expected to believe that *The Guardian's* solicitor, Geraldine Proudler, who is one of the cleverest libel lawyers in the country, had also failed to appreciate the significance of the name "Iris" in Fayed's message book, yet she had had that in her possession for months or even years, whilst Marvin (a US-based outsider, who was only visiting the UK) had supposedly appreciated the significance in five minutes flat.

'Do you think,' I said to Malcolm, ironically, 'it is likely that two lawyers of the calibre of Proudler and Robertson honestly needed to have the significance of the name "Iris" in the telephone message book explained to them by an American lawyer who had only been on the case for five minutes?'

'It's total crap,' Malcolm replied, again subconsciously paraphrasing Ratner. 'And have you seen the letter Rusbridger wrote to Downey on 18 February?'

'Can't remember.'

'Well, in referring to the period prior to the libel trial Rusbridger says this . . .' Malcolm picked up volume two again. ' "Over the previous two months, *The Guardian* had five lawyers, five journalists and two accountants working full-time on the case, producing and requisitioning the evidence necessary to justify the story at trial." So how come no one in *The Guardian's* football-team-sized task force of super-sleuths thought of asking Bond, Bozek, and Bromfield if they were involved in paying Hamilton?'

It was a serious investigation we were conducting, but there was always room for a little humour at times it certainly helped to keep us going but the stark fact was, *The Guardian's* and Fayed's explanations for the emergence of Bond, Bozek and Bromfield were so contradictory and ridiculous, they *were* amusing.

'And to suggest that Bond and Bromfield wouldn't have thought once of suggesting to their boss that they could help him, during the two years that Fayed was preparing his libel case, is just nonsense,' Malcolm added. 'Yet Marvin's version was the one Downey accepted. What the hell was Downey on? Evo-Stik?'

I thought I would play devil's advocate for once. 'Perhaps Downey hadn't read *Sleaze*,' I said.

Malcolm looked at me with a "who do you think you're kidding" expression. 'Are you checking to see if I've done my homework?'

'No,' I replied, honestly. I was enjoying winding him up instead.

'You know full well that he quotes the bloody book throughout his report. You'll be saying next that perhaps he was distracted when Rusbridger gave his evidence. And while we're on the subject of Downey, he can't claim that he never saw Carlile's letter to the Members' Interests Committee, either, because he quotes from it in volume one.' He thumbed through the pages. 'Page three... but Downey never mentioned Carlile's next sentence, which contains the reference to the employees. I'm telling you there's something . . .'

'And how come Downey didn't mention Fayed's willingness to put forward i.e. "persuade" his employees back in 1994, having quoted from Carlile's letter? And his treatment of Francesca Pollard and Christoph Bettermann has been niggling me for some time too, and all the rest of them. All this is in the same vein. No one can be that stupid, surely?'

'This whole story stinks from top to bottom,' Malcolm said. 'And when I said "top" I meant it.'

But the facts are that Downey accepted this irreconcilably conflicting, tenuous and bogus story about a visiting American lawyer "discovering" Bozek, Bond and Bromfield just as he accepted so many other unlikely stories that were unfavourable to Hamilton, without apparent qualm. And it was the testimony of these three witnesses that were crucial in leading Downey to conclude that there was "compelling evidence" that Neil had taken the money. Evidence we had examined and exposed as worthless.

I returned to examining a few more of the witnesses whom wise Sir Gordon Downey had decided he didn't need to call to testify.

Elizabeth Swindin was one. She had worked as Ian Greer's secretary in IGA from early 1987 to October 1996, covering the period when Fayed belatedly alleged that he paid Greer cash every quarter in brown envelopes. Her duties included opening and distributing the mail and receiving and distributing courier packages and all other incoming matter within the office.

Fayed's secretary, Iris Bond, said in her witness statement for the libel trial: 'On these occasions (i.e. Greer's alleged demands for quarterly cash payments of £5,000) I would then inform Mr Al Fayed that either Ian Greer *or his secretary* had telephoned asking for payment. Mr Al Fayed would then in my presence place two bundles of £2,500 notes (sic) in £50 denominations in a plain envelope which he would then instruct me to deliver to Mr Greer.

'I would then arrange for a porter to deliver these to Mr Greer at his office, though sometimes Mr Greer personally collected these envelopes from the reception desk, and I believe on some occasions he arranged for a courier to make collection.'

Since Bond had implicated her, Elizabeth Swindin expected to be called by Downey to testify before his Inquiry, to confirm or contest Bond's allegations. When no call came she wrote to Downey before he concluded his oral examinations of witnesses.

My duties included the opening of mail marked for Mr Greer's attention, the placing of a large proportion of his telephone calls . . . In the course of my duties, I have spoken from time to time, to Ms Iris Bond and Ms Alison Bozek.

On no occasion have I left messages, with any client, requesting payment of moneys owing to either the company or to Mr Greer at anytime . . . Any deliveries made to the office marked for Mr Greer's attention would have been given to me by the company's receptionist.

On no occasion have I ever received, opened or witnessed any envelopes containing cash from either Mr Fayed's office or indeed from any other client.

Considering this contradicts what Bond, a principal witness against Neil and Ian Greer, says, it would seem logical for

Downey, after receiving this letter, to invite Swindin to give evidence. He did not.

Now, it could be argued that Downey would have considered her evidence, as a loyal Greer employee, to be insufficiently impartial. I would have no argument with that *if he had also, by the same yardstick, discounted the evidence of Fayed's employees* instead of building his "compelling" case against Neil entirely around what they said.

Then there was Christine Hamilton herself. She had worked as Neil's secretary ever since he entered Parliament in 1983. At around the same time as Downey received Elizabeth Swindin's letter, Neil telephoned Downey to ask if Christine could accompany him when he was orally examined by the Inquiry on 20 February. Downey said no, on the grounds that he intended to call Christine as a witness later on. This at least made sense, as four weeks earlier, Iris Bond had made the same allegation against Christine as she had made against Elizabeth Swindin.

'Did you answer the phone to Mr or indeed Mrs Hamilton when there were requests (for cash in envelopes)?' Nigel Pleming asked Iris Bond.

'Mrs Hamilton or Mr Hamilton would not ring up and say "can we have our £2,500", but they would say "is there an envelope ready?" ' Bond replied.

This is completely at odds with Christine's very public defence of her husband. Given this important conflict, one could be forgiven for thinking that Downey would have called Christine to give evidence before the Inquiry, exactly in line with his earlier stated intention. In the event, however, he did not. Why? Who can say? Perhaps she would have been just that bit too credible. Or perhaps something happened after 20 February to make him change his mind.

Peter Clarke is a journalist and a weekly columnist on the Scottish edition of the *Sunday Times*. He is also a mutual friend of both David Hencke, (the journalist who wrote the original *Guardian* article about Neil) and Neil himself, having known them for six and thirty years respectively.

On 15 May 1995 Clarke met Hencke for lunch, during which Hencke introduced the subject of Hamilton's impending libel case against *The Guardian*. Clarke cautioned Hencke that he was a friend of Neil and that, whilst he offered himself as a mediator between the two parties, Hencke should not be "too indiscreet" with regard to what he revealed, because he felt he would have to report back to Neil. Hencke said he understood his position, but that as the two "legal machines" were locked-in, nothing Clarke said to Neil could help him.

As a result of what was said, Peter Clarke did indeed report back to Neil Hamilton, who then asked him to write down his recollection of what Hencke had said. Clarke subsequently wrote and signed a witness statement, dated 24 May 1995, to be used in the libel trial. Neil then referred to Peter Clarke's report of the conversation in his submission to the Inquiry and, in his forensic demolition of the case against him, quoted a small extract from Clarke's witness statement. Neil, in his naivity, thought this might have been sufficient to raise Downey's interest.

The following is a larger extract from Clarke's statement:

> He (David Hencke) stated that his lawyers, including the articled clerks, were enjoying the case. Part of the pleasure was because the credibility of the Government probably, and Conservative Central Office definitely, would be dented. He said that The Guardian would win even if they lost the case because the publicity would be so good . . . I was told that even if no sums had been received by Neil Hamilton, either Mr Greer, or someone else, had told Mohamed Al Fayed he was 'buying' Mr Hamilton in some sense . . . He said that even if no cash had changed hands, the hospitality Mr Hamilton had received would appear as a 'trade off.' He told me that The Guardian felt that laughter would be their greatest weapon and that George Carman [The Guardian's original QC who was replaced by Geoffrey Robertson] would be able to taunt Neil Hamilton over the details of the Ritz bill and that even the most reasonable explanation could be made to look risible. He told me that the reality mattered to a juror less than the impression and that the evidence would be affected by the Government's popularity.

Hencke's *de facto* admission that *The Guardian* had no evidence against Neil, save for the Ritz hotel bill, and his cocky opinion that "the reality mattered less to a juror than the impression," exposed the weakness of *The Guardian*'s case.

Once again you would expect Downey to call Peter Clarke to give evidence, since his statement completely undermined the credibility of Hencke and the integrity of *The Guardian's* allegations, but once again he did not.

I obtained Peter Clarke's telephone number from Neil and called him at his home in Scotland, for a out first hand rendition what the conversation with David Hencke was like.

'It was difficult for me,' Clarke said, 'being a friend of both David (Hencke) and Neil, and I thought that in some way I could have helped. I have never had any reason to doubt either of them before, but David is definitely going to have to walk the plank on this one.'

Timothy O'Sullivan was the author and friend whom Neil Hamilton introduced to Fayed on 20 February 1988 – a date when Fayed alleged he made a payment of gift vouchers to Neil. O'Sullivan signed a statement confirming that he had been alongside Neil throughout the meeting and that Fayed could not have given him gift vouchers or anything else without his knowledge.

As Fayed later withdrew the allegation that he paid Neil on that date, O'Sullivan's appearance before the Inquiry would, it could be argued, be totally superfluous – except that his deposition would have drawn attention to the fact that Fayed had been caught out fabricating allegations. Another witness who was not called. Because his testimony would have been helpful to Hamilton?

Norman Lawrence, yet another witness whom Downey did not call, was a financial adviser to the music industry in general and the pop group, Pink Floyd, in particular. He came across Fayed when his client, Pink Floyd drummer, Nick Mason, entered into a dispute with Fayed's company Modena Engineering, a specialist Ferrari car dealer.

Lawrence wrote to Downey:

Through this matter I came to know Graham Jones, Teron Schaeffer and Christoph Bettermann, all former senior directors of the House of Fraser and/or Harrods, and I have learnt a great deal about Mr Fayed both at first hand and through those gentlemen. I think it would be useful back-ground for you in assessing whether Mr Fayed is someone whose word you can believe.

He is exceedingly vindictive and prone to making wild and completely unfounded allegations about former executives and indeed others with whom he has 'fallen out' and against whom he has conducted the most extraordinary and appalling vendettas.

I can be reached by phone in business hours or after hours at home . . . I look forward to hearing from you,

Downey subsequently contacted Lawrence who sent a wealth of information regarding his case, detailing how Fayed had prosecuted an amazing vendetta against former House of Fraser Director, Graham Jones.

But though he had diligently requested Lawrence's material, Downey did not reprint any of it, despite its importance. Instead he provided a footnote that referred to Neil's second-hand discussion of Jones's case in his submission and once more Downey did not discuss its merits.

Lord Harris of High Cross is one of the foremost economists of our time. He was personally responsible for the establishment of the Institute for Economic Affairs in 1957, which fuelled free-market thinking among intellectuals when such ideas were widely discounted in favour of regulated economies. The IEA was the bedrock for the exchange of ideas that were first embraced by radical right-wing Tories before being largely accepted by mainstream politicians. Harris, therefore, was instrumental in furthering the intellectual climate in which Thatcherism flourished and New Labour was born.

In response to Fayed's allegations and *The Guardian's* campaign against Neil, Harris wrote a letter of support to the *Daily Telegraph* in October 1996 and also to Downey in February 1997 to make clear his views on the possibility that Neil could be bought by Fayed or anyone else.

I am venturing to write as one who has known Neil Hamilton well since his student days and who has followed his career closely ever since. I am therefore able to declare from direct knowledge over almost 30 years that he has been unwaveringly consistent in the causes he has espoused and I know of no exceptions to that course of conduct.

Indeed, it was because I largely share his dedication and

beliefs that I felt no hesitation in composing the attached letter which was published in the Telegraph. Accordingly, I would say that Guardian *and other journalists who have repeated the foul accusation by Mr Fayed, that he is principally motivated by money and his opinions could be bought, demonstrate that they simply do not know the man.*

Harris went on to recall his observations from the time he first met Neil in 1969, when he, Neil, was a student at Aberystwyth. He described him as being high-spirited and articulate, and an exponent of a free society. He also noted Neil's "irrepressible sense of fun and tomfoolery." As to his intellectual prowess, "his deep commitment to monetarist and free market ideas predated by many years the emergence of Thatcherism after 1979."

Harris finished with the words:

It must be admitted that in debate he could employ a caustic turn of phrase that must have made some enemies, especially among the slower-witted or ideologically opposed. The Guardian *can at least be credited with having singled out for destruction one of that highly ideological paper's most formidable political foes.*

Harris stood to gain nothing by volunteering such an endorsement. On the contrary he would have suffered a great loss of prestige if Neil was proven to be corrupt. Most reasonable people might, therefore, have thought that Harris's words should have carried some weight.

Downey considered the submissions volunteered by Harris and Lawrence thus:

I received two other pieces of evidence relevant to Mr Hamilton's good character;
– a letter from Lord Harris of High Cross testifying to Mr Hamilton's good character.
– a letter from Norman Lawrence, a financial adviser to the music industry, and an acquaintance of Mr Bettermann, claiming that Mr Al Fayed had conducted vendettas based

on unfounded allegations, against a number of former business associates.

And that was all. No assessment, no summing up. No discussion of the many tributes that Harris had made or assessment of the worth of this reference vis-à-vis the worth of references of the Fayed employees, all of whom were financially dependent on Fayed.

So, by our calculations, there were at least eight witnesses whose testimony would have dramatically strengthened Neil's case and equally dramatically weakened Fayed's and *The Guardian's*, all of whom contacted Downey, but *none of whom he called upon to testify at the Inquiry.*

Harris's words about how *The Guardian* had chosen the right political foe to attack stuck in my mind, coupled with David Hencke's admission over lunch to Peter Clarke that they were all "enjoying the case," because it was bound to dent the credibility of the Government and Conservative Central Office.

Both Malcolm and I felt that we were now making important progress. The evidence was building, brick by tortuous brick, into a case that at worst seriously discredited the Fayed and *Guardian* camps, and at best as good as cleared Neil Hamilton of all charges. If we just pushed on a little further into the jungle of paperwork we would suddenly break through into the light, then everyone would be able to see what was already blindingly obvious to us.

But there were still important conflicts to reconcile. The biggest of all comprised of the differing versions of Neil's interview on the Commons Terrace, which took place in July 1993 over a year before *The Guardian* printed its story.

Neil insisted that he wasn't asked about "cash for questions", and that Fayed most likely made his allegations out of spite in September 1994 when the European Court of Human Rights rejected his application to quash the DTI report into his acquisition of Harrods. And I believed him.

However, *The Guardian* journalist who penned the story, David Hencke and his then editor, Peter Preston, claimed otherwise. They said that Fayed first made his allegations against Hamilton back in 1993, and that that was specifically what journalists David Hencke and John Mullin went to interview

Hamilton about. In other words, Fayed couldn't have been motivated by spite, as he had made his allegations a year prior to the ECHR ruling.

But little did *The Guardian* realise that they and their friends had left enough clues to enable the truth to be discovered.

11

How The Seeds Were Sown

I WAS BEGINNING TO THINK THAT PERHAPS WE SHOULD BE looking more deeply at the motivations of *The Guardian*, rather than concentrating so much of our effort on uncovering the well-documented duplicity of Fayed. So, Malcolm and I went all the way back to David Hencke's original article of 20 October 1994 and dissected it again. Why, we jointly wondered, did the *Guardian's* editor, Peter Preston, print a story in the first place that he has not, so far, been able to support with any evidence?

The first clue was to be found towards the end of the article, where Hencke referred to a fax that Ian Greer sent to Fayed on 29 March 1989:

> *The most detailed connection between Mr Hamilton and Mr Greer is shown in two faxes from Mr Greer to Mr Fayed and his legal adviser on March 29 and April 4 1989. In them it is made quite clear that the tabling of parliamentary questions by Mr Hamilton was being arranged by Mr Greer as part of his parliamentary services fee. "Tried to contact you earlier today without success. Spoke to Brian Basham's (City PR company) office last night and today. Agreed with Neil Hamilton four questions (faxed to you earlier today) which have now been sent to Brian for use in tomorrow's press. Believe it will be possible to put more questions down next week. Suggest you mention that I will be in contact when you see Michael Grylls MP (the only MP who declares*

a link with Ian Greer Associates) because I believe he would
want to help."

Hencke himself had put in the bracketed note at the end about
Sir Michael Grylls being "the only MP who declares a link with
Ian Greer Associates." What was the relevance of that piece of
information? Why would Hencke draw attention to a "declared
link" between Grylls and Greer in a story about "cash for
questions" involving two other MPs, Tim Smith and Neil
Hamilton?

I pulled out our file of press cuttings to see what John Mullin,
who had partnered Hencke during Neil's interview in July 1993
the year before, had written, if anything. After a few minutes'
searching I came across an article by him that had been printed
the day after Hecke's article appeared. Significantly, Mullin
emphasised exactly the same points. He was describing a function organised by Ian Greer in 1985, at which Mohamed Fayed
met the members of the Conservative backbench Trade and
Industry Committee. A few paragraphs in, Mullin wrote:

> *'Neil Hamilton, who entered Parliament in 1983, a year*
> *after Mr Smith [Tim Smith] won a by-election in*
> *Beaconsfield, was also there. He had long known Mr Greer.*
> *Sir Michael Grylls, the only MP ever to have declared a*
> *financial link to the lobbyist, was a long term friend of both*
> *men . . .'*

For the second time in two days, one of the two *Guardian*
journalist who interviewed Smith, Hamilton and Greer in
1993 had made a point of mentioning that Sir Michael Grylls
was the only MP to declare a financial link with Ian Greer.
Frankly, Malcolm and I couldn't understand the significance. But
then I found another major clue towards the end of Mullin's
article.

> *'. . . In his interview with the Guardian, Mr Greer said*
> *several MPs had sought commission. Only two MPs other*
> *than Sir Michael . . . are known to have received payments*
> *from him for introducing clients, and that was more than a*
> *decade ago.'*

This tallied with something else that had been on my mind for a while. I pulled out my file containing submissions for the 1996 libel trial and turned to *The Guardian*'s witness statements. I knew I had seen it somewhere, but where? And then I found it, right at the front of David Hencke's statement, in the second paragraph:

> *As* The Guardian's *Westminster correspondent, I have an ongoing interest in the issue of parliamentary lobbyists generally and their role in the political process. The role of lobbyists at Westminster has become increasingly important over the past 10 years; indeed, during the House of Commons session 1989–1990, the Select Committee on Members' Interests examined the issue of parliamentary lobbying. Ian Greer, the Chairman of Ian Greer Associates ("IGA"), is probably the best known parliamentary lobbyist at Westminster. Mr Greer gave evidence to the Select Committee enquiry in April 1990. Prior to writing my first article about Ian Greer in mid-1993, I was aware that in the course of giving evidence to the Select Committee Mr Greer had said that he had made payments to three MPs in return for them introducing business to IGA.*

The Select Committee to which Hencke was referring had carried out an investigation in 1990 into Greer's convention of giving commissions to people who introduced business to his company. Hencke obviously thought this significant, because he attached the whole transcript of Greer's oral examination by the Committee to his witness statement.

'Why is that so significant?' I asked Malcolm. 'Why is Greer's practice of paying commissions relevant to a story that's supposed to be about Smith and Hamilton being paid to ask questions?'

We studied the transcript to find out exactly what the Select Committee had questioned Greer about and, once more, Grylls' name came up.

'We need to look further back to work out what sparked the Committee's interest in Greer and Grylls in the first place,' Malcolm suggested.

This led us back to another Select Committee that investigated the emerging phenomenon of parliamentary lobbying in 1988.

Greer had also given evidence to this Committee, during which he stated that his company maintained a strict policy of political independence. He did not retain any MPs as advisers, Greer said, unlike other lobbying companies, which, he claimed, did.

Nothing much happened as a result of this investigation, but in the following summer of 1989 Parliament's interest in Greer was stirred a second time. On this occasion another Select Committee was investigating how Secretary of State, Nicholas Ridley, was thwarted in the mid-1980s, when his plan to hive off certain British Airways routes to British Caledonian was over-ruled by the Cabinet. Greer, as BA's lobbyist, was the person chiefly responsible for successfully swinging opinion in the Cabinet against Ridley's scheme.

His success did not go unnoticed, and many people did not like the idea that a lowly lobbyist could wield such influence in Parliament . . . and a journalist called Andrew Roth was particularly harsh in his condemnation.

Roth has made a career out of identifying and publicising all aspects of MP's parliamentary activities and their outside consultancies, which he encompasses each Parliament in a journal titled "Parliamentary Profiles." He had already stated that he was convinced Greer was a "uniquely corruptive influence in the lobbying field" long before the "cash for questions" scandal blew up. It is not surprising then, that he paid close attention to Greer's activities and his contacts with Conservative MPs, especially those on the Tory back-bench Trade and Industry Committee.

At around the same time, in 1989, Roth met a disaffected former employee of IGA, who disclosed that Greer gave commission payments to people who introduced business. Among those who had benefited from this practice was Sir Michael Grylls, who had helped Greer win the BA account from another lobbying company, Shandwick.

Consequently, in his description of Grylls in his next "Parliamentary Profiles," Roth propounded:

Grylls, Sir Michael: The smoothly handsome face of hard Right economics and politics; the high profile of small business as projected by the Conservative Party and the Institute of Directors; linked to Ian Greer . . . warned of consequence of GEC takeover of Plessey (his friend, Ian

Former Conservative MP Neil Hamilton, with his wife Christine.

(photo Tim Jervis, Northwich Chronicle

Melissa Bell and her father, Martin, electioneering in Tatton during April 1997.

The 'Battle of Knutsford Heath,' April 8 1997.

The world-famous Harrods department store, Knightsbridge, London. It was acquired by the Fayed brothers in March 1985.

Mohamed Fayed during a light-hearted moment.

The entrance to Mohamed Fayed's office and apartment block at 60 Park Lane, where Neil Hamilton is alleged to have collected 'cash in brown envelopes'.

The Terrace of the House of Commons: scene of Neil Hamilton's only interview with *The Guardian* (22nd July 1993)

Parliamentary Commissioner for Standards, Sir Gordon Downey, with his report of 3 July 1997. He described the evidence as 'compelling' that Neil Hamilton had taken bribes from Mohamed Fayed.

Ian Greer, formerly London's most successful lobbyist. He was cleared by Sir Gordon Downey of paying MPs to ask questions..

119 Farrington Road, London. Headquarters of *The Guardian* and *The Observer* newspaper

The editor and former editor of *The Guardian* , Alan Rusbridger and Peter Preston, pictured outside the High Court after defeating the libel action brought by former Conservative MP Jonathan Aitken.

Tease all Thursday.

Smith:

extremely nervous.

Linked to House of Fraser - he was an accountant with Peat Marwick in 1971 - they did work on the Lonhro account - he says he was disgusted by what he saw, and took an interest thereafter.

As secretary of the (Tory?) Trade and Industry committee (run by Grylls) be and all officials were invited to an Ian Greer function for House of Fraser crica 1985. (must set the context here - who was secretary of state, what was happening in the bid etc).

Put down 17 questions on House of Fraser between 28 Ocotber 1987 and 23 January 1989. They then stopped, right after Lonhro's letter (quote line about how much and when and the last par). He admits to being frightened by that letter.

Says Greer offered MPs visits to the Ritz. He turned it down because he didn't think it was right. But he did accept big teddy bears for his children from Harrods. He values them at £100 (check the price). Put it in register of interests, which he says is updated every couple of weeks, bug had it take out before it became the published version.

Denies receiving payment for asking questions: 'That's not true'

Q: '£2,000) inb a brown envelope'

'That's certainly not true.'

(Interesting use of phraseology, don't you think?)

No role to play in fundraising, only came on board at central office in July 1992.

Hasn't received any money for any parliamentary business.

Hamilton: Ludicruous to suggest an MP or Minister is influenced by lobbying. It's a con, waste of money.

Friend of Greer for 15 years, introduced through Grylls, who was Christine's boss. She's his wife.

Introduced to House of Fraser through Sir Peter Horden, its consultant.

It appealed to his liberatarian insticnt, (oh yeah, pull anoth)
.....questioned about hotel:
OK then might have stayed a night at the hotel.

Taken Opera tickets worht hundreds of pounds as well

Paid his own fares.

Can't remember or explain why he didn't declare it.

Never received any payment other than those in the register of interests.

On the record: Rules himslef out of DTI questions on House of Fraser-Lonhro battle re European Court.

But not on British Gas, one of Greer's recently introduced cleint, which is facing MMC probe.

(And apparently, none others)

Asked about the brown paper bag, he was by this stagd somewhat agitated and began his increasing level of threats about Peter Carter-Ruck: "I'm a man who sees it through...etc"

John Mullin's contemporaneous notes of Neil Hamilton's interview on the Terrace. They do not record a 'cash' allegation was put to him.

The computerised transcription of Mullin's notes of both Smith's and Hamilton's interviews, (separated by a double line). It is the only document to show a 'cash' allegation existed against Neil Hamilton before September 1994. It is a forgery.

These and other documents discussed in this book can be viewed on the author's Internet website (www.coverup.net)

1am, 2nd May 1997. The end of a career in politics?

Always good advice.

Greer, was its lobbyist) July '86 . . . Urged speedy takeover of BCal by British Airways (to whom he recommended his friend Ian Greer as its lobbyist) July '87. . . Approved Lord Young's refusal to refer House of Fraser takeover to MMC but opposed GEC/Siemens bid for Plessey (for whom Ian Greer was lobbying) Jan '88 . . . Allowed unprecedented presence of lobbyist Ian Greer at meeting of Tories' Trade and Industry Committee Apr '89 . . . Consultant: Unitary Tax Campaign (representing 50 leading companies opposed to double taxation) '79; Beneficiary of Ian Greer Associates, in connection with Unitary Tax Campaign for which he had until Apr '89 a 'research assistant' and a percentage (5%?/10%?) of business recommended '84.

Roth's reference to Grylls' commissions from Ian Greer was marked. Grylls had not registered these because, he claimed, the rules did not require payments that carried no obligation to be registered. Nevertheless, the tenor of Roth's prose clearly implied that Grylls' commissions were related to the support he gave certain of Greer's clients, and that his relationship with Greer was therefore corrupt. As a consequence, Grylls consulted the Registrar of Members' Interests, Jim Hastings, who recommended thereafter that he register Ian Greer as a "client." Hastings also wrote to Greer for clarification of his earlier statement to the 1988 Select Committee that he "did not retain any MPs."

In his reply Ian Greer explained that it was his practice to grant commission payments to people who introduced new clients to his lobbying company, and that MPs had figured among them. Greer insisted that there was no obligation sought or implied, and that once the commission had been granted that was the end of the matter. Greer claimed that this was a practice that was well known in the profession and merely his way of saying "thank you" for introducing business.

Nevertheless, Roth's piece prompted Jim Hastings to circulate a memo in December 1989 to every MP, stating that, in the future, all payments of whatever nature should be registered.

Labour MP Dale Campbell-Savours, who sat on the 1989 Select Committee of Members' Interests, was so concerned about the insinuations in "Parliamentary Profiles" that he met Roth at his office to discuss exactly what he suspected lay behind Greer's commissions to Grylls. After hearing what Roth had to say, Campbell-Savours then persuaded the Tory Members of the Committee to undertake yet another investigation into Ian Greer.

And so, a few months later on 3 April 1990, Ian Greer once again appeared before the Select Committee on Members' Interests. Which brings us to where our paper-chase started, for it was the transcript of this hearing that Hencke had attached to his witness statement. Malcolm and I studied the transcript closely. This hearing was obviously immensely significant as far as *The Guardian* and David Hencke were concerned.

Under relentless questioning by Campbell-Savours, Greer confirmed that it was his normal practice to give "thank you" payments to people who introduced clients, and that these were always calculated at 10% of the client's first year's billing. When asked, Greer disclosed that three MPs had figured among the many people to whom he had given such payments, but he declined to name them, on the grounds that it was not his position to do so. Campbell-Savours henceforth referred to the three MPs as X, Y and Z, thereby increasing the aura of mystery around the whole issue.

Then the Committee's Chairman, Geoffrey Johnson-Smith, quoted from Roth's book the fact that Sir Michael Grylls had introduced BA to Greer. So right away it was obvious to all present that Grylls was one of the three mystery MPs.

'Do you think,' I said to Malcolm, 'that Andrew Roth, Peter Preston and David Hencke had all come to the conclusion that Greer's commission payments were really covert payments to reward MPs for parliamentary favours?'

'You mean like putting down questions?'

'Among other things, yes.'

'Maybe,' he said. 'It would explain why *The Guardian* had suspicions about Greer's liaison with Tim Smith and Neil Hamilton when they supported Fayed. It would also explain why the paper attached so much significance to Greer's commissions that Hencke attached a copy of that Select Committee's investigation to his witness statement.'

The complex jigsaw was beginning to take shape.

I thought about it a little further. 'But if *The Guardian* suspected that Greer's commissions were a secret way of rewarding MPs for asking questions etcetera, why didn't they make any allegations against Grylls? And why did they decide that Hamilton and Smith were the other two unnamed MPs? Leaving aside the common thread linking Grylls, Smith and Hamilton i.e. they all sat on the Tories' back-bench Trade and Industry Committee, there were other MPs who also had supported Fayed's battle against Tiny Rowland.'

So, we put ourselves in *The Guardian*'s shoes and looked at the evidence that was available to them at that time, that might have thrown light on the identities of "X, Y and Z."

The full list of Fayed's Parliamentary sympathisers, in descending order of Parliamentary activity, comprised Labour MP Campbell-Savours, and Tories Sir Peter Hordern, Tim Smith, Neil Hamilton, Sir Michael Grylls and Sir Andrew Bowden.

Labour MP Dale Campbell-Savours would not have been even considered. Although his Fayed-backed parliamentary activity during 1989-90 exceeded all Fayed's Tories' activity during 1985-1990 put together, Campbell-Savours was the MP that met Roth in 1989 and then persuaded the whole Members' Interests Committee to investigate Roth's theory about Ian Greer's commissions. It was almost as it he was acting as *The Guardian's* own Parliamentary Consultant.

Sir Peter Hordern would have been crossed off the list too, as he was House of Fraser's registered parliamentary consultant, so any payments he might have received would have been covered by his entry in the Register of Members' Interests anyway. Apart from which, he didn't actually ask any questions, as his activity was limited to organising support among other MPs, such as arranging delegations to ministers.

Sir Andrew Bowden's period of support was the shortest, extending over just a few weeks from 27 March to 22 April 1987. And, although his activity, pro-rata, outstripped everyone else's (having put down as many written questions (6) in those four and a half weeks as Neil had put down in two and a half years), the brevity of his involvement would have resulted in his being struck off the list next.

So while X was obviously Grylls, it seemed possible that, in the eyes of Roth and *The Guardian*, Y and Z would have been Hamilton and Smith.

'I bet Andrew Roth and *The Guardian* suspected Tim Smith and Neil Hamilton were the other two unnamed MPs, you know, Y and Z.' I said. 'This would explain why *The Guardian* were so prepared to believe Fayed when he alleged, falsely, that

Ian Greer had paid Tim Smith. And when you add the fact that Tim Smith was the Secretary of the Tories' backbench Trade and Industry Committee, Hamilton was its Vice Chairman, and Grylls was its Chairman, it becomes even stronger, because it was Grylls' commissions that sparked off the whole hullabaloo in the first place.'

Malcolm and I tested our hypothesis endlessly. But, if our deductions were sound, then *The Guardian*'s original intention would have been to make allegations against all three MPs, not just Neil and Tim Smith. So why, we wondered, didn't they make allegations against Grylls too?

The answer lay in Hencke's and Mullin's original articles of 20 October and 21 October 1994, which both stated the fact that Grylls had already registered a connection with Greer as a consultant to the Greer-organised Unitary Tax Campaign (the UTC was an all-party group of MPs that lobbied the U.S. Government to introduce legislation to stop certain states taxing British companies unfairly). Equally important, Grylls' support, like Sir Peter Hordern's, was limited to lobbying ministers, so *The Guardian* could hardly have alleged that Grylls had been paid to put down questions, as he hadn't actually put any questions down.

That just left Neil Hamilton and Tim Smith, both of whom had put down questions in support of Fayed, both of whom were members of the back-bench Trade and Industry Committee, both of whom were enlisted by Greer into helping Fayed.

We were sure that we had cracked the case and found the real reason that *The Guardian* had printed Fayed's unsupported allegations. It was because Fayed's (false) allegation that Ian Greer had paid Tim Smith dovetailed with Roth's theory about Greer's commissions. And as Roth was a known associate of *Guardian* journalists, such as David Leigh, it follows that Peter Preston and David Hencke would have been well aware of Roth's theory even before Fayed came onto the scene.

'If we're right, and I think we are, this means that Roth and *The Guardian* would have believed that Smith's resignation confirmed Fayed's allegation that Greer paid Smith. Whereas we both know that Smith *actually* resigned because he had been paid by Fayed himself.'

'When Hamilton and Greer issued their libel writs,' I postulated to Malcolm, 'Roth, Preston, Hencke and whoever else at

The Guardian must have still believed Andrew Roth's theory about Greer's commissions.'

'But they also knew they couldn't prove anything,' Malcolm said.

'Exactly. That would have made them panic, because if Greer won his libel action it would cost them £10 million in compensation for the collapse of his business.'

Malcolm nodded.

'It's not surprising that Fayed and *The Guardian* pulled out all the stops. Fayed was the first to bolster his defence with new face-to-face allegations two months later. *The Guardian* probably had nothing to do with concocting these, but Rusbridger and co. would nevertheless have been happy Fayed made them because it took the heat off them.'

'All this is making sense. But can you prove it?' Malcolm asked.

'I'm sure I can'. To my ears I sounded more confident than I felt. 'A year later in 1995, *The Guardian* were obviously still convinced that they were on the right track with Roth's theory, as evidenced by Hencke's heavy reliance on Greer's commissions in the construction of his witness statement, dated 26 June 1995. But then, in late 1996, Greer's books revealed that *Brown* was the third MP to receive a commission, instead of *Smith* as they thought. That's when *The Guardian*'s whole world must have fallen apart right before the libel trial was due to begin!'

Malcolm chipped in. 'So what you're saying is this: *The Guardian* couldn't claim Hamilton's two commissions as a back-door method of payment from Greer, because Smith had never received a commission from Greer. Similarly, Brown *had* received a commission from Greer, yet he had given Fayed no support whatsoever.'

'Exactly!'

'Actually, I think you're right,' Malcolm said. 'I've noticed that in all of Rusbridger's letters to Downey, he refers to Hamilton's commissions always in inverted commas, implying that they're not really commissions at all. 'Yes, here it is, even in his oral examination by the inquiry, Rusbridger says, "While undoubtedly convenient for Mr Hamilton and also Mr Greer to be able to present this payment as an introductory commission, it is questionable if it was indeed so." '

'It all fits, doesn't it?' I said.

Malcolm picked up his copy of *Sleaze* from his desk. 'David Leigh does exactly the same in here . . . which also makes sense, because in Roth's letter to Downey he admits that Leigh visited him during his research for the book.'

'In other words, *Sleaze* is based on Roth's screwed-up theory too. I guess he must have had to do a tad rewriting when they found out that Brown was the third MP, instead of Smith,' I added.

'Can you imagine all their faces when they found out?' Malcolm said, grinning broadly. 'They must have crapped themselves.'

'It looks as though they all screwed up in a big way,' I agreed.

It was time to take stock and figure out how our discovery fitted in to the wider pattern of events between 1993 and 1997.

'Okay,' I said. 'Let's work out slowly what happened from the beginning. Hamilton says that he wasn't asked about cash for questions in July 1993, when Hencke and Mullin interviewed him. Right?'

'Right. Hamilton's stance is supported by his letter of 1 October 1993, in which he threatens legal action if Preston printed any article that misconstrued his stay at the Ritz, but makes no threat regarding the publication of cash for questions allegations, which would be ten times more damaging . . .'

I could see that something was troubling Malcolm. 'What's the problem?' I asked.

'Why would it have taken so long for *The Guardian* to find out that the third MP was Brown and not Smith?'

'Because they could have only found that out from Greer's books, and *The Guardian* didn't get sight of those until the accountants assessing Greer's special damages claim handed them over in September 1996, just before the libel trial.'

'Okay. Can I just summarise what I think we're saying. Even if Fayed had *not* made his "cash for questions" allegations against Hamilton in 1993, *The Guardian* would still have suspected that he was one of the three mystery MPs, and that Greer might have paid him to ask questions under the disguise, as they saw it, of commission payments.'

'Correct! Because, one: he was a friend of Ian Greer; two: he was a member of the Tories' back-bench Trade and Industry Committee like Smith and Grylls; and three: because he put down some written questions in support of Fayed.'

'Got it in one. I mean three. They went to see Hamilton to try and substantiate Roth's theory!'

'As all the evidence shows that Fayed didn't make his cash for questions allegations against Hamilton until September 1994. We'll need to look pretty carefully at any evidence *The Guardian* has put forward to support their contention that Fayed's allegations existed against him in July 1993.'

'All this fits together perfectly,' Malcolm said, 'and it certainly fits the facts. But we've got one massive problem to overcome.'

'What's that?'

'So far, all this is based on circumstantial evidence. We need solid proof that Roth and the rest of them believed that Greer's commissions were secret payments for Parliamentary favours from MPs.'

'I agree.'

'Which means we need solid proof that they thought Tim Smith was the third MP to receive a commission payment from Ian Greer.'

12

The Vendettas

LATE ONE SUNDAY MORNING I DROVE OVER THE HAMILTONS'
house to ask a few questions on some new material that had
turned up. The door was ajar so I stuck my head around it.

'Anybody home?' I called.

'In here, Jonathan,' came a muted response from the direction
of the kitchen. I went on through and found Christine in the
office next door, looking desolate.

'Are you all right?' I asked.

'Oh . . .' Her voice was small and cracked, her shoulders
sagging as if under a terrible weight. 'It just all gets too much
sometimes.'

'Why? What's happened?'

'Oh, nothing special. It's just one of those days.'

'Tell me, what's happened?'

She made a dismissive gesture, then, as if thinking the better of
it, said resignedly, 'People who've been our friends for years cut
me dead in the street. I can't even go to the supermarket without
something happening. And Peter Carter-Ruck has written to tell
us they'll have to charge us interest on the fees we owe them
now. It's all so unfair when we haven't done anything wrong.'

I knew what she meant. When she and Neil attended a village
fête in Great Budworth I had heard rumours that a number of
villagers had expressed their disquiet. I put my arm round her
and she sank her head into my shoulder.

'Don't worry,' I kept patting her shoulder. 'The truth will
come out, I promise. Whatever happens, I won't give up.'

It was not the first time that I had seen Christine, supposedly a diamond-hard battleaxe, crumbling beneath the pressure, and it made me all the more determined to ensure that the truth was told. The first time I had witnessed her devastation was on a previous Sunday, immediately after the election. I had called in just after they had arrived back from church to find her in quite bad shape: 'We've just been to church and the vicar said we should all pray for the new members of Parliament and it all seems so unbelievable. When I think about that Martin Bell walking in and stealing our livelihood when he hasn't got a clue about Neil, and there he is telling everyone Neil is corrupt.'

One of the reasons I was prepared to believe that Neil might be an innocent victim, was because of Fayed's well-documented capacity for prosecuting vendettas against innocent people. This on its own was enough to cast doubt on Neil's guilt, to my way of thinking. The Hamilton scenario seemed to fit perfectly with Fayed's modus operandi, which he had allegedly developed into a near-science over the years.

We had seen how he had crossed writs with Tiny Rowland. We had heard Christoph Bettermann's story of being persecuted through the courts in Dubai. Others on the receiving end of his vengeance included Michael Howard, Peter Bolliger, Ken Warren, Professor Barry Rider, Graham Jones, Eamon Coyle, Teddy Taylor and even, perhaps, the disgraced Conservative MP Jonathan Aitken – in spite of what *The Guardian* and their pals at "World in Action" said. The list seemed never ending. Neil was just the latest in a long line of honourable victims.

'It might be useful if we were to look at some of the other people who had suffered at his hands,' I suggested to Malcolm one leaden Manchester morning. 'Let's put them all together and see if a pattern emerges.'

We now had Francesca Pollard's evidence to throw new light on Fayed's psyche and the methods he had used against those who had fallen foul of him. One of Fayed's earliest campaigns was against Hugh Aldous FCA, when Aldous and Henry Brooke QC began their investigation into his acquisition of House of Fraser.

The first of a series of nine letters to Aldous went out on 6 August 1987. Like almost all the letters that were sent out in

Pollard's name, it had been written by Richard New, Fayed's private detective, under Royston Webb. These early letters contained no threats or insults or, indeed, anything defamatory and this first was merely a plea to the inspectors that, instead of investigating him, their time would be better spent investigating Tiny Rowland, whom Fayed described as the "colossus of corruption." It actually revealed more about the way Fayed thinks, than it did about Rowland:

Dear Mr Aldous, (New, on behalf of Fayed, wrote)
"The dog (Rowland) barked and the caravan (Inspectors) moved on" – Ismail.

You will remember that I wrote to you on 6th August last year, concerning that colossus of corruption, Tiny Rowland . . . I am now writing in your capacity as one of the Inspectors appointed to investigate Rowland's dealing in the shares of Harrods . . . while I envy you your task, I am not optimistic that you will succeed in exposing Rowland's corrupt empire. What can ordinary decent people, like you and I, do against a man who, behind his "sincere" mask is a master perjurer. A man whose whole life is a lie. As his "Mr Fix it" security chief, ETHERIDGE (former Scotland Yard Detective Chief Superintendent Ken Etheridge), the fraud squad chief who was investigating Rowland and Lonrho for years, and who then saw where his future lay . . . That Rowland is like an octopus whose corrupt tentacles of bribery, blackmail and threats now extends (sic) everywhere is well known. Firstly, like J Edgar Hoover, he has something on everybody, and that is why the establishment is now so scared of him . . . he will view you as a fish – to be played. He has lied to every previous Inquiry, and has bombarded them, and everyone else he thinks appropriate, with reams and volumes of lies and red herrings. His purpose is, of course, to create a smoke-screen in order to divert attention away from the truth. So you see, Sir, the reasons for my pessimism, and my belief that you too will be duped by Rowland and his allies . . . You may rest assured, Sir, that if Rowland is displeased with your report, then you will be "crucified" in the "independent" Observer. I trust that this will not influence you.

Nearly a year later, on 17 July 1988, New wrote and despatched his final semi-literate "Pollard" invective to Aldous again, copying it to his colleague, Brooke. Even after a year's development, there was still nothing defamatory contained within, but more an attempt to influence their inquiry by suggesting that any information Rowland had supplied to them was tainted and that to concur with it would amount to being his puppet. The letter was sent just seven days before the report was delivered to the Secretary of State for Trade, Nicholas Ridley.

When the report on the Fayeds was finally delivered, Ridley immediately despatched a copy to the Serious Fraud Office for consideration of possible criminal charges against the Fayeds. Meanwhile, many MPs were growing impatient at the delay to publication of the report. Labour MP Jeff Rooker started to raise awkward questions in the Commons, following which he too was to receive one of New's letters, ostensibly from Pollard.

One such letter, posted on 17 January 1989, contained a fair amount of unprintable material. The printable highlights, however, were:

Dear Mr Rooker,

Thank you for your undated and offensive note received earlier this month . . . It does not surprise me that you found my last letter to you offensive. I make no apologies . . . That is why your support for such an evil man (Rowland) is so offensive to ordinary people, given that you are an MP, and given that you know what a bullying, crooked thug he is . . . Why are you furthering the interests of Rowland, a man who makes Al Capone look like a saint . . . Are you a paid consultant to Rowland/Lonrho or any of their associates, or have you received any benefits? . . . I expect Rowland's "front man", the chairman of Lonrho, Sir Edward du Cann, has been putting the arm on you as well . . . And you wonder why you receive what you consider to be offensive letters from ordinary victims like me. It is you that give offence, not I.

But not only had New written this, he had forged Pollard's signature and disseminated it widely without Pollard even knowing. One thing is for sure – it was authorised by Fayed.

Six months later, on the Tory back-benches, Teddy Taylor had also got into his stride and demanded to know the whereabouts of the report. As Fayed was not one to discriminate between parties at this stage, Taylor received a torrent of letters, all written by Richard New, in the name of Francesca Pollard, as usual, but carrying her forged signature, also as usual. Edited highlights from one sent on 10 July 1989:

Dear Mr Taylor,

Thank you for your letter of 16 June. I am sorry that you felt unwilling to answer the questions that I put to you concerning your inexplicable support for Rowland and Lonrho . . . it is the very fact that you are so obviously hypocritically selective in your public views regarding Rowland/Lonrho that causes such concern and creates the atmosphere of suspicion as to your motivation.

You know, and I know, and every other informed person knows, that Rowland is a cheap bullying crook who should have been put behind bars long ago . . . that is what makes your continued (almost demented) support for him totally baseless, and sinister. That you fly in the face of all the facts must be increasingly worrying to both your Parliamentary colleagues and to the public. It must now be quite clear to everyone that you are Rowland/Lonrho's "man" in the House (seemingly their only one). You act as if you are a paid consultant to them . . . Your attempts to justify your blatant support for Rowland simply have no credibility . . . How can you therefore have the gall to say . . . Equally you have the gall to say . . .

No Mr Taylor, when history is examined, your stance is staggeringly hypocritical and you apply the most blatant double standards. You cannot expect anyone to believe that your fanatical support for Lonrho is honourable . . . I am also told that you have bought, or are planning to buy, a new home or a second car. If true, where has all this money come from?

As in his letter to Jeff Rooker, Fayed implied that Teddy Taylor might have been paid secretly for his Parliamentary stance. In retrospect, these can be seen as being the very first signs of Fayed's now legendary practice of making bribery allegations.

One person for whom Fayed reserved particular ire was Conservative MP Michael Howard who, as Corporate Affairs Minister, appointed the DTI inspectors in 1987. According to Pollard, acting on Fayed's instruction, Fayed's PR man Michael Cole organised the production of a pamphlet titled "Twenty things you ought to know about Michael Howard MP". It contained all sorts of allegations that Howard had been involved in unsavoury deal makings and had appointed the Inspectors because he was under Rowland's sway.

Fayed organised the pamphlet to be printed in hundreds. Richard New also produced a placard on Fayed's instruction, bearing an allegation that he helped advise Tiny Rowland how to rob the Israel British Bank. It was intended that Pollard parade with this, whilst she distributed the pamphlets in Howard's constituency. Amazing stuff indeed.

Shortly afterwards, during the weekends of 10/11 February 1990 and 23/24 February 1990, Pollard distributed the leaflets in Ashford and Folkestone, Kent, which both lie in Michael Howard's constituency. Her activities were picked up by the local press and reported, harming Michael Howard's reputation. Later still, as Fayed's ire against Howard increased further, Fayed requested that Pollard parade Howard's constituency bearing another placard, this time alleging that he had been bribed £5 million by Tiny Rowland to appoint the Inspectors.

The DTI Inspectors' report into House of Fraser showed Mohamed Fayed and his brother, Ali, to have lied constantly to their Inquiry, but that no charges could be brought against them because lying to Government inspectors did not at that time constitute a criminal offence. The Committee decided to examine all aspects of Government inspections and the legislation that covered their procedures.

Though the Fayeds could not be prosecuted retrospectively (if the Government followed a recommendation to pass new legislation), DTI Minister Nicholas Ridley nevertheless could have applied to have the Fayeds disqualified as company directors. So, in an attempt to stymie criticism that could have forced Ridley's hand, Fayed embarked on all sorts of scurrilous smear tactics against the members of, and advisors to, the Committee, whom he thought were against him.

Professor Barry Rider PhD (Lond); PhD (Cantab); Hon LLD, Fellow and Dean of Jesus College, Cambridge was a special adviser to the 1987 Trade and Industry Select Committee. An expert in company law and now Director of the Institute of Advanced Legal Studies, he was formerly the Head of the Commercial Crime unit at the Commonwealth Secretariat. There, his job involved exposing company frauds like tax evasion and money laundering, and his exploits often resulted in very powerful people being consigned to HM prisons.

In September 1989, one of the many villains his expertise had helped put behind bars started putting it about that Rider himself was guilty of fiddling his expenses. The Secretariat held an internal inquiry that subsequently cleared him completely. However, Rider was incensed that they had felt the need to investigate him and moved on to the Trade and Industry Select Committee. Fayed discovered that Rider had been the subject of allegations and that the Secretariat was investigating him. So Richard New spun out a story that he had been sacked and leaked it to *Private Eye*, the satirical gossip sheet read by everyone in Fleet Street. The story appeared in the 11 May 1990 issue:

> . . . *Sadly Dr Ryder's* (sic) *departure from the secretariat was less than amicable. He was effectively sacked on 18 September last year for – among other things – alleged fraud, fiddling expenses, threatening staff and sending non-secretariat personnel to Interpol meetings while passing them off as bona-fide Commonwealth Secretariat employees.*

Leaking damaging stories about his perceived detractors to the Press, as distinct from making allegations himself, was a new move by Fayed. The result was satisfyingly damaging and Rider's reputation was greatly harmed. Rider explained what then happened in a letter to Downey.

> . . . *I have reason to believe that the Fayeds remain vindictive to me. Frankly, I cannot understand why this should be the case. I can only assume that they and perhaps their advisers, consider that my role in advising the Com-mittee was more significant than it was. Indeed, I find the whole saga bemusing to say the least. I remain, however, saddened that what was a serious attempt to undermine the*

proper working of a Select Committee and impugn the personal and professional integrity of those who did absolutely nothing wrong and sought only to perform their public duty, has been allowed to pass without criticism.

Fayed had indeed got away with everything he'd been up to so far. So he pushed the boat out a little further when New composed one of his egregious "Pollard" letters to Kenneth Warren MP, Chairman of the Select Committee a few weeks later.

Dear Mr Warren,

As like any "warren" you are normally so full of "rabbit, rabbit" that I was surprised when you scampered off and refused to talk to me when I sought to question you at the House on the day of the publication of the Select Committee's report on DTI Inquiries.

All I wished to ask you was why I had the distinction of being the only person whose evidence to your committee was not reproduced in your report, but was instead shunted off to the obscurity of the House library leaving only my name and an otherwise blank page in your report (page xlvii). Despite the fact that I appear to have been the only person to give evidence who has actually been the victim of fraud (by Rowland and his henchmen).

Your appointment of Barry Rider to the key position of legal adviser to your committee was simply staggering. Was it representative? You must have been aware that on the 18th September last year he had been effectively sacked – for alleged fraud, fiddling expenses and threatening staff – from his position as head of the crime unit of the Commonwealth Secretariat (Eyes 11th and 25th May) and that it is also alleged that parts of his "CV" are fictitious. You must also have known that it was in his position at the Secretariat that he had come to know Rowland so well.

As can be seen from your report, it was solely on Rider's say so that you scurrilously dreamt up various "hypothetical" charges against those running House of Fraser – flying totally in the face of the evidence of all the investigating bodies, and furthering Rowland's vendetta . . .

. . . My moderate views on Mr Rowland are by now well

known. He is a conniving, thieving, crook, as are most of his cronies. In his ten year vendetta against House of Fraser, he and his assorted lackeys may have been able to hijack and hoodwink a couple of naïve DTI inspectors into chasing nannies and birth certificates and rubber-stamping a "Rowland" report, but to ordinary people the affair is simple.

Mr Rowland's background manifestly makes him an "unfit person" to run even an ice cream stall, let alone to have gained control of the House of Fraser – a known master criminal, thief, blackmailer, briber, perjurer and ex-Nazi sympathiser.

Contrary to the impression given, Francesca Pollard had not harassed Ken Warren outside the Commons at all. She just happened to be standing outside by the Lords entrance when she noticed Warren and his secretary walking by briskly. But after she casually mentioned this to Fayed, he got New to invent the scenario that Warren had "scampered off," thus giving the impression that he had retreated from a confrontation with Pollard.

Once again, out of invention came forth policy, because as a result of this fabricated story about harassment, that was exactly what Fayed ordered Pollard to do thereafter to Warren and other Members of the Select Committee on Trade and Industry – harass them. Fayed even provided her with a Mazda van, complete with a driver and bodyguards from a respected security company, to enable her to distribute propaganda in their constituencies unhindered.

And so, on Friday 12 April 1991, out of misplaced loyalty to the man who had promised to help with her legal battle, Francesca Pollard organised a family outing to Warren's constituency in Sussex, with Fayed bodyguard, Julian Smith, as driver. There she was to deliver leaflets to homes and commercial buildings close to Warren's constituency office.

On arrival in Hastings, Pollard, her common law husband, her daughter, and Julian Smith duly distributed Fayed's smear material, putting scores of leaflets through the letterboxes of local houses, Ken Warren's constituency office, and the office of the local newspaper. The job done, the party then set off to Warren's village of Goudhurst, Kent, some 45 minutes' drive north. There they leafleted the street where Warren lived.

Fayed was pleased with the result, and induced Pollard to do exactly the same in the constituencies of three other Members of the Committee, namely Tory MP Robin Maxwell-Hyslop and two Labour Members, Stan Crowther and Doug Hoyle. According to Pollard, Fayed and New had even discussed the idea of hiring women to pose as prostitutes to harass Warren and Maxwell-Hyslop.

However, in the weeks following her visit to Sussex and Kent, Pollard, reflected on her involvement and during her visit to the constituency of Maxwell-Hyslop, developed grave misgivings about her role. Her thoughts must have been affected to some degree by Fayed's insistence that she parade with the bribery placard and harass Maxwell-Hyslop on his walk to church. In the event, she opted to do nothing more than go to the seaside with her family instead.

On her return, Fayed was unhappy at her change of heart and insisted that she become even more involved in his campaign against Tiny Rowland. Fayed wanted to put her name to a book about Rowland that he, Fayed, had paid Richard New to write. On reading it, Pollard refused point-blank. Fayed also demanded that she should go to Rowland's country retreat of Bourne End and sell toilet seats bearing the logo "I shit on Tiny Rowland" at car boot sales for £5 each (they cost Fayed £50 each to make). He also tried to persuade her to demonstrate outside Lonrho's headquarters in Cheapside for two days a week, whilst continuing, on his behalf, her attacks on Members of the all-party Select Committee on Trade and Industry.

But Pollard had had enough and quit. In a state of exhaustion and confusion she approached her brother, Benjamin, and confided in him in all that she had done, and been asked to do. Benjamin contacted Lonrho, and Pollard subsequently met Rowland and spilled the beans. In due course, she swore an affidavit detailing all her nefarious activities on Fayed's behalf.

Having perfected this mix of intimidation, bribery allegations, smearing and poison pen-work, Fayed started to direct his spleen towards those Harrods executives whom he considered to be open to attack.

Graham Jones was Fayed's Finance Director from 1987 to January 1990, and had undertaken a valuation of Modena

Engineering (a Ferrari specialist), prior to Fayed's purchase of the company for his son, Dodi. Fayed subsequently decided that he had paid too much for the company and accused Jones of having taken a bribe from Modena's vendors to over-value the company. He then sacked Jones and started a vendetta involving the dissemination of false allegations to the press.

Jones decided to return to his native Australia where he secured an executive position with its national airline, Qantas. On 18 June 1990 he boarded an aircraft at Heathrow bound for Sydney. The doors closed and the plane prepared for take-off as the air staff settled the passengers into their seats. But the aircraft did not move. Several minutes passed then the doors dramatically opened up again to admit four heavies from Surrey Police. Jones was arrested, dragged off the plane and spirited away to Guildford Police Station where he was interrogated for over an hour and a half about financial matters relating to Modena, with a view to possible corruption charges being brought.

Having satisfied themselves that there were no grounds for any charges, the police apologised and admitted they had been persuaded to take such draconian action by Fayed's adviser, Royston Webb and Fayed's head of security John MacNamara – two of Downey's most trusted witnesses. They released Jones, put him up in an hotel at the expense of the Surrey Police, until he could take another flight the following day.

While Jones' flight cruised towards Australia, Michael Cole, Fayed's spokesman, was contacting the *Daily Express* with a story. The *Express* reporters did not validate the allegations. Twenty-four hours later Qantas executives were able to read all about their new high-flyer when their London office faxed over the article titled, "VAT men's flight inquiry flattens Graham's champers take-off," alleging that Jones had been responsible for serious VAT irregularities. Jones, notwithstanding the crude attempts to discredit him, retained his new job and prospered in it.

Fayed, however, does not readily abandon old grudges. Nearly two years later, in early 1993, he heard that Qantas had promoted Jones to the post of Financial Director. He instructed Royston Webb to send off to the airline and its shareholders, (the Australian Government and British Airways), a dossier listing all his allegations of Jones' corruption and financial incompetence. Regrettably Qantas took them seriously and immediately despatched their head of security, Ron Armstrong, to London to interview Webb, MacNamara, the police, Jones's solicitors and Norman Lawrence. After Armstrong found nothing to substantiate Fayed's allegations, Webb confessed that Fayed had asked him to distribute them because he wanted to "crush Jones" and "pursue him to the grave."

A few weeks later Fayed called a stooge on the *Mail on Sunday* and gave him another black story about Jones, which the paper carried under the headline; "Past catches up with Qantas boss – new airline chief faces fraud probe." A Melbourne newspaper picked up the story off "the wires" and ran it next day under the headline "Qantas boss in $9 million row." Two weeks later they were forced to print a full retraction and an apology.

Many other employees, such as Christoph Bettermann and Peter Bolliger, the former managing director of House of Fraser, suffered similar campaigns and even as I write details of the goings-on at Harrods over the last few years continue to find their way into the papers on a regular basis. Probably the most shocking is Fayed's treatment of Eamon Coyle.

Eamon Coyle was Harrods' deputy director of security. He worked for the store between 1979 and 1995, after which he offered his inside knowledge to the American society magazine *Vanity Fair*, then embroiled in a legal battle with Fayed. Fayed had sued the magazine over an article by Maureen Orth, in which she catalogued for the first time Fayed's lying, thieving, surveillance methods, sexual shenanigans and true background, as well as his propensity for vendettas (Fayed withdrew his action against the magazine in the first days of December 1997.) Coyle also gave testimony to ITV's "The Big Story," which carried out its own investigation based on the bugging, harassment, vendettas and racism allegations first aired in Orth's *Vanity Fair* article.

In February 1998 Coyle was then informed by Harrods legal director, Michael Rogers, that a Harrods' staff training videotape had "come into his possession," which contained intimate film of Coyle and his homosexual lover. This had been dubbed, by Harrods, from Coyle's own videotape that he had made privately with his partner. Rogers then "invited" Coyle to provide his "input" on another ex-Harrod's employee, whom Fayed wished to discredit, in advance of a complaint being made over the "theft" of the training video, value £5. Coyle refused to succumb to the "invitation" and voluntarily contacted the police himself, reporting the crude attempt to pressurise him into smearing his former colleague.

And so, back in the summer of 1993 when Fayed first called in Peter Preston of *The Guardian*, Fayed had already established a track record of reckless allegations and unjustified vendettas though only his victims and closest employees knew what he was capable of. His early success at manipulating the media against his enemies, however, must have made Fayed wonder how he could harness this power in other ways. It was a good five months since his brother had applied for citizenship and the process seemed to be at a standstill. So he decided to start a new vendetta. On the surface, this was directed at his lobbyist, Ian Greer, to whom he felt he had paid good money for what he saw as very little return. In fact it was a shot across the Tory Government's bows as to what they could expect if his brother, and later Fayed himself, didn't get their British passports. However, from these small beginnings, it developed and developed into arguably the biggest vendetta of all time – a vendetta perpetrated by one man against the entire Conservative Government.

On 14 July 1993, after being contacted the month earlier, Peter Preston of *The Guardian* went to see Fayed. At the meeting Fayed complained constantly about Greer and the Tories.

On the basis of what he heard, Preston nominated journalists David Hencke and John Mullin to interview MPs Tim Smith and Neil Hamilton, and Fayed's own lobbyist Ian Greer. The two journalists interviewed Smith and Hamilton separately at the House of Commons on 22 July, and interviewed Ian Greer the following day at his offices. Neil claims that at this, his one-and-only interview with *The Guardian* (or indeed any newspaper) he was *not* asked about "cash for questions." The journalists insist that he was.

A year later, when the European Court of Human Rights rejected his appeal to have the damning DTI report quashed, Fayed focused his ire on the two Ministers most directly involved: Michael Howard for appointing the inspectors and Neil Hamilton for not withdrawing their report. Tim Smith was tossed into the campaign, perhaps simply because he knew Smith *was* guilty of taking cash from Fayed and therefore it would have been a waste of opportunity not to accuse him. After all, he was a Tory Minister. But even then Fayed couldn't quite bring himself to tell the whole truth immediately, alleging that Smith had been paid by Greer rather than by himself. Perhaps he reasoned that by placing an intermediary between himself and the recipient of his bribes, he could avoid allegations being levelled in his direction.

It is likely that the Minister for Defence Procurement, Jonathan Aitken, was also targeted at this stage, because in September 1993 he too had stayed at the Ritz – in the company of some high-ranking Saudi Arabians connected with the massive £5 billion Al Yamamah arms contract. That would have provided Fayed with an opportunity to do what his record has proved he is most adept at doing: fabricating allegations so they appear to match real events and relationships, thus giving them an aura of credibility.

In October 1994 the year-old Hencke story was printed, with no further interviewing of Smith or Neil. But when Hamilton and Greer issued libel proceedings, it suddenly became very important whether the "cash for questions" allegation was put to Neil or not, during the interview on the Commons Terrace the previous year. Hamilton asserts that the allegations were most likely made out of spite around 21 September 1994, when the ECHR rejected Fayed's appeal. He is adamant that he would definitely remember such a controversial and potentially damaging question being asked, had one been put during his interview on the Terrace in July 1993. He insists that the interview was almost exclusively concerned with general questions about lobbying, followed by more specific questions about his consultancies and his stay at the Paris Ritz. *The Guardian*, on the other hand, has consistently claimed that Fayed made his corruption allegations against Neil in his meeting with Preston back in July 1993, and therefore could not have been motivated by spite.

'To begin with I was hesitant about discussing the stay at the Ritz,' he admitted to me, 'and *The Guardian* and Downey have made a capital of that reticence. But, given *The Guardian's* track record in representing any event that could be used against the Tories in the worst possible light, I was just being cautious. I never denied that I had stayed at the Ritz, though I'm sure they would have preferred me to lie.'

But if it could be *proved* that Hencke and Mullin had not put a specific "cash for questions" allegation to Neil, it would show that at the time that *The Guardian's* investigations started in 1993, Fayed had not made any specific allegations to *The Guardian* that Hamilton had taken cash. If he had taken cash, Fayed would certainly have mentioned it to Preston at that stage. If he did not mention it, then it is likely that the allegations *were* made out of spite. It comes down to the fact that either *The Guardian* or Hamilton must be lying about the questions asked in that interview. So if one or other side can be proved to have been telling the truth, the case for the other would be severely discredited.

After identifying the importance of establishing which of the two conflicting accounts of the crucial interview was the true one, Malcolm and I put in hundreds of hours of research, analysing every scrap of evidence to find out.

At this stage it's worth restating a few important points: Tim Smith does not dispute that, during *his* interview with Hencke and Mullin, they put allegations to him that he had taken cash. But when he resigned on the article appearing, he did so because he had received money from Fayed, not from Greer as was alleged in the article. Tragically, Smith did not clarify this in his resignation statement, thus giving *The Guardian* and everyone else the impression that the allegations against him, and therefore by association Hamilton and Ian Greer, were true. Hamilton, on the other hand, denied vociferously being paid by anyone to ask questions for cash, and continues to deny it to this day.

Neil's interview on the Commons Terrace happened immediately prior to the 1993 summer recess. As already mentioned, a few months later, just before Parliament returned from the recess, he heard that *The Guardian* was about to print a damaging story about him based on the interview. So, in an attempt to prevent anything defamatory being printed, he wrote to Peter Preston, *making reference only to his interrogation about the Ritz*, threatening a legal response if the paper misconstrued his stay. The genuineness of his letter has never been disputed by anyone.

It seems unlikely that he would respond vigorously to anticipated misrepresentation concerning his stay at the Ritz (a relatively minor matter) and not also respond to the much graver charges about corruptly taking cash in payment for putting down questions, if such questions had been put at the interview. So it would be absurd to suggest he wouldn't have even mentioned them in his letter of 1993 *if the allegations had in fact been put to him.*

Downey never alluded to this glaring paradox at all. Even worse, in the chronological sequence of events that Downey constructed in his report, he totally misrepresented Neil's letter, giving any reader the impression that the allegations *did* exist in 1993. He stated:

– 1 October: Mr Hamilton writes to the editor of The Guardian *in an attempt to forestall publication of the allegations against him, and threatens a libel suit.*

But, as we have said, the only allegations that Neil attempted to forestall the publication of, were those he feared *The Guardian* might misconstrue regarding his stay at the Ritz. Downey's account was grossly misleading. Downey also took no account of other aspects of the evidence that should have had alarms ringing.

In his witness statement Hencke stated:

We then confronted him with the cash for questions allegation. Either John or I directly asked him: 'Have you received any cash from Mohammed Al Fayed in return for asking questions on his behalf?' I also recollect that we mentioned the figure of £2,000 per question asked.

It seemed strange to us that Hencke could not remember which of them asked a Minister of the Crown if he was taking cash bribes. Is the memory loss really a lie, aimed at avoiding responsibility for the other lie – that the question was ever asked?

In his submission to Downey, Neil was categorical in his denial of Hencke's version of events:

This is a lie. It is not surprising that Hencke professes not to remember who asked the question, as neither of them did. At this time, Hencke had not spoken to Fayed personally and was dependent for his information on Preston, who had met Fayed only once. Fayed had not, at this point, made his allegation of direct cash payments. [Author: This is highly significant.]

No "cash for questions" allegation was put to me at this meeting, which was entirely about the Ritz. I did not hear of such an allegation until the Sunday Times *published a report of its entrapment exercise a year later.*

Without giving any reasons, as well as rejecting the logic of Neil's letter to Peter Preston, Downey also rejected the logic of Neil's examination of Hencke's statement. Instead, he concluded that Hencke and Mullin *did* put the "cash" question during the interview, stating:

However, contemporaneous documentation in the form of meeting notes which I have examined, and whose authenticity I have no reason to doubt, appear to support the account given by Mr Hencke and Mr Mullin.

When I first read this, in my mind a thousand horses at full gallop suddenly stopped dead. For the evidence to which Downey referred was the evidence *The Guardian* put forward to support their claim that Fayed had made his allegations against Hamilton way back in 1993. This was counter to Hamilton's claim, and counter to our conclusion that, back in 1993, at least as far as Hamilton was concerned *The Guardian* had only been trying to substantiate Andrew Roth's theory about Greer's commissions. Nothing more.

This evidence of *The Guardian's* was the evidence that Malcolm and I knew we would have to test to destruction on one criterion alone: did it prove that Neil was asked about "cash for questions" during the interview on 22 July 1993?

Malcolm and I focused on our next step, and we decided that I should return to Nether Alderley for yet another interview, this time concentrating on just one issue – his interview on the Commons Terrace by Hencke and Mullin. Malcolm, meanwhile, settled down to some serious analysis.

Christine opened the front door. 'How many more sessions do you need?' she said, exasperated, 'I'm running short of tea!'

'Yes please,' I said, as she went into the kitchen. 'Don't mind if I do.'

Neil emerged from the library and we both went into the dining room, where we settled in our usual confrontation postures on opposite sides of the table.

'Sorry about the short notice, but I'm going to need a detailed account of your interview on the Terrace. It's fundamental to where we're at in our research right now,' I said.

'Fire away.'

'Just before I come to that, I've been meaning to ask you about *The Guardian's* allegation that you lied to Michael Heseltine. Rusbridger says that you lied to Michael Heseltine when you gave him an "absolute assurance that you had no financial relationship with Ian Greer." What do you say to that?'

'It's just another of *The Guardian's* tortuous use of semantics to misrepresent what happened. It's just like all the rest of their charges that we've been through, where they say I lied. When you scrutinise what they say none of it holds water.

'When the allegations first broke in *The Guardian* on 20 October 1994, Michael Heseltine put a call through to me at a school in Wilmslow where I was conducting my constituency duties. He then conveyed the essence of this conversation to the Cabinet Secretary, Sir Robin Butler, and Butler duly made a minute of what he understood had been said, which was that "Mr Hamilton has given him (Heseltine) an absolute assurance that he had no financial relationship with Mr Greer."

'The important thing to understand here, is this: as Michael (Heseltine) has confirmed, Sir Robin was not party to the conversation, so his second-hand understanding should not be relied on as a verbatim account anyway. Michael's letter to Downey supports fully the account I've been giving of his question and my reply. It certainly does not support the version that Rusbridger and his cronies have concocted from Butler's second-hand understanding, which itself was most likely based a rather less specific account from Michael than the one he gave Downey.

Michael's letter to Downey supports what I've been saying all along, that is, he asked me if I had a financial relationship that could put me under *obligation* to Ian Greer.' His voice rose as emotion took over. 'His question was deliberately specific, to which I gave a truthful answer you can search through Hansard until you're blue in the face and you won't find anything to suggest I ever favoured Ian Greer.'

Instead I thumbed through the report until I found Heseltine's letter:

> *As Sir Robin's note accurately reflects, my concern was to ascertain whether Mr Hamilton had had any financial relationship with Mr Greer* **which might have put him under an obligation to him** [my emphasis], *I did not have to consider at the time what might or might not constitute a financial relationship because the reply I received was "no." I did not ask any further questions, because the answer was unqualified.*

'The truth is,' Neil said, 'if there was any misunderstanding it wasn't between Michael and me, but between Michael and Sir Robin Butler, which Michael obviously sought to mask by describing Butler's note as "accurately reflecting" our conversation. I'm just glad Michael then went on to contradict that, because it couldn't have "accurately reflected" our conversation if Butler's interpretation was different to the clarification that Michael then gave in the same sentence.

'And while we're on the subject,' Neil said, indignantly, 'Downey didn't provide me with a copy of that letter prior to my oral examination. If he had, it would have been immensely useful in the construction of my defence.'

'Did he ever say why he didn't let you see it?' I asked.

'He said it was "not relevant" to me.'

I was amazed. 'But it's one of the most important pieces in the whole Inquiry for establishing your credibility. Especially in the media.'

'Exactly. But, when it comes to the media, an individual like me or you has got no chance if you happen to be up against a newspaper. What with their journalists propagating their version of this or that in the lobbies to their chums from all the other newspapers, radio and TV.'

But nothing could detract from the truth, regardless of *The Guardian's* massive influence. Because the fact is, Heseltine's letter confirmed that he had not asked a catch-all question, *but a particularly specific one*, requiring a particularly specific answer, just like Neil said, centred on whether he had been placed under an obligation to Ian Greer.

Crucially, Heseltine's focus on the issue of *obligation* accords exactly with Neil's account, which he gave five months earlier when the libel trial collapsed. With delicious irony, this was reported by David Leigh himself in *The Guardian* on 2 October 1996.

> *When the media were baying for my resignation in 1994, and besieging me whilst on a visit to a school in my constituency, I had a fraught telephone conversation with the President of the Board of Trade, Michael Heseltine. He asked me if I had a financial relationship with Ian Greer. I responded that I had not. It was my view, then and now, that the receipt of two payments many years ago did not constitute a financial relationship which implies some kind of continuing obligation . . . The commissions placed me under no obligation whatsoever, either to Ian Greer or his company. They were wholly unconnected to my position as an MP, and similar payments are frequently made throughout industry to people in all walks of life.*

The only issue, therefore, was whether these commission payments *had* placed him under an obligation to Greer. As Neil's interest in the House of Fraser/Lonrho battle pre-dated Fayed's engagement of Greer by nearly two years, and as Neil was among the least active of those whom Greer had enlisted to give Fayed support, there was no reason for him to be under obligation to the lobbyist at all.

As if to prove the point, in 1993/4, after Neil became Minister for Corporate Affairs, British Gas plc engaged Ian Greer to win parliamentary support for the company's desire not to be broken up or lose its monopoly status. But, despite exerting the same kind of effort that he had put into his similar, successful campaign for British Airways, Neil initiated and then saw through both the break-up of British Gas and the introduction of new competition. There could be no better illustration that he took no account of Greer's interests when they conflicted with his responsibilities.

In fact, of the many representations that Ian Greer made to Neil's ministerial office on behalf of his clients, the only one that succeeded was the one he made on behalf of the "Big Eight" accountancy companies. These financial bulwarks were seeking limited-liability legislation after the collapse of companies such as the Bank of Credit and Commerce International, Polly Peck, and Maxwell Communications put them at risk of massive negligence claims from creditors.

But considering that the newly-elected Labour Government revealed in the *Sunday Telegraph* on 6 June 1997 that it was in favour of the introduction of this same limited-liability legislation, Hamilton's decision to consider Greer's clients' case could hardly be construed as arising out a sense of obligation to him.

Christine put her head around the door. 'More tea? Silly question, I know.' She took the tray out for refuelling.

'Thanks Christine.' I turned to Neil. 'I thought that Heseltine business was going to take about ten minutes. We spent nearly an hour on it.'

'Well,' he sighed, 'I suppose in many ways that bothers me more than Fayed's allegations. There's an awful lot of people who think that Fayed's a liar and Downey's an idiot. But when people like Charles Moore (editor of the *Daily Telegraph*) start believing all this "lie to Heseltine" stuff it's enough to make you despair.

'I wouldn't mind,' he added, 'but we have Geoffrey Robinson and Christ knows who in the present lot dissembling and lying and deceiving, yet I've been hung out to dry because a newspaper dishonestly interprets a civil servant's note which was itself an inaccurate record of his second-hand understanding of what he thought was said between two other people . . .' he took a breath '. . . which he never even witnessed for Christ's sake.'

I started laughing. 'Okay, I've got the idea.' His outburst reminded me of an old Monty Python sketch where John Cleese turns to the camera and says something like 'before you can get anything done in this country you've got to go blue in the face.'

As Christine entered with more brain fuel, we chatted about some other related matter, allowing the passion to subside before going on to the subject that was my real reason for being there that day. That is, Neil's 1993 interview on the Terrace.

'So what exactly happened that afternoon that Hencke and Mullin came to see you at the House?'

He thought back for a moment. 'As you know, I invited them

out onto the Terrace for a cup of tea. We exchanged a few pleasantries and then they got down to business. They asked what I knew about Ian Greer. They had formed the impression that he and I were pretty close.'

'What did you tell them?'

'I explained the background – how Christine worked for Michael Grylls from 1973 to 1983. How Grylls and Greer were old friends and I had met Greer through him. In particular, one of Greer's clients had been the Unitary Tax Campaign, established by big British multi-nationals to try to stop US States from imposing double taxation on part of their earnings worldwide. Grylls was Parliamentary Consultant to the UTC.'

'What was your interest in UTC?'

'I was a fledgling tax barrister in 1979 and was writing a book on the US/UK Double Taxation Treaty. Through Greer's contacts in the US Congress, which he gained via the UTC, I was able to obtain a lot of helpful documents relevant to my book. This was how I originally came to know Greer well, as I've said before.

'Four years later I was elected an MP and immediately became secretary of the back-bench Trade and Industry Committee, chaired by Grylls. He was also a friend of Ian's.'

'How intensively did Hencke and Mullin question you on your relationship with Ian Greer?'

'As I said, they were certainly interested but I think they were just letting me speak freely at that stage. Perhaps to get me to relax, put me off-guard. I told them I was sceptical about the value of lobbyists in general. Many were bullshitters taking money under false pretences. But, as the job went, Greer was very good at it. I cited his famous success with the British Airways defence of its dominance at Heathrow and its defeat of BCal, who had tried to get the Government to intervene to reduce BA's dominance by allocating more slots to independent airlines.'

'Did they ask you about your relationship with Fayed?' I asked him.

'They seemed to be more interested in my involvement with Greer's campaign for him. I explained the background to my interest – my belief in competition, the fact there could be no conceivable public interest in who owns a chain of department stores. I said I could see no case for Government intervention and I admitted I harboured an antipathy towards Tiny Rowland, but principally as an enemy of Thatcher and so forth, not because of any grudge against Rowland personally. I didn't even know the man.'

'How did Hencke and Mullin work together as a team?'

'Mullin was the hard man,' he said, with a reflective smile, 'to Hencke's soft. He started to probe in a politely menacing way. Had I received any benefits in return for my support? They had been told by "someone who should know" that I had had an unregistered stay at the Ritz. I gave nothing away at first, answering with another question – "That's interesting. Who told you that?" They said they had proof. I said "Well, let's see it, then." Hencke refused.

'By then the tone of the conversation had completely changed. I had originally thought Hencke merely wanted some gossip. Now it was clear I was the subject of a rather disconcerting line of inquiry.

'I said that I had been to the Ritz and had made no secret of it. The purpose of the visit had been to see the Windsor villa at Fayed's invitation. I had not registered the stay because I did not think it was registrable. I had met my own travel costs and Fayed had said we could stay in his private rooms.

'I could not remember exactly how many nights we had spent there, but the idea that anyone was going to be influenced into acting out of character by such an invitation was absurd. Anyway, apart from the most exceptional cases, no back-bench MP could have the slightest effect on ministerial decisions in matters like DTI Inquiries.

'I went on to say that the Register was largely hypocrisy, that it hid more than it revealed and was a triumph of form over substance. What about the ministers who received thousands of pounds worth of hospitality at the Opera, Wimbledon, Ascot and so forth? Nobody bothered to register any of that.

'Similarly, Andrew Roth had complained to me that I had not registered an upgrade on a BA flight somewhere. My response had been, "Nobody else does, why should I?" The Ritz stay was no different. An upgrade costs an airline nothing. Our stay at the Ritz had cost Fayed nothing apart from the price of the ingredients of the meals we ate and the wine we drank, a tiny fraction of the exorbitant charges clocked up. The invitation was a mark of friendship and merely incidental to our relationship.

No doubt *Guardian* conspiracy theorists could read something sinister into it.'

Though he was suppressing it well, it was clear that just below the urbane surface anger was bubbling away. He paused for a few moments, perhaps to collect himself, before resuming his account of the interview.

'I went on to say that Parliamentary lobbying was largely confidence trickery. Lunches and dinners with MPs were held mainly to impress the lobbyist's clients. Early Day Motions or interventions in the Chamber were most unlikely to bring about changes in policy – apart from very exceptional cases where a real furore could be generated. The BA case was one of these exceptions and Greer had handled it exceptionally well, knitting together constituency interests and chauvinist "national champion" notions.

'But such cases were rare and the most that an MP could achieve was to get the client in to see the Minister. This in itself was no big deal – though no doubt it would mightily impress the client. What they didn't know was that they could achieve as much by going to their own MP. But access to the Minister would not make much difference. What really mattered was the strength of the case.

'I explained that ministerial decision-taking was a labyrinthine process, with many civil servants and, perhaps, other Departments and Ministers involved. Everything would be copiously minuted throughout and full records kept. Anything that smacked of being out of character could easily give rise to "embarrassing leaks" and this militated against corruption. So, although the media became orgasmic about supposed undue influence by lobbyists and "MPs on the make," the truth was rather more mundane and unsensational.'

Once again, I asked him the question that had at that time become the focus of our whole investigation. 'So did they ask you about cash for questions?' I had to ask it, if only for the record.

'I've told you this so many times absolutely not. They never mentioned it. After all, the phrase "cash for questions" didn't even enter the English vernacular until July 1994, one year later, when the *Sunday Times* coined it for their entrapment "sting" on Riddick and Tredinnick.'

'Did they ask you about your commission payments from Ian Greer?'

'No. They never mentioned them.'

'Did they ask you about the support you gave to companies which were also clients of Ian Greer's?'

He paused in thought for a moment or two. 'Come to think of it, yes, they did. How did you know that? They wanted to know my motivation for supporting House of Fraser and United States Tobacco. They were both clients of his.'

But not only were these companies clients of Ian Greer, what's more, when UST engaged Greer, Hamilton received a commission for the introduction.

It all made perfect sense. Hencke and Mullin didn't go to see him to ask about "cash for questions" at all. They really went to see if they could flush anything out about his relationship with Greer, to try and substantiate Roth's theory that Greer's commission payments were secret corrupt payments in return for parliamentary favours.

'Did Hencke or Mullin ask you about whether you had undertaken any parliamentary services for payment, or did they ask you any questions about your registered consultancies?'

'I can't remember them asking me anything about "being paid for Parliamentary services," as you put it,' he said. 'If they did, they certainly didn't phrase it that starkly, because I would have remembered. But they were certainly interested in my consultancies, because Hencke had made notes of them from the Register of Members' Interests before the interview.'

'How do you know that?'

'*The Guardian* surrendered them for the libel trial.'

I hadn't remembered seeing these in our files. 'Dig them out Neil, I need to see them.'

'They're only scribbles. They're meaningless.'

'Nevertheless.'

Neil went out of the room and returned in due course with a few sheets of A4 photocopies of the notes Hencke had made. I cast my eyes over the pages. They didn't just consist of Neil Hamilton's consultancies, they also consisted of the registered consultancies of Sir Michael Grylls and Tim Smith for the years 1986–1989 i.e. the period that Ian Greer organised support from them in the Commons.

'Don't you see the significance of this?' I asked.

'The significance of what?'

'The significance of Hencke's interest in the registered consultancies that you, Smith and Grylls had.'

'I don't see what you're getting at.'

'Hencke and Mullin were looking to see if you had any registered interests with Greer, or with Greer's clients. Think about it after Hastings' memo in 1989, Grylls registered Greer as a client, remember? And the fact that they were interested in you three is further proof that they imagined you were the three MPs who had received Greer's commissions – X,Y and Z. In fact, they were *damn sure* that you three were the three mystery MPs, otherwise they wouldn't have had the confidence to surrender all this stuff for the libel trial!'

Neil looked bewildered. 'But Smith hadn't received a commission payment.'

'I know!' I said, in exasperation. 'That's the whole bloody point! *The Guardian* thought he had!'

13

Finding Questions For The Answers

I DROVE STRAIGHT BACK TO BASE WITH OUR NEW EVIDENCE – meaningless scribbles! But, of course, before we had started to put the jigsaw together, that's exactly what they appeared to be. We shouldn't blame Neil for not seeing their significance. Carter-Rucks hadn't, and they're pretty sharp, and we had read documents three or four times ourselves before the penny dropped on some point.

I burst into the office to see Malcolm poring over the Downey Report.

'Have you found anything?' I asked.

'Yes, I think so.' He held up four documents labelled A,B,C and D. I recognised them from our "bits and pieces" file. 'These are the documents that *The Guardian* claims prove Hencke and Mullin asked Hamilton about cash for questions during the interview on the Terrace.'

'So, what have you spotted?'

'I'll tell you in a minute, but whilst I was checking up on them, I came across something else that's quite interesting. You know that letter Hamilton sent to Peter Preston in October 1993?'

'The one threatening legal action if anything was printed about the Ritz?'

'Correct. Well, in *Sleaze,* David Leigh describes it as containing "five direct lies," and Rusbridger says the same in one of his letters to Downey.'

'What page?'

'Top of page 130, volume two.'

'Okay. So they're singing from the same hymn sheet. So what?'

'Flip back to page 73, to David Hencke's witness statement for the libel trial. Got it? Paragraph 13 . . . interesting, isn't it?'

I read out the extract from Hencke's statement: ' *"Neil Hamilton wrote a letter to Peter Preston at The Guardian, dated 1 October 1993 . . . In the event that letter contained a number of **inaccuracies"**.*'

I glanced across at my smug colleague. 'Yes, it is interesting how "inaccuracies" back in June 1995 can suddenly transform into "direct lies" by the time 1997 comes along. I must have read that statement at least three times and still never spotted that.'

'Same here. That's the problem with this project,' Malcolm remarked. 'As soon as you discover something new you have to go through all the files again to see how it fits in with everything else. It's not a major discovery, I know, but I thought you'd like it anyway.'

'No, I think it's quite important. It all adds up death by a thousand cuts and all that. But to get back to the important stuff . . .'

'Okay, these four documents are the only evidence *The Guardian* submitted to Downey to support their contention that Hamilton was confronted with Fayed's allegations during his interview.'

'You're certain?'

'Yes, I'm sure. Downey cites extracts from all four on page 78 vol. 1 to refute Hamilton's denial that he was asked about cash for questions.'

We sat down and studied them. The first document, document "A", was described by Downey as: *a shorthand note of the conversation with Mr Hamilton made by Mr Mullin immediately after leaving the interview.* Downey quoted one line from the last paragraph, which Alan Rusbridger claimed was Neil's response to a "cash for questions" allegation put by his journalists. Downey wrote: *A translation provided by The Guardian reads: "never received any payment other than those declared in the Register of Members' Interests."*

If Downey had reproduced these notes photographically it would have drawn attention to the fact that this entry (*which is supposed to refer to the most important part of the interview*), is limited to just a line or so at the bottom of the page, and could therefore easily have been added some time later. Downey should also have had these notes examined forensically, as he did other less important documents. But it is actually of no consequence because, as we were to discover, these notes are genuine, but that Neil's response *was to a completely different question.*

We put ourselves in Hamilton's shoes and imagined being propositioned with a corruption allegation. Would it be likely that he would have given such a long-winded answer discussing the niceties of whether he had registered payments of cash in envelopes? More likely he would have blown his top.

If, however, Neil had been asked an oblique question that the two journalists had asked to try and substantiate Roth's theory about Greer's commission payments, it fits perfectly. Such a question could be 'Have you ever undertaken any consultancy work without registering it?' The logic of this explanation was bullet-proof, because Hencke had scribbled Grylls', Smith's and Neil's registered consultancies on pieces of paper prior to the interview and we knew that it was Roth's theory they were trying to substantiate anyway.

'So you think this note is genuine, then?' I asked Malcolm.

'Well, if this note recorded a response to a "cash" allegation, it would be far more direct. Such as "of course not" or "never" or "that's preposterous!" Somehow, I don't think *"never received any payment other than those declared in the Register of Members' Interests"* quite rings true. But, like you say, that *does* fit a different question about unregistered parliamentary consultancies, business, services, etcetera.'

'And if it was a forgery, Rusbridger or whoever would have made sure it was specific.'

'What's the point of forging something that's unclear?'

'Quite.' I summarised its status: 'Okay, so we assume it's genuine, but it contains an answer to a question that Hencke and Mullin asked fishing to bear out Roth's theory. It doesn't record a response to a cash for questions allegation. All right so far. What's the next one?'

'Now this really is interesting,' Malcolm enthused.

We studied document "B". This was described by Downey as: *a note keyed into Mr Mullin's computer on his return to the office after the meeting with Mr Hamilton.*

Downey then quoted an extract from this document too, also to support Rusbridger's claim that the allegation was put: *"Asked about the brown paper bag, he became by this stgd* [sic] *somewhat agitated and began his increasing level of threats about Peter Carter Ruck."*

'This computer note of Mullin's,' Malcolm said, thoughtfully, 'is supposed to be a transcription of his shorthand notes.'

'Is it?' I said, peering over his shoulder.

'Yeah, look. It all matches. But there's something funny about it.'

'What's that?'

'See if *you* can spot it,' Malcolm challenged.

I pulled up a chair and concentrated hard. The first part of this computer note recorded aspects from Tim Smith's interview, but Rusbridger had not supplied to Downey any shorthand notes of that.

The second half of this computer note recorded aspects of Hamilton's interview. It recorded that Neil said that he:

– *thought lobbying was a ludicrous waste of money.*
– *had been introduced to House of Fraser through Sir Peter Hordern, its consultant.*
– *had stayed at the Ritz but not declared it and had been given Opera tickets too.*
– *had never received any payment other than that declared in the Register of Members' Interests . . .*

I noticed that this last entry tallied with the entry in the shorthand notes which we had decided was an answer to a different question about consultancies or similar. I continued reading. There were a number of other entries which seemed to tally, such as this next one:

– *had ruled himself out of dealing with House of Fraser (when he became Minister).*

But the last entry, which Downey quoted in his report, stood out like a sore thumb:

– *Asked about the brown paper bag, he became by this stgd [sic] somewhat agitated and began his increasing level of threats about Peter Carter Ruck.*

'Well?,' Malcolm asked.

I went back to the shorthand note to compare the two. 'It's not there, is it?' I said.

'No, it's not. Interesting, eh? I mean, here we have the most important response a response to a cash in brown envelopes question and yet it's not in the shorthand notes from which this note was translated. And that comment about Hamilton threatening libel lawyers isn't in the shorthand notes either, yet the rest of it tallies perfectly with the shorthand notes. What do you think?'

I knew what I thought, but this was Malcolm's discovery. 'No, what do *you* think?'

'I think it's been added later, that's what. It looks more bent than something dreamt up by the West Midlands Serious Crime Squad. But we're going to have to be very careful before we start accusing newspaper editors of submitting forged documents. Very careful. We'll have to come back to this and look at it again a few times.'

I agreed.

In his report, Downey reproduced the full extract accurately, right down to the typographical error, which, perhaps, could have been done deliberately to make it look authentic. Similarly, the confusing use of the term "brown paper bag," instead of "brown envelope," would also lead one to believe that it was authentic. But it does not take too much sophistication to appreciate that, if this was a forgery, then such distractions can be seen to be intentional.

Computer-generated notes can all too easily be amended, and even made to look authentic by introducing typographical errors and inaccuracies to convey the impression that they are exactly as they were laid down. The note in question is the only supposed contemporaneous document produced by *The Guardian*, to support their contention that a specific "cash for questions" allegation against Neil existed before the 1994 European Court of Human Rights ruling, Accordingly Downey should have examined it with far greater circumspection.

'Okay, next one,' I said.

'Right then, Document "C." Now this one is a real oddball,' Malcolm said.

'How do you mean?'

'Well, someone's scribbled at the top, "John Mullin statement," but I couldn't remember seeing a statement by John

Mullin in my libel file, and I've checked. There isn't one. Have you got one in yours?'

I checked. 'No. I thought Mullin didn't give a statement anyway, on the grounds that he was in Bosnia when the solicitors prepared them?'

'That's nonsense,' Malcolm asserted. 'Preston and Hencke both signed their statements in June 1995. The libel trial wasn't until September the following year. Mullin must have had *some* home leave in which he could have signed a statement, he wouldn't have been stuck in Bosnia for over a year.'

We studied this document very closely. Only pages seven and eight of an unknown total number were sent to Downey. There was no signature or date at the bottom of each sheet, as was the case with Hencke's and Preston's witness statements, nor was the final sheet provided, which would have been expected to include the date and signature.

There was a crucial section that had been highlighted by *The Guardian*, presumably Alan Rusbridger. It read: "*We then went on the record, and I asked Mr Hamilton formally about the allegation that he had accepted payments from Mohamed Al Fayed, and that these consisted of £2,000 per question paid in cash. He denied that this was the case . . .*" On the second page, there was another highlighted section. It read: "*It was specifically put to Mr Hamilton that he was paid money by Mr Al Fayed to ask questions. By this stage he was visibly agitated. He mentioned Peter Carter-Ruck and Partners . . .*"

'Curiouser and curiouser, said Alice,' I remarked.

'Malcolm chipped in: 'So, despite the fact that John Mullin's shorthand notes contain no reference whatsoever, for some reason in his 'statement' he makes two unequivocal declarations that he put a specific allegation that Hamilton had taken Fayed's cash.'

'What does Downey say about this then?' I asked.

Malcolm sighed. 'Your not going to believe me when I tell you. No, I retract that. After seeing what a pig's ear he's made of this whole affair, I think you will.'

'What?'

'Downey cites the extract from this 'statement' as being an extract from "Mr Hencke's statement for the libel trial". Not only does Downey not scrutinise the damn thing, he can't even attribute it to the person whose name is scribbled on the top! But the question is, has Mullin really signed it? Without the final page, there's no way of knowing. What do you think?'

'I wouldn't be surprised if he hasn't. It seems to me that our friend Mullin has been trying to keep his nose clean right from the word go. After all, it wasn't Mullin's article that caused the problem and, unlike the others, Mullin wouldn't have had any great motive to lie. Once you start lying, you never know where it leads you. Not blowing the whistle is one thing, it's something quite different to be part of a major cover-up. I'll ask Neil to write to Downey. We'll soon find out.'

'So, for the moment, that gets categorised as bent too, like the computer note,' Malcolm said. 'Another West Midlands Serious Crime Squad job.'

He then took a deep breath. 'And so to the statement by our erudite friend Mr Hencke. Document "D" – the only one of the four that was produced as part of *The Guardian's* original submission to the Downey Inquiry. Hamilton's already pulled this apart in his submission, so there's little more that we need to say.'

I disagreed. 'I think there's a couple of things he's missed about Hencke's statement. Hamilton did, of course, make a big issue of the fact that Hencke couldn't remember which one of the two it was who supposedly asked him the "cash" question. Just to recap, Hencke writes: *"Either John or I directly asked him: 'Have you received any cash from Mohamed Al Fayed in return for asking questions on his behalf.' I also recollect that we mentioned the figure of £2,000 per question asked. Neil Hamilton denied the allegation."* We both agree with Hamilton that it's preposterous for Hencke to claim to forget which one of them asked a Government Minister whether he'd accepted corrupt payments, right?' Malcolm nodded. 'Especially when he quotes the question itself in direct speech, which would be much harder to remember than who asked it.

'But this is the bit I found really interesting. Hencke then goes on to say: *"He said that he had never received any payment from Mohamed Al Fayed or anyone else other than those declared in the Register of Interests."*

'That sounds familiar,' Malcolm said, turning over the pages until he came back to "A" Mullin's shorthand note. 'Hencke has used exactly the same words that Mullin used in his shorthand notes, but with the words "from Mohamed Al Fayed or anyone else" inserted in the middle. Now why would he do that?'

'I'll brew up while you think about it. It took me about fifteen minutes once I'd noticed the similarity – I'll expect the answer when I come back with the teas.'

About five minutes later I returned to the office with two hot steaming mugs of Kenya's best. Malcolm was leaning back on his chair against the wall, with his hands on his head. He rocked forward to take his mug off me.

'Well ?' I said. 'Figured it out yet?'

'They're a tricky bunch, aren't they?' he said.

'You figured it out?'

'Yeah, I figured it out all right. Tricky bastards.'

'Go on then.'

'Well, I've not had as long as you have to think about this, so correct me if I'm wrong. Here goes: Hamilton has denied vehemently from the outset that Hencke and Mullin asked him about "cash for questions" during the interview.' I nodded. He paused for a few moments to collect his thoughts. 'So, up until we figured out that Hencke and Mullin asked some different question to try and substantiate Roth's theory, Hamilton would have denounced any evidence that supported *The Guardian's* claim as being false. Am I right so far?'

'Bang on track.'

'So, if the libel trial had gone ahead, when Hencke went into the witness box he would naturally be questioned on his witness statement. Right?' I smiled and nodded again. 'So, when it comes to the crunch question of whether Fayed's allegations were made out of spite in 1994, Hencke says "Oh no they weren't, I asked Mr Hamilton about cash for questions in July 1993." Then Hencke recites Hamilton's response, as written in Mullin's short-hand notes, but with the extra words inserted to make it appear like a response to Fayed's "cash" allegations.'

'You're doing all right so far.'

'Hamilton then says Hencke is lying, and that he was never asked in 1993, but Hencke refers to the shorthand notes to back up his claim. No one takes account of the missing words "from Mohamed Al Fayed or anyone else," as they think the shorthand notes are just an abridged version of what Hencke claims Hamilton said. No one twigs that it's actually the other way round – that Hencke's statement is an expanded version of Hamilton's complete response to a different question.' He took a deep breath and looked across. 'QED. How did I do?'

'You've stopped short of the goal,' I said.

Malcolm stared into the middle distance then turned to me as the second penny dropped.

'Hamilton would naturally be forced to denounce Mullin's shorthand notes as forgeries because he swears they never asked him about cash for questions . . .'

He gave me an enquiring look.

'And so,' I said, giving him a leg-up, '*The Guardian* says "lets get them forensically examined," to which Hamilton agrees readily . . .'

He nodded. 'And then the best forensic lab in the country submits a report stating they are genuine through and through, citing Mullin's other contemporaneous notes on other stories in the pages that follow, which confirms the book was from 1993 . . .'

'Libel trial collapses,' I said, smacking my palms together. 'Hamilton devastated and destroyed forever! Well done, *The Guardian!*'

'Nice bit of work, chum' Malcolm said.

'Nice bit of work yourself, partner.'

Solving the puzzle of *The Guardian*'s forgeries and misrepresentations was an invigorating yet, paradoxically, exhausting task. The rush of adrenaline when solving one problem always seemed to be counterbalanced by fatigue, especially when the new discovery had to be articulated in our report. This was a complex story with all sorts of sub plots, some of which I have yet to reveal. Our ever-growing report took so much revising and re-jigging I seemed to spend as much time writing and typesetting as I did examining the evidence itself.

The effort that went into solving the puzzle of the last four documents was considerable, and although the pennies all seemed to drop at once, in a manner not too dissimilar from that just described. Other documents took significantly less examination. The following two fall into this category.

Fayed's telephone message pad and diary were held up by *The Guardian* and Fayed to be among the most important documents to support their allegations that Hamilton took Fayed's cash. The importance that Downey attached to them is remarkable, and is another cause for concern as to his handling of the Inquiry.

In the event, Neil questioned the message pad's authenticity regarding any document that Fayed put forward. It was subsequently sent for forensic examination by a respectable lab and found to be genuine in all respects. Downey then treated it and the diary with a conspicuous reverence out of all proportion to their real evidential worth. The stark fact is that they confirm only that messages were taken and that arrangements for meetings were made – they do not prove the messages themselves are genuine nor do they confirm that meetings on the days bearing entries ever took place. And of course they certainly do not confirm that cash was passed. Since Neil has acknowledged the possibility that he might have attended meetings which were not even logged, they contribute absolutely zero.

After Downey published his report, Neil found his diary for 1988 and discovered that on a date in March when Downey stated "Mr Hamilton was attending a briefing meeting with other members, Mr Greer and Mr Webb," he was actually in New Zealand, a trip that was registered in the Members' Interests Register!

This showed how wrong it was of Downey to make assumptions and then extrapolate from them and draw inferences that were harmful to Neil Hamilton. In similar vein, Downey extrapolated that on 15 December 1988 Hamilton met Fayed and was paid in gift vouchers, although he himself had already rejected the gift voucher allegations. Clearly he did not rate his own evidence very highly!

Other evidence was far more significant. From reading Ian Greer's witness statement for the libel trial, we learned that he was interviewed at his IGA offices by Hencke and Mullin on 23 July 1993, the very day after they had interviewed Hamilton and Smith. I suddenly remembered that Andrew Smith, Ian Greer's former managing director, had told me that Greer had tape-recorded the whole thing.

When I was first told this we had not started to develop any notions about when Fayed made his allegations, but since this had now become central to our investigation, Greer's tape suddenly became of paramount importance. If any allegations against Neil had existed at that time, surely Hencke and Mullin would have mentioned them. I phoned Ian Greer.

'Ian, I believe you have a tape of your interview by Hencke and Mullin on 23 July 1993?'

'Yes.'

'Do you have a copy or a transcript?'

'I have a transcript done by Tellex Monitors. Why?'

'Oh, just some idea we're thrashing out. Could I borrow it?'

'I'll stick it in the post. Don't lose it, it's the only one I've got.'

When it arrived I made three copies: one each for Malcolm and me, and one for Neil. As soon as I'd run them off we sat down to scrutinise it from beginning to end.

Despite Hencke's claim that Preston had given them concrete information about Neil being paid cash and gift vouchers beforehand, the transcript shows that Hencke and Mullin only suggested that Smith had been accused of taking cash to ask questions and Neil had only been accused of staying at the Paris Ritz.

'*Yes!*' I leapt from my chair and punched the air. Yet another substantial piece of evidence supporting fully everything we said. Malcolm was still reading, but already the first indications of satisfaction were evident in his expression.

The 33-page document showed that Hencke and Mullin's questions were all about lobbying in general, until page 20 when the subject of introductory commissions to Sir Michael Grylls was raised. Once more, this was consistent with the inquiries that Hencke and Mullin would have made to try and substantiate Andrew Roth's theory. After about ten exchanges on this subject the issue of Neil's stay at the Ritz was brought up. After a further ten or so exchanges the subject turned to the conduct of MPs; John Mullin brought up the subject of "cash for questions:"

'Can I put one thing to you which is nothing to do with Ian Greer, which you may be able to throw light on and if you want to do that on an off the record basis, fine. One allegation which has been made about the House of Fraser that has to do with Ian Greer in the sense that House of Fraser are an Ian Greer client, one allegation that's been made about House of Fraser is, that in return for a Parliamentary question being asked by a friendly MP, a brown envelope stuffed with fivers would be passed to the MP.'

'I've absolutely no knowledge,' Greer replied. 'I find it . . . I would be amazed that any Member of Parliament would allow themselves to enter into that sort of . . . for God's sake . . .'

'We were surprised,' Hencke agreed with him. 'The extraordinary thing is, it came from sources who in theory should know about it. That's why we took it seriously. And we checked in questions (Hansard), and it is true. In fact we actually talked to Tim Smith, because he put down 17 questions.'

'I can't . . . *Tim?*' Greer was stunned.

'Yes,' Hencke continued. 'We then got interested in why people would put it to us that this may have happened.' Hencke then changed the subject to donations to the Tory Party, with no mention having been made of Neil Hamilton. If any cash for questions allegations had existed against him at this time it is inconceivable that Hencke and Mullin would have refrained from airing them in conjunction with their reference to Tim Smith.

We made a few more observations. The way John Mullin put the cash in envelopes proposition could not have been more vague if he tried, and he deliberately couched his question in such a way that it gave Ian Greer no inkling that it was *he* who was the person they suspected of handing out fivers in envelopes. This tallies with our contention that a similarly vague question was put to Hamilton the previous day, instead of the completely contrasting direct and authoritative version in the suspicious so-called Mullin statement: "I formerly went on the record etc. etc."

Another observation is Greer's obviously genuine incredulity at Mullin's suggestion that Tim Smith had taken cash. But the most interesting feature is that Mullin suggested that a 'brown envelope stuffed with *fivers*' would be passed to a friendly MP. This is curious, because all the cash-in-face-to-face-with-Fayed allegations, which didn't even surface until two months after *The Guardian* printed its Greer-paid-MPs story, were that £50 notes changed hands, not fivers. So was Mullin repeating an allegation, or was he fishing to substantiate Roth's theory, using "brown envelopes" as a metaphor? We shall see in due course.

But before we leave this transcript, it's worth pointing out that when Hencke recalled the interview in his witness statement for the libel trial he referred, inaccurately, to the Hamiltons' stay at the Ritz followed immediately by Mullin's suggestion that "a friendly MP would receive a stuffed envelope." This would lead any reader to the inference that, during the meeting, Neil Hamilton was the MP they suggested had taken cash for questions. Hencke omitted the reference to Tim Smith that showed that it was *him* under discussion, not Neil.

Not only did Downey fail to examine properly the facts relating to whether Hencke and Mullin put the cash allegation during Hamilton's interview, he didn't even address the paradox of their admitted failure to put the gift voucher allegations to him, also supposed to have existed in 1993, but which didn't appear until over a year later.

In his witness statement for the libel trial Hencke stated: *Peter Preston had certainly told me that Mohamed Al Fayed had given shopping vouchers to Neil Hamilton. I was not as interested in the vouchers as I was in the cash.*

It seems unbelievable that Hencke would have been interested in the stay at the Ritz and yet not be interested in gift vouchers, a far more newsworthy story.

One explanation would be that Fayed had not invented them back in 1993, just as it was becoming clear that he had not invented his cash allegations then, either. This would explain why the gift voucher story did not even appear first in *The Guardian*. The first journalist to break the gift voucher allegations was actually Gordon Greig of the *Daily Mail* on 22 October 1994, and his article even suggested that Fayed originally intended to level these new allegations against a different Tory MP.

> *It was revealed that two more Ministers have been asked to answer allegations of corruption by the Downing Street inquiry into the "cash for questions" scandal. And Harrods boss Mohamed Al Fayed, whose accusations sparked the affair, claimed that a 'senior Tory MP' had accepted Harrods gift certificates worth 'thousands of pounds' from him. He said: "This man must be very thick skinned – he cannot have any dignity or honour left." Neither the Ministers nor the MP have been named.*

As Fayed differentiated between Ministers and MPs and said it was an *MP* who had taken the gift vouchers, it is reasonable to deduce that the allegations were not originally intended to be made against a Minister, which Neil was. Furthermore, if *The*

Guardian did already have knowledge about Hamilton and gift vouchers, surely it would have named him. Logical, yes? But Hamilton was actually first referred to by name in the *News of the World*, the day after the *Daily Mail* story:

> *Embattled minister Neil Hamilton denied last night he received £15,000 of shopping vouchers from Harrods boss Mohamed Fayed. Mr Hamilton said: "I categorically deny it. I never received any vouchers from Harrods." Mr Al Fayed has claimed the senior Tory demanded vouchers on frequent visits to the store.*

It is pure tosh that Hencke and Mullin would not be interested enough in the gift voucher allegations to ask Neil about them. Think of all those juicy tales about swanning around the store, stuffing baskets full of caviar and Champagne. It is equally untenable that Peter Preston would allow a rival newspaper, the *Daily Mail*, to break the story and another rival newspaper, the *News of the World*, to be the first to name Hamilton as having received vouchers, if Fayed had given him (Preston) exclusive information about gift vouchers a year earlier.

Sorting the lies from the truth when there were so many people who had vested interests in putting up smoke-screens, was proving the challenge of our lives. Our heads were spinning with all the machiavellian ploys and tricks, smoke screens, false statements, forgeries and the sheer magnitude of the conspiracy.

It seemed impossible that it was limited to those we knew were involved, namely Peter Preston, David Hencke, Alan Rusbridger and David Leigh for *The Guardian*; and Bond, Bromfield, Bozek, and of courser Fayed himself, for the Fayed camp. What about *The Guardian's* other senior political journalists, such as Hugo Young and Michael White?

Michael White, for example, is *The Guardian's* Political Editor, and he wrote a number of stories about the paper's "cash for questions" campaign. Hugo Young, as well as being a contributing columnist on *The Guardian*, is also Chairman on the secretive Scott Trust, which owns the Guardian Media Group. And as the Group was on the receiving end of a libel action from Ian Greer that would have crippled the paper, it seems, on the face of it, that they would have been unaware of what their comrades were up to.

Of course, it is entirely possible that neither did.

As for Downey, was it possible that he had found himself similarly bogged down in all the detail and had simply been unable to work out what was going on? The evidence did not suggest he was incapable; in the early weeks of his investigation he took evidence from Hamilton's supportive witnesses with due diligence. Prior to the start of the Inquiry, he even wrote a letter to the *Times* complaining about *The Guardian's* delaying tactics. And then, when Alan Rusbridger tried to parry his criticism, Downey lambasted him for disingenuously interpreting what he had said.

So what caused Downey's change of heart.

But in contrast to these almost unfathomable questions and the devious goings-on, Neil Hamilton continued to be a small, quiet, consistent yet ignored voice in the storm of accusations, claims and arguments.

It was around this time that Princess Diana and Dodi Fayed were killed in the tragic car accident in Paris. A week or so later, Panorama broadcast an investigation by one of their journalists, Jane Corbin. But while everyone else up to that point seemed to tow Fayed's and his employees' line that it was all the fault of the paparazzi, she appeared not to buy all their nonsense. By the end of the documentary it was clear that she saw it as a false story, designed to cover up the fact that the driver, Fayed employee Henri Paul, was drunk. She was the first journalist to publish the simple truth.

I knew in an instant that we must recruit this woman to our cause. I inveigled her number from the BBC and rang her on her mobile the same evening. I told her how impressed I was with her programme.

'These days, it's hard to find someone who hasn't been suckered by Fayed,' I said.

'I have been doing this job for some time, you know,' she said coolly.

'Yes. Of course.' I realised how patronising I must have sounded. 'The fact remains you're probably the only journalist so far who's not been taken in by Fayed's lie machine. Two of us have been working on the "cash for questions" case for some months now and the media have collectively swallowed this "brown envelopes" thing as if it really happened. But it didn't! Not involving Neil Hamilton anyway. Can we come and talk to you about our research?'

'You've already spoken to my producer haven't you? Thea Guest, remember? Look, it doesn't look like we'll be running our programme on Fayed now that he's lost his son, but I'm really busy right now, Jonathan.' I could feel her slipping away from me as she went on about her heavy workload. 'Perhaps some time in the future?'

'Sure,' I said, deflated as a Branson balloon. 'I'll be in touch.' As I hung up I carefully typed her name into our file of media contacts whom I felt might, at some stage, be persuaded to look beneath the surface of this case. The list was now several pages long, but still the moment hadn't come when one of them was ready to give us air time or page space.

Meanwhile, our report continued to grow, covering more and more evidence, exposing more and more deception. Every day I persuaded myself, "just another few pages and we'll be finished," and then a new piece of evidence would turn up and we would be off on a fresh paper trail.

Perhaps it was destined to be never-ending.

14

Guardiangate

IT HAD BECOME AS CLEAR AS CLEAR COULD BE THAT THERE WAS something about John Mullin's role in the whole affair that needed further examination. We asked ourselves: why hadn't he given a statement for the libel trial, despite having a year to make one? Why didn't he give evidence to the Downey Inquiry? Why was *The Guardian*'s evidence, which supported its contention that Fayed made his allegations against Neil back in 1993, exclusively in Mullin's name?

The next morning I telephoned Neil. 'Neil, hi, just need to ask a few questions.' It was an almost daily routine.

'Carry on.'

'John Mullin didn't give a statement for the libel trial. Why not?'

'Well, he did, actually, but it was just a one-paragraph job saying that he agreed with what Hencke said. Something like that, anyway.'

'I need to see it. I don't have a copy.'

'We're just packing to go away to stay with some friends in America for a break,' he said, 'and we've got a hundred other things to do before we go. I'm sorry, Jonathan, but I just don't have the time to dig it out just now. But if you're desperate you can come over and root for it yourself.'

I felt slightly irritated about this, grumbling to myself as I drove to the house about having to do all the work to clear his name and he wouldn't even dig out one document for me. By the time I reached the door I had got it out of my system, realising that he was under pressure just as much as I was.

He let me in, took me to the dining room and pointed me towards the boxes of files stacked under a side table. 'It's in there somewhere, Jonathan,' he told me, and bounded back up the stairs.

Sitting down at the dining room table with a box of papers, I started to flick through all the witness statements from the libel trial. Neil's, Christine's, Peter Clarke's, Timothy O'Sullivan's, Ian Greer's, Greer's employees', Preston's, Hencke's, Fayed's, Bond's, Bozek's, Bromfield's . . . John Mullin's!

It was a single paragraph as Neil had said, with an introduction:

> *The Defendants intend to adduce the following evidence from John Mullin, the nature of which is as follows:*
>
> *Confirmation that insofar as it refers to investigations carried out by John Mullin and conversations to which John Mullin was a party, the Witness Statement of David Hencke is accurate and that John Mullin has nothing further to add to David Hencke's witness statement.*

I was not surprised, by now, to see that Mullin had not signed even this pathetic effort. And Neil had missed the introduction, making it clear that *The Guardian's* solicitors were *hoping* that Mullin would sign it.

I was about to shout Neil to tell him, but had seconds thoughts and decided to rummage through the files in case there were others Neil had forgotten.

I then came across another file containing a sheaf of *Guardian* documents that, from reading the contents page, it became clear had been prepared by *The Guardian's* solicitors. It was dated 14 June 1995 in satisfaction of a Court Order that had been served on the paper by Hamilton's and Greer's solicitors. The papers inside had not been surrendered to the Downey Inquiry and I had never seen them before. I flicked through them and began to read.

There were six computerised documents and other papers. They all had a common typeface that I noticed was completely different to the document Alan Rusbridger had sent to Downey as being "John Mullin's computer note." Additionally, they all had computer-generated ID marks of one sort or another at the top of each page, which "John Mullin's computer note" didn't have, either. But then one particular document at eight pages, the biggest caught my attention. It was a computerised document listed as being "Peter Preston's computer queue." A quick scan revealed it to be *The Guardian*'s file on the "cash for questions" story.

Most major newspapers have an internal computer network that allows journalists to communicate with each other and share information on various stories. This document was clearly a file into which information was accumulated and exchanged between *Guardian* journalists about day-to-day developments on the cash for questions affair.

Because it had been surrendered before *The Guardian* had seen Hamilton's and Greer's witness statements dated 27 June 1995, which disclosed and explained Neil's two commission payments, *The Guardian,* therefore, at the time the documents were surrendered, would still have been convinced (despite having no evidence), that they were on the right track with their "Greer's commission payments are a covert method of paying to have questions asked" story.

Since *The Guardian* could hardly have claimed that no computer files existed (and were therefore obliged to produce something), they would have had little reason to withhold documents which they could not have foreseen would damage their case.

The eight pages of "Peter Preston's computer queue" contained twenty-two entries – nineteen from David Hencke and three from Political Editor Michael White, covering a period from 15 September 1993 to 17 October 1994. I was seized by a feeling of dread. If I read this document and found that there was an entry linking Neil to any cash or gift voucher allegations before September 1994 our whole case would fall to pieces. I started to read, turning each page as if it might detonate a bomb, wondering whether months of hard work was about to explode in my face.

The first entry, dated 15 September 1993 (just seven weeks after the interview on the Terrace), and the longest entry of all, listed seven points relating to Neil's stay at the Ritz. And, though there was much discussion of how damaging this could be to his ministerial career, there was no mention of "cash for questions" or gift vouchers, either or both of which would be incalculably more damaging. So far so good. I had managed to snip through several wires and not detonate the bomb. I took a deep gulp of air and pressed on.

Another entry, dated 11 July 1994, (the day after the *Sunday Times* published their "cash for questions" sting about MPs David Treddinick and Graham Riddick), contained another mention of the stay at the Ritz, followed by a completely separate and unrelated reference to the *Sunday Times* story. But still no mention of Neil in the context of "cash for questions." Each of the remaining entries related to Hencke's investigation into the perceived lobbying activities of Ian Greer, without any mention of Neil in *any* context.

Except one.

My stomach turned over. It mentioned Neil in what was obviously a "cash for questions" context. David Hencke had written: "seems to me our lobby friend and minister banged completely to rights over PQs [Parliamentary questions] by documents . . . but will need a strong statement by our Egyptian friend over payments to push it through." But what was the date? I looked at the date entry and the relief flooded through me. It was dated 17 October 1994, i.e. just two days before the allegations appeared in *The Guardian* and, crucially, one year and three months after Rusbridger, Preston, Hencke and, David Leigh all claimed Fayed first alleged that he had given Neil cash and gift vouchers. Interestingly, it was 17 October that Peter Preston admitted was the day when documents from Fayed started to arrive at *The Guardian* after Preston's first meeting with Fayed, following the failure of Fayed's appeal to the European Court of Human Rights.

I had defused the bomb and lived to tell the tale. For a moment I couldn't believe that we were in the clear. I took a deep breath to keep myself calm for long enough to read it again, to double-check what I was seeing. And after double-checking every single entry I checked them all again a third time. I knew that this document confirmed our conclusion that *the allegations about "cash for questions" never existed until after the European Court ruling.* It was absolutely inconceivable that Hencke would not record at least once during fifteen months of his investigation, any reference whatsoever to Neil taking cash or gift vouchers if those allegations had ever existed. Especially as

Peter Preston had admitted to having had ten or eleven meetings and many telephone calls with Fayed over the same period. Every claim we had made on Neil's behalf was vindicated. I actually felt tears of relief starting to well up.

I shouted Neil to come down.

'What's the matter?' he asked, obviously noticing my moist eyes.

'I've just found something that vindicates everything you suspected and which we've been saying is borne out by our research,' I said, emotionally.

'What?' Not himself given to such displays, he couldn't work out what was wrong with me. 'What are you so upset about?'

'I'm not upset, I'm just . . .' I shrugged. 'I don't know what I feel. When did you get these documents?'

'1995.'

I was flabbergasted. My euphoria went out of the window like a cat with Coleman's English Mustard up its backside. '*You mean you've had them in this box all the flipping time?*'

'Sorry. I thought I'd given you everything.'

I used a word I only use at times of extreme frustration.

'I could have sworn . . .' he said helplessly.

'Okay,' I said. 'It's my fault. I should have rummaged through this lot months ago. Anyway, I want to show you something else. Can you dig out those four documents that Rusbridger sent Downey. You know – A, B, C, D.'

Looking somewhat crestfallen, he opened up another couple of boxes before disappearing into the library. While he was hunting out the Rusbridger documents, I retrieved the complete file that I had just discovered.

A few minutes later Neil came back into the dining room and sat down alongside me with the four documents. I turned to "B" "John Mullin's computer note," and compared its appearance with the other six computerised notes.

'What are you looking for?' Neil enquired.

'I'm comparing this document, which Rusbridger claims proves you were asked about brown envelopes in 1993, with these documents that have been festering in your box for the last two years.'

'They're different in appearance,' Neil exclaimed.

'They're totally different! They have a completely different typeface. Plus, the documents that were surrendered in 1995 all show log-in log-out details and the name of the journalist who accessed each document. This one,' I said, holding the "John Mullin Computer note," doesn't show any of that!'

'Actually,' Neil said, 'come to think of it, if Peter Carter-Ruck had a Court Order served on *The Guardian*, how come this document, this one called "John Mullin's computer note", how come it wasn't surrendered? Because if it existed in 1993, it should have been.'

'Another good point,' I said. 'Malcolm and I reckon Mullin is the key to all this. In your submission you denied being asked about "cash for questions" in 1993. You also pointed out that Hencke couldn't remember whether it was he or Mullin who asked the question, though he was insistent that the question was asked.'

'What are you driving at?' I could see he was thoroughly bemused.

'Well, that one-paragraph statement that Mullin made that you told me about wasn't a statement at all. Mullin never signed it, and he had a full year to do so. Yet here in this statement, which appeared from nowhere in the middle of the Downey Inquiry . . .' I held aloft document "C" 'Mullin gives the most emphatic, unambiguous, totally unequivocal statement that he absolutely, categorically, most definitely asked you about Fayed's allegations in 1993. Don't you smell a rat? Because I do! And where's the signature at the bottom of each page like Hencke's and Preston's statements had? Why wasn't the last page included, which would also show a signature? I'll tell you why. It's because Mullin's refused to sign this statement just like he refused to sign the last one! That's why!

'As for this document called "Mullin's computer note," *Why wasn't it submitted to the libel trial as the others were?* And why is it totally different from all the other computerised notes? And, best of the lot, why does it show that you were asked about "brown envelopes" when the shorthand notes from which it was translated don't include that crucial entry?'

'Don't they?'

'No, I was going to tell you that later. Anyway, to get to the sixty-four thousand-dollar question, why is "John Mullin's computer note" the only document *The Guardian* has produced to show that Fayed made his allegations before the European Court ruling?'

Neil and I spoke in unison. 'Because it's a forgery!'

'I wouldn't mind betting,' I went on, 'that Mullin is not part of the cover-up at all. He didn't give oral evidence before Downey either . . .'

'Didn't he?' Neil said. 'Are you *sure*?'

'Certain. Which is decidedly iffy, as the most crucial evidence Rusbridger put forward is all in Mullin's name.'

'You know,' Neil said, 'you might be on to something. This calls for champagne, well, fizzy wine anyway. This'll cheer Christine up, she's been very depressed today.' He called up the stairs to her and she came down, puzzled by the sight of us both so cheerful, unable to believe that anything could actually be going right for us after so long.

'It was always your suspicion,' I reminded them as we walked into the kitchen, 'that the European Court of Human Rights' ruling was the trigger that set Fayed off, and this proves it.' I waved the "computer queue" at them as Neil popped the cork.

Christine and I sat at the kitchen table and sipped wine and chatted for the next quarter of an hour, while Neil read the extracts from the four documents "A", "B", "C" and "D".

'I've seen that statement of Mullin's in the Downey report,' he said at one point. 'Doesn't Downey ascribe the extract to David Hencke?'

'Yes,' I confirmed. 'Unbelievable, isn't it.' I confirmed.

'I'd spotted that myself and was going to ask you about it. He's such a useless twerp!'

'Look,' I said to Neil, 'it's all right us three celebrating, but the fact remains we need to establish whether Mullin signed that statement, the one marked "C." We need to know if Mullin was involved with all the rest of them. You'll have to write to Downey today before you leave for the States.'

'I'll do it right now,' Neil said, and strode across to the adjoining office, sitting down at his computer. He started typing. 'Dear Sir Gormless Dopey . . .' he muttered, as he pounded the keys.

After lunch I headed back to the office, eager to share the news with Malcolm. 'You were absolutely right about Mullin's computer note,' I gushed, 'it definitely comes into the "bent" category.'

He took the file from me. 'What's all this lot?' he asked.

'Some stuff that *The Guardian* surrendered for the libel trial after Carter-Rucks hit them with a Court Order to disclose all relevant documents.' He looked at me incredulously. 'I know, I know – there was a misunderstanding between Hamilton and me. Anyway, compare "John Mullin's computer note" with all the computerised documents in this file.'

Malcolm studied the new documents. 'It's totally different in appearance,' he said.

'I know great stuff, eh?' I replied, cocky as they come. And then a dreadful thought struck me as I remembered Malcolm's warning that my eagerness to prove Neil's innocence would be "my undoing." 'I suppose Rusbridger could claim that Mullin went straight home and wrote this up on his PC in his bedroom,' I said, just a touch less cocky than two seconds before.

Malcolm continued scanning through the documents. After a few minutes, he looked across at me. 'No, actually, he can't,' Malcolm reassured. 'You want to spend a bit more time doing your homework.' He reached over for his copy of Downey, volume two. 'It's in here somewhere 'cause I saw it last night.' He thumbed through the pages for what seemed a very long time while I sat wondering what he'd found.

'Here it is,' he announced. 'Page 141 volume 2, near the bottom.' As I flicked through the pages Malcolm spoke again. 'Incidentally, Rusbridger didn't send Downey those four documents we looked at yesterday until 19 February, in response to Hamilton's submission, so Mullin's statement and computer note look even iffier than we thought.'

He found what he was looking for. 'Anyway, here's how Rusbridger described Mullin's computer note when he submitted them: "Mr Mullin's note written on the computer on his return to the office (Exhibit B)". That's straight from the horse's mouth, so there's no excuse for all these differences in its appearance when compared to these other documents.'

'That's bloody marvellous. Thanks, Malcolm.'

'What are you thanking me for? There's something else as well. Alan Rusbridger describes the bent "Mullin statement" as John Mullin's *affidavit*, in other words its been sworn by Mullin on oath, so if it turns out it hasn't even been signed by Mullin, Rusbridger's really in the shit.'

'I'm brewing up again,' I said decisively. 'The excitement's too much.'

When I returned with the tea Malcolm was reading "Peter Preston's computer queue."

'Hencke might claim that he didn't make an entry about "cash for questions" because he was waiting for evidence,' he said, once he had finished reading.

'He can't,' I crowed. 'Check it for yourself. The whole document is littered with unsubstantiated tittle-tattle about Ian Greer. It also contains an entry about Hamilton's stay at the Ritz, and even Hencke and Preston admit they didn't possess any evidence about that until 18 October 1994.'

'Hencke might try and claim that he wasn't interested in Hamilton as much as Greer during this period,' Malcolm said, doing his devil's advocate bit.

'He can't, he can't,' I chanted, rubbing my hands together vigorously. 'Because the very first entry of 15 September 1993 is a list of his thoughts on just how damaging Hamilton's stay at the Ritz would be to his ministerial career – and that is the largest entry in this document by far. If he was excited enough to fill in an A4 page with seven damaging points regarding Hamilton's stay at the Ritz, it's impossible to imagine that he wouldn't have made a single entry about him taking cash or gift vouchers in thirteen months, if Fayed really had made the allegations when he met Peter Preston in July 1993, as they claim!'

The evidence was piling up that we had proved the unthinkable a major cover-up within a British newspaper.

The picture of what must have happened was forming in my mind: Hencke and Mullin *did* return to *The Guardian* after their interview with Neil and Mullin *did* enter up a transcription of his shorthand note onto the office computer, just as Rusbridger stated. However, this was held back in defiance of the Court Order so it seemed safe to assume that it must have contained wording that supported Neil's account of the interview. However, when Neil made an issue out of the date that Fayed had made his allegations, *Guardian* editor, Alan Rusbridger, must have gone to this hitherto unused document and then authorised its transfer, *via floppy disk*, from the office computer onto a PC.

Once it had been downloaded, it was presumably amended retrospectively to show that a "cash for questions" allegation had been put to Neil. And the reason for the different typeface and lack of log-in details would be explained by the PC onto which it was transferred not supporting the font used by the office computer. And, of course, a PC would not generate automatic log-in details on the tops of documents, like the main, network computer.

'But why transfer it?' Malcolm asked. 'Why not amend it on the main office computer?'

'One or both of two reasons,' I replied. 'The main network computer probably has a security system whereby once documents have been "put to bed" they can't be amended.'

'What's the other one?'

'This is Mullin's computer note, right?'

'Right.'

'And Mullin, so far, has shown no signs of being involved in the cover-up, right?'

'Come on, out with it.'

'Well, to get into the document to amend it, if it is amendable, would probably need Mullin's password.'

Malcolm looked at me as the penny dropped. 'And without Mullin's password Rusbridger or Leigh, or whoever, would have had to copy it onto a floppy then onto another PC to amend it!'

'You've got it.'

'The sneaky bastards probably haven't even told Mullin that they've amended his note and sent it into the Downey Inquiry as evidence in his name.'

We sat there staring at each other, rendered temporarily speechless by our discovery – and its significance. We had in our possession hard evidence that the Editor of a British national newspaper was heavily involved in the fabrication of evidence as part of a cover-up. For all we knew, Alan Rusbridger might have forged it himself.

Furthermore, because "Peter Preston's computer queue" shows that *Guardian* Political Editor, Michael White, had access to their data and discussed Hencke's investigation with him, there were serious implications that White knew, along with John Mullin, that his colleagues conspired in a cover-up too.

'What a fine mess they've got themselves into,' Malcolm mused, as we gazed in amazement at all the evidence we now had.

I looked at my watch. 'Come on,' I said, 'let's go and have a pint. I think we damn well deserve one.'

'Here,' Malcolm said. 'You'd better deal with this first.' He passed me a fax asking if I would be booking a table for the North Western Royal Television Society Awards ceremony in Manchester, as I had the previous year.

'Just hold on a minute, Malcolm.' I telephoned the organising company.

'What's the catchment period for the broadcast of programmes submitted for awards?' I asked.

'September '96 to September '97,' the woman said.

'Is it too late to put an entry in?'

'No,' she said. 'You've got another week or so.'

I pulled out a tape of the "Openshaw" programme, which was the last item I did for Granada, broadcast in December 1996, scribbled out a quick note, stuck them in a Jiffy bag and wrote on the address for the girls downstairs in the lobby to post. 'Come on, lets go to the pub.'

A few minutes later in the Toll Gate Arms, we discussed our discoveries again. We could believe that, in the space of a few months ago, arising out nothing more significant than a common curiosity about Hamilton's protestations of innocence, we had come so far.

'You know, Jonathan,' Malcolm, said, taking a long, deep breath, 'these people made the Watergate conspiracy look like kindergarten.'

'There's a big difference,' I said. 'Watergate was about straight journalists and bent politicians. We're looking at a reverse situation. How do you think they all managed to get so involved?'

'I think that when they printed the first cash allegations against Hamilton and Greer,' Malcolm said, as he took another swig, 'they did believe them to be true. I think they had probably been seduced by a combination of eagerness to get the Tories out of office, coupled to the fact that Fayed's allegations against Ian Greer, Tim Smith and Hamilton, all seemed to support Andrew Roth's theory about Greer's commission payments which we still need more evidence on,' he reminded me.

He took another swig. 'And then, when Fayed's allegations about Hamilton's stay at the Ritz turned out to be true, and Fayed's allegations against Greer paying Tim Smith *seemed* to be confirmed by Smith's uneasiness throughout the interview, everything they had suspected slotted into place – as they saw it. The last thing they would have expected was that Hamilton and Greer would issue libel writs the same day.'

'After that, the rot really set in.' I agreed, finishing off my pint. 'False statements, misrepresented documents, forged documents, smoke screens. And the bastards nearly got away with it, too.'

'There's another little difference between Watergate and this affair,' Malcolm said, banging down his empty glass on the bar. 'Woodward and Bernstein got paid!'

15

Going Public

WE WERE NOW READY TO LAUNCH OUR REPORT ON A WAITING world. We knew that, if we weren't careful, we could go on working on it forever and still dig up every scrap of evidence needed. But there had to be a moment when we felt we had enough material to make a convincing case to the media and handed over the results of our investigations to date.

'Before we go public with this report,' I said to Malcolm one morning in September, 'we really need to get Preston, Hencke and Mullin on film.'

'What about Rusbridger and Leigh?'

'At the moment let's stick with the three who were involved at the start of the "cash for questions" story. The only concrete evidence we have against Leigh is his false explanation for the late emergence of the three employees. He could always wriggle out of that using the "dramatic licence" plea. Apart from the wider charge of being guilty of deliberately misinterpreting reporting, we don't really have anything else on him, he's been too careful. As for Rusbridger, we still don't have anything absolutely cast iron on him either. We'll need confirmation from Mullin that he didn't amend his computer note, and either confirmation from Mullin or Downey that Rusbridger submitted a false witness statement.'

'You mean affidavit,' interrupted Malcolm. 'That's how Rusbridger described it in his letter to Downey.'

'Whatever. We'll still need confirmation from Downey before we can pin the charge on Rusbridger that he masterminded the forgery and fabrication of documents. But we're going to have to talk to the other three now before they rumble that we're onto them or they'll never talk to us.'

He agreed and that afternoon we sent off a fax to Peter Preston, requesting interviews with himself, David Hencke and John Mullin. When we received no reply Malcolm followed up with phone calls. They didn't actually say "no," but they certainly didn't say "yes" either. They stone-walled.

We carried on excavating. More evidence. Still more evidence. An embarrassment of riches that was causing me all sorts of problems, for the relevance of each piece of evidence needed articulating in our report in a logical, understandable fashion. It was not an easy task.

Then, on 8 October 1997, at around 10.00am, I received a phone call at the office from Neil. He and Christine had just arrived back from their trip to America.

'Jonathan, it's Neil, we're back,' he said, excitedly. In fact, I had never heard him so excited before. 'Downey's replied to my letter. You and Malcolm were right! That statement of John Mullin's wasn't signed by Mullin at all! In fact, Downey says it wasn't even written by Mullin, but that it was prepared by someone else for him! Brilliant detective work! Brilliant! Absolutely brilliant! You're geniuses, the pair of you.'

'What does Downey say about the fact that Rusbridger submitted it to the inquiry as an affidavit?' I asked, trying to keep my own excitement well damped in case it proved to be another false dawn.

'He doesn't comment! All he says is that the section that Rusbridger submitted was cleared for accuracy.'

'Cleared for accuracy by Rusbridger or by Mullin?'

'He doesn't say,' Neil replied. 'So you can bet your life it was cleared by Rusbridger.'

'You know Neil,' I said, 'Rusbridger is going to be putting Mullin under tremendous pressure to authenticate it. And his computer note too. Don't be surprised if he does.'

'Well, if he does then he will have to explain all these anomalies you've found.'

'Does Downey acknowledge that he ascribed it to the wrong journalist?'

'He just passes it off as a simple error.'

'On one of the most crucial pieces of evidence to the inquiry,' I sneered.

After a further few minutes chat I put the phone down

'We were right, I take it?' Malcolm asked. 'About Mullin not signing his own affidavit, I mean.'

'One hundred per cent,' I replied. 'It turns out he didn't even write it, never mind sign it or swear it.'

'Well you'd better get that in the report too,' Malcolm said, 'because Hamilton is going to want to hand it in to the Select Committee when he gives his televised address next Tuesday.'

The Select Committee on Standards and Privileges, with whom Neil had an appointment to present his case, had the power to reject Downey's conclusions.

The proof of yet another of our conclusions was a massive boost to all our morale, and it confirmed beyond any doubt the involvement of Alan Rusbridger in the cover-up. What's more, Rusbridger could clearly be seen to be the orchestrator of the whole thing because he was the one who had submitted to Downey the unsworn, unsigned and undated "Mullin statement" as an affidavit. As if to underline how slippery a character he really was he had also tried to pass the unsworn Hencke statement off as an affidavit, not to mention the unauthorised and forged "Mullin's computer note" and the misrepresentation of Mullin's shorthand note. And he had submitted all these on 19 February *after* having sight of Neil's submission and nine days after *The Guardian*'s oral examination.

'I think it's time we contacted Jim Hancock,' I said to Malcolm. 'Hamilton says he's been pretty straight, so you never know, he might do a piece on what we've been up to.'

Jim Hancock was the BBC Northwest's political correspondent, based at the Oxford Road studios in Manchester. Along with the *Knutsford Guardian* and *Northwich Chronicle*, he was one of few who had reported the allegations against Hamilton more or less neutrally from the outset. I told him over the phone about the draft report we had compiled and he made the right noises.

'We're going to go public with it soon,' I told him. 'And we're giving it to Neil Hamilton to use when he faces the Select Committee next week. Would you like to see a copy?'

'Yes, of course, I'm very interested. But why have you done it? What's *your* interest in all this? No offence meant, but I have to ask – is Hamilton paying you? Is anyone paying you? Tiny Rowland, for instance?'

'No Jim, no one's been paying us.' I took no offence at his line of questioning at all. In his place, it would have been the first question I would have asked.

Malcolm and I personally delivered the report, which by now had grown to over a hundred pages of detailed evidence, to him at the BBC in Oxford Road. The three of us ascended to the canteen there to sit around a table drinking undrinkable tea in polystyrene cups while he skimmed through it.

'My God,' he said at last. 'I didn't think it would be anything like this. What's it all about? What's the bottom line?'

'It can't be summed up that easily, Jim,' I said. 'There's plots and sub-plots and God-knows-what.'

'Try and give me some idea.'

'You're going to have to spend some time on this,' I insisted, 'but basically there's been a stitch-up. *The Guardian* was suckered into printing Fayed's false allegations and then had to cover-up. Hamilton's innocent.'

'You're joking!' He was more than just a little incredulous. 'Are you sure? You're really swimming against the current, you two.'

'We know that, but we're certain.'

'You know,' he said, 'I've always tried to treat Hamilton fairly.'

'I know, you don't have to persuade us. Why do you think we've come to you?'

Like every other reporter in the media today, Jim was over-worked, with little time for his own investigations. He started to interrogate us. When he had run out of questions we said our goodbyes and left, knowing we had put up a convincing case, but having no idea whether the BBC would do anything about it.

A few days later Jim rang the office. 'You're not going to believe this,' he said. 'I gave your report to my producer, Liam Fogarty. He's OK'd it and referred it upstairs and the top brass have cleared me to do a piece about you two for transmission.'

'What do you mean?' I couldn't believe that we were finally seeing a crack in the wall of indifference.

'Look, I'm telling you we wouldn't stick our necks out here on offbeat stories and I'm telling you your report has gone all the way to the top and they've cleared me to do a piece. We want to do a feature on you two guys and your investigation and the fact that you're going against everyone else. It'll be broadcast on GMR radio too.'

A few days later Jim came round with the crew and did his interviews and 'piece to camera' at the business centre, and the items went out on the BBC's morning, noon and evening regional news bulletins on 13 October '97 – the eve of Hamilton's address to the Select Committee. It showed film of Malcolm and me beavering away in the office and explaining what we were up for the benefit of the cameras. It was only a short item but it was the first time anyone had actually acknowledged in the media that our case existed at all. That morning *The Guardian*'s Northern Correspondent rang Jim.

'What's this about two investigators trying to clear Hamilton?' he asked him.

'It's not really for me to say,' Jim said. 'Why don't I give you their number and you can talk to them yourself?'

He gave him our number, but we never received a call.

The next day Neil gave his televised address, often referring directly to our 'Magnum Opus,' as he called it. The first time he quoted from our report, he said this:

'This issue is exhaustively gone into in a document which I have not been responsible for producing (and I am grateful to the authors for pointing all this out to me), in a document which I shall be giving to the Committee, produced by two independent journalists wholly unconnected with me, who after the General Election decided there was a story here worth investigating because they wanted to make a TV programme about it. They have been working at their own expense, without income, putting their own money from their own meagre resources into the investigation. I have given them free run of all the papers that everybody produced for the inquiry and they have gone on and done it . . .'

Neil went on to give an excellent performance, tearing into Fayed's and *The Guardian*'s evidence and ripping it to shreds. Tory Members Ann Widdecombe and Quentin Davies obviously listened.

After his address, which lasted two and a half hours, he handed it in to the Clerk to the Committee, who copied it for each Member, including Labour MPs Dale-Campbell-Savours, a friend of David Leigh, and Alan Williams, a friend of David Hencke.

A few days later, Malcolm and I were working in the office when Malcolm suggested I should contact Granada to try and create some interest in our work. I telephoned Helen Michael, PA to Granada's head of regional political programmes.

'Helen, it's Jonathan Hunt. Is Rob McGloughlan there?'

'Congratulations,' she said.

'What for?'

'Being short-listed.'

'Short-listed for what?'

'You've been short-listed for News Reporter of the Year by the North West RTS. Didn't you know?'

When I put the phone down I looked across at Malcolm. 'You'll never guess what. I've just been short-listed for Television News Reporter of the Year.'

'Congratulations,' he said warmly. 'You're a lad, aren't you? I didn't even realise you were in the running.'

'Thanks. You know, it won't do us any harm, this. When you're shifting a mountain you need every bit of explosive you can get your hands on. This might just help prevent *The Guardian* from destroying us.'

I knew that something like this could enhance our chances of having our findings accepted, because that was the way the media worked. They did not look at what was being said, they looked at who was saying it. You needed credibility, credentials.

Then, on Friday 24 October 1997 at 11.25 am, the phone rang in the office. I was there on my own.

'Is Malcolm Keith-Hill there?'

'No,' I replied. 'This is Jonathan Hunt, his colleague. Who's speaking?'

'It's David Leigh.'

Well, well, I thought, what does *he* want?

'Is that David Leigh the eminent journalist?' I enquired ironically.

'Yes.'

'Your reputation precedes you, David. How can I help you?'

'I'm just interested in what you two chaps are doing. I hear you've compiled a report saying all sorts of wild things. Like the allegations against Hamilton didn't exist in 1993. And he was never asked about "cash for questions" that year. And that there's been a cover-up in *The Guardian*.'

I wondered from which one of the two *Guardian* stooges on the Committee he had heard – his own, or Hencke's.

'That's right, David,' I said, feeling sure that Rusbridger had sanctioned his making (and, no doubt, taping) this call. I decided to play along with it and act happy-daft. 'I know you've written a book called *Sleaze,* but we haven't included you in our report at all. So, if I were you, I would be very circumspect about any relationship I had with Alan Rusbridger, Peter Preston or David Hencke, because these people are at the heart of the cover-up, you know.'

'These are strong allegations you're making, Jonathan.'

'I know they are,' I said. 'But, as journalists, we have to carry on with what we think is right, just as you would.'

'Did you see Peter Preston's article on Monday this week?' he enquired.

'No, I didn't, actually.'

'Well, he said the allegations definitely existed in 1993. So if you are going to publish anything that says they didn't exist, that would be calling him a liar and that would be a libel, and I feel fairly certain that Peter Preston would take out a libel action against you.'

'Well, Peter will have to do what Peter thinks is right. But you can tell him from me that we are going to publish, and that if he wants to start a libel action against us then I look forward to receiving the writ. We're not going to be frightened off writing the truth. As a journalist yourself, David, I'm sure you agree with me.'

I was beginning to think that if David Leigh was willing to make a call like this he must be as deep in the cover-up as the rest of them. I made a mental note to scrutinise everything that Leigh said and wrote down to the last comma.

'Tell me a bit about yourself, anyway,' he said and being an obliging sort of fellow, with nothing to hide, I launched into my life story. I went into laborious detail about the haulage company I built up and why I closed it down. I mentioned my subsequent six-month sabbatical touring the States in an old Austin Vanden Plas limousine I exported for the trip and how, in turn, that led me into becoming, as an interim measure, an importer of classic cars into Britain from America, until the collapse of values resulted in me shutting shop again.

I told him how I had gone on to take a job as a computer operator in the Libyan oil exploration industry by exaggerating my computer skills, and how I ended up as a 'well tester' – a job that entailed flowing wildcat oil and gas wells. I had lasted three years before tiring of sand in my sandwiches, whereupon I returned to England in search of a new career. I waxed lyrical about the long year of unemployment, that ended when I was offered a position in a PR company, which led, eventually, into television journalism. And I was happy to give him all this information because I knew it would annoy him.

It had been my experience at Granada that some people, who had been journalists throughout their working lives, resented outsiders breaking into their profession and stripping away some of the mystique. They like to give the impression that you have to be "trained for the job." The reality is that much of today's journalistic expertise consists of little more than re-jigging press releases and downloading stories from the wire agencies.

'Well, Jonathan,' he said, 'you seem to have a good career ahead of you in television and I can only repeat what I said to you before – I wouldn't print anything about these allegations, if I were you.'

With that caveat, ended my first contact with David Leigh.

A couple of days later we sent out news releases to the Press Association and all the newspapers, giving notice of our press conference, which was scheduled to take place three days later, on 29 October in Westminster.

Mindful of the resistance we were facing from the British media, having been rebuffed so many times for so many different reasons, (including the BBC's *Rough Justice* programme who declined to take up the story because Neil Hamilton isn't in prison), I also contacted the CNN *Impact* documentary team in Washington, USA, and got through to Steve Daly, one of the production staff.

Daly seemed mildly intrigued, so I spent about an hour or so going through the story from its very beginnings all the way to Fayed's vendetta against Neil Hamilton, and how *The Guardian* had embarked on a massive cover-up after realising that Andrew Roth and Fayed had each sold them a pup.

Steve Daly grew more and more absorbed as I reeled off the

evidence. When I told him how Fayed had seduced the British Press, and that all the signs were that it would need an intervention from the Americans to expose the corruption within *The Guardian*, he promised to arrange for a London-based CNN crew to be present at our Press conference.

The following evening, as I was leaving the office to barrel down the M6 to London, I received a call from Ian Greer on my mobile phone. 'Jonathan,' he said, 'this press conference you're holding tomorrow to release your report . . .'

'Yes?'

'I've just had a phone call from an intermediary. I can't give you his name. I feel duty-bound to tell you that it may not be in your best interests to go ahead.'

'Why do you say that, Ian?'

'Apparently *The Guardian* are gunning for you. They say they'll smear you in their columns about all these debts that you've got and the illegal trading that you've been involved with in Libya.'

That rocked me. 'What debts?'

'From your previous companies.'

'I don't have any debts,' I said. 'I used to run a limited haulage company which I closed down, but everyone was paid off. I could have milked it and gone bust and bought a big house in Cheshire like everyone else.'

'What about this illegal trading in Libya?'

I laughed. It seemed David Leigh had swallowed the bait. 'I was working in the desert in oil exploration,' I said. 'I have some good references. I may not have known quite as much about computers as they thought when they took me on, but that was the extent of my deception.'

'So there's no truth in any of these accusations?'

'None whatsoever. They're trying to frighten me.'

'Oh, right. Well, I just thought I should tell you.'

'Don't worry about it, Ian. Nothing is going to stop us.'

'Good for you. Good luck, good luck.'

Ian Greer's warning did not deter me, and when I told Malcolm it didn't put him off either. In convoy with most of the other car owners in Britain we headed down the M6 to London with all our files and 50 copies of our report. We were ready to face whatever *The Guardian* might throw at us, confident that we had done our research and had a story that would rock the

Establishment. The press releases had gone out to everyone we could think of who might be interested in our findings. We expected a good-sized crowd.

The conference was going to be held in a Parliamentary outbuilding in Millbank. I was sure that accusations of corruption in the press would be enough for most of the major news organisations to send someone down just to check it out. We carried all our boxes into the room we had booked and laid it out on the table, then went to fetch a couple of glasses of water. Amongst the first to arrive were David Leigh and David Hencke, with their photographer, Graham Turner. I shook Leigh by the hand and nodded a greeting to Hencke who had great wads of papers under his arm.

'You still planning to go ahead?' Leigh asked.

'Very much so, David.'

'You really shouldn't be doing this,' he said, his face full of spurious concern for our well-being. 'I'm sure you're going to regret it. Do you realise the ramifications? You're going to end up swamped by libel actions and God knows what other problems.'

'We feel we have to do it,' I said, determined not to be intimidated.

'What about you, Malcolm?' Leigh turned his attention to Malcolm, enquiring about his background in a slightly intimidating manner. Malcolm responded to his questions equably.

A quarter of an hour before we were due to kick off our audience was still thinly spread. Not one camera crew. 'This doesn't look good at all,' I said to Malcolm. 'Where are all the rest of the press?'

I dashed out of the building and went a few doors down to the Westminster television studios. I burst into Sky News and asked if they had received our press release. I was met with blank looks. Talking fast, I persuaded them to send a reporter along and then ran down to the BBC and to encounter the same puzzled expressions. I managed to track down Robin Crystal, a reporter whom I knew slightly.

'Robin,' I almost pleaded. 'I thought you were covering our press conference. We're releasing our report on the cash for questions affair.'

'I've heard nothing about it. Jim told me to expect details but I've not seen anything.'

'Isn't there anything on the PA? Didn't you get our news release?'

'I've seen nothing anywhere.'

'We need you to cover it if you can. It starts in about 10 minutes. Do you have a crew?'

'Leave it with me,' he said, reassuringly. 'I'll be there.'

I dashed down the stairs to ITN. Same story. Nothing on "the wires" and never saw our release. I begged for a crew to be sent but none was available. I rushed back to join Malcolm. In my absence a solitary reporter from the *Independent* had drifted in. Edward Leigh MP and a researcher for Dale Campbell-Savours had also appeared, but empty seats abounded. Neil and Christine were there and it turned out that the man from the *Independent* had actually come to talk to them about a cookery feature or some such. But at least he was there. Leigh and Hencke were in the front row, well-placed to hurl brickbats. Hencke's papers were stacked on the seat beside him.

As Malcolm and I stood chatting, trying to cover up the delay in starting, the BBC camera crew arrived, followed by Gaby Hinscliffe from the *Daily Mail*. I had spoken to Gaby the previous day and she had seemed very keen. I felt my confidence rising. Mark Lyons, the Westminster correspondent from my old programme, "Granada Tonight," strolled in, looking very dour. A few days earlier I had received a fax from Granada, stressing that I was a freelance reporter throughout the period I worked for them. They were obviously keen to distance themselves from me and to make sure that I did not claim the status of a staff reporter.

Feeling that it was unlikely our audience would swell further, and being keen to start before the camera crew got called away, I handed out copies of the report and opened the conference by introducing Malcolm. He then kicked off with our statement. Nobody barracked him as he spoke. He sounded confident and authoritative. Then he handed over to me; it was my job to fill in with some of the evidence we had accumulated in support of our claims. But the moment I opened my mouth David Leigh started barracking.

'Just who are you to be saying all these things? I've talked to Sue Woodward at Granada (my old boss), and she says that all you've done is presented stories about leaky pipes. You have no journalistic background or training. You're just a presenter, not even a reporter.

I remained very calm. 'I would be surprised if Sue really did use those words; in fact, I can't believe she did. I'd be very disappointed with Granada Television, considering how hard I worked for them. I don't think I should be put in a position where I have to say this, but I was short-listed for Television News Reporter of the Year just a few days ago.'

'We didn't nominate you,' Mark Lyons piped up.

'So what?' Privately, I was taken aback by his disassociation. I wondered at his motives for being there – to attack me or to hear the evidence? Were *The Guardian*'s ties with Granada *that* strong?

Leigh kept up his heckling all through the presentation of the evidence, while Hencke noisily shuffled his stack of papers, ensuring that at least the racket they made between them was stereophonic. And while all this was going on, Graham Turner, *The Guardian*'s staff photographer, was standing about two feet in front of me, letting his camera off in my face like a machine gun as I tried to talk. I just kept on going, determined to out-last them. I flourished the piece of paper that was supposed to be Mullin's affidavit but wasn't even written by him, let alone signed, and explained what it was. The hecklers went strangely quiet. I moved on to read out Alex Carlile's letter from 1994 which proved that Leigh's explanation for the late emergence of the three Fayed witnesses was a lie. The two naughty boys went as silent as lambs. Clearly, on that subject Leigh had nothing to heckle about.

Eventually the BBC reporter, Robin Crystal, obviously keen to wrap his film up and go, asked, 'Have you been paid by anybody to do this?'

'I can confirm,' I said for the cameras and the record, 'we have not been paid by anybody, not even Tiny Rowland.'

As they got up to leave I said to David Leigh, 'Okay David? You know where to send the libel writ.'

'You're not worth suing,' he said and walked out. Hencke shuffled along behind him, bowed beneath the weight of his papers.

Malcolm and I packed up all our paraphernalia and went to the pub for a pint.

'Did you see David Leigh's face when we discussed the evidence?' I said as we quaffed.

'He soon stopped shooting off at the mouth, didn't he?'

'They know we've got them on the run, that's why.'

That afternoon Malcolm went back to Manchester while I stayed overnight to try and stir the media out of their apathy somehow. I descended into frustrated depression. So few people at our press conference. No CNN crew either. I guessed that none of the few reporters at the press conference would be ready to break the story anyway. Every door I hammered on seemed to be so tightly shut I couldn't imagine ever being able to wake anyone up to what was going on. The more time that elapsed since the election, the more likely the public would forget all about the *Sleaze* issues, and the less likely we would be to get a hearing for the truth. More than once I had found myself singing the old Danny Kaye number: *"The King is in the all-together, the all-together, the all-together . . ."*

Back at the hotel that evening, I telephoned Steve Daly in Washington. To save my phone bill, he offered to ring me back immediately

'What happened, Steve? Where was your crew?'

'Hey, Jonathan,' he said in lowered tones, 'I'm really sorry. I had it all lined up but I was overruled. I'm sorry man.'

'It was your English boss who put the blocks on, correct? Peter Bergen?'

'Er . . . how did you know?'

'I spoke to Peter a few moths ago when he was in London researching Fayed after Princess Diana's death. What reason did Peter give, Steve?'

'Look, Jonathan, I can't help you.'

'It was because he is now a drinking friend of *The Guardian*'s new Washington correspondent, Ed Vulliamy, wasn't it?'

'How do you know? Look, Ed does some work for us out here and he and Peter are pretty close.' We spoke for a further five minutes or so and then Daly signed off. 'I really am sorry man . . . but don't give up, you'll eventually get there. Good luck man . . . you take care of yourself.'

I put the phone down and made a cup of tea. I opened the window and stared out into the Rest of Britain. There I was, on my own, knowing the truth of the biggest scandal in the British press since the printing press was invented, and 58 million people were totally ignorant of the truth. I reflected on Daly's parting words of advice: "don't give up and you'll get there." Of course, he was right. One day, someone in British television would grasp the nettle. But I thought to myself that it would be a shame if it had to take ten years before "Timewatch," "Witness" or "Secret History" got around to examining the real story behind the "cash for questions" affair the media witch-hunt of all time when the evidence is available now.

I roused myself. There was work to be done. Where was Jane Corbin's number? I retrieved the print-out of our contact sheet from my briefcase and rang her on her mobile.

'Jane,' I said when she answered. 'It's Jonathan Hunt. We really need you to do this programme.'

'Jonathan! I'm up to my neck right now. I'm in Germany at the moment.'

'Jane, we *need* you and "Panorama" to do the programme,' I wheedled.

'I'm just too busy right now . . .' That was not what I wanted to hear and I was in no mood for any put-downs. Not after the CNN lark, anyway.

'Jane!' I yelled down the phone. 'I need to see you!'

'Okay! Okay! Okay!' she yelled back. 'White City. Next Tuesday, at ten!'

The following morning, filled with new resolve to get some-where, I phoned up the office of Charles Moore, Editor of the *Daily Telegraph* and got his secretary, Frances Banks.

'Miss Banks,' I said, 'I need to speak to two journalists urgently about the Hamilton affair. I'd like to come over to Canary Wharf to brief them on our investigation into the "cash for questions" affair. I explained what we had uncovered.

'Why two?' she asked, more curious about the number than the purpose.

'If I only talk to one person they'll have to relay it all to someone else. I would rather have someone else there who can vouch for what's said.'

Half an hour later she rang back to tell me she had fixed up a meeting with Barbie Dutter and Philip Johnston at twelve o'clock. Perfect.

At Canary Wharf, closeted with Dutter and Johnston, whom I had never met before, I went through my usual routine, showing all the evidence and explaining why we now knew that it was all a cover-up.

'I've read the Downey report,' Johnston said, 'and I have

to say I didn't find anything compelling in it at all. Downey doesn't say how he's come to his conclusions.'

This was encouraging, as not many journalists of my acquaintance had bothered to even read the report and I had been told that Granada Television didn't even have a copy. I left the meeting feeling that perhaps the mountain had moved another millimetre or so. The *Telegraph* pair weren't promising to do anything about it yet, but at least they were listening to me, and they seemed to accept that our evidence made sense.

But was anyone in the media prepared to *do* anything?

16

Onto The Floor of The House

BACK IN MANCHESTER, JIM HANCOCK AT THE BBC WAS KEEN TO interview someone from *The Guardian* for inclusion in the second, longer piece about us that he was now preparing for BBC Northwest's "NorthWestminster" political programme. He wasn't having much luck, which didn't surprise me. I happened to be BBC newsroom in Manchester when he took a call from a public relations woman down at *The Guardian*'s office in London. I overheard him say, 'so they definitely asked him the question that day?' and I signalled him frantically.

'Excuse me a minute,' he said into the mouthpiece, and covered it with his hand to listen to me.

'I can absolutely prove that they *didn't* ask the question,' I hissed.

He nodded and went back to the phone. 'Well, I have Mr Hunt here, and he says . . . I'm sorry? Yes, he's in the room here with me . . . Well, what's the difference? He's just in the room, that's all . . . But that's . . . but that's ridiculous!' He covered the phone again and told me, 'They don't want to talk to me if you're in the room!'

He tried to reason with the PR woman again, half laughing at the absurdity of the situation. Eventually he gave up and slammed the phone onto its stand.

'That's disgraceful,' he said, shaking his head in disbelief. 'You've obviously got them rattled.'

'I'm telling you, Jim,' I said, 'they're frightened to death.'

In the end he managed to get Hencke to agree to an interview, by which time he was as convinced as Malcolm and I that *The Guardian* journalists were running scared. It showed in his interviewing technique. When he pressed Hencke about the interview with Neil in 1993, the journalist looked shifty.

'We definitely asked Neil Hamilton about the "cash for questions" question,' he said, his head bobbing around and his eyes rolling. 'If I had lied about this I could lose my job,' he added, as if to emphasise the truth of his words.

Well, I thought, Neil Hamilton lost his, so that would be a fair trade.

The following Tuesday Malcolm and I set off south once more in my trusty diesel Montego. We had a packed day ahead of us. The first meeting was with Jane at the BBC Centre in White City, armed with briefcases and boxes bulging with material. Afterwards, at lunchtime, we were doing the filming with Jim, and immediately after that we were due to see Baroness Turner, a Labour peeress who is both a former trade unionist and a former director of Ian Greer's lobbying company. She was also Blair's front-bench employment spokesman in the House of Lords until he insisted she stand down, following *The Guardian*'s allegations about Greer.

Jane welcomed us into her office, warning us that she only had half an hour to spare. A television in the corner was tuned to a Sky TV channel and a reporter, coincidentally called Jonathan Hunt, was interviewing a woman called Sue Woodward, mother of accused nanny, Louise. I thought to myself, there's one or two questions a different Jonathan Hunt wouldn't mind asking a different Sue Woodward (Sue Woodward was also the name of my boss at Granada whom David Leigh alleged had rubbished my credentials).

Malcolm and I spent the next thirty minutes bombarding Jane Corbin with facts, like a couple of tennis ball machines. Every now and then I could see that we were catching her attention with some detail or other that struck her as odd. During optimistic moments I felt that we might be getting through the outer shell of preconceived ideas that everyone seems to have in the Hamilton case, wearing it away. But the going wasn't getting any easier.

'I'm really sorry,' she said after half an hour. 'I do have to go. I fitted you in between two other projects.'

I was disappointed, but kept it hidden.

'Don't worry,' I said, exuding false cheer. 'We'll be back.'

'I had a feeling you might be,' she smiled wryly.

'This isn't going to go away, Jane.'

'No,' she stood up to go. 'I realise that. Let's make another appointment when my producer and I can spend a couple of hours with you going over everything in more detail.'

Heading back to the Montego, which we had had to park on a pavement in front of someone's house because the security guards wouldn't let us into the BBC car park (which was half empty), we drove up to Westminster to a pub just round the corner from Parliament called the Westminster Arms. We were due to meet Jim Hancock again; he wanted to film us lobbying Parliament for inclusion in a second programme he was making about our investigation. Our appointment with Baroness Turner was after lunch.

We made good time to the pub. Jim hadn't arrived, so we settled down with our pints to wait. Our table was at the top of a staircase going down to a basement restaurant. John Sweeney from the *Observer* came in from the street with a couple of girls and headed for the stairs that led down to the restaurant. Recalling how he had been willing to listen to the other side of the argument during Downey Day, after previously whipping up the press at Millbank like some demented warm-up man, I called out to him.

'Hello there, John, how are you doing?'

He looked our way and an expression of recognition flickered across his face. He called out a greeting but carried on and disappeared down the stairs. When Jim turned up we all went downstairs to eat and Jim briefed us on what he wanted to get from us that afternoon.

'We're not going to screen anything controversial,' he warned. 'We don't want you slagging off any journalists. If you're not careful what you say on camera, it will be cut out in the editing suite.'

'We're not going to be slagging off anybody,' I assured him. Not that we didn't have just cause.

All the time we were talking I was thinking about John Sweeney on the other side of the restaurant. I was very keen to talk to him about the case. I suspected that he had only taken his ferociously anti-Hamilton stance simply because he was a passionate person who didn't know what he was talking about.

Eventually he came by us on his way to the Gents, so I asked if he could spare us a few minutes. I was encouraged that he seemed quite willing to talk to us.

We put our heads together over the table and spent some time going over the evidence; for my part, trying to convince the doubting Sweeney that Neil had never done anything that every other MP hadn't done.

'Look, John.' I laid my metaphorical cards face up before him. 'We would really like to get someone like you, who is known to be a critic of Hamilton, on our side. When can we meet up so that we put the facts to you properly?'

'I really don't have that kind of time . . .' he started to protest.

'It will only take an hour,' I chopped through his protests, like a salesman determined to make a sale, refusing to be put off. 'Two at the most. And I guarantee you will be frightened to death by what we can show you. Forged documents, false witness statements. Your boss is in it up to his neck.'

'I can't . . . really . . .' I sensed that he was afraid. He knew we had at least some right on our side, but he worked for a paper that was owned by *The Guardian*. He wasn't a free agent.

'All right then,' I said, backing off. 'Humour me, will you? Tell me – how many times did Neil Hamilton spoke from the floor of the House on behalf of Fayed, do you think?'

He looked confused and I knew I had him. 'I can't remember exactly . . .'

'Remember roughly then. How many oral questions did he ask, for example?'

'Off the top of my head I can't remember the *exact* number . . .' He was stalling; he didn't really have a clue.

'It was *nil*,' I snapped. 'You couldn't forget nil, John. You can't confuse nil with anything else. Nil is just about the easiest figure to remember.'

Aware that he had betrayed his ignorance of the case, he became embarrassed. 'Can you keep that off the record?' he said, in a pleading voice.

'Of course,' I replied. 'We're not *Guardian* journalists.' But, on second thoughts, I decided that we needed every bit of ammunition we could get. This man had manically pursued Neil Hamilton in the General Election and claimed to know all about him, and even written a book implying he was a fascist. Yet here he was, not even able to say how many questions Neil put down in the "cash for questions" affair. That's akin to an authority on the "Dambusters" not knowing that their job was all about busting dams.

After a few more pleasantries he left us, looking uncomfortable, as well he might. I was not displeased with the outcome of the session. We walked back to the green outside Parliament (where else?) to do the filming with Jim and then made our way to the Commons lobby where we had arranged to meet Baroness Turner.

We arrived 20 minutes late, the filming session having overrun, and were naturally ill-at-ease as a result. Parrying our apologies she instead greeted us warmly as if we were friends. After the introductions she led us through to one of the Lords bars and ordered some tea.

'Ian Greer has told me all about you and I'd just like to say how much I appreciate what you're doing,' the Baroness said once we were settled. 'It's terrible what *The Guardian* has done to Ian and it's all false. It's a wicked newspaper these days run by wicked people. It's terrible . . . and it used to be such a wonderful newspaper too.

'As a director of IGA,' she continued, 'I have a strong personal interest in this whole affair. When the media started on Ian they came after me too. Not long afterwards, I began to receive a lot of unsolicited mail and goods. Not only that, but Tony Blair pressurised me into standing down from the front bench.' She was referring to her role as Labour's employment spokesman in the Lords. 'It's absurd the way Parliament has been subjugated by the media. The tale is wagging the dog these days. Everyone is frightened of the media.'

'Who do you think was sending you the stuff?' I asked, recalling that Christine Hamilton had been subjected to a similar campaign.

'I can only speculate,' she replied. 'But it would have to have been organised by someone with time on their hands. I think it would be safe to say that it was someone in "Fayed's machine".'

'Did any of it change your opinions of how Ian Greer ran his business?' I asked.

'Absolutely not. I remain a staunch supporter of Ian to this day. But I would defend the media's right to investigate. I am a firm believer in the total freedom of the press. Nevertheless, I am constantly campaigning for the appointment of a Press

Ombudsman, someone independent of the press to whom aggrieved parties can complain. The Press Complaints' Commission is hopeless, totally useless.'

'Greer made donations to twenty six constituency associations,' I said. 'Twenty one of which were Tory. What's your view on that?'

She pooh-poohed it. 'Political donations are completely normal. All sorts of people, like the unions, do it all the time. They were all up front and on the books, there was nothing covert about them.'

Malcolm gave her a précis of our investigations.

'You know,' she said at one stage of the interview, 'I admire you two for your courage. There are a number of peers who have told me privately that they support Greer and Hamilton, but they're afraid to stand up and say so on the record.'

We parted as firm friends and soul-mates. She impressed me as being a very courageous and principled lady indeed.

A couple of days later the all-Party Select Committee on Standards and Privileges adjudicated on Sir Gordon Downey's report. Ann Widdecombe and Quentin Davies refused to endorse it, withstanding tremendous pressure from all sides to get the matter rubber-stamped and out of the way. It was an unprecedented split of the Committee. Davies and Widdecombe have both earned reputations for savaging Conservative ministers during the previous administration, so it can be taken as read that their actions were not prompted by Party considerations.

A Commons debate on Downey was scheduled to take place two weeks later on 17 November. A few days beforehand, Gerald Howarth organised a seminar for MPs supportive of Neil and who expressed an interest in speaking in the debate. Gerald asked if either Malcolm or I would be willing to make the journey down to support Neil's address to the meeting, which was proposed to last just an hour or so. Malcolm decided that for such a short meeting one of us was enough, and so a few days later I was back down the motorway to London, arriving at the Commons at bang on five o'clock.

A number of prominent Conservatives were present, including Sir Peter Tapsell, Nicholas Winterton, Teresa Gorman Edward Leigh and, of course, Gerald Howarth himself. Neil was going to address them all and Gerald Howarth asked me to talk as well. I was more than happy to agree, always keen to bend the ears of people who might be influential in helping to break down the resistance to the truth that we met at every turn. This was a receptive group of listeners, all of them keen to hear our findings.

This case is my obsession. I admit it. Once I have a captive audience, I do tend to get carried away. I wanted to spend several hours with this audience, explaining every last detail, but these were busy people and I knew I had to edit myself without mercy. I was worried that I wouldn't have enough time to be really convincing. So I handed out copies of the report in advance. Probably I was giving them too much material for what they probably expected would just be a briefing. In the event, I had about half an hour with them and the two points I was most anxious to get across were (a) that the emergence of the three Fayed employee witnesses was a charade, and (b) that documents had been faked in order to prove that the allegations about "cash for questions" existed *before* the first *Guardian* article.

'We have been told through intermediaries,' I said at one point, 'that if we released this material we will be destroyed in the columns of *The Guardian*.'

Nick Winterton's nose emerged from his copy of the report like a missile from its silo. 'What do you mean?' he demanded.

I said, 'We were told a few weeks ago that they would dig around in our backgrounds to find material to discredit us if we released this material.'

'Who told you that?'

'It was communicated to us via Ian Greer.'

'I think,' Winterton said, turning to his fellow MPs, 'that if Mr Hunt and his colleague have been receiving threats like that we should take it up.'

There was a general murmur of agreement. Or at any rate, ever the optimist, I interpreted it as agreement.

By the end of the meeting I was not sure how much they had really soaked up, but at least I had managed to establish that there was a great deal of material backing up our claims. I had given it my best shot. After a quick half with Gerald in one of the bars, we said our goodbyes again and I headed for home. What with all the stress and long-distance driving I arrived home absolutely whacked.

A couple of days later was the NW Royal Television Society

Awards evening. So, having collected Adele from her home in Hartford on the outskirts of Northwich, we set off to meet Malcolm and a group of our friends and relatives at a packed Palace Hotel. It was a night of relaxation and we had been looking forward to it. I had not seen my friends from "Granada Tonight" for quite a while and it was nice to be able to keep in touch.

During the evening I bumped into a few of them and caught up with the gossip, noticing a certain guardedness in one or two whom I had expected to be more friendly. Andy Spinoza was also there, the gossip columnist from the *Manchester Evening News* who had been very supportive. Sue Woodward, my old chief from "Granada Tonight" expressed her concern that the Hamilton investigation would damage my career.

'The truth is addictive, Sue,' I said. 'Nothing would persuade me to let go of the story now.'

'I sometimes wonder why I ever introduced you to television,' she said. And I wondered if she had been getting flak about me from Granada's factual department, who are thick as thieves with *The Guardian*.

I was amazed to discover that was the celebrity handing out the awards was none other than the white knight of Tatton, Martin Bell. I couldn't help thinking that it would be the supreme irony if he, after a tumultuous welcome from all the media people in the room, had to give me a prize while I was engaged in compiling a report about his being duped by *The Guardian*.

Adele looked radiant, and, of course, wanted so much for me to win. I had been shortlisted, and I figured that was a good result on its own. In the end though, I didn't win, and the award went to a BBC journalist for a report about child abuse. When the nominations were read out I was introduced as, "Jonathan Hunt, who doesn't mind who he upsets in his quest for the truth." An ambiguous accolade.

As soon as the result was announced I went out through a fire exit into the street and phoned Neil to tell him the news.

'I didn't get it,' I said. 'For your sake, I'm sorry, Neil.'

'Never mind me,' Neil said gruffly. 'Still, I am disappointed for you, Jonathan.'

'Don't worry,' I assured him. 'I'm not discouraged. It would just have been helpful to our cause to have won, that's all.'

I was surprised to find that I actually didn't feel too bad about losing. Perhaps, deep down, I had known I couldn't win. To become NW Television News Reporter of the Year in my first year in the business was the stuff of fantasy.

On the way to the toilets later in the evening, I bumped into Steve Boulton, chief of "World in Action," whom I knew had done programmes with journalists like David Leigh, and was, moreover, a friend of Alan Rusbridger's.

'I've got a great story for you,' I teased, straight-faced. 'I've been investigating *The Guardian* newspaper now for about a year and we've uncovered a great story involving Peter Preston and Alan Rusbridger and a whole nest of other vipers. Corruption in the press, wouldn't that be great for "World in Action?" '

Boulton was not impressed. 'Oh, don't tell me about Hamilton,' he grunted. 'He took all those commission payments. And that support for United States Tobacco was disgraceful.'

Here we go again, I thought. I decided to rev him up. 'Well, he was supporting a company which had been induced by the Government to spend God-knows-how-much to build a factory to manufacture a product that Swedish Government research proved was 140 times less dangerous than cigarettes. So, arguably, if smokers could be weaned off cigarettes and onto them, they would be a lot safer. I think it was a cause worth supporting. Don't you?'

Unable to absorb my counter punches, he stalked off muttering, back into the ballroom. Just then, Rob McGloughlan, head of regional political programmes, walked by. I thought I'd test his mettle, too.

'Hi, Rob. As you know I've been investigating the "cash for questions" affair for the last year . . .'

'Not now, Jonathan,' he said, as he brushed by and walked on. So much for my lobbying efforts.

As I was walking back to our table I bumped into Martin Bell and daughter, Melissa. Bell seemed decidedly edgy in my presence. I told him how the investigation was going, that there was no evidence whatsoever against Hamilton and that he was a victim of a *Guardian* conspiracy. Bell mumbled a few insincere platitudes of support for Neil, made excuses, and walked off with Melissa, speaking in *sotto voce* in her ear as they made their way through the dinner-jacketed crowd.

I thought, one of these days I'm going to test those pledges of support of yours.

A few days later I motored down to London yet again, to attend the Commons debate, during which I was asked if I could brief Neil's supportive MPs as it actually took place. Teresa Gorman and Gerald Howarth met me in the lobby. Teresa showed me through a door into a small panelled-off section at the end of the Opposition benches where the Members themselves sat. She signed me in and, once I was inside the Chamber, the door was locked behind me. I caught Nick Winterton's eye and he gave me an encouraging smile. Martin Bell was sitting a few seats away, his back to me. In the press gallery above the speaker I could see David Hencke. If I could see him, presumably he could see me. I quashed the temptation to wave to him.

I couldn't believe that our investigation had actually brought me this far, to sit feet away from the Members as they debated in the crucible of British democracy.

The Speaker, Betty Boothroyd, started the debate by calling a succession of pro-Downey Select Committee Members to speak. They all droned on and on about Downey and how many documents he had studied and how he had found the evidence "compelling."

Robert Sheldon, Chairman of the Select Committee and a personal friend of Sir Gordon Downey, read out a list of Fayed employees and *Guardian* journalists, and asked the House, 'Can all these people be lying?'

I had to muster all my self control not to shout back, 'Of course they are, you idiot!' But I managed to keep stumm.

One of the most impressive speakers was left-wing Labour MP Tony Benn. Notwithstanding his assumption that Neil Hamilton was as guilty as Downey had stated, he gave a passionate speech trashing the whole inquiry process. Tory MP Tom King also stood up and suggested that perhaps the previous Government hadn't appreciated quite how big an issue this was going to be when they decided to appoint Sir Gordon Downey. I took that be Parliamentary coded language for "Downey had been found to be well out of his depth."

Ann Widdecombe and Quentin Davies, the two Select Committee Members who had rejected Downey's findings, were standing by the Speaker's chair, trying to attract the Speaker's attention. But Betty Boothroyd sent them back to their benches like naughty schoolchildren and ignored them for the rest of the debate. But whenever they contrived an intervention they let rip like tigers.

Robert Sheldon, who I'm ashamed to say is the MP for the constituency in which I was born, even reneged on his earlier undertaking to Ann Widdecombe not to represent her abstention on Downey as an endorsement. Widdecombe was incandescent. 'Let me put it plainly on the record,' she blasted. 'I do *not* endorse the Commissioner's findings.'

Guardian stooge Dale Campbell-Savours rambled on about the 1990 Members' Interests Committee's investigation into Sir Michael Grylls' commission payments from Ian Greer, and how that Committee had been "meddled with." What he didn't let on was the fact that he was the very engine of the whole "cash for questions" affair in the first place. It was he who used that same Members' Interests investigation to try and substantiate Andrew Roth's and *The Guardian*'s theory about Greer's commissions, a theory that he knew full-well had been destroyed by the circumstances surrounding Tim Smith's resignation.

Quentin Davies jumped to his feet more than once to intervene. He eventually succeeded. 'I am afraid that the Hon. Gentleman is trying to divert attention from the subject under discussion because he is worried about the role he played on that Committee.'

Campbell-Savours tried to lay down a smoke-screen of smears against Davies. Davies was having none of it. Jumping to his feet once more, he proclaimed, 'The Hon. Gentleman's emotional attack on me may have something to do with the fact that he put down 55 Early Day Motions on behalf of Mr Al Fayed and vociferously and vituperatively tried to prevent me from calling Mr Al Fayed before the Committee!'

Campbell-Savours had no answer to that charge.

As the debate progressed, both Teresa Gorman and Gerald Howarth came over to ask me questions. Subsequently, Gerald gave a rousingly-supportive speech for Neil. It was a fine and moving address, the *cri de coeur* of a true friend. But if only he had read our report thoroughly he could have waved specific *Guardian* documents in the air and denounced them as forgeries and accused *The Guardian* editor and his staff of a cover-up. He could have done some real damage and grabbed the headlines for the following day. I was impressed by the extent of his support, but disappointed by the lost opportunity. I was also enraged by the amount of uninformed waffle I had had to listen to from those who believed Downey had pronounced some great truth.

One of the worst was Labour Committee Member Tom Levitt, MP for High Peak, who rambled on interminably, praising Sir Gordon Downey for his "thoroughness," the "14,000 pages of documents" that he said Downey had considered, and Downey's conclusion that the evidence that Neil Hamilton had taken Fayed's cash was "compelling." Yawn-inducing.

When the debate broke up, the MPs started to leave the chamber and the door behind me was unlocked. I left the chamber myself and awaited Levitt in the Members' lobby. I thought to myself, considering his forthright views, I'm going to see just how much this man knows. Levitt came through, and I approached him.

'Mr Levitt,' I said, standing with a copy of our report cradled in my right forearm, 'I couldn't help hearing your speech and your praise for Sir Gordon Downey, the 14000 pages of documents he examined, and the compelling evidence.' He smiled, obviously thinking what a good speech it must have been. 'I'd be interested to know, what did *you* find compelling about the evidence?'

His face started to redden, his Adam's apple disappeared into his shirt collar actually causing his tie to move forward. Then he cast his eyes downwards to see our report. 'You're the journalist that's written this report, aren't you?' he accused.

'Yes, I am,' I replied.

'Fascinating!' he exclaimed, and with that he turned on his heels and stamped off. What was it Baroness Turner had said about the tail wagging the dog?

Teresa Gorman and Gerald Howarth came through. 'Good Speech Gerald,' I said.

'Come on, lets go for a drink,' he said, and so the three of us navigated our way to one of the bars. Tony Banks, the Labour MP and Sports Minister, was seated at a table by the door as we walked in. When he saw Teresa he recoiled and made a sign of the cross against his chest, in mock-fear-of-Dracula-style. We laughed at Banks' good humoured send-up.

As we sat there chatting, the performances by Widdecombe and Davies came up in the conversation. Teresa Gorman told me that they had both been heavily influenced by our report in their refusal to accept Downey's findings. It seemed that we were beginning to gather some powerful supporters, but still not enough to push the issue onto the front pages. After half hour or so, we split up and I went back to my hotel in Paddington.

It was an exhilarating evening to round off a long and frustrating day.

17

The Heat Goes On

THE NEXT MORNING I DROVE ROUND TO HOLLOWAY TO THE home of James Heartfield, the only national journalist to have interviewed Neil personally during the period when the "cash for questions" issue was all over the front pages.

He was sent to question Neil at his flat in London by *Living Marxism*. Despite its pejorative title, *LM*, as it prefers to be known, had been following Neil's treatment by the media. Heartfield ended up writing a very positive piece about Neil, and I arranged to meet him to provide a full de-briefing on all our research.

Once settled down, I went through some of the mountains of evidence, including John Mullin's (forged) computer note. He read it studiously, and when he came to the "brown paper bag" entry the one we concluded was a forgery he drew my attention to something that had escaped Malcolm and I.

'It breaks into prose at the end,' he exclaimed. 'All the other entries read like shorthand, which is what you'd expect of a transcription of a shorthand note. But this one reads like a grammatical sentence.'

I looked at it again. He was right! Another discordant note to join the long, long list.

In all, I spent three hours with James, before getting in the car to drive home. But no sooner had I started the engine when my mobile phone began to burble. It was Stephen Glover, a renowned journalist, currently with the *Daily Mail*, who was working for the *Spectator* at the time.

'We're interested in this report of yours,' Glover said. 'Would you like to talk about it?'

'Absolutely,' I said. 'I'm in London right now, if that's convenient. Shall I come to your office?'

"Sure. I'm in Oxford right now but I can meet you there later this afternoon. Can you be there for five o'clock?'

'I'll be there.'

When I arrived with my bag full of documents, I was escorted up to editor Frank Johnson's panelled office, where I unpacked all my documents while Frank handed me a glass of chilled white wine. About fifteen minutes later, Stephen Glover showed up. They proceeded to grill me on the case and then on my own background.

It turned out that their interest arose out of an article in the *Spectator* by Paul Johnson, headlined, "Is Nice Mr Rusbridger Britain's Biggest Porkie?" In it he gave examples of some lies that Rusbridger had told about Johnson over the years.

Johnson was prompted to write it after *The Guardian* dishonestly reported the Standards Committee as having endorsed Downey 9-0, whilst all the other papers reported faithfully that on "cash for questions," the committee did not endorse Downey, being split 7-2 (thanks to Quentin Davies and Ann Widdecombe). A deliberate error by *The Guardian*? A Freudian slip?

I immediately fired off a copy of our report to Johnson, delighted that someone else had rumbled Rusbridger, albeit from an altogether opposite direction. I also sent a copy to Frank Johnson, the editor of the *Spectator*. Paul Johnson had sent his copy into the *Spectator* as well, so they had two copies sitting in the office.

'Do you have any skeletons in your own cupboard?' Glover asked.

I took a breath. 'Yes,' I admitted. 'In 1990 I was importing cars from America and I undervalued many of them to reduce the duties payable. I was cautioned and had to pay the back duties and a small penalty. Everything is paid off now.'

'Does *The Guardian* know about this?'

'They're bound to find out, once they know we're onto them.'

Johnson raised his immaculate eyebrows. 'And you're still willing to do it?'

'Oh yes, I've never made a secret of it. As soon as Ian Greer warned me that they planned to smear us I telephoned the Customs officer who carried out the enquiry. He told me that as far as he's concerned It was a routine offence and I co-operated fully.'

'What are your politics?'

'Usually Conservative, but I didn't vote Tory at the last election.'

'Why not?'

'The Tory candidate was pro-European integration. I'm not a Federalist.'

'What are the politics of your colleague, Malcolm Keith-Hill?'

'Left wing,' I said flatly. 'Very.'

'Okay, let's hear your evidence.'

Pacing up and down the office as I talked, I launched into a detailed dissertation on why we were sure there had been a cover-up. I referred them from one document to another, like Perry Mason on his day in court, interjecting my display with ironic side-swipes at Downey and Rusbridger. It was a good performance, I was flying.

'You'd make a good QC,' Frank Johnston quipped drily, when I finally sat down.

'I know this case inside out,' I said.

They exchanged looks.

'We can tell you do,' Glover said with a grin.

By the time I was back in the Montego, my papers in the boot, I felt good. If I could get an organisation like the *Spectator* on my side, as well as someone like *Living Marxism*, I had a chance. It seemed ironic that two publications at the extreme ends of the political spectrum could both see the truth, when the mass in the middle couldn't.

Two weeks later Glover put the story out in the *Spectator*, using our report as source material, suggesting that what was really needed after Downey was a "real" inquiry into the Hamilton Affair. Like most of his work it was a masterclass example of measured yet devastating prose. But he didn't, alas, refer to *The Guardian's* cover-up.

As I headed back home through the London traffic, I vowed that I would carry on producing and explaining the evidence until he did.

Around this time Malcolm's involvement in the story started to recede. Whereas I was on a "mission," and cared little about the debts I was running up with my parents as long as they felt the same way, Malcolm had real financial worries. We had been working on the case for over six months without pay. He decided he would have to return to his home in Brazil and re-start his career there as a documentary film-maker.

'I'm sorry, mate,' he said, 'but I can't keep hanging around hoping someone is going to commission this programme. I've got to go home and earn some money.' Accordingly, over the next few weeks he was busy tying up the loose ends as he prepared to leave England.

While Malcolm busied himself, I carried on with my lobbying of the media. In early December I went back to Jane Corbin at "Panorama" and we sat down together, this time with her producer, Thea Guest, for a whole two hours or more studying the evidence. Both acknowledged that we had identified and provided enough evidence to make a *prima facie* case for a massive cover-up at *The Guardian*. But in the end their new editor decided the story was too heavily political, and Jane passed it to the BBC's offices at Millbank, to the department responsible for political documentaries.

A couple of days later I rendezvoused with Malcolm at the office for a cup of tea and chat about what we had achieved to date. He was due to fly out of Manchester the following morning at 4.00 am. We had come a long way together. We had started off as strangers, coming from two opposite standpoints, with one common belief: that the media had not done the Right Thing in the "cash for questions" affair. From the early days when neither of us had understood anything, we had put together the jigsaw to reveal the truth. We had become almost like brothers. He asked me to look after his Fiesta until his planned return to England the following summer.

It was an emotional parting. We felt we had been through a lot together, like a couple of comrades in arms parting before the outcome of the war is finally decided. From now on, I was on my own.

I carried on researching related aspects to the affair and writing up my findings. Then, on January 20 1998, I donned suit and tie and journeyed wearily southwards again to meet with yet another set of programme-makers.

'We want to do a documentary on how standards in

Parliament have changed,' they told me, 'since the "cash for questions" affair.'

I shook my head. 'But that suggests that you believe standards were bad and have improved or not improved. That's not where I'm coming from. Our research shows that the whole "cash for questions" affair was a media stunt.'

It was obvious that they had obtained most of their information from Fayed, Fayed's employees and/or *Guardian* journalists, and made up their minds, along with most of the population, that Neil was a liar.

'You should hear what Fayed's legal adviser, Royston Webb, has to say about Hamilton,' the woman said.

'You mean the same Royston Webb who, in 1994, said he knew nothing about MPs being paid, but who, for the Downey Inquiry, said that he knew that Fayed had been paying Neil Hamilton all along? You mean the Royston Webb who Fayed is reported to be paying a £1 million retainer, spread over five years up to September 2001, for no discernible reason? Is this the Royston Webb you're talking about?'

'But how can you believe someone like Neil Hamilton?' she asked.

'Easy,' I replied. 'I've researched this story for the past eight months and I know what I'm talking about. If you think Hamilton's a liar, give me one example of him lying.'

She didn't. But there was obviously no point in me hanging around.

Another wasted meeting. But before setting off, I also made use of my trip to set up an appointment with Ambrose Evans-Pritchard, one of *Daily Telegraph's* top investigative journalists. We went down to a pub on the quayside at Canary Wharf and I ran through my spiel again. By the end of lunch he seemed interested, and so I gave him a copy of our report to digest, without any expectation that I would hear further from him.

Then, right out of the blue, a few days later, Evans-Pritchard called to tell me he was about to leave for America to follow up the Clinton sex scandal.

'I've read your report, Jonathan and I think you've made an good case. As soon as I get back I'll need to satisfy myself first by going through the evidence. If it checks out we'll go for *The Guardian*. We'll ask some awkward questions.'

He sounded as if he meant it.

But by the time he returned to London, his editor had decided to put the story on hold. Further proof that newspapers are reluctant to stick it to one another.

Perhaps the problem is that once this story comes to the surface, every editor in Fleet Street, even the one who exposes the conspiracy, will be discredited or at least be embarrassed for never having asked Neil for his side of the story. And even though the BBC in Manchester reported the story neutrally, the BBC nationally would not gain much credit. Any prominent person accused of wrongdoing is entitled to a fair hearing, yet no such right was ever accorded Neil Hamilton.

But there were some hopeful signs from unlikely quarters. Three days later, on January 23 1998, the *Mirror* broke the story that Martin Bell, the ex-BBC reporter who ousted Neil Hamilton on an anti-corruption platform, had benefited from £9,400 of legal advice that was paid for by the Labour and Liberal Democrat parties, but which he had not registered. Bell gave notice of a Press conference in Knutsford that lunchtime to answer the Mirror's charges.

This gave me an idea. In the previous two months Bell had been showing increasing contrition. Since winning the election, he had progressively modified his stance from "anti-corruption" to "behaviour unbecoming of an MP." Notwithstanding that his "unbecoming behaviour" charges were concocted by *The Guardian* from dishonestly interpreting facts and events, Bell had been saying some quite supportive things about Neil in the press and on television.

For example, in an article by Bell in the *Daily Mail* on 19 November 1997 titled: "Neil has been shabbily treated," he challenged the lack of appeals procedure. Then, on 3 December 1997 in the *Northwich Guardian*, Martin Bell wrote another positive piece titled: "Justice? Neil deserved better." Leaving aside the fact that Bell's piece began: "It is possible to arrive at the right destination and yet have doubts about the road that got you there," which implied that he agreed with Downey's verdict, it was very uplifting to see him end his piece with his most vocal support ever for his former adversary: "But it seemed that Mr Hamilton was abandoned, in his own eloquent words, to a 'lifetime of opprobrium and unemployment.' That is a harsh sentence. There has to be more than justice. There has to be *manifest* justice."

So, as it was manifest justice that I also had in mind, I drove to Knutsford to attend his Press conference. I entered his small constituency office, pushed through reporters and, in the full glare of live Sky TV cameras, handed him a copy of our report. In a clear voice, in front of millions of witnesses, and reporters from all the main media organisations, I told him of our conclusions that Neil Hamilton had been a victim of corrupt journalism at *The Guardian*. Bell accepted the report and promised to read it.

But though our report contained copious detailed evidence that Neil Hamilton had been a victim of a terrible miscarriage of justice, and despite living across the street from my parents in Great Budworth (where I moved to complete my book), Bell has not used our research to take up Hamilton's case in Parliament, nor has he taken up my invitation to view the evidence or request a debriefing.

I thought this was rather odd. But like all conundrums, there's usually an answer to be found somewhere. I found one answer in the Guardian Group newspaper *The Manchester Evening News*, where Bell stated in his column on 16 July 1997:

As far as I am concerned, the Downey Report is the end of the matter, leaving little more to be said.

I found another answer in a videotape of BBC NW television news, recorded on 3 July 1997, when Downey's report was published:

'The people of Tatton having spoken on the first of May,' Bell said, 'and now, the Downey report having come out, I really think that's the, that's the end of it – and I would hope that we can put it behind us now.' And when asked to comment on Hamilton's protestations of innocence, he said: 'I think it's time for Mr Hamilton to return to private life and for me to get on with being a member of Parliament for Tatton.'

Martin Bell has hardly lifted a finger to help Neil Hamilton, and it may be that the above declaration reflects his true opinion, rather than his photo-opportunity promise of help outside the Commons and his noble gestures of support in the press, months later.

After our report had been with him for a week without any acknowledgement, I decided that there was only one thing for it.

I would have to flush out Rusbridger and his corrupt journalists with a head-on approach.

On Friday 30 January 1998 I fed the letter to Alan Rusbridger into my fax machine and punched out his number. I was going to offer him and his fellow journalists a chance to answer our questions in a video-recorded interview before I published the latest version of the report and started work on this book. It would be obvious to him that we were going in for the kill. It was a direct challenge to the cover-up's orchestrator and to the powerful global empire that employed him. It was David against Goliath.

I copied my letter to Lord Wakeham of the Press Complaints Commission, suggesting that it would be appropriate if he nominated someone to be present throughout the proposed interviews. Rusbridger would have no choice, he would *have* to respond.

The single sheet of paper was gobbled up by the fax machine. There was no backing down now. That'll give him something to think about over the weekend, I thought to myself.

The following Monday his two-page faxed reply came through. He refused the interviews, on the grounds of my "ethical standards," and because of "the torrent of malicious lies about *The Guardian*" that we had written in our report. He invited me to submit my questions in writing, presumably so he would have time to concoct answers to the anomalies we had identified in his and his colleagues' evidence. He signed off by suggesting that we were "being covertly funded by one of Mr Hamilton's supporters." (I fell about laughing). At least that was a different line from that of his Political Editor, Michael White, who had been putting it about that we were being paid by Tiny Rowland.

I faxed back a response the following day with a two-page blast, pointing out that there were no intentionally false statements in our report, but that as a draft document, it might, of course, contain the occasional typo. I invited him to highlight any he had spotted. As for being paid by anyone, I stated formally that not only had we not received a penny contribution from any source, I personally was seriously in debt as a result of our investigation. I repeated my request for interviews with himself and six other *Guardian* journalists.

Rusbridger's three-page reply came through by fax the next

day. This time he questioned the notice we gave *The Guardian* prior to releasing our report to the Select Committee and the press a few months earlier, accusing me of telling a "direct lie" in my earlier letter. He also sought to make an issue of my describing our report as a "draft," claiming that I had a "reckless disregard for the truth."

Interestingly, he also suggested our report contained an allegation that John Mullin lied. This was a figment of his own duplicity. It was a bravura performance from the master of disingenuousness.

It was time to do the business, so I fired off a five-page cannonade of chain shot:

5 February, 1998

Alan Rusbridger
Guardian
Farringdon Road
London EC1R 3ER

By Fax Transmission 0171 239 9997

Dear Mr. Rusbridger,
Thank you for your letter of 4 February 1998. You state that Peter Preston states that he did not receive our fax requesting interviews with himself, David Hencke and John Mullin. We have a fax transmission sheet to prove that a fax was sent, and the fax itself proves that a request was made to Peter Preston for interviews with David Hencke and John Mullin. It was sent to fax number 0171 713 4225 at 16 38 hrs on 29 9 97. The transmission took 52 seconds for the one sheet, and was successful.

In addition, a number of telephone calls were made to the Guardian by my colleague Malcolm Keith-Hill chasing up our request, but no response was forthcoming.

You refer to our draft report of 21 10 97, and a list of our conclusions from pages 51/52. Your summary is not accurate. Importantly, this summary was preceded by a qualifying proposition. For the understanding of others, the full extract is reproduced below. Incidentally, this list does not appear in this form in our current report, though we stand by what was written earlier.

Conclusions

From a careful scrutiny of all the evidence relating to Hamilton's interview on the Terrace in 1993 and other documentary evidence, it is clear that Hencke, Mullin and Preston had no knowledge whatsoever in July 1993 of any allegations that Hamilton had taken Fayed's cash or gift vouchers.

The only evidence which The Guardian cites to substantiate their assertion that a specific 'cash for questions' allegation had existed against Hamilton before September 21st 1994 is in the form of notes made on a computer – which can be fabricated without any possibility of forensic detection.

And if both the cash allegations and the gift voucher allegations did not exist at the time of Hamilton's interview, there can be only one logical conclusion to be drawn:

Journalist of the Year David Hencke, his former editor Peter Preston and current editor Alan Rusbridger conspired and knowingly allowed fabricated evidence to be put forward. They did this in an attempt to show that allegations which Fayed later invented after September 21st 1994 had an earlier history dating back to July 1993.

Specifically:

1. Peter Preston lied in his witness statement for the libel trial and lied when he testified before Downey, when he stated that: in his only meeting with Fayed prior to Hencke and Mullin's interview with Hamilton, Fayed had stated that he had paid Neil Hamilton cash and gift vouchers to ask questions in Parliament.

2. Peter Preston lied in his witness statement for the libel trial and lied when he testified before Downey, when he stated that: he had told David Hencke that, in his only meeting with Fayed prior to Hencke and Mullin's interview with Hamilton, Fayed had stated that he had paid Neil Hamilton cash and gift vouchers to ask questions in Parliament.

3. David Hencke lied in his witness statement for the libel trial and lied when he testified before Downey, when he stated that: Peter Preston had told him that, in his interview with Fayed, Fayed had stated that he had paid Neil Hamilton cash and gift vouchers to ask questions in Parliament.

4. David Hencke lied in his witness statement for the libel trial and lied when he testified before Downey, when he stated that: during the interview on the Commons terrace in July 1993, Neil Hamilton had been asked by either himself or John Mullin about taking cash from Fayed to ask questions in Parliament.

5. Peter Preston or David Hencke or Alan Rusbridger or another person fabricated evidence which was represented to have been made by John Mullin vis: 'John Mullin's computer note' which they purport to be a truthful account of the interview on the Commons terrace and which is purported to show that Neil Hamilton had been asked about taking cash from Fayed to ask questions in Parliament.

6. Peter Preston and David Hencke and Alan Rusbridger conspired and knowingly allowed fabricated evidence to be put forward by The Guardian before Sir Gordon Downey vis: 'John Mullin's computer note', which they purported to be a truthful account of the interview on the Commons terrace and which showed that Neil Hamilton had been asked in July 1993 about taking cash from Fayed to ask questions in Parliament.

7. Peter Preston and David Hencke and Alan Rusbridger conspired to misrepresent evidence vis: 'John Mullin's shorthand notes', which they purported to represent as containing a genuine response from Neil Hamilton to a proposition that Neil Hamilton had taken cash from Fayed to ask questions in Parliament.

8. Peter Preston and David Hencke and Alan Rusbridger conspired to misrepresent evidence vis: 'John Mullin's shorthand notes', which they knew to contain a response to a question other than a question that Neil Hamilton had taken cash from Fayed to ask questions in Parliament.

9. Alan Rusbridger submitted to Sir Gordon Downey evidence to his Inquiry which he knew to be false vis: David Hencke's statement; Peter Preston's statement; a witness statement purported to be the unadulterated work of John

Mullin; a computer note purported to be the unadulterated work of John Mullin.

10. Alan Rusbridger deceived Sir Gordon Downey vis: submitting to Sir Gordon Downey a statement purported to be by John Mullin without disclosing that this statement had not been available for the libel trial, which led to Sir Gordon printing this statement as a Witness Statement for the libel trial. and, if the statement and computer note purported to have been made by John Mullin are, in the future, authenticated by John Mullin as being his own un-adulterated work:

11. John Mullin lied in his statement [which Downey ascribed to David Hencke] when he stated that: during the interview on the Commons Terrace in July 1993, he had asked Neil Hamilton about taking cash from Fayed to ask questions in Parliament.

12. John Mullin made a false entry in his computer note which purported to be a truthful account of the interview on the Commons terrace and which showed that Neil Hamilton had been asked in July 1993 about taking cash from Fayed to ask questions in Parliament.

Please note that, contrary to the impression given by your letter, there are two distinct qualifying propositions: one at the head of the list and another before items 11 and 12.

Contrary to your assertion, at the time that this list was compiled in October last year, we had not drawn any conclusions about John Mullin's involvement in any un-ethical goings-on. In fact, it seemed to us that John Mullin had deliberately gone out of his way not to involve himself in giving false evidence.

For example, despite the fact that he was one of only two reporters who were initially involved in the Guardian's investigation, Mullin gave no statement for the libel trial, nor did he appear before Downey for oral examination, nor as we have since established did he authorise a statement which you falsely presented to the Downey Inquiry as being his affidavit.

In this regard, the statement which you represented to Sir Gordon on 19 February 1997 as being John Mullin's [sworn] affidavit was confirmed by Sir Gordon four months after his Inquiry was published as being neither sworn, nor written, nor even signed by John Mullin. Sir Gordon's letter of 7 October 1997 to Neil Hamilton confirms that this statement was actually prepared for John Mullin by someone else, but that John Mullin had not authorised it.

In other words, this document had about as much evidential value to the Inquiry as a book on fly-fishing by J R Hartley, but your misrepresentation of it ensured that it was pivotal to Sir Gordon's conclusions.

Even though Sir Gordon has now stated that John Mullin has recently authorised this document as being true, I am unsure as to what John Mullin's position is. This is why I would like to ask him some questions.

Moving on, you assert that I am guilty of " a weasel step to describe this document [our earlier report] *as being a <u>draft</u> document" and you contend that my reasoning for doing so is "laughable".*

According to the Oxford Dictionary (ninth edition), 'draft' in this context is defined as: 'a preliminary written version of a speech, document etc.' Given that this earlier document carried the words (Draft Document) on the front page; and given that our report has since grown from 48,000 words to 78,000 words, I am at a loss as to why you would try and make a contentious issue out of this. It was and is a preliminary written version of our current report.

Regarding the allegations that you make against me, I am perfectly happy to answer any questions you and your staff may have, in any amount of interviews you may wish to hold with me. All I ask is that I am provided with the same facility to interview you and your staff.

However I am not willing to give you my questions in writing. It is certain, as our correspondence over these last few days shows only too clearly, that whatever you say in reply will give rise to one or more other questions. We could go on like this forever, and we are both busy people. Also, I wish to learn first-hand what you and your staff's immediate responses are to my questions. I do not wish you to be able to confer with one another beforehand.

Once more, I reiterate my request for interviews with David Hencke; David Leigh; John Mullin; David Pallister;

Peter Preston; and Michael White. I also repeat my sugges-
tion that someone nominated by the PCC should attend. Of
course, it is entirely up to the PCC whether they would
agree to so doing.

If you prefer, I am perfectly content to have other
journalists standing in instead, and I would not object to
many journalists from the Guardian such as Simon Hoggart
or Andrew Rawnsley being nominated.

Whatever you allege about my motives and ethics, what
cannot be denied is that I now am giving you the oppor-
tunity to answer questions which have been raised by
our investigation. I cannot see any validity in the reasons
you have put forward so far for not agreeing to inter-
views.

For your information, my book on the 'cash for questions'
affair Trial by Conspiracy will be published later this
year. It is my view that you should not deny access to
your staff thus preventing them from addressing certain
issues.

If, like me, you have nothing to hide, then you have
nothing to fear from answering a few questions. Indeed, on
31 October 1997 you were personally responsible for
launching a major PR conference in Manchester, whose
main theme was, er, 'accountability.'

Unless you agree to my request for interviews, I do not see
any point in further correspondence between us.

Yours sincerely,
Jonathan Hunt.

c.c. The Right Honourable The Lord Wakeham

I think it would be fair to say that Rusbridger would have
acquired a good understanding of my position.

Over the following weeks I spent most of my time either at
Companies House or at Central Library, in Manchester, building
up a picture of *The Guardian's* power and influence in the media
(more of this later). Then, on March 6th, I went down to
London to meet Baroness Turner.

The Baroness and I had been invited to address the Politics
Society of St John's College, Southsea, for an evening billed:

"Sleaze and the Press." Southsea is where Neil's family settled after upping sticks from South Wales, and Neil taught politics and economics there in the mid-seventies upon graduating from Aberystwyth University.

On my way down in the train I received a call on the mobile from Ambrose Evans-Pritchard. I got up and took the call between carriages, which was noisy but at least private. He was doing some more research on our analysis of the evidence. He came at me with the most direct of questions: 'Downey says the evidence that Hamilton took Fayed's cash is compelling. What do you say to that?'

'It's very simple. Downey had forensic accountants crawling all over both Christine and Neil Hamilton's financial records, including building society accounts, credit card accounts and bank accounts, going all the way back to when Hamilton first gave Fayed his support. Downey found no evidence whatsoever of any cash payments or changes in spending patterns, nor did he find any income that could not be accounted for. Similarly, Downey found no evidence whatsoever of gift voucher payments. Downey's compelling evidence punch-line was based *exclusively* on the testimony of Fayed, Royston Webb, Bozek, Bond and Bromfield.

'Only Fayed claimed to have direct knowledge of gift voucher payments, which Iris Bond corroborated with hearsay evidence. Downey dismissed the gift voucher allegation on grounds of insufficient evidence. Royston Webb's hearsay evidence corroborating the cash allegation can be dismissed because in 1994 he told Ian Greer that he had no knowledge of MPs being paid. Greer taped the conversation so he can prove that Webb lied to the Inquiry.

'Under questioning for the inquiry, Bromfield testified to giving Smith brown envelopes, but Smith, who admitted receiving more from Fayed than Fayed alleged and so undoubtedly told the truth, denied he had ever taken a brown envelope from Bromfield. So Bromfield's evidence can be dismissed.

'That leaves one person, Alison Bozek. Bozek is the only person who testified to having a direct hand in paying cash. However, she was castigated as a liar by Francesca Pollard and Christoph Bettermann, both of whom wrote to Downey, but whom he did not call to give evidence.

'So, what it boils down to is this: in the eyes of Sir Gordon

Downey, the difference between *compelling* evidence and *insufficient* evidence is the evidence of one person who at least two independent people say is a liar.'

'Thanks for that,' Ambrose said. 'It was very useful. I'll give you a ring next week.'

A few days later, the March issue of *Living Marxism* magazine hit the streets, carrying James Heartfield's provocative feature on our investigation as their lead story. It was titled "Cash, Questions and Answers." (For those interested this is on *LM's* website: http://www.informinc.co.uk/LM/LM108/ LM108_Hamilton.html)

Heartfield zeroed in on the central issues: did Fayed make his allegations in 1993, as *The Guardian* claimed, or in September 1994, at the time of the European Court of Human Rights ruling? Did Hencke and Mullin put a specific "cash-from-Fayed" allegation to Neil Hamilton in 1993? Is John Mullin's computer note, which happens to be the only document to substantiate this claim, a forgery?

Heartfield told me later that he had been informed by a *Guardian* insider that the article caused a maelstrom at their offices, with much gnashing of teeth into the night. *The Independent's* "Pandora's Box" gossip-column reported all sorts of rackets and power-struggles down at Farringdon Road, but whether they were related or not, I couldn't say.

Heartfield's article had other important ramifications. Firstly, it worried Rusbridger and his poisonous colleagues enough to cause him to let loose *The Guardian's* Head of Legal affairs, Siobahn Butterworth, to try and frighten me (and my publisher) off. The second effect is that it aroused the interest once more of Stephen Glover of the *Daily Telegraph*.

The first missive from Butterworth followed the disingenuous style of her boss. She rambled on for a bit about the lack of notice we gave *The Guardian* before we published our report in October. Then she made noises about denying our allegations. She finished off by making other noises about reserving their position.

'You can get up at six o'clock in the morning and put a few towels down for all I care,' I thought to myself. And so Ms Butterworth became the recipient of another broadside from the city that gave birth to their newspaper.

11 March, 1998

Siobhain Butterworth
Head of Legal Affairs
Guardian
Farringdon Road
London EC1R 3ER

Dear Ms. Butterworth,
Thank you for your letter of 9 March 1998.

I would like to set out my response to the points that you raise. Firstly, you state that my report of October 1997, which was based on research by me and my colleague, Malcolm Keith-Hill, contained the most defamatory allegations against four Guardian journalists. You also state that, in the six months prior to publishing this report, we had not made any attempt to contact three of them.

This is ground which is covered comprehensively by my letters to Alan Rusbridger of 3 and 5 February 1998. You state that you have read these, yet you continue to bring this issue to the fore. The only purpose you can have of regurgitating this is to draw focus away from the fact that Alan Rusbridger now shies away from giving interviews on the grounds that 'I have shut the stable door after the horse has bolted', to paraphrase your own words.

This will not do. Our earlier draft report was circulated only to a few dozen people in the Press and Parliament and was in any event, as I have stated, after our requests for interviews went unheeded. Your argument that this is realistic justification for Alan Rusbridger's current refusal to give interviews, prior to my book being published, is a specious one.

My book will be available to the public and will, in all likelihood, be printed in many thousands. It will contain the most serious allegations ever printed against a British newspaper editor and a number of his staff. It is, therefore, of paramount importance that the accused parties have the opportunity before publication to explain a number of anomalies in the Guardian's reporting of the 'cash for questions' issue, and further anomalies in the Guardian's

*submissions before Sir Gordon Downey, about which the
allegations against them are centred.*

*However, in the absence of any consent from the
Guardian to give interviews, as far as I am concerned it
then becomes just as important that I can demonstrate
my many attempts to secure interviews prior to the book
being published. This being such an opportunity, I repeat
my request to interview David Hencke; David Leigh;
John Mullin; David Pallister; Peter Preston; and Michael
White.*

*Whilst I am on this subject, I would also like to register a
new request for an interview with Guardian journalist Jamie
Wilson, on his role in the production of the 'Dispatches'
programme on 'cash for questions', about which Neil
Hamilton has recently issued a libel writ against Channel 4,
Fulcrum Productions and Mohamed Fayed.*

*You repeat Alan Rusbridger's offer to receive my ques-
tions in writing. This is not acceptable to me, for the reasons
I have already given in my letter of 5 February 1997. So
there may be no misunderstanding, I believe that there exists
the strong possibility that Alan Rusbridger and certain of his
staff will concoct all manner of false explanations to my
questions if I were to do so.*

*You may rest assured that my publisher is aware of the
Guardian's concern about the allegations contained in early
drafts of our report. You may also rest assured that the
allegations in my book will be no less severe.*

*For your information, they will be along the lines of: A
major conspiracy involving the fabrication and misrepresentation of evidence, and the giving of false testimony both
orally and in writing to the Downey Inquiry, between Alan
Rusbridger, Peter Preston and David Hencke, to create the
false impression that Mohamed Fayed made his cash and
gift voucher allegations against Neil Hamilton in July 1993,
rather than at the time that the European Court of Human
Rights rejected Mohamed Fayed's application to have the
damning DTI report quashed, which was in September
1994.*

*The book will show that Fayed made his cash and gift
voucher allegations against Neil Hamilton at the time of
the ECHR ruling out of spite, because, as Minister for*

Corporate Affairs at the DTI, Neil Hamilton was perfectly positioned to help Fayed, but did not.

No doubt more 'new evidence' and 'new corroborative testimony' could be produced by the Guardian to support its contention that the cash and gift voucher allegations against Neil Hamilton existed in 1993. My publisher and I expect such 'new evidence' to be produced. If this happens, then as far as we are concerned, what has been done so far by the Guardian will merely be compounded.

Finally, you state that I admit that our earlier draft report of October 1997 contains errors, which I have made no attempt to rectify. I stated no such thing. I actually stated that, as it was a draft report, it might contain the occasional error, and I also invited Alan Rusbridger to point out any errors he has identified. As it happens he has not, so far, identified any.

A small point, but an important one.

Yours sincerely,

Jonathan Hunt.

c.c. Lord Wakeham
Alan Rusbridger

Meanwhile, Stephen Glover had been reading Heartfield's article and decided that there was enough in it to warrant an airing of our investigation in the *Daily Telegraph*. I was working in Manchester Central Library when the mobile rang.

'I'm just putting an article to bed for tomorrow's *Telegraph*,' he said. 'Tell me, why would *The Guardian* fabricate documents to show that Fayed made his allegations in 1993, instead of 1994 as you say?'

We had a short, too short, conversation, in which I attempted to explain the story. It was akin to trying to explain the history of the Second World War in 4 minutes flat.

Glover's piece came out the next day. It was the lead article on the editorial page, very critical of the process that had done Neil down, and, for the first time for a major national paper, mentioned our investigation and our radical conclusion that there had been a cover-up at *The Guardian*. But the impact of the last point was largely negated when he went on to say that he knew *The Guardian* people personally and couldn't imagine anything like that happening. And there was worse to come. Commenting on Rusbridger's description of our report as "a work of malevolent fantasy," Glover said:

"I think that much of Mr Hunt's report is off the wall, though I see no reason to impugn his integrity. He simply allows his imagination to run riot"

I could hardly believe what I was reading. We had solved with solid evidence a highly complex story, exposing how Andrew Roth's/*The Guardian's* conspiracy theory about Greer's commissions dovetailed with Fayed's false allegations that Greer paid Smith, thus resulting in the 'confirmation' (as *The Guardian* would have seen it) of their theory. This led in turn to the publishing of Hencke's original article.

Stephen Glover is one of this country's most cerebral journalists. To have been written off by him in those few words was ten times as bad as an infinite number of brick-bats from Farringdon Road.

I was furious. By now I had been on the project for nearly a year, and had been junked as a lunatic on five minutes' explanation. I phoned him up the moment I read it and left a acerbic message on his answerphone.

Next, I phoned the *Telegraph* and spoke to Frances Banks in an effort to get hold of Charles Moore and demand to know when he planned to let Ambrose Pritchard-Evans off the leash. Ms Banks was very protective of Moore.

'What's Charles Moore holding back for?' I protested down the line. 'Is it because he can't believe it happened? The Holocaust happened, yet he can't believe that a newspaper editor and his staff can be involved in a cover-up? During the war the Jews were ringing the BBC for years telling them about the Trains Heading East and nobody believe them either, but *that* happened. Nobody believed that the *Titanic* could go down on its maiden voyage, and *that* happened. What's the big deal about a handful of corrupt journalists running a major newspaper?'

'Why don't you write him a letter?' she suggested.

'Okay, I'll write a letter. Thanks, Frances.' I tried not to slam down the phone too hard.

I then rang Frank Johnson at the *Spectator* and demanded that he let me write an article.

'You've got it,' he agreed.

'When do you want it by?'

'Two weeks.'

Having subsided a little, I sent Glover a fax telling him that I did appreciate his bringing the matter into the public arena, and apologising for what I had said into his answering machine. I then sat down and penned a letter of response to the *Telegraph*, which I then faxed off. Ambrose rang up later to say that he had read the faxed letter and thought it was "measured" and good (it was printed in the Letters page a few days later).

'We're going to have to get involved in this,' Ambrose said. 'We can't just sit around. I'll do something on it but we can't simply attack *The Guardian*, we'll have to introduce the story sideways. We'll do a profile on you and Malcolm to start off.'

'Well, as long as it's more about the evidence than about us.'

'Leave it with me.'

I left the office that evening feeling encouraged. Perhaps we were getting somewhere at last, I hoped for the umpteenth time. When I got home I found a message from Glover apologising for his article. He obviously hadn't seen my second fax when he left the message, so our apologies had crossed.

My article for the *Spectator* was about the influence that the news agencies "news wires" had on the press. Frank said he liked it, but didn't publish it in the end as he didn't have room. At least I had got it off my chest and felt a tad better for that. It was like pouring out the contents of a broken heart in a letter to an ex-lover that ends up in the bin after second thought about sending it.

Back in the library the following Wednesday afternoon, my phone trilled again and I hastily silenced it under the disapproving gaze of other readers and researchers.

It was Ambrose. 'I'm just putting this article on you and Malcolm to bed . . .'

Under the glares of nearby readers I nipped out into the entrance hall to continue the conversation. Ambrose read through the text of the article to me. When he'd finished he asked, 'What about Hamilton's admitted wrong-doing?'

'The only wrong-doing was Neil not registering his stay at the Ritz. If he had registered it he would have been the first MP in history ever to do such a thing. People have taken his deference to Parliament's authority and crucified him with it.'

'Okay,' he said. 'This'll probably come out tomorrow.'

It didn't. Nor the next day. It turned out that Charles Moore had blocked it after all. The mainstream media *still* wasn't ready to face the facts.

But I was at least learning to accept the repeated let-downs philosophically. And I was more determined than ever to prove that we were right, and, for that matter, that Ambrose Evan-Pritchard of the august *Daily Telegraph* and Jane Corbin of *Panorama* were right to back us.

The next day I took the tram back into Manchester and back to Central Library. Once inside I went back to my seat at the newspaper microfilm viewers and scanned the columns of *The Guardian* and the *Observer* again. As I sat there, I couldn't help thinking that there must be something, somewhere in the library that would convince even the cautious Stephen Glover. And then Malcolm's words from months earlier entered my mind:

'We need solid proof that Roth and the rest of them believed that Greer's commissions were secret payments for Parliamentary favours from MPs . . . we need solid proof that they thought Tim Smith was the third MP to receive a commission payment from Ian Greer.'

I scoured the rolls and rolls of film of *The Guardian*, looking for anything related to Roth's theory about Greer's commission payments. Then, as so often had happened in the months before, it came to me in a flash. I needed to be looking for *Roth's* words of wisdom, not Hencke's or Mullin's!

I left the microfilm viewer and went up to the inquiry desk.

'Excuse me, I would like to find out if a journalist called Andrew Roth has written anything in any periodicals in 1994. What would be the easiest way without having to go through the whole library?'

The woman led me to a computer terminal. 'We have a number of publications printed on CD-ROM, just type in the author's name and if there's anything, it will come up in a list.'

'Thank you,' I said, and settled down at the monitor. I wasn't used to the system, but soon got the hang of it, zapping around from this to that. Roth's name came up as the author of a number of articles, but none of them were any significance to me. But there was another facility to search the database using words that might be included in articles' text. So, out of curiosity, I typed in his name "Andrew Roth." Once again, a few articles came up but nothing of any significance. And then I noticed that one referred to his being a contributor to the left-wing magazine *New Statesman*.

The fact that David Hencke's 1995 witness statement relied so heavily on Ian Greer's commissions to three anonymous MPs confirms that Tim Smith's *unclear* resignation led *The Guardian* to believe that he actually resigned because Roth's theory was correct. So, if *The Guardian* still believed this in 1995, Roth would have been pretty cocky about Smith's resignation in 1994, wouldn't he? But would he be cocky enough to claim that it proved his theory? I asked myself. Would he write anything in the *New Statesman*, claiming as much?

I left the terminal and went back to the desk. 'Excuse me, but do you archive the *New Statesman*?' She told me where to look for it. And so in hope more than expectation I went to the appropriate section and pulled one of the magazine's files from 1994. I went straight to the issue published immediately after *The Guardian's* original article of 20 October 1994 on which Smith resigned, to see what Roth had written, if anything. It was dated 21 October. I scanned its pages until I came across Roth's column. There was nothing at all about Greer and his commissions, nor was there anything about Grylls, Hamilton, or Smith. Nothing. Zero. Zilch. Not a sausage.

But then the obvious struck me. Supposing that the 21 October edition of the *New Statesman* went to press before the 20 October edition of *The Guardian*?

I went to the 28 October edition and thumbed through its pages. And there it was, in all its wonderful, glorious, Technicolor black-and-white. Roth wrote:

In 1989 I first disclosed that Tory MP Sir Michael Grylls was taking an unregistered commission from Ian Greer for referring business to him . . . just before the Committee learned he had registered, the Tory majority voted for an investigation to clear Mr Grylls' name. During the investigation Ian Greer admitted that, in addition to Grylls, he had paid two other MPs. We now know for sure that Tim Smith was one.

But Tim Smith wasn't one, Mr Roth. The third MP to receive a commission was Michael Brown MP, and he had given no support to Fayed's cause at all. I read it again and again. And then again. In just a few choice words, the cocksure Roth had vindicated research by Malcolm and me that had taken us literally over a thousand hours to compile. We were right. Confirmed by the man himself. The man whose theory inspired David Hencke's article and on which David Leigh's book, *Sleaze,* was based.

Little did Roth imagine that his misplaced bragging would give the game away years later. In a few words he had destroyed any chance *The Guardian* had of concealing that their whole "cash for questions" adventure was really a gross cover-up, designed to conceal that the paper had printed an entirely false story, based on the allegations of a vengeful liar, simply because those allegations 'substantiated' their conspiracy theory. A conspiracy theory adopted from Andrew Roth.

A theory which not only was destroyed, but which we had succeeded in exposing as being destroyed.

18

Dirty Tricks PLC

I ARRIVED BACK AT THE OFFICE ON 23 MARCH TO FIND ANOTHER missive awaiting me from *The Guardian's* Head of Legal Affairs, Ms. Butterworth.

> *Thank you for your letter of 11 March, which arrived on 13 March.*
>
> *The purpose of my letter of 9 March is to put you on notice that The Guardian denies the original defamatory allegations made by you and that it does not consent to the repetition of these allegations or the publication of any further defamatory allegations.*
>
> *The letter also puts you on notice that The Guardian requires you to put any further allegations you intend to publish in writing so that The Guardian and the journalists concerned are given the right to reply.*
>
> *You refuse to put your allegations in writing because you believe that Alan Rusbridger and certain of his staff "will concoct all manner of false explanations to [your] sic questions if [you] sic were to do so." But you want to interview them. The position you have adopted is not credible and we take it as a further indication that you are not acting in good faith.*
>
> *There is little point in our litigating this matter by correspondence. You are now fully appraised of The Guardian's*

*views about the allegations you make and the way you have
conducted your investigation.*
 Yours sincerely,
 Siobhain Butterworth

This was getting bothersome. It took me a few days to collate
the necessary material and then off went a blistering broadside to
silence their guns once and for all.

27 March, 1998

Siobhain Butterworth
Head of Legal Affairs
Guardian
Farringdon Road
London EC1R 3ER

Dear Ms. Butterworth,
Thank you for your letter of 20 March 1998.
 *Thank you for notification that the Guardian denies the
allegations contained within our report (of October 1997),
and that the Guardian does not consent to the repetition or
publication of these allegations.*
 *With regard to your request that I put in writing all
further allegations to The Guardian, the most serious allegations I make are listed in my letters to Alan Rusbridger,
dated 3 and 5 February 1998, and in my letter to you, dated
11 March 1998. I may make other allegations in due course,
but the nature of these will be dependant on whether
The Guardian gives interviews, during which satisfactory
answers are provided to my questions. Ergo, as I have not,
so far, been granted interviews, I do not intend to furnish
The Guardian with any further allegations. Nor, for the
reasons I have already given, do I intend to provide written
questions.*
 *You continue to contrive to establish that I have not
acted in good faith on the single issue of the notice that
my colleague and I gave to the Guardian, prior to the
release of early versions of our report. As I have pointed out
many times, my colleague Malcolm Keith-Hill requested*

interviews with the Guardian by fax on 29.9.97 and thereafter twice by telephone shortly after. However then, as now, the Guardian stonewalled our requests.

Keith-Hill made our requests over two weeks before our earlier draft report was first presented to the Select Committee by Neil Hamilton on 14 October 1997, and over four weeks before we released a later version at our press conference in Westminster on 29 October 1997 which was attended by Guardian journalists David Hencke and David Leigh. Incidentally, despite the fact that we had not circulated our report before, David Hencke boasted that he had already obtained a copy some time earlier, "from one of [his] sources". I postulated that his source was probably his friend Alan Williams MP, who sits on the Committee. Hencke did not dispute this.

So, given that we requested interviews two weeks prior to our report first being released to the Select Committee, and given that The Guardian possessed a copy of this report in advance of our notice of its release to the Press, it is pure tosh that you assert that we have acted in bad faith.

Your proposition is even more absurd, given that Neil Hamilton and Ian Greer received no warning from The Guardian prior to it publishing, on 20 October 1994, Fayed's/The Guardian's corruption allegations against them.

In fact, the only notice that Hamilton and Greer received was by fax from David Hencke at 4.13 p.m. and 4.16 p.m. respectively on the very eve of publication, and even then there was no inkling that any article would be published imminently, least of all an article containing defamatory allegations.

For your information, the full text of Hencke's faxes to Hamilton and Greer (they were worded similarly, as was probably a third fax that was sent to Tim Smith), was:

"Dear Mr Greer [/Hamilton],
I am approaching you by fax to make sure that my enquiry is drawn to your attention. I am working on the story of your association with Mr Al-Fayed in the Harrods campaign against Lonrho. I have many of the documents involved in that campaign. If you would like to comment I can be reached on 071-239-9716 or by fax on 071-239-9997."

You will see that Hencke made no suggestion whatsoever that The Guardian was about to publish an article, least of all an article containing corruption allegations. But despite the lateness in the day that the Guardian sent these no doubt (ostensibly) to satisfy journalistic guidelines Greer responded minutes later. The full text of his reply was:

"We received your fax at 16.16 hours and have given attention to it.

We will certainly consider a response to any questions which you wish to fax to us. We would obviously expect to hear from you during normal office hours (9.00am–6.00pm)."

But despite Greer's explicit invitation to receive questions about "the story" that Hencke stated he was "working on", The Guardian ignored his offer and sent the story to press (that is, if it hadn't already been sent) to appear in the following day's paper.

In recalling these events eight months later, David Hencke stated, on 26 June 1995, in his witness statement for the libel trial:

"I cannot now locate the copies of the faxes that I sent to Tim Smith and Ian Greer but of the three facsimiles, only Ian Greer replied. I recollect that the only thing he said was that he would sue."

Of course, Hencke could (try and) excuse his grossly-false recollection on the basis that this had all happened eight months earlier. Except for the fact that, on 26 October 1994, just one week after this exchange of faxes had taken place, Hencke wrote in the Guardian:

"On Wednesday afternoon [19 October 1994] *The Guardian* put the allegations to Messrs. Greer, Smith and Hamilton. Only Mr Greer responded by denying them and threatening legal action."

You will see for yourself that Hencke did not put any such allegations to Greer at all. Ergo, it is not surprising that, completely contrary to Hencke's false statements, Greer did not deny any such allegations nor did he make any threat of legal action either. Of course, the criterion that determines whether Hencke's false statements are lies, is whether he made them intentionally.

Perhaps instead Hencke has a memory like a sieve. Or maybe he does not understand the subtle distinctions between offers of co-operation and threats of legal action; and working on a story and putting allegations.

Alan Rusbridger's and your own moralising to me is undermined further by Peter Preston's behaviour. For in his witness statement for the libel trial dated 26 June 1995, Preston recalled these events thus:

"On the morning of 19 October 1994, I remember sitting down with David Hencke and helping him write the introduction to the story that was to be published on 20 October. It was of course an important story. The lawyers took a look at it and I then agreed with David Hencke that we should send a short facsimile to Ian Greer, Neil Hamilton and Tim Smith informing them that we were about to write an article. I didn't expect any particular response to these facsimiles".

Once again, the sole criterion that determines whether Preston lied, when he falsely stated that he and Hencke had informed Hamilton and Greer that they were "about to write an article", is whether he made this false statement intentionally. It could be that Preston also has a memory like a sieve. But it would be surprising if Peter Preston attempts to excuse his false statement on the grounds that he hadn't seen Hencke's faxes, as the identification on them shows that they were sent from his own office.

As for Preston's statement that he "didn't expect any particular response", I'm not surprised, given their vague nature and timing.

Whilst we are exploring this subject of journalistic ethics, I now refer you to The Guardian's only interviews of Neil Hamilton and Ian Greer, which were conducted by David Hencke and John Mullin on 22 and 23 July 1993 respectively, over a year before the Guardian printed its article on 20 October 1994 (this article, of course, centred exclusively on Fayed's disproved allegations that Ian Greer paid Neil Hamilton and Tim Smith to ask questions in Parliament).

For your information, Hamilton and Greer have both stated that they were not confronted during their interviews with any allegations of either taking or giving 'cash for questions'. However, Peter Preston stated in his witness statement:

"All the allegations we were going to make in the article had of course been put fairly and squarely to all three protagonists 12 months before [the article being published] and they had been denied. I believed by then that all three had lied."

Although I have accumulated overwhelming evidence that Neil Hamilton was not asked about 'cash for questions' during his interview, he cannot prove 100% that he was not asked because he did not tape-record it. However Ian Greer did tape-record his interview (having secured Hencke's and Mullin's consent first). And the transcript shows that John Mullin said to Greer:

"Can I put one thing to you **which is nothing to do with Ian Greer**, which you may be able to throw light on and if you want to do that on an off-the-record basis, fine. One allegation which has been made about the House of Fraser that has to do with Ian Greer in the sense that House of Fraser are an Ian Greer client, one allegation that's been made about House of Fraser is, that in return for a Parliamentary question being asked by a friendly MP, a brown envelope stuffed with fivers would be passed to the MP."

[Note: the only MP that Mullin and Hencke disclosed as having been accused of taking 'cash for questions' was Tim Smith. Subsequently, Smith denied the Guardian's allegation that he had been paid by Greer, but instead confessed privately to John Major to taking payments from Mohamed Fayed directly which was not an allegation that the Guardian printed. Downey was later forced by evidence to

dismiss all the *Guardian's* original allegations that Ian Greer had paid Hamilton and Smith to undertake parliamentary activity at his behest.]

Completely contrary to Preston's statement, this transcript shows that Hencke and Mullin did not put to Greer, "fairly and squarely" any allegation that he had been involved in 'cash for questions'. Once again, whether Preston lied about this is wholly dependent on whether he knew his statement to be false, at the time that he made it.

You attempt to justify the *Guardian's* refusal to grant interviews, by attempting to undermine my credibility, and you attempt to achieve this by questioning the adequacy of the notice we gave The Guardian prior to releasing our report last October. But your posture is destroyed by the fact that The Guardian gave substantially less notice to Ian Greer and Neil Hamilton, and contrived to couch its 'warnings' so as to amount to no notice at all.

This contrasts completely with my own notice now of the nature of the allegations that will be in my book 'Trial by Conspiracy.' The stark fact is, I am now giving Alan Rusbridger and his staff ample opportunity to answer my questions months in advance of any allegations about them being widely disseminated to the public. This is totally unlike the *Guardian's* own disgraceful behaviour.

After nearly a year's examination of all the evidence before Downey, plus other evidence from the libel trial, I have identified countless gross anomalies in The *Guardian's* evidence and reporting. Therefore, once again I formerly request that I am provided interviews with: David Hencke; David Leigh; John Mullin; David Pallister; Peter Preston; Alan Rusbridger; Michael White and Jamie Wilson.

If Alan Rusbridger has nothing to fear, then the opportunity I am giving The Guardian to answer my questions is surely something he would welcome.

Yours sincerely,
Jonathan Hunt.

c.c. Lord Wakeham
Alan Rusbridger

I enclosed copies of four documents, including all the faxes referred to and the relevant page from Telex Monitors' transcript of the tape-recorded interview by David Hencke and John Mullin of Ian Greer, dated 23.7.93.

I guess they got the message. Having realised that threats of legal action were not going to work, Rusbridger resorted to intimidation of the underhand variety.

On Tuesday 31 March, just after lunch, I received a call from *Guardian* journalist Luke Harding, requesting an interview. I had not come across his name before during our investigation, though I knew him to be one of David Leigh's co-authors on the *Liar* book, about former Tory minister Jonathan Aitken. Not, it seemed to me, to be the sort of credentials I would boast about in polite company.

Harding told me that *The Guardian* wanted to run a feature on Malcolm Keith-Hill and myself.

'Oh, really?' I said, sarcastically. 'You mean like the one you did on Neil Hamilton? No, thanks. I've requested interviews with Rusbridger and his staff five times and he's declined every time, so I don't see why I should talk to you.'

Harding's oily bedside manner belied his intentions. 'No, it's not like that, Jonathan, I mean, this report you've done, it's very interesting though I don't agree with it . . .'

I kept on trying to end the conversation and get off the phone but Harding's skill at keeping me on the line exceeded my own.

'What's your motivation for supporting someone like Neil Hamilton?' he asked, as if Neil Hamilton was the devil incarnate himself.

'Well, he's innocent and just because he's a right-wing Tory who wears a dickey-bow isn't a good enough reason to stitch him up,' I replied.

He repeated his question.

'Look,' I said, 'if you want to know my motivation you should talk to other people who know me and who can give you their own independent views. You should talk to Jim Hancock at the BBC in Manchester, or Baroness Turner of Camden, or Andy Spinoza from the *Manchester Evening News*. Now there's a good person to speak to, he's one of your own a journalist on a Guardian Group Newspaper. I'll spell it out for you: S – P – I . . .'

'No, it's okay,' Harding said. 'But why do you think someone with your record is qualified to make corruption allegations against *Guardian* journalists?' Harding asked.

'What do you mean, *my* record? I have an honourable record in business, I was a good employer, I treated my staff well, and I got out of business with no debts.'

'Well, someone like you, a tax fraudster, evading tax?'

My heart jumped. He'd found out about my misdemeanour from 1990 when I had under-declared the duties on many of the classic cars I imported from California.

He continued: 'I have a document from Customs and Excise that says you had evaded £115,000 of VAT and had to pay a £22,000 fine. Why should anyone believe a person like you who had been involved in tax evasion?'

Harding was bluffing. His figures were wildly inaccurate. The total amount I had to pay Customs was £23,000 inclusive of penalty.

'That's factually wrong,' I said. 'I don't know where you got this document from but I'd like to see it. I'd be very surprised if Customs gave out these figures because they are wrong.'

'Do you deny that you evaded tax?'

'I don't deny that I undervalued certain cars I was bringing through from America, but before you run any story I insist that you check first with the Customs Officer who carried out the investigation. Look, Luke, Rusbridger's obviously put you up to this for another stitch-up job. I don't know you from Adam, and you could be an honourable journalist for all I know, but I will say this. You're not going to help yourself by taking any orders from Rusbridger or Preston because they're in it up to their necks. Unless you want to be shackled to *The Guardian* for the rest of your life I suggest you think this through carefully.'

I became aware that someone else was listening in on the call Rusbridger perhaps? It was time to turn the tables and have some fun.

I said mischievously, 'What I'm really looking for is someone on the inside at *The Guardian* to really blow the lid off what's been going on down there. Why don't I come down to Farringdon Road with all the evidence and we can have a chat about it? There's definitely been a conspiracy, and Rusbridger and Preston are definitely behind it. I can bring down all the files, everything. How about it?'

There was some rustling during the pause as he spoke to

someone. He put the handset back to his mouth. 'No, I don't think I can let you do that,' he said.

What a surprise, I thought.

'Could I arrange to have some photographs taken of you?' he enquired.

'No,' I replied. 'But if you contact your staff photographer, Graham Turner, who attended our press conference in Westminster in October last year, you will find he has plenty of pictures of me and Malcolm Keith-Hill.'

'When's the story coming out, anyway?' I asked.

'In about a week,' he said.

I disclosed, with a sense of triumph, that I was working on this book and that I expected it to be published. 'Well make sure you get your facts right from Customs and Excise in Manchester first.'

And with that the call ended.

I fired up the Montego and tore down to Customs House at Ralli Quays, Manchester, to see the Martin Lennon, investigating officer who cleaned me out back in 1990.

He agreed to see me and took me off to the canteen.

'Good to see you, Martin,' I said, as we sat down with a tea apiece.

'Good to see you too,' he replied. 'What's the problem?'

'Do you remember me ringing you up last year?'

'Yes, of course.'

I was referring to my call to him in November 1997 after Ian Greer warned me of *The Guardian's* intentions to smear Malcolm and me should we publish our report. I explained to Martin what we had uncovered, and the warnings we had received, and asked him where I stood if *The Guardian* started digging around in my past and found out about my misdemeanour. At the time he said that as far as he was concerned I had co-operated fully, the matter was settled, no charges were brought, and I was one among many doing the same.

'Well,' I said, 'I received a call about half an hour ago from a *Guardian* journalist called Luke Harding. He says he has a document from Customs stating that I evaded £115,000 of VAT and had to pay a £22,000 fine. I know that's wildly out, but is it possible someone got their wires crossed upstairs and gave the wrong figures?'

'They wouldn't have got anything from us. We don't give confidential information out. They're trying it on. Believe me. Someone else with a grudge has told them.'

'What can I expect from Customs if they ask for a statement?'

'Exactly what I said last year. When confronted you co-operated fully and we found no reason to bring any charges. It happens all the time. I'll see if anyone has been trying to breach security.'

The next day Martin Lennon rang me on the mobile. 'The only thing I'm authorised to disclose is that Customs and Excise has not given any information out from the file we have on you. However, a person by the name of a Mr Harding has been recorded as trying to acquire it.'

'Thanks Martin.'

He promised to get back to me and we parted company.

Three days later, on Friday, I thought I'd better touch base with my old supporter from *The Manchester Evening News*, Andy Spinoza, the gossip columnist on "Mr Manchester's Diary." I telephoned the News and was told he'd left to start his own PR company. I obtained his cellphone number and called him.

He sounded pleased to hear from me. 'What can I do for you?'

'You remember I told you a few months ago about my investigation into *The Guardian*? Well, they might give you a call to try and dig something up on me. Give me a shout if you hear from them, will you?'

'I've been meaning to phone you but I lost your number. They've already been to see me.'

'*What?* Was it Luke Harding?'

'Yes. He wanted to know all about you.'

'Thanks, Andy. Good luck with the business. Bye.'

After getting back to the flat I telephoned just about everyone I could think of who I had been in contact with on the story. And then, over the weekend, I thought that, for the purposes of this book, I had better get the day correct. I thought about it for a second or two. As I had given Harding Spinoza's name on the Tuesday, and Spinoza had already been visited by Friday, then Harding must have journeyed up from London on either the Wednesday or the Thursday.' I needed confirmation of the day.

On Monday I phoned Spinoza again. 'Andy, it's Jonathan Hunt again. Can you just tell me which day it was last week when Harding came up? Was it Wednesday or Thursday?'

'No,' Andy said. 'Luke Harding came up here about three weeks ago.'

For Harding to have been up to see Spinoza three weeks *before* I had given him Spinoza's name, *The Guardian* must have put some serious time into researching me. And yet, though he claimed to want to know all about me for a 'profile,' he didn't contact me when he was in Manchester.

Harding had also been busy elsewhere. On Thursday 16 April, Malcolm called me from Brazil. 'You're not going to believe this,' he said, 'but I've had a visit from a *Guardian* journalist named Alex Bellos,' The line was a very poor and with a lot of interference. I got the gist of what he was saying, but decided it would be handy to have it on record, and asked him to write with the details.

Which he did. The letter ran:

Dear Jonathan,
You asked me to let you have a written statement regarding the visit of the Guardian reporter to my home here in Rio.

  Toward the end of March 1998 at around midday, I was surprised to find a young Englishman on my doorstep here in Barra de Guaratiba. He introduced himself as Alex Bellos and gave me his card, which showed him to be a reporter from the Guardian.

  The purpose of his visit was, he explained, to find out more about me and my present activities! He had received a call from London asking him to go and find me, providing him with my above address which they had apparently got from my mother, in Cornwall.

  What was I doing here in Brazil? What was I running away from? Who had paid me to come out here? – and for this house? Whose house is this? Oh – it's yours! Where did the money come from? Are you working at present on any production? And so on . . . The subject then turned to Hamilton and our report, etc.

  Why did you produce this report? Who put you up to it? Who paid for you to do it, and how much? What are your motives for wanting to criticise the Guardian?, etc. . . . What did you find during your research? What are your criticisms/denunciations of the Guardian and its staff? Why do you think you are right and the Guardian are wrong? Do you really think Neil Hamilton is innocent, or what? And so on . . .

Naturally, I only had to tell him the truth and he soon realised that he was on a loser. Apparently he had thought he was going to discover some hidden secrets or facts about me and you, in order to discredit us and the work we have done on this.

About an hour and a half later, he took off in the taxi he had arrived in which had been waiting for him in the lane must have cost them a fortune, the Guardian that is! Before he went, he asked me if he could take a photo of me on the veranda with the fabulous view we have here in the background sort of Ronald Biggs and the good life in Rio style of shot!! Naturally I refused. He gave me his telephone number in Rio and promised me a copy of his article when published. Since then I have neither seen nor heard anything from him, so I don't know if the Guardian have printed his report yet.

Looking forward to seeing you in the not too distant future. Remember I need the money from the car to buy my passage back to England! Keep up the good work, I hope you are going to like what I have been doing out here when you see it.

Please give my kind regards to Neil and Christine thank them for looking after the car and please apologise for me not writing to them all this time I think this is the first letter I have written since arriving here in December '97!

All the best, friend.
Malcolm.

P.S. Regards to everyone Jim Hancock , your folks, etc.

Malcolm telephoned me a few weeks later and provided his parents' telephone number. I subsequently rang Mrs Keith-Hill and she told me how she had been deceived into disclosing her son's address. As with Malcolm, I asked her to put her experience into writing.

Dear Jonathan,

It was nice to make your acquaintance over the phone after you and Malcolm have been working together for so long and he had mentioned your name so many times.

I hope the following résumé of my contact with Mr Harding [Guardian journalist Luke Harding] will be of some use to you.

On the morning of 31 March this year I had a phone call from a Mr Harding, who seemed by his manner to be a friend of my son Malcolm, especially as he knew my home address and phone number (which is ex-directory). He asked me if Malcolm was still in Brazil and if so could I let him know his address. I agreed and dictated it to him over the phone.

He told me that he wanted to do an article about Malcolm and would like to have some photographs of him. Would I be agreeable to a photographer calling that afternoon and taking some copies? He asked if we were anywhere near Falmouth or Truro and I told him we were some distance away – 20-25 miles in fact. He said he would arrange with a photographer and let me know.

Shortly afterwards I had a call from a Nick Robinson of 17 St George's Road, Truro, Cornwall TR1 3JD, who said he was on his way. I found three photographs of Malcolm. Two of them were from some years ago but one was a recent one of him holding his little son in his arms, which, of course, would have been a great help in identifying him! He copied all three, left his card with me and departed. When I asked him if he knew Mr Harding's 'phone number, he said he had no idea as he was only given instructions and that was that.

When I spoke to my son a few days later he asked me if I had revealed his address to anyone, as he had had someone call on him in Rio de Janeiro who made himself very unpleasant. I was naturally very upset to hear this as I had acted in good faith, thinking that Mr Harding was intending to do Malcolm a good turn and all the time he was intending just the opposite. In fact, he had deceived me in a very cunning and underhand manner. He did not tell me he was from the 'Guardian' newspaper – otherwise my suspicions would have been aroused. I only found that out later.

Will keep in contact, Jonathan. Till then all the best!
Affectionately,
Joyce Keith-Hill.

It was clear that *The Guardian* had put far more time into investigating Malcolm and me than they had put into investigating the "cash for questions" story itself. Not only had The Guardian acquired the ex-directory telephone number of his parents, they had also traced Malcolm to his home in Brazil.

It beggars belief that a British national newspaper could stoop to such levels, and yet claim the high ground as justification for refusing a lowly freelance journalist such as myself interviews. But what is really frightening is the way that this Organisation from Hell has managed to spread its tentacles in the British media.

19

The Evil Empire

AFTER THE APPALLING BEHAVIOUR OF *THE GUARDIAN*, BOTH IN ITS 'reporting' of the "cash for questions" affair and in its attempts to intimidate Malcolm and myself, I decided that I needed to look a little more closely into the extent of *The Guardian*'s influence over the rest of the British media.

I began to travel to Companies House in Manchester daily, paying out a tidy sum in fees as I ordered company reports and then photocopied hundreds of sheets of microfiche in search of the true picture of their power.

During all the time when no journalist approached Neil Hamilton to interview him for his story, the media received all their information about the case from two main sources: *The Guardian* and Britain's leading press agency, the Press Association (PA), which relied heavily for its information from *The Guardian*. The vast majority of news reporting and investigation these days is done over the wires and the screen. Once a story has been accepted as true by one of the main sources of news, such as the PA, all the others simply follow on.

The PA, however, may not be as independent and impartial as most people suppose, for it is owned jointly by *The Guardian* and other major newspapers. Normally its impartiality would never be questioned. But in a case where one of its member newspapers has a vested interest in news being partial, as is demonstrably the case in *The Guardian*'s and later the *Mail on Sunday*'s reporting of the "cash for questions" story, the influence that one newspaper can exert over the PA is worrying.

I recalled when, on Tuesday 2 December 1997, at around 9.30 a.m., I telephoned PA News and spoke to staff reporter Katherine Road, whom I had spoken to at length outside Neil and Christine's flat in Battersea the day after Downey's report was released. I told her I was intending to release our report at that time onto the Internet, at my special website (www.coverup.net) . She remembered me and seemed quite keen on the idea of writing that up, until I explained that we had uncovered evidence of a criminal conspiracy within *The Guardian* to pervert the course of justice in the libel trial, followed by the deception of Sir Gordon Downey.

'We wouldn't be interested in a story like that,' she said with a shudder in her voice. 'Didn't you know – we're part-owned by *The Guardian.*'

'But this is a major story of national interest,' I protested. 'Couldn't you at least do a basic bulletin stating that our investigation questions *The Guardian*'s evidence and Downey's conclusions?'

'I'll speak to my editor,' she said. 'If we're interested we'll give you a call.'

Needless to say, she didn't call. Their shame at they way they had covered the story, coupled to the interests of the PA's shareholders, outweighed their duty to maintain freedom of information and promote factual reporting.

Incorporated as a limited company in 1868, the PA was founded to provide a non-partisan news service to the hundreds of independent newspapers that served towns and cities across Britain and Ireland. In 1904, a total issue of 3708 shares was divided amongst 191 shareholders. The highest holding of 54 shares was held by two newspapers (each representing less than 1½% of the issue), and the most common tenure was between 6 and 36 shares.

At the time of writing the disparate ownership that safe-guarded the PA's impartiality has gone, with just five news-paper groups owning over 60% of the 7,965,000 shares: Mirror Group plc (1,455,000 shares or 18%), Associated Newspaper Holdings Ltd (1,120,000 shares or 14%), News International plc (1,042,500 shares or 13%), United News and Media Group Ltd (900,000 shares or 11%) and Guardian Media Group plc (314,000 shares or 4%).

This is, of course, no different from the centralisation that has evolved across all sorts of businesses, from tissue manufacture to clothes retailing. But a democracy does not depend to the same extent on the integrity of its toilet rolls or T-shirts as it does on the integrity of its news. Any employee who values his or her job is naturally averse to acting against the interests of his or her employer, so it is hardly surprising that the PA's editorial staff did not question *The Guardian*'s line.

It is even less surprising when you consider that the PA's chairman, Henry (Harry) Roche, was the chairman of Guardian Media Group during the period that the Hamilton saga raged in the press, right up to 10 January 1997. As if that wasn't enough, the same solicitor, Simon Olswang, whose firm Roche paid to defend Hamilton's and Greer's £10 million+ libel action, had a seat on the PA board.

The words "conflict" and "interests" spring to mind. Of course, it would be hard to imagine Roche or Olswang inter-fering in the PA's day-to-day business, but then they wouldn't have needed to. To quote Matthew Parris of *The Times*, when commenting on his newspaper's subdued coverage of China where Rupert Murdoch has business interests: "a journalist has to 'tread carefully' when writing a story that conflicts with the interests of the proprietor."

This would explain why certain PA bulletins described Neil Hamilton pejoratively as "the MP at the centre of the sleaze allegations," rather than "the MP accused by Mohamed Fayed." It would also explain why the PA didn't emphasise that *The Guardian*'s allegations against Ian Greer and Neil Hamilton were founded on the word of a man who had been officially condemned as an habitual liar.

With all this in mind, it is hardly to be wondered at that the PA refused to consider reporting our findings, or why our press conference in Westminster, in late October 1997, was so poorly attended. Any PA sub-editor who contemplated putting out news undermining *The Guardian*'s evidence "on the wires" would probably have feared being strung up by one.

The Guardian Media Group has publishing interests across Europe (including Eastern Europe), Africa, North and South America, Australia and New Zealand. In addition to its holding in PA, it runs its own news agency, Guardian News Service. It not only publishes *The Guardian* and the *Observer* (which it bought from Lonrho in 1993), it is also directly responsible for publishing the *Manchester Evening News*. It also owns five regional news publishing companies that publish or distribute, (or both), a total of 71 newspapers, including two free-sheet papers that are distributed heavily in Neil Hamilton's former constituency of Tatton.

The "cash for questions" affair was a national issue that affected every constituency in the May 1997 election, including, of course, all those in which Guardian Group local newspapers were distributed. But out of all Britain's constituencies, the sleaze issue was most dominant in Tatton, where the *Wilmslow Express Advertiser* and *Knutsford Express Advertiser* slavishly followed *The Guardian*'s editorial line (unlike other non-*Guardian* local newspapers). Both these papers reprinted copious extracts from *The Guardian*'s book, *Sleaze,* as if it were the definitive reference work on Parliamentary standards, the way *Fowler's English Usage* is on grammar.

Neil subsequently complained to Mike Quilley, the editor of both *Express Advertisers* and asked him to print his response, which included extracts from the damning DTI report into Fayed's takeover of the House of Fraser. Quilley declined on the grounds that the DTI report was "highly libellous" against Fayed – even though the report was covered by Parliamentary Privilege and therefore could not give rise to any libel action.

On 3 February 1997, Alan Rusbridger addressed this anti-Hamilton coverage by *The Guardian*'s subsidiary newspapers in a letter to Downey.

> *I can confirm that the editor of the* Wilmslow Express, *Michael Quilley, is entirely right to say that there has never been any pressure on the* Wilmslow Express *regarding anything to do with Mr Hamilton (the same is incidentally true of the* Manchester Evening News*).*

However, Rusbridger's assurances were undermined just seven weeks later by the *Manchester Evening News* itself when, on March 24 1997, just weeks away from the election, it carried Fayed's full page advertisement promoting the book, *Sleaze,* (cost of the ad – £5,000). The display carried a personal message from Fayed:

Because of threats from Mr Hamilton's lawyers, some book-shops have decided not to stock this book. I believe it is a book that everyone has a right to read and therefore I have ensured that stocks of it are available at the Harrods bookshop.

Details of how to obtain copies were provided, and the ad. concluded:

However powerful an MP may believe himself to be, he has no right to prevent other people from reading a book published in the public interest by a reputable publishing house. Why should Mr Hamilton fear the facts? Read Sleaze *and find out.*

The Group's influence does not stop with the printed word, it also extends to the broadcast media.

Few jobs in broadcasting last long and personnel move from programme to programme, sideways, upwards and outwards constantly. This, no doubt, contributes to the nervous energy that permeates the industry. But *The Guardian* has a unique role in the working of the broadcast media. The weighty "jobs" pages in its Monday classified section emphasises the media's unhealthy dependence on this one newspaper. Whether you are a department head, a commissioning editor, a TV journalist, a programme producer or a director, a grip or a scene-shifter, *The Guardian* is the best place to look for work. And, as everyone in the business is keeping an eye out for that new opportunity, it is no wonder that *The Guardian* has become the media's favourite paper.

The *Guardian*'s subliminal influence over broadcast media is strengthened by the its involvement in television. Guardian Media Group owns Broadcast Communications plc, the third largest 'independent' producer of TV programmes, and the parent of TV companies Initial Film and Television, Bazal Productions, Hawkshead and Lomond Television. Together they supply around 700 hours of programmes every year to the BBC, ITV, Channel 4, Channel 5 and BSkyB. And, according to a recent annual report of The Guardian Media Group, stronger links are also being forged between Broadcast Communications and Fourth Estate, publishers of David Leigh's vile fantasy, *Sleaze.*

The Guardian also wields direct influence; its staff work hand-in-hand with factual programme-makers for (and within) some of the biggest television companies in Britain. There is, of course, nothing immoral or unethical about broadcast television companies employing journalists from Fleet Street. Many of them from all newspapers fill our screens on all sorts of programmes, but *The Guardian* is probably the only newspaper to cultivate relationships with television personnel specifically to have its conspiracy-theory stories made into documentaries.

For instance, Granada Television's "World in Action" documentary, "Jonathan of Arabia," which levelled allegations against the former Tory Minister Jonathan Aitken, was produced by David Leigh, assisted by his colleagues David Pallister and Alan Rusbridger. This trio also penned articles related to the "cash for questions" story.

So, since "World in Action" commissions its own programmes from *Guardian* journalists, you could hardly expect them to commission a story telling how Preston and Hencke were duped by Fayed and, in collusion with Rusbridger, Leigh and others, embarked on the most scandalous cover-up in the British press's history – even though by all that is fair and just, this criminal conspiracy should be bigger news by far than the original "cash for questions" affair.

"Jonathan of Arabia" was also based on information supplied by Fayed. Although Aitken's subsequent libel action against Granada and *The Guardian* collapsed when *The Guardian* produced evidence to show that he had lied about who had paid his bill at the Paris Ritz, Granada and *The Guardian* had already withdrawn their most damaging allegations – that Aitken had procured prostitutes and had been involved in illegal arms trading – before the case went to trial.

Central Television's "The Cook Report," was also embroiled in a story by *The Guardian*, this time by David Hencke. In October 1993, after seeing an article by Hencke, Sylvia Hones, a researcher on the programme contacted him. Hencke then persuaded Central's Clive Entwhistle to investigate *The Guardian*'s theory that Ian Greer paid MPs to act on his behalf in Parliament. He then worked alongside the production staff in a sting operation to trap Greer into stating that he could get an MP to put down a question in Parliament by paying him.

Greer made no such admission despite being induced to do so.

The sting failed and the programme was aborted. But this shows how *The Guardian*'s influence in television resulted in one of Britain's best investigative TV programmes embarking on a wild goose chase.

"Dispatches" is one of the most respected current affairs programmes in British television. However, *The Guardian* and Fayed's media campaign to demonise Neil Hamilton obviously softened up Channel 4's commissioning editor, David Lloyd, to the point where he accepted as fact that Neil Hamilton was corrupt to the bone. On 16 January 1997, timed to coincide exactly with Rusbridger's delayed submission to Sir Gordon Downey's Inquiry, Channel 4 broadcast Fulcrum Productions' 45 minute documentary on the "cash for questions" affair, piling more pressure on Downey. Made in full collaboration with *The Guardian*, it told the paper's story in an identical propagandist style.

It opened with shots of Parliament and a voice-over stating that the Major Government depended on the support of a number of MPs who were "fighting to save their reputations." In a darkened room a slide-projected photograph of Neil Hamilton appeared. An earnest voice-over introduced him: 'Neil Hamilton. Conservative MP for Tatton. Former Minister for Trade and Industry, and the man who dropped his libel action in the "cash for questions" scandal. A man battling to be believed.'

Fayed then appeared to relate how he had given Neil free shopping, gift vouchers, and a free holiday. 'If he is innocent,' Fayed thundered, 'why did he run from the court case?' No explanation was made of the real reason.

Slow-motion archive footage of Neil leaving the High Court was coupled to a droning soundtrack: 'But the "cash for questions" scandal reaches beyond the reputation of a few MPs,' the voice-over continued. 'Many are now questioning whether Parliament is fit to govern itself, let alone the nation.'

Vernon Bogdanor, Professor of Government at Oxford University, who writes occasionally for the *Telegraph*, *The Guardian* and *New Statesman*, pronounced: 'I think the "Neil Hamilton Affair" and the problems associated with it, which seem to cast a pall on a number of MPs, do require something much more than Parliamentary self-regulation.' The voice-over continued over a darkened-room slide photo of Neil and night-time views of the Houses of Parliament. 'This call is being made louder and more frequently today than ever before, but more and more MPs seem willing to exploit their positions.'

'When I first started working in Parliament in the early '50s,' proclaimed discredited conspiracy-theorist Andrew Roth, 'most of the Tory MPs had inherited wealth, and didn't go chasing after money. The later generation – the Thatcherite generation – they're looking for a substantial supplement to their pay, so that they can live in the manner which they would like to become accustomed.'

'Lobbying really is the interface between the public and Whitehall and Parliament,' explained lobbyist, Andrew Gifford. 'There was a growing number of lobbying companies and public relations companies engaging in lobbying, and it was apparent that some of them were definitely what I would call "cutting corners." '

Gifford was a rival to Ian Greer and also holds a shareholding and a seat on the board of publishers, Fourth Estate. This successful company is not only 50% owned by *The Guardian,* but also published *Sleaze.* Gifford lost out to IGA for a contract to represent the so-called group of "Big 8" accountancy companies.

Ex-Tory MP and health minister Edwina Currie also appeared in the documentary. 'Well, the fact that people were being paid to lobby was far from unusual,' she said. 'It is fairly common, it was widely known, it was widely understood, some of them boasted about it . . . they regarded it as a very successful bandwagon.' She was referring to the wider issue of MPs consultancies, but the juxtaposition of her comments help create the false impression that the production company desired.

It was noticeable that, while their accusers were shown in favourable settings such as panelled offices and gothic buildings, Neil Hamilton and Ian Greer and the other accused were shown in slow motion or in black-and-white slides, projected in a darkened room.

Two other clearly impartial witnesses testified for Fayed in the film: Brian Basham, who has since been re-engaged as Fayed's PR consultant, and David Alton (now Lord Alton), who received £1 million from Fayed to help him establish a political anti-sleaze body, "The People's Trust." News of Fayed's donation leaked out three days before the programme went out. We have yet to discover where the money has gone.

'Hamilton's true relationship with Ian Greer,' the voice-over stated, 'only emerged when Mohamed Al Fayed gave his story to *The Guardian*. Fellow Member for Harrods (sic), Tim Smith, owned up and resigned.'

But Smith did not own up and resign because he was paid by Greer. He resigned after admitting to an activity that Fayed and *The Guardian* had not made at the time – that of receiving direct payments from Fayed. This is exactly the same method that *The Guardian* uses to skate around the circumstances of Smith's resignation. Why? Because when Smith's role is examined, it destroys *The Guardian*'s whole premise about Greer's commission payments, on which their story was founded.

It beggars belief that Channel 4 could broadcast such an unmitigated stitch-up. So who are Fulcrum Productions Ltd, and why would they follow the *Guardian*'s line so faithfully?

Fulcrum is run by the programme's producer, Richard Belfield, and its reporter Christopher Hird two radical journalists who have written occasional articles for the *Guardian* (including one that Rusbridger reviewed himself). Hird has also written for the *New Statesman* and the *New Left Review*. This in itself may not be significant. But their contacts with the *Guardian* certainly seem to have ensured their eagerness to collaborate with the newspaper on a documentary about its 'exposure of Tory sleaze'.

But, though their programme bore every hallmark of the *Guardian*'s involvement, Alan Rusbridger wrote to Downey on 16 January 1997 (the day of transmission) and stated:

> 'You will be aware that Channel 4 is showing a Dispatches programme tonight on related matters. **I have not been at all involved** in the making of this . . . but I believe that it contains important new material which you should consider.'

But *Guardian* journalist Jamie Wilson, who worked on the paper's "cash for questions" story, was listed on the programme's credits. So as the authorisation for Wilson's attachment to the programme would have been the editor's responsibility, it is interesting that Alan Rusbridger claims to have had no involvement at all.

In short, from the opening shots to the closing credits,

the programme was designed to mislead by selective omission; distortion; misrepresentation; and dishonest juxtaposition.

This was exactly the style that Richard Belfield used when he became Fayed's mouthpiece for the second time seventeen months later, in a brilliantly-crafted nonsense-documentary about the circumstances surrounding the car crash in Paris that caused the death of Diana, Princess of Wales.

Commissioned from Granada Television by ITV's controller of news and current affairs, Steve Anderson, and broadcast by ITV on 3 June 1998, Fulcrum's *'The Secrets Behind the Crash'* sought to give credence to Fayed's outrageous ideas that the British Royal family could have been behind an assassination plot perpetrated in league with the British security forces.

The programme implied that this could have been carried out because Dodi and Diana were supposedly about to marry (Fayed's butler said so), and so the Royal family had a reason to bump them both off because they would not have wanted a Muslim entering the dynasty.

Belfield used the same techniques that he used for the 'cash for questions' documentary the year before. Decidedly dubious witnesses bearing odd testimonies were juxtaposed with comments from the presenter to lead the viewer to ideas that all sorts of goings-on were going on. This was all interwoven with reputable witnesses raising valid points on related issues. Their inclusion on the programme conferred credibility on the dubious witnesses by association. It was a class act.

The key witness was a certain François Levistre (who had already been questioned and dismissed as a crank by the French police), who claimed to have been driving his Ford Ka ahead of the Mercedes as it entered and negotiated the Pont D'Alma underpass. He said that he remembered clearly seeing the Mercedes being overtaken by a weaving paparazzi motorcyclist and pillion-rider, then seeing a blinding flash, after which he saw the Mercedes run into the support pillar. And Levistre supposedly saw all this happen through his rear view mirror.

The presenter suggested, archly, that this was akin to the kind of blinding flash that is produced by a stun-device used by security forces like the British security forces. The programme then put forward the proposition that this alleged motorcyclist and pillion rider overtook the Mercedes on the bend into the down-ramp and then, once it had sped past the Mercedes, the pillion rider had turned round and blinded driver Henri Paul with the anti-terrorist flash stun-device.

Two months later the programme's credibility was vaporised. On 2 August 1998, the *Sunday People* printed a front-page story by Rachael Bletchly and Pascale Palmer, focusing on a forthcoming book on the death of Diana by Nick Farrell. It concerned an interview with the same 'key witness' on whose testimony Belfield's documentary had hung its whole premise: François Levistre.

The People's headline screamed: 'I CAUSED DIANA DEATH CRASH'

"A FRENCH motorist has sensationally admitted last night that his reckless high-speed driving was a major factor in the car crash which killed Princess Diana. François Levistre has confessed: "Thinking about it carefully I now understand how I could have helped cause the crash. I was close behind the car, as much as 10 metres, and my driving may have caused it to swerve and lose control."

Levistre's new story could not be more different to the one he gave on the programme. The new version is that Levistre emerged in his Ka from a slip road, just ahead of the down ramp, at speed when the Mercedes and a white Fiat Uno were passing. This caused the Fiat to swerve, which in turn caused Henri Paul to lose control of the Mercedes and collide into the post. The new version has no mention of flash stun-devices. No mention of Levistre being ahead of the Mercedes and observing, through his mirror, the Mercedes' headlights dance with the headlight of a motorcycle.

So instead of a conspiracy involving MI5/MI6/the Duke of Edinburgh/Mossad/Barbara Cartland etc, the amended version centres on a simple combination of two reckless speeding drivers, one of whom was drunk, coming together at the wrong time. Whatever the veracity of this new story, one thing is certain. Belfield had crafted his documentary out of total fantasy, which a commissioning editor on a British network television channel then bought and broadcast.

Which is exactly what he did the year earlier for Channel 4's *Dispatches*, in league with *The Guardian*.

And there lies a good story that Britain's newspapers and

documentary makers really should investigate (if they had the courage). It concerns the role of Richard Belfield, and Mohamed Fayed. For it is rather strange that Belfield should be Fayed's mouthpiece a second time, after having produced the *Guardian*'s 'cash for questions' documentary that gave Fayed a platform to spout his false allegations against Neil Hamilton. For example, it would be interesting to learn whether Belfield received money from Fayed for producing these two programmes.

Another avenue involving Belfield that investigative journalists could explore is the case of the curious interweaving links between Fayed and: Granada TV factuals; the *Guardian*; and Fulcrum.

Because Granada TV's first 'Fayed factual' (based on Fayed's allegations against Tory minister Jonathan Aitken) was co-produced with *Granada's* friends at the *Guardian*; whereas Fulcrum Production's first 'Fayed factual' (based on Fayed's allegations against Tory minister Neil Hamilton) was co-produced with *Fulcrum's* friends at the *Guardian*; whilst Fulcrum's second 'Fayed Factual' (based on Fayed's allegations of an Establishment conspiracy to murder his son and Diana the Princess of Wales), was co-produced with the *Guardian*'s friends at *Granada* again.

Which is where *La Ronde* began.

This means that, of all the TV production companies, newspapers and TV broadcast companies, the same ones from each sector were involved in producing the three TV documentaries which promoted Fayed's allegations. And all three organisations were involved in the production of two programmes, which were co-productions with each of the other two organisations.

Of course, it could be just a bizarre coincidence that Granada TV's factual programmes department, the *Guardian*, and Fulcrum Productions are the only organisations to have produced programmes based on Fayed's allegations. Yet, when it actually comes to examining Fayed's erratic behaviour and outlandish lies and vendettas, the *Guardian* and Granada TV have displayed a curious lack of interest. One is left pondering whether the *Guardian*'s and Granada's journalists would have been as eager in becoming Fayed's mouthpieces if he had turned on his sympathisers/allies in the Labour and Liberal Democrat Parties, such as Dale Campbell-Savours, and Alex Carlile.

Interestingly, the controller of news and current affairs at ITV who preceded Steve Anderson, and who commissioned the *World in Action* programme on Jonathan Aitken, was Marion Bowman, who is the wife of Richard Belfield, who, of course, produced the other two Fayed-based documentaries. Also, Steve Anderson, who commissioned from Granada Fulcrum's Fayed-based documentary on Diana's death, is the brother of Jeff Anderson, who is Granada's new chief of *World in Action*.

However, Britain's television industry is incestuous, therefore this is not unusual. But what cannot be doubted is that if any (Conservative) Member of Parliament had such relationships and conflicts of interest, the *Guardian*; *World in Action* and *Fulcrum* would be crawling all over themselves to co-produce a television documentary about it.

When I first started my investigation, just after the election, I imagined that the whole of Fleet Street would be queuing up to hear Neil Hamilton's side of the story. But, despite the fact that he had been ousted from the fifth safest Tory seat in Britain, and though he had shouted his innocence from the rooftops, not one national reporter ever interviewed him about Fayed's and *The Guardian*'s allegations. But this is not their fault, either individually or collectively. It is the fault of the system itself.

Initially, many newspapers reported Fayed's allegations at arm's length as a *Guardian* story. But it didn't take long for *The Guardian*'s influence to cause the great majority to suspend their critical faculties and accept, without scrutiny, the paper's propaganda. Even the BBC got carried along with "Mohamed Al Fayed's allegations" seamlessly transforming them into generic "sleaze allegations," without any accreditation to Fayed or *The Guardian* at all.

So Britain's journalists formed their views and wrote their columns, based purely on the prevailing received wisdom. And then the allegations acquired even more credibility from their repetition. Doubledoubletalk. It is the stuff of Big Brother.

But there is always hope. There remain many independent-minded commentators throughout Britain's press who have, at one time or another, expressed concern at the way this story has been covered, and how it has been allowed to develop unchecked. My lobbying of the media has brought me into contact with many such people who seem, however, to consider themselves powerless against the media's self-perpetuating reliance on centralised thought and quick turnaround of stories. Some have supported Neil Hamilton and expressed reservations about Fayed and his employees' evidence and probity. Others have tried and failed.

In September '97 I discussed the affair with Andrew Roberts, a respected columnist on the *Sunday Times,* the newspaper that first introduced the phrase "cash for questions" into the British psyche with their alleged entrapment of the two MPs, Riddick and Tredinnick. Roberts has been very sceptical of Fayed's allegations and *The Guardian's* reporting from the word go. He assured me he had tried to persuade his editor to allow him to write a supportive article, but that he had been turned down repeatedly.

'My editor has treated Hamilton shittily throughout his editorship,' he told me, in some disgust. I have absolutely no compunction about repeating Roberts' words. The cause of freedom of thought and words is too great and, in any event, it is Roberts and his ilk whom history will judge as the moral victors.

This stifling of opinion, and the vacant-headed coverage given to Fayed's allegations over the last few years should give rise to a major debate on three central issues: the rights of an individual to sufficient column inches and air-time to answer allegations (for it takes only an instant to make an allegation, but forever to refute it); the effect of wire-driven news services on free thought and balanced coverage; and the ease with which this enables news to be manipulated in Britain by those with the power to do so.

The DTI Inspectors' report from 1990 gives us some insight into how easy it was:

> *In the present case it appears to us that two processes were at work concurrently. On one hand Mohamed Fayed was telling lies about himself and his family to representatives of the press, and once those stories were on a cuttings file or in a press cuttings library they grew and multiplied without much further inquiry into their accuracy. As a result of what happened, the lies of Mohamed Fayed and his success in "gagging" the press created, as Mr Fisher would put it, new fact: that lies were truth and that the truth was a lie.*

It is a disgrace that the British media be deceived twice in ten years, by the same man, using the same, highly-documented methods. It must never be allowed to happen again.

20

The Evidence Cupboard

THE STRESS OF THE INVESTIGATION WAS BEGINNING TO WEAR ME down. It was time to relax, take a break from things. We had achieved everything we set out to achieve and more, stumbling on and exposing one of the greatest stories of the century. All that was needed was a little more work to our report. A little tightening-up here, a little expansion there.

There was nothing more to do, surely? But I had thought, and said as much before, and yet this had often been the precursor to an investigation into yet another of the myriad sub-plots or other aspects that make up this story. And idle thought provided the catalyst once again.

It was during such a moment of reflection that I remembered my own words to Ambrose Evans-Pritchard on the train en route to the meeting at Southsea:

'What it boils down to is this: in the eyes of Sir Gordon Downey, the difference between *compelling* evidence and *insufficient* evidence is the evidence of one person who at least two independent people say is a liar.'

Those two people were Christoph Betterman, Fayed's former Deputy Chairman of Harrods, and Francesca Pollard, whose lone battle for her inheritance had driven her into Fayed's clutches, only to be tricked, exploited and betrayed.

But both these people had been handed to us on a plate. Christoph Bettermann's evidence was comprehensively documented in volume two of the Downey report. Francesca Pollard had come forward herself, writing first to Downey, and then, on her own initiative, to Gerald Howarth. Gerald, in turn, passed on her letter to Neil, and so on to me.

These two witnesses were not rooted out as a result of our investigations, but emerged of their own volition. It seemed to me that a little positive ferreting might well turn up some others.

I pulled out the videotape recording I made on 16 December 1997, of ITV's 'The Big Story.' The programme was a devastating exposé of Fayed's lying, surveillance methods; sexual shenanigans; propensity for vendettas etc. A number of witnesses appeared, including Christoph Bettermann, who told his harrowing tale of how Fayed tried to have him incarcerated in an Arab jail on trumped-up fraud charges. He was only saved from such a fate by Arab justice, which threw out Fayed's allegations time and time again.

Two other witnesses on the programme were believed to have been subjected to some kind of 'treatment' too, for they spoke with conspicuous passion. They were Bob Loftus, Fayed's former Director of Security, and Eamon Coyle, Loftus's former right-hand man. I decided to track them down. In the event, it took just one call – to Ambrose Evans-Pritchard, who provided Coyle's number.

I rang Coyle up. Mindful of the people he had cause to worry about, when he answered I explained quickly who I was, what I was doing, and where I had acquired his telephone number.

'If Ambrose gave it to you, you must be all right,' he said. 'But you must appreciate my position. I don't know you. I'd like to speak with Ambrose first, if that's okay.' I rattled off an impressive list of people I had come to know as a result of the investigation, and gave him my telephone number. 'I'll call you back,' he said.

An hour or so later Eamon Coyle rang back, as good as his word. We spoke at length about Fayed's crude attempt to blackmail him into giving false evidence against another Harrods employee, and about his other experiences working for the "Phoney Pharaoh," as Tiny Rowland had dubbed him. We went on to discuss the breaking-in of Rowland's safety-deposit box, and that led naturally on to Bob Loftus.

'Bob's very cautious who he speaks to,' he said. 'I'll give him a call and tell him you're okay. With any luck, he'll ring you back tonight.'

And Bob Loftus did indeed ring up later that evening. Thanks to Coyle's endorsement he seemed perfectly at ease speaking with me. However, he wasn't going to say much on the phone, as he suspected the line was tapped.

'If you want anything from me,' he stipulated, 'you're going to have to come down here and get it face-to-face.'

So, three days later I journeyed down to his home in Northamptonshire. After greeting me warmly, he led me inside his house. I looked around. It was a neat, well kept home, with framed collections of cigarette cards from the '40s and collectors' editions of British Army campaign medal ribbons adorning the walls.

Bob Loftus was formerly a Royal Military Policeman from 1958–1986, reaching the rank of Major in 1981. Armed with a distinguished service record, he joined Harrods in September 1987 as Fayed's Director of Security. He became one of Fayed's most trusted staff.

His wife, Janice, brought in the teas and we started.

He told me how, under instruction from Fayed's chief of security, John MacNamara, he organised the bugging of Fayed's staff's private telephone conversations; the surveillance of Fayed's senior executives; the organisation of protection for Francesca Pollard as she went about her business harassing Kenneth Warren MP and suchlike, and other sundry activities.

However, he fell from favour owing to his increasing dissent, which culminated with the breaking-in of Tiny Rowland's safe-deposit box at Harrods and refusing to have anything to do with two further break-ins. Fayed dismissed him, offering him £90,000 to sign a confidentiality agreement. He refused. Instead, he fought Fayed for his legal minimum entitlement of just £39,000, and subsequently got in touch with Tiny Rowland to inform him of the interference with his box. He assured me that he had neither requested nor received any inducement for his help.

He seemed to be an honourable man; a man whose testimony could be relied on. We chatted on for over four hours about how things were done at Harrods and at Fayed's offices. And, of course, we covered the subject of Bozek and Bond's standing as witnesses.

He told me that Alison Bozek would undoubtedly have been given to lying on Fayed's behalf. 'She was the "Queen Bee" when she said "shit," you jumped on the shovel,' he said. 'Bozek was deliberately lying when she claimed to have had no recollection of processing large cash handouts to people on Fayed's behalf. She did it all the time.'

I changed the subject to Iris Bond, and told him that she claimed to have received a request from Fayed to send over £5,000 to Harrods because Neil Hamilton was visiting him there later that day.

'That's a massive porkie,' he said. 'He wouldn't have needed to. He had a facility for £30,000 in cash every single day from Harrods' bank in the basement of the store, and when Fayed was at Harrods and needed cash, that's always where he got it from.'

In other words, Bob contradicted the two Fayed employees who testified against Hamilton on their testimony and probity.

Bob also expressed disbelief at the "brown envelopes at the door of 60 Park Lane" allegation on two counts: firstly, he stated that Fayed would never have given 'bungs' to such a prominent person as an MP unless they were face-to-face (Tim Smith said that he was *always* paid face-to-face). He also stated that he had knowledge of cash being passed to a host of people in *white* envelopes, but that he had never known Fayed to give cash in *brown* envelopes. When he said this something jangled in my brain, but not loudly enough for the thought to come through.

'Here, what do you make of this?' Bob said.

He passed me a transcript of a secret tape recording he made of a meeting between Fayed and Tiny Rowland on 20 October 1994. When I read it my eyes popped out. The transcript showed that Rowland pressed Fayed constantly to explain his allegations against Smith and Hamilton that had been printed in that morning's edition of *The Guardian*.

'What about this man Hamilton who denies . . . ?' asked Rowland.

'He can't deny,' said Fayed. 'How can he deny?'

'Did Hamilton actually ask for cash?'

'Yes, of course, he took maybe £30,000 cash, that's between us. I didn't say I'll give him cash. Greer was taking the cash to him and giving him maybe £500 instead.'

Within three short statements Fayed stated that Neil asked for and received £30,000 directly; then contradicted himself by denying that he paid Hamilton directly; then contradicted the story in that morning's *Guardian* that Greer paid Hamilton

£2,000 per question by suggesting that Greer 'maybe' gave Hamilton '£500'.

In other words, this transcript shows that Fayed not only contradicted the allegations that appeared in *The Guardian* that morning; it shows that Fayed also contradicted all the other allegations that were made subsequently in the two years that followed.

I could hardly believe it. This was the transcript that Downey cited in his report as *supporting* Fayed's allegations. I pulled out my copy of the Downey Report from my briefcase and thumbed through the pages. When I found it I read out to Bob what Downey had said.

' "However, the main thrust of Mr. Al Fayed's allegations namely that Mr. Hamilton accepted cash from him *has remained constant** even in private conversations." ' [*my emphasis]

Bob told me that his father-in-law, Lieutenant-Colonel Ward, shared his doubts about Fayed's allegations and he submitted a copy of the transcript to his local MP, who happened to be Standards Committee Member Quentin Davies. Quentin Davies passed it on immediately to Downey prior to start of the inquiry. It would be reasonable to suppose, therefore, that Downey knew of Bob Loftus's existence and his possible availability to testify to the inquiry. However, Downey, predictably, did not call him to testify.

'What does Downey mean when he calls it a private conversation?' Bob pondered. 'I set that recording up myself on Fayed's instructions, for the sole purpose of trying to entrap Tiny Rowland into saying that he had bribed Michael Howard £1 million to appoint the DTI inspectors.'

It seems very strange of Downey to deem this recording to be of a private conversation, and even more curious that he cited it to support the case against Neil. Especially when Fayed denied direct payments, and ended his sentence by only suggesting that Greer gave Hamilton "maybe £500", because Downey dismissed all allegations that Greer paid MPs "cash for questions" anyway.

Downey withheld both the recording and the transcript of it from Neil on the wholly specious grounds that it was 'the property of Mr Al Fayed.' The fact that Downey misrepresented the evidence and then withheld it, only serves to fuel speculation about his motives.

As I was just about to leave, Tiny Rowland rang Bob from his floating palace in the Mediterranean. After speaking with him about the safety-deposit box proceedings, Bob passed him across to me. He was keen to know how our exposé was progressing. I assured him it was close to completion, and he seemed well pleased.

'You really must come and see me in London,' he said. Little did I know that it would be the last time I spoke with him before he died.

When I arrived back in Cheshire, I asked Eamon Coyle if he would read the transcripts of Bond and Bozek's oral examination, and see if anything caught his eye. He agreed and I posted off volume three of the Downey report.

About three or four days later he rang me up and corroborated all that Bob Loftus had said. But Coyle had seen something else, too.

'Bozek was definitely lying when she said Fayed had written Neil Hamilton's name on envelopes,' he said. 'In all my time there I never saw Fayed write once on anything, and that includes all the envelopes of cash he handed out.'

'What about Bozek's story that she used to put these white envelopes inside brown ones to be left at the door?' I asked.

'I've never saw any brown envelopes all the time I was there. It just wasn't Fayed's thing. Everything had to be crisp and clean. Always brand new £50 notes. Always white envelopes. I'm not saying it's impossible, it's just that I never saw them.'

I called Bob Loftus back and asked him whether Fayed wrote names on the envelopes he handed out.

'I never saw him write anything while I was there,' he said.

So, with just the minimum of effort, I had established that there were four independent witnesses who would have testified against Alison Bozek, on whose lone testimony the case against Neil Hamilton ultimately rests. That made over ten witnesses in all who could have contradicted the Fayed and *Guardian* camps had they been given the opportunity to do so.

A few weeks later, as happened more than once since I started on this quest, I woke up one morning with a clearer view of something than I remembered having had the night before. It was if, while I was asleep, all the data in my head was being reorganised, reclassified, and filed. It was no wonder I was becoming fatigued. It was Loftus's and Coyle's scepticism about "brown envelopes" that did it.

I cast my mind back to my thoughts from months before, when I had been considering what John Mullin suggested to Ian Greer during his interview back in July 1993.

> '... that in return for a Parliamentary question being asked by a friendly MP, a brown envelope stuffed with fivers would be passed to the MP.'

The Guardian's and Fayed's whole case rests on the three corroborating employees and the "cash in brown envelopes" allegation. But, although this allegation didn't appear until two years after the first, John Mullin's proposition *seemed* to be evidence that Fayed's "brown envelope" allegation existed as far back as July 1993. And that *seemed* to bear out Alison Bozek's testimony, when she made a big point of saying that she always put Fayed's alleged white envelopes into brown ones.

But Malcolm and I had established beyond doubt that Fayed's admission of giving Tim Smith cash directly, and also his claim to have given Neil Hamilton cash directly, both emerged a year later, *after The Guardian* printed allegations that claimed *Ian Greer* was the paymaster.

This made sense, because if Mullin *was* putting Fayed's direct-payments allegations to Greer, he wouldn't have said "stuffed with fivers" because all of Fayed's allegations were referred to £50 notes, not *fivers* (and who would use five pound notes for such an amount). In fact, Mullin wouldn't have had any reason to put such an allegation to Greer at all. If Fayed was paying MPs cash himself, why would that have anything to do with Ian Greer?

Then it clicked. Mullin must have been using the "brown envelope" term *metaphorically*, and probably even invented the phrase himself the instant before he used it.

As they knew that a tape-recording existed of this conversation, Fayed and The Guardian had obviously briefed Alison Bozek to say that she put white envelopes into brown ones for one reason: it was so that Mullin's tape-recorded *metaphorical* use of the term could be cited in the libel trial as supporting their false contention that he was, in fact, relating a 'brown envelope' *allegation* back in 1993.

The Guardian and Fayed had simply looked into their "evidence cupboard" and fashioned an allegation to fit what was on the shelves. Except that close examination shows that it doesn't fit anything.

However, it would have been very easy to confuse a jury that Mullin's metaphor corroborated Bozek's story, and a few good QCs would have scratched their heads over it too especially if they hadn't been allowed to dwell on it for long, which is the most likely reason that the allegation wasn't made public until a couple of days before the libel trial was due to begin.

The Guardian might have pulled it off, just like they might have got away with their misrepresentation of Mullin's genuine shorthand notes.

I telephoned Neil and told him that I had worked out why Bozek made such an issue out of always putting the supposed white envelopes into brown ones.

'You know,' he said, 'I've been puzzled about that and I've also been trying to work out how and why Mullin used the 'brown envelope' phrase when he interviewed Greer back in 1993. Now it all makes sense. There's something else I couldn't work out as well.'

'What's that?' I asked.

'Well, in Mullin's article on 21 October 1994, Mullin says that when he interviewed Smith on 22 July 1993, he put the proposition to him that he had put down a question for £2,000 in a brown envelope. But Smith was never paid in brown envelopes, so that didn't add up either. Now it all makes perfect sense. Mullin obviously got so attached to his metaphor he inserted it into the allegation to juice it up a bit. Being accused of being paid £2,000 to put down questions is bad enough, but being paid £2,000 in a brown envelope conjures up all sorts of mental images.'

I drove back to the office and pulled out our press cuttings file, flicked the pages and found the article. Neil was right. And then I read further to see what Mullin said about Neil's interview. I phoned Neil immediately.

'I've just read that article of Mullin's. Well spotted and well missed, too.'

'What do you mean, well missed?'

'Mullin's article is clearly based on his notes from the two interviews he had with you and Smith. But guess what – Mullin makes no mention of asking you about cash for questions. And he doesn't mention you threatening libel lawyers, either. It's yet more proof that his computer note was tampered with by someone else for the Downey inquiry.'

'Well done, Jonathan!'

'There's nothing well done about it. If you hadn't mentioned Mullin's article I wouldn't have even bothered to look it up. I can't believe that I've read this before at least twice and never noticed it.'

'What does Mullin say about the interview with me?'

'All he says is that you asked five questions on House of Fraser . . .'

'Seeing as I actually asked nine, no doubt Rusbridger and Leigh will call him a liar!' he quipped.

'Quite. Mullin also says you stayed at the Ritz and didn't think much of the view, and that you didn't register the visit. He then goes on to say, and I quote: "In an unpublished briefing with The Guardian last year in the Terrace Bar at the Commons, he – that's you – said he had received scores of tickets for the opera and he pondered, rhetorically, whether he should have registered them," end of quote. That's all he says about your interview.'

'Well, that puts concrete boots on it,' Neil said.

'It already had concrete boots. Now its got about 40 tons of Blue Circle cement on top as well.'

In the final weeks, prior to converting the story of our investigation into this book, I rekindled contacts with some of the journalists I had come to know during the investigation.

On the whole Stephen Glover had been very supportive and we spoke frequently on the telephone. When The Guardian's dirty tricks against us went into gear, Stephen made it quite clear that if The Guardian tried to smear us he was going to take them to task.

Ambrose Evans-Pritchard of the Daily Telegraph had been another rock. Evans-Pritchard won national acclaim for being the first journalist to blow the lid off Bill Clinton's peccadilloes before the Americans would even go near the story. In fact, as I write this now, that's exactly where he is, covering the same story. It was his baby and his persistence came good.

In mid July 1998, I met up with Ambrose again at Canary Wharf, at the same waterfront pub where I first met him in

January. It was good to see him and chat about the developments over the previous six months. I rabbited on about the case and mentioned Roth's article in the New Statesman, which proved conclusively that our theory that *The Guardian*'s theory was wrong was right.

He smiled and nodded. 'It makes sense,' he agreed.

Among other issues we talked about were the lengths to which Rusbridger, Harding, Leigh, and Hencke went, to prevent this book from coming out. He sat silently soaking it all up.

'You've got them, Jonathan. Rusbridger must have thought he was going to get away with it. He couldn't have imagined that you two would turn up out of nowhere. You must be his worst nightmare.'

During another visit to London, I called on Graham Forrester down at the ITN studios in Millbank. When, on Downey Day, the world went mad, he had spared me time and taken an interest in what Malcolm and I were doing. I had chatted to him infrequently over the year that followed and I always came off the telephone feeling heartened.

'Hi, Graham, what are you sucking off the wires today?' I jibed.

He smiled. 'You've touched a point we're going to have to address,' he said. 'Anyway, tell me what's it all about.'

We spent a half hour or so while I gave a concise account of what we had uncovered. When we finished, he picked up on one of the story's central features.

'You know, if Smith had only made clear the circumstances of his resignation, this story would never have been driven the way it was.'

Graham was right, but as it has turned out, if Smith's resignation letter *had* made clear the falseness of *The Guardian*'s allegation that he took cash from Ian Greer, then neither Andrew Roth nor *The Guardian* would have revealed their hand, as Roth did in the *New Statesman* and *The Guardian* did in their papers for the libel trial. Which helped us to expose their rotten journalism and their conspiracy.

On 23 July I met Lorana Sullivan for the first time, after over six months of getting to know her over the telephone. Lorana is an American journalist who worked on the *Observer* City desk in the days when Tiny Rowland owned the newspaper. Along with colleagues Melvyn Marckus and Michael Gillard, and freelancer Peter Wickman, she blew wide open Fayed's 1985 deceit of the British press, the City of London, and the Department of Trade and Industry itself.

We first started our telephone relationship after she read my letter in the 1997 Christmas issue of the *Spectator*, which gave notice of our intention at that time to release our report on the Internet. She wrote to me enquiring when it was going to happen, so I sent her a hard copy through the post.

From that day we became firm 'telephone' friends and her knowledge of Tiny Rowland (who she says was grossly misrepresented by the British media, regardless of his sins) and Mohamed Fayed made her a very useful ally. Throughout the months that followed, especially when I became frustrated or just plain browned off, I would ring her and invariably my spirits would be enlivened. No matter how busy she was, and though she was fighting a serious illness, she still had time to talk to me whenever I called. Eventually, I contacted her in July 1998, suggesting that we should meet one Thursday when I happened to be in London.

'I'm going to be in the London Clinic in Harley Street,' she told me. 'Why don't you come and talk to me while I'm having my treatment.'

I dropped by in the mid-afternoon whilst she was receiving her medication. After handshakes and smiles we chatted for hours about Fayed and our report. I showed her selected pieces of evidence from the thousands of pages we had amassed.

'You've won,' she sighed in her soft American accent. 'The case is overwhelming.'

In the middle of our chat I had to pop out to the toilet, walking along hushed corridors, past the other closed doors on the same floor. What I didn't know, until a few days later, was that Tiny Rowland was dying in one of those rooms.

In the course of our phone calls from his yacht and to his homes in London and Buckinghamshire over the previous year, Tiny had been full of suggestions about introducing me to people who had inside information on Fayed. He had even offered to fly me to India on an executive jet. In the end, none of it came to anything and his life slipped away just a few yards from the room where I sat with Lorana.

When I read about his death, it occurred to me that things had now gone full circle. In many ways he was the man who started the whole thing. If it hadn't been for him Fayed would never have got his hands on Harrods and probably would never have met Neil Hamilton. It was Tiny's exposure of Fayed that set the man off on his campaign of mischief and mass character destruction.

A campaign in which Fayed joined forces with a corrupt British newspaper to hoodwink the entire British media and Parliament itself. All because one man acquired a position of influence and couldn't be corrupted.

Mostyn Neil Hamilton.

The Main Players

Jonathan **AITKEN**
Former Conservative government minister for Defence Procurement.

Following the failure of Mohamed Fayed's appeal to the European Court of Human Rights to have the DTI report quashed, and following weeks of effort thereafter by Fayed to try to get John Major to withdraw the DTI report and give him a British passport, the *Guardian* published Fayed's allegations that Aitken had procured prostitutes for prominent Saudis; had earned commissions from arms dealing with Saudis; and had his hotel bill paid for by a Saudi national, Said Ayas, when Aitken and Ayas stayed at the Paris Ritz following a meeting between the two in September 1993.

These allegations were broadcast in a *Guardian*/Granada TV co-produced *World in Action*, which *Guardian* journalist David Leigh, author of *Sleaze*, produced, and in which Alan Rusbridger and other *Guardian* journalists also had a heavy involvement. The chief of *World in Action*, at that time, was Steve Boulton, who is also a personal friend of *Guardian* editor Alan Rusbridger.

Aitken denied all the allegations and sued the *Guardian* and Granada, who dropped the majority of them subsequently, prior to going to Court.

However, Aitken was forced to withdraw from his libel action, when Granada and the *Guardian* produced evidence, supplied by Fayed, which exposed Aitken as having lied about who paid his hotel bill. Neither Granada nor the *Guardian* have produced any reliable evidence to substantiate their other original allegations.

Paddy **ASHDOWN**
Leader of the Liberal Democrat Party before, during and since Fayed's

war against the Tories. He became a personal friend of Martin Bell from shared opinions on the Bosnian civil war.

He supported the Liberal Democrat candidate's withdrawal from the Tatton constituency in the general election of 1 May 1997, to provide the best chance of Martin Bell ousting Neil Hamilton from Parliament. He authorised his staff to help Bell's campaign.

Martin BELL

Award-winning former foreign correspondent for BBC TV news, who became famous for wearing his 'lucky' white suit during his reporting of the Bosnian civil war. He quit to stand as an 'anti-corruption' candidate in Neil Hamilton's Tatton constituency in the general election of 1 May 1997, after being persuaded by his friends in the media and the Labour and Liberal Democrat parties. Before announcing his candidature, he secured the assent of Tony Blair, Paddy Ashdown, and the Tatton Labour and Liberal Democrat parties to withdraw their candidates.

During the first two days of his campaign, he failed to give any cogent reasons for standing. On the third day he was briefed by *Guardian* journalists David Leigh and Ed Vulliamy on 'wrongdoing' that they claimed Hamilton had admitted. The *Guardian* had trumped these up from papers that Neil Hamilton and Ian Greer had disclosed freely in preparation for their libel trial. Thereafter Bell cited Hamilton's 'admitted wrongdoing', though Hamilton denies he had made any such admissions.

Bell claims he stood on Hamilton's 'wrongdoing', not 'cash for questions'. Yet his original 'anti-corruption' stance can only relate to 'cash for questions' and Bell didn't learn Hamilton's 'wrongdoing' until three days into his campaign.

In the straight head-to-head with Hamilton, Bell won a landslide victory.

Christoph BETTERMANN

Former junior judge in Germany; House of Fraser executive between 1984 and 1991; becoming eventually Mohamed Fayed's deputy chairman of Harrods. He left Fayed in 1991 and became subjected to Fayed's false, invented allegations of fraud, and had to endure 25 court appearances on criminal and civil charges in Dubai as a result When he was acquitted at last, Bettermann sued Fayed for libel in London. A letter from Fayed was also read out in open court admitting that all his allegations against Bettermann were false. Fayed paid him substantial damages. Bettermann wrote to Downey and submitted a wealth of information about Fayed's vendetta against him. He also offered to testify before the Inquiry to give his knowledge about the activities of:

Mohamed Fayed; Alison Bozek; Royston Webb; John MacNamara; Michael Cole; and other Fayed employees.

Downey rejected Bettermann's submission, and declined his offer to testify. Instead, Downey accepted the evidence of Fayed's chief of security, John MacNamara, who claimed that Bettermann had lied. In Downey's earlier investigation of Fayed's allegations against Michael Howard, Downey disregarded MacNamara's evidence on the grounds that it may have been false.

Tony BLAIR
Leader of the Labour Party installed as Prime Minister in the 1 May 1997 general election. Leader of the Opposition at the height of Fayed's war against the Tories.

He supported the Labour candidate's withdrawal from the Tatton constituency in the general election, to provide the best chance of Martin Bell ousting Neil Hamilton from Parliament. He authorised his staff to help Bell's campaign.

Iris BOND
Since 1979, Mohamed Fayed's most senior secretary at his offices in 60 Park Lane. She worked alongside Alison Bozek. Along with Bozek and Philip Bromfield, she emerged to give evidence supporting Fayed's allegations in the final days before Hamilton and Greer's libel trial, a full two years after the *Guardian* printed Fayed's original allegations.

She claimed to have received telephone calls from: Ian Greer; Ian Greer's secretary Elizabeth Swindin; Neil Hamilton; and Neil Hamilton's wife, Christine; all asking for their 'envelopes'. She also claimed to have received a telephone call from Fayed at Harrods requesting that she send over £5,000, so that Fayed could pay Neil Hamilton, who was meeting Fayed at Harrods later that day.

She is alleged by: Neil Hamilton, Christine Hamilton, Ian Greer, and Elizabeth Swindin, to have lied before the Inquiry. Bob Loftus, and Eamon Coyle also reject completely her evidence on crucial points. She was also exposed by Nigel Pleming QC as having lied before the Inquiry on crucial points.

Peter BOTTOMLEY
One of three Tory MPs who sat on the 1997 Select Committee on Standards and Privileges, which deliberated Sir Gordon Downey's report on the cash for questions affair. He endorsed the Select Committee's rubber-stamping of Downey's report.

Sir Andrew BOWDEN
Former Tory MP until May 1997, and a Fayed supporter for just 3½

weeks in early 1987. He is also a friend of lobbyist Ian Greer, and was among 26 (mainly Tory) MPs who benefited from Greer's donations to their constituency associations, prior to the 1987 general election. Bowden's constituency's benefit totalled £5,319.90 of office equipment. The majority of the other associations (which did not include Neil Hamilton's nor Tim Smith's) received £500 or thereabouts.

Bowden rejects completely Downey's conclusion that Greer's donation and his support for Fayed were linked, and rejects Downey's report itself as 'distorted'.

Alison **BOZEK** (nee FOSTER)

From 1981–1994, the personal assistant to Mohamed Fayed at his offices in 60 Park Lane, London. She left Fayed to work as a trainee for one of Fayed's solicitors, Allen and Overy, after Fayed gave her a gushing reference. Along with Iris Bond and Philip Bromfield, she emerged to give evidence in the final days before Neil Hamilton's and Ian Greer's libel action.

Downey found no material evidence of either gift vouchers or cash having been given to Neil Hamilton. Given that Downey dismissed the gift voucher allegations, which were corroborated by Iris Bond, on grounds of insufficient evidence; this means that, as far as Downey is concerned, the difference between 'compelling' and 'insufficient' is the word of this one person, Alison Bozek.

Neil Hamilton, Ian Greer, Francesca Pollard, and Christoph Bettermann all allege that she lied before the Downey Inquiry. In addition, Bob Loftus and Eamon Coyle both strongly contest her evidence on crucial points. Bozek's evidence also conflicted with Philip Bromfield's evidence on crucial points.

Philip **BROMFIELD**

Since 1983, Mohamed Fayed's doorman at his offices in 60 Park Lane. Along with Alison Bozek and Iris Bond, he emerged to give evidence in the final days before the libel trial. He claimed to have remembered giving Neil Hamilton two brown envelopes in 1987–1988. Neil Hamilton alleges that he lied before the Inquiry. Bob Loftus and Eamon Coyle also contested Bromfield's evidence. Bromfield's evidence also conflicted with Alison Bozek's evidence and Tim Smith's evidence.

Michael **BROWN**

Along with Neil Hamilton and Sir Michael Grylls, Brown was one of three MPs who figured among the people who had received commission payments from Ian Greer for introducing clients. Brown was not a sympathiser of Mohamed Fayed and gave no parliamentary support at any time.

Sir Robin BUTLER

John Major's Cabinet Secretary at the height of Fayed's war against the Tories. His second-hand account of Hamilton's telephone conversation with Michael Heseltine was represented by the *Guardian* as showing that Hamilton lied about his relationship with Ian Greer. The detail of Heseltine's letter to Downey supported Hamilton's account of their conversation, and the evidence, when examined properly, bears out that Hamilton told the truth.

However, Downey withheld Heseltine's letter from Hamilton prior to it being published in his report and he contended that Heseltine had deliberately been misled. Heseltine was not called to give his opinion on the matter.

Dale CAMPBELL-SAVOURS

Long-standing Labour MP, and an associate of *Guardian* journalist David Leigh. Following the publication of Andrew Roth's book, *Parliamentary Profiles*, in 1989, Campbell-Savours met Roth privately and learned Roth's (later discredited) theory that lobbyist Ian Greer's commission payments to people who introduced business were instead covert payments to reward MPs for parliamentary services. Consequently, Campbell-Savours persuaded his colleagues on the 1989 Members' Interests committee to investigate Greer. When Greer appeared before the committee Campbell-Savours questioned him unrelentingly in his efforts to substantiate Roth's theory.

Like many Opposition MPs, in 1986–1987 Campbell-Savours asked many questions supporting Tiny Rowland's troublesome barracking of the Tory government over its handling of Fayed's acquisition of House of Fraser. However, when the appalling facts became known in 1989, Campbell-Savours ignored the opportunity to embarrass the government and instead allied himself, ostensibly, with Fayed's cause, putting down 11 questions and 58 motions attacking Rowland's ownership of the *Observer* newspaper, which *The Guardian* had decided it wanted to buy. All in all, Campbell-Savours' activity exceeded all Fayed's Tory sympathisers' put together by a large margin. On 1 June 1993 Lonrho sold the *Observer* to the *Guardian*, partly as a result of his covert campaign.

Ironically, Ian Greer believes he recruited Campbell-Savours to the Fayed cause, through the late Labour MP Allan Roberts and Neil Kinnock. The truth is the reverse: Campbell-Savours recruited Fayed in his quest to deliver the *Observer* into *The Guardian*'s hands.

When Fayed's allegations were published by the *Guardian* on 20 October 1994, Ian Greer spoke to Royston Webb on the telephone and taped the conversation. The transcript shows that Webb denied emphatically any knowledge that Fayed had paid any MPs. Webb also stated that he had spoken to Campbell-Savours earlier that day. This would mean that Campbell-Savours knew Royston Webb lied to the Downey Inquiry when Webb claimed that Fayed had told him years earlier that he had given Hamilton thousands of pounds.

Furthermore, Fayed's ex-director of security, Bob Loftus, claims that, after Fayed's allegations were published, he witnessed on at least two occasions Campbell-Savours entering and leaving the vicinity of Fayed's office at Harrods. If Campbell-Savours did have meetings with Fayed, as Loftus surmises, then this would be at odds with Fayed's testimony to the Downey Inquiry when Fayed stated twice that he had never met Campbell-Savours. This would also mean that Campbell-Savours knew that Fayed had lied to the Inquiry, as well as Webb.

Despite his monumental conflicts of interest, Campbell-Savours sat on the 1997 Standards Committee that deliberated Downey's report on Fayed's 'cash for questions' allegations. Yet in spite of his reputation for assiduousness, he was, according to his colleague on the Committee, Quentin Davies, the most 'vociferous and vituperative' objector on the Committee to Davies's call to have Fayed questioned on oath about his allegations against Neil Hamilton.

Alex CARLILE QC

Former Liberal Democrat MP. A former critic of Fayed who became a friend on first name terms. He communicated Mohamed Fayed's second version of his allegations in two letters to Geoffrey Johnson-Smith, chairman of the 1994 Members' Interests Committee.

Carlile stood down at the 1997 General Election and immediately became a director of three of Mohamed Fayed's companies: Liberty Radio; Liberty Publishing and Punch.

Peter CLARKE

Former BBC Economics Correspondent; a columnist on the Scottish edition of the *Sunday Times*, and a mutual friend of David Hencke and Neil Hamilton.

He met Hencke in May 1995 and offered to mediate between the *Guardian* and Neil Hamilton in Hamilton's libel action against the newspaper. During the conversation, Hencke made a number of admissions, including a *de facto* admission that the *Guardian* had no evidence of payments to Neil Hamilton.

Hamilton included an extract from Clarke's witness statement in his original submission to Downey. Downey made no reference to it nor did he call Clarke to testify.

Michael COLE

Mohamed Fayed's and Harrods' fiercely-protective PR spokesman.

Formerly an award-winning BBC reporter and newsreader, before becoming the BBC's royal correspondent. He was demoted to arts correspondent in December 1987 after journalist Andrew Morton published details of the Queen's Christmas speech, which Cole had given in confidence. Cole left the BBC of his own accord in October 1988 after being head-hunted by Fayed.

Francesca Pollard alleges that, along with Richard New, Cole wrote defamatory material against Fayed's perceived enemies, which Pollard and New disseminated in Pollard's name.

Within a few days of the *Guardian*'s original 'cash for questions' article being printed in October 1994, Cole successfully embroiled the majority of the British Press, using the technique of feeding individual newspapers exclusive stories on different aspects. Cole resigned from House of Fraser in nebulous circumstances on 20 February 1998 after over nine years' loyal service.

Eamon COYLE

Harrods former deputy Director of security, reporting to Bob Loftus. Along with Bob Loftus, he broke ranks with Fayed after falling foul of John MacNamara.

After leaving, Coyle helped American publishers Condé Nast prepare their defence to Fayed's libel action regarding an article which appeared in the September 1995 issue of American magazine *Vanity Fair*.

Coyle also helped Bob Loftus's claim for unfair dismissal against Harrods in April 1997, and he also assisted the ITV's *'The Big Story'* do an exposé on Fayed's phone-tapping and the other surveillance methods used on his staff and others, which was transmitted on 16 December 1997.

Following his involvement in these, Coyle was subjected to a crude attempt by Harrods' legal director, Michael Rogers, to pressurise him into giving false testimony against another ex-security guard, upon pain of trumped-up theft charges being filed against him if he declined to co-operate.

Coyle refused to be part of Rogers'/Fayed's scheme. Instead he informed the police and Ambrose Evans-Pritchard of the *Daily Telegraph*. Nevertheless, Fayed filed theft charges against Coyle anyway, in vengeance.

Having since read the transcripts of the oral examinations of Mohamed Fayed, Alison Bozek, Iris Bond and Philip Bromfield from the Downey Inquiry, Coyle rejects completely their testimonies against Ian Greer and Neil Hamilton on a number of crucial points.

Quentin DAVIES

One of three Tory MPs who sat on the 1997 Select Committee on

Standards and Privileges, which deliberated upon Sir Gordon Downey's report on the 'cash for questions' affair. Known for his independent mind, he once famously savaged former Tory Whip David Willetts during an earlier Committee investigation.

Along with fellow Tory committee member Ann Widdecombe, Davies refused to endorse Downey's report. Yet, though he was one of only two highly-vocal dissenters on the Committee, Speaker Betty Boothroyd did not call him to speak on November 17 1997 during the Commons debate on the Downey report.

Sir Gordon **DOWNEY**

A civil servant with no legal training, he was appointed by John Major to the post of Parliamentary Commissioner for Standards: the watchdog on MPs' probity.

He is also a personal friend of the Chairman of the 1997 Select Committee on Standards and Privileges, Robert Sheldon, from the period they worked closely together when Sheldon was Chairman of the Public Accounts Committee and Downey was Chairman of the National Audit Office.

In his investigation into Fayed's and the *Guardian*'s plethora of allegations against former Conservative MP Neil Hamilton, Downey rejected Hamilton's request to have evidence taken on oath in spite of the Standards Committee's specific provision for evidence to be taken on oath; he failed to take account of the glaring discrepancies in Fayed's and Fayed's employees' evidence; he failed to identify any of the glaring discrepancies in the *Guardian*'s evidence; he dismissed evidence from an ex-Fayed employee of unblemished integrity whose word had been tested many times in Courts of Law on the evidence of a Fayed employee whose word he had previously rejected, and who was implicated subsequently in the unlawful entry into Harrods' safe-deposit boxes; he rejected offers from witnesses who wrote to him contradicting the testimony of Fayed and Fayed's employees; he failed to call witnesses against whom he knew Fayed and his employees had made false allegations, including respected Members of a Parliamentary Select Committee and an adviser to that Committee; he failed to call four ex-Fayed employees who had offered to give evidence supporting Neil Hamilton from their personal experience of Fayed and Fayed's employees Bond, Bozek and Bromfield; he did not disclose that two of these ex-employees had offered to testify; he took no account of Fayed's propensity for vendettas; he attached great significance to documents that had no significance and attached no significance to those that did; he took at face value the veracity of pivotal documents that have since been proven to be false; he claimed to have taken no account of Fayed's uncorroborated word but took it; he cited the supposed similarity between Fayed's allegations against Tim Smith and Fayed's allegations against Neil Hamilton as having evidential worth, though Fayed had not made any 'cash-in-hand' allegations against Tim Smith originally nor made any 'brown envelopes' allegations against Tim Smith subsequently and despite the fact that he dismissed Fayed's original allegations against Tim Smith; he found no material evidence whatsoever that Hamilton had received any cash payments but charged Hamilton with concealing between £18,000–£25,000; he made no attempt to examine the fundamentally different stories given by Fayed's U.S. lawyer and the *Guardian* to explain the late emergence of Fayed's employees Bond, Bozek and Bromfield; he denied Hamilton sight of important evidence prior to publishing it in his report, and he denied Hamilton access to other evidence that he cited in his summing-up completely; he took no account of the DTI report by Aldous and Brooke; he took no account of Francesca Pollard's affidavit detailing how she was employed by Fayed to make outlandish bribery allegations against respected MPs whom Fayed perceived were his enemies; he rejected Hamilton's character reference from a cross-bench Peer of the highest eminence and accepted a character reference for two Fayed employees from ex-Fayed employee Royston Webb whom Fayed has retained for no obvious reason up to the year 2001 for an annual fee reported to be £200,000; he took no account of any of the points in Hamilton's 133-page forensic demolition of the evidence against him; and he accepted uncritically, except where he had no choice, the *Guardian*'s submission, even citing the *Guardian*'s book *Sleaze* as a work of reference.

In his report of 3 July 1997, he castigated Hamilton vehemently over a handful of technical breaches of parliamentary rules, which had been culled from a stringent scrutiny of Hamilton's fourteen years as an MP, which are equal or less significant than other MPs' breaches of the rules; including those by former Prime Minister Lord Callaghan; the current Prime Minister Tony Blair; the current Deputy Prime Minister John Prescott; the current Paymaster General Geoffrey Robinson; and scores of MPs from both sides of the House, including former cabinet ministers from the last Conservative government.

On the central issue, having found no evidence whatsoever, in the face of overwhelming evidence to the contrary, Downey concluded on the conflicting evidence alone of Fayed and his three employees Bond, Bozek and Bromfield, that the evidence that Hamilton had been paid by Mohamed Fayed was 'compelling'.

The British Press, so far, has not questioned his perverse treatment of the evidence or his perverse reasoning, nor has the Press explored the possible reasons that could lay behind it.

Mohamed **FAYED** (a.k.a. AL-FAYED)
Together with his brother, Ali Fayed, the joint-owner of Harrods, the famous London department store. He also owns the Paris Ritz hotel and leases the late Duke and Duchess of Windsor's former home outside Paris.

Born the son of a respectable but humble Egyptian family; raised in the slums of Alexandria; he worked his way up the ladder until he became a confidant of the richest man in the world: the Sultan of Brunei.

His 1985 acquisition of House of Fraser was investigated by the government's Department of Trade and Industry in 1987. Their March 1990 report blackened Fayed as a liar, briber, character assassin and thief, which prevented Fayed from attaining his life-long ambition of British citizenship.

In January 1987, Fayed forged an alliance with Francesca Pollard, whereby Pollard distributed black propaganda against Tiny Rowland and Fayed's perceived enemies, in return for Fayed's help with her own legal battle against Rowland.

In September 1994, when, on appeal, the European Court of Human Rights rejected Fayed's last hope of having the DTI report quashed, Fayed went public with corruption allegations against a number of Tory Ministers. These were: Michael Howard, the former minister for Corporate Affairs at the DTI who commissioned the DTI report; Neil Hamilton, who was Howard's replacement with responsibilities for the self-same report; Tim Smith, Junior Northern Ireland minister; and Jonathan Aitken, Minister of Defence Procurement.

Between 1987 and 1998, either indirectly through Francesca Pollard, or directly himself, Fayed made allegations of bribery against at least fifteen MPs including four ministers and five former prime ministers; accused at least three Harrods directors of fraud; accused his own lobbyist of bribing MPs; tried to blackmail his staff; claimed that Diana, Princess of Wales, uttered dying words whilst unconscious; implied that the Royal family had conspired with MI5 to murder Diana; and called Diana's grieving mother, Mrs Shand Kydd, a snob and a bad mother.

Fayed's most startling traits are his generosity to those loyal to him, and his capacity for vengeful vendettas against those who he feels have been disloyal.

Countless witnesses and the evidence suggests overwhelmingly that Fayed lied throughout Downey's Inquiry into his allegations against Neil Hamilton.

Michael **FOSTER**
Labour MP and a Member of the 1997 Select Committee on Standards,

which deliberated Sir Gordon Downey's report on the cash for questions affair. He endorsed Downey's report.

Andrew GIFFORD
One of two principal shareholders in lobbying company GJW Government Relations Ltd. He gave damaging testimony against his biggest rival Ian Greer in a *Guardian* co-produced *'Dispatches'* television documentary, which replicated the *Guardian*'s 'cash for questions' story.

Gifford also held personally 39,700 shares and a seat on the board of *Guardian* publishing company Fourth Estate, which is 50% owned by the *Guardian*, and which published David Leigh and Ed Vulliamy's book on the 'cash for questions' affair: *'Sleaze: the corruption of Parliament'*. Gifford's shareholding was the highest of any of Fourth Estate's directors at the time.

Sitting on Fourth Estate's board with Gifford was Jim Markwick, who was the Managing Director of the *Guardian* when the paper published the original 'cash for questions' article. Markwick was also a director of Guardian Media Group.

The *Guardian*, *'Dispatches'*, and *Sleaze*, together blackened and destroyed Greer and Hamilton. This removed any possibility that Greer would return to compete for business against Gifford, and almost eliminated the possibility that Greer or Hamilton would return to the courts with a libel action against the *Guardian* which in Greer's case would have wiped out up to a year's profits of the entire £300 million-turnover Guardian Media Group.

After five years of zero growth, GJW's turnover increased 57% in the first year following Greer's forced departure from lobbying. GJW also replaced Greer as London's top lobbying firm.

Ian GREER
Formerly London's most successful lobbyist. He ran his own lobbying company, Ian Greer Associates (IGA), until the loss of business caused by the *Guardian*'s article in October 1994 forced it into liquidation.

He was Fayed's lobbyist from Nov 1985–mid 1990, and Fayed's parliamentary monitor thereafter until September 1994. During the earlier period Greer helped orchestrate Parliamentary support for Fayed from his Tory sympathisers Tim Smith, Neil Hamilton, Sir Michael Grylls, and Sir Andrew Bowden. Greer also believes he was responsible for recruiting to Fayed's cause the Labour MP Dale Campbell-Savours. However, Campbell-Savours was only using Fayed as a source of information to discredit Tiny Rowland's ownership of the *Observer*, as he was acting on behalf of *The Guardian* who had designs on acquiring the Sunday paper. Greer had no contact with Campbell-Savours, who instead liaised directly with Fayed's legal adviser, Royston Webb, and *Observer* journalist David Leigh.

After journalist Andrew Roth's lurid disclosure in 1989 that Greer had given commissions to Sir Michael Grylls for introducing business, Greer appeared before the Members' Interests Committee in early 1990 and was questioned by Campbell-Savours, who was seeking to substantiate a theory of Andrew Roth's that Greer's commissions were covert payments to MPs for Parliamentary favours. Greer stated that, in addition to Grylls, he had paid two other unnamed MPs commissions for introducing clients to his company. Roth, the *Guardian* and Campbell-Savours believed that this strengthened Roth's theory, which then became the foundation for the *Guardian*'s cash for questions story. Roth and the *Guardian* believed that these two other MPs were Neil Hamilton and Tim Smith. This was subsequently discredited when Tim Smith was revealed not to have received a commission from Greer, but had, instead, been paid by Fayed directly.

The *Guardian*'s original story was that Fayed paid Greer, and that it was Greer who then paid Hamilton and Smith to ask questions in Parliament. The *Guardian* has not at any time put forward any evidence to support these allegations. Two years after the *Guardian*'s article Fayed then alleged that he had paid Greer £5,000 cash per quarter in brown envelopes.

Greer's subsequent £10 million libel action for loss of business at that time would have wiped out up to a year's profits of the entire £300 million-turnover Guardian Media Group. The *Guardian*'s campaign and immense influence helped create public opinion that was universally condemnatory of Ian Greer, thus ensuring that any flaw in Greer's case would have been fatal to his chances in court. Such a flaw emerged when it was revealed that Greer had given four more commission payments to Grylls than he had previously testified in 1990. So, on this unrelated infraction, Greer had to withdraw his libel action. Downey was forced by documentary evidence to dismiss all allegations that Greer paid MPs for Parliamentary services, which included asking questions.

Sir Michael **GRYLLS**

Former Tory MP and former chairman of the Conservative back-bench Trade and Industry Committee. He was one of three MPs who had introduced new clients to Greer's lobbying company, IGA, earning commission fees for so doing. The other two MPs were Neil Hamilton and Michael Brown.

In his book 'Parliamentary Profiles', published in 1989, parliamentary journalist Andrew Roth publicised luridly Greer's commissions to Grylls, implying a corrupt link between the lobbyist and the MP. This provided the genesis of his (later discredited) theory, which was adopted by Labour MP Dale Campbell-Savours and the *Guardian*, that they were covert payments to reward MPs for Parliamentary services.

Roth's allegations were investigated subsequently by the Members' Interests Committee in April 1990. The Committee concluded that: 'It may not be readily apparent from the description of each category contained in the introduction of the annual Register, that commission payments of a minor or casual kind should be registered, or where they should be registered.'

Grylls was a Fayed sympathiser, and he supported Fayed's cause in delegations to ministers, though he did not put down any questions.

Neil HAMILTON

Former Tory MP from 1983–1997, and former vice-chairman of the Conservative back-bench Trade and Industry Committee. He was appointed to government as a Whip in 1990, then Minister for Corporate Affairs at the DTI in April 1992.

As a back-bench MP he had received two commission payments from lobbyist Ian Greer when two companies engaged Greer in 1987–1988. Hamilton did not register these in the Register of Members' Interests because, he claimed, the rules were not clear that they should, and that there was no category in the Register to cover them. In 1990 the Members' Interests Committee agreed.

Hamilton was a sympathiser of Mohamed Fayed for three-and-a-half years between Nov 1985–April 1989, during which period he put down nine written questions, three Parliamentary motions and joined two of Sir Peter Horden's four delegations to ministers. Hamilton's total activity over this 3½ year period was eclipsed by Labour MP Dale Campbell-Savours in one five-day period (24 July–28 July 1989). In similar vein, Hamilton's total activity in his most active year, 1989, was equalled by Dale Campbell-Savours' total activity in his most active day, 1 March 1989.

Hamilton also enjoyed Fayed's hospitality, visiting the Duke and Duchess of Windsor's former home outside Paris, coupled to a stay at the Ritz. Similar visits to the Ritz and the Windsor's home have been enjoyed by many other MPs, none of whom have registered their trips.

When he became Minister for Corporate Affairs in April 1992, with responsibilities for the DTI report that Fayed was trying to have quashed in the European Court of Human Rights, Hamilton, acting on advice, spurned Fayed's attempts to contact him and instead passed on his apologies to Fayed through intermediaries. Nevertheless, Hamilton's officials at the DTI advised him that he was entitled to take decisions relating to House of Fraser and Lonrho, but regardless of this, Hamilton delegated matters relating thereto, to another minister, Edward Leigh MP.

On September 21 1994 Fayed's appeal to the European Court of Human Rights to have the DTI report quashed was rejected unanimously. Subsequently, in the weeks that followed, Fayed tried to pressurise John Major to withdraw the DTI report and give him a British Passport, upon pain of allegations against a number of Ministers being made to the Press. Major refused to succumb for the final time on 18 October 1994. The next day, Fayed gave the go-ahead to the *Guardian* to publish allegations that his lobbyist, Ian Greer, had paid Neil Hamilton and Tim Smith to ask questions in Parliament. When the article appeared on 20 October 1994, Tim Smith resigned but denied privately that he had been paid by Greer, admitting instead to being paid by Fayed himself. This had not been alleged in the article. Hamilton denied that he had been paid by anyone to support Fayed, but he was pressurised into resigning his ministerial post a few days later.

Two months after Smith's (unpublished) admission of being paid by Fayed directly, Fayed alleged that he had paid Hamilton directly also. Hamilton denied this new charge too. Nineteen months later still, days before the libel trial was due to be heard, Fayed then alleged that Neil Hamilton had been paid in 'cash in brown envelopes', which had been processed by three of his staff at 60 Park Lane: Alison Bozek, Iris Bond, and Philip Bromfield. Hamilton denied this also.

When Hamilton was forced to withdraw his libel action, the *Guardian* continued their campaign against him. One of the main weapons in this action was the concoction of 'wrongdoing' and 'admitted wrong-doing' allegations, which the *Guardian* had mainly wrung out of information surrounding the two isolated commission payments that Hamilton had received from Ian Greer. Hamilton and Greer had volunteered this information freely in preparation for their libel trial. Close examination shows these charges to have zero substance.

Neil Hamilton lost his seat to Martin Bell after the Labour and Liberal Democrat candidates stood down.

Hamilton denies any wrongdoing (in the sense of improper behaviour) and all allegations of corruption or dishonesty. Exhaustive scrutiny of the evidence and the evidence of ten witnesses, nine of whom contacted Downey but were not called to testify, supports Hamilton's contentions and vindicates his claims of innocence.

Christine HAMILTON

Wife and staunch defender of Neil Hamilton. Prior to the start of proceedings, Neil Hamilton telephoned Downey for permission to have her accompany him when he was orally examined by the Inquiry. Downey declined to give it.

Hamilton made this call to Downey a few days before his examination on 20 February 1997. However, four weeks earlier on 22 January, Fayed employee Iris Bond testified before Downey that Christine Hamilton had telephoned her on occasions asking for her husband's 'envelope'. Christine Hamilton says that Bond lied. Downey did not call Christine Hamilton to testify before the Inquiry.

Luke HARDING

Guardian journalist who was despatched by Alan Rusbridger in March 1998 to investigate the background of author Jonathan Hunt and Hunt's fellow investigator, ex-pat TV producer/director Malcolm Keith-Hill.

Lord HARRIS of High Cross

Celebrated economist and cross-bench Peer. He founded the Institute for Economic Affairs in 1957, which provided the exchange of ideas and created what became known as Thatcherism, since adopted by most centrist politicians.

Harris has been a close friend of Hamilton for 30 years since Hamilton was a student at Aberystwyth. He has supported Hamilton throughout the 'cash for questions' saga, and wrote to Downey voicing his affirmation of Hamilton's integrity. Downey dismissed Harris's endorsement, opting instead to accept the endorsement of Fayed's retained legal adviser Royston Webb as a character witness for Fayed employees Iris Bond and Alison Bozek.

David HENCKE

Guardian journalist who penned the original story of 20 October 1994, which alleged that Fayed's lobbyist, Ian Greer, paid MPs Tim Smith and Neil Hamilton 'cash for questions'. No evidence has been offered by the *Guardian* to support the allegations in the article, and the principal charge that Greer was a conduit for corrupt payments to any MP has been positively disproved by documentary evidence. Hencke won 'Journalist of the Year' for his article.

Hencke's investigation into Greer began over a year earlier in July 1993, when Fayed met Hencke's editor, Peter Preston, and alleged that Greer had paid Tim Smith MP for his support in Parliament. This prompted Hencke and his colleague, John Mullin, to try and substantiate a theory they had held about Greer since 1989: that Greer's convention of granting commission payments for introducing business was really a cover for secret payments to three MPs on the Tory back-bench Trade and Industry Committee, to reward them for providing parliamentary services. The *Guardian*'s belief in this theory was bolstered by the fact that the committee's chairman, Sir Michael Grylls, was known to have received commission payments from Greer, whilst Tim Smith and Neil Hamilton were the committee's secretary and vice-chairman respectively and all three had expressed sympathy for Fayed in Parliament during the mid 1980s.

When Hamilton and Greer issued their libel writs against the *Guardian*, Fayed and the *Guardian* made a plethora of new allegations, including allegations that he had paid Hamilton cash and gift vouchers in face-to-face in meetings. Two years later in September 1996, Fayed and the *Guardian* alleged that Hamilton had received 'cash in brown envelopes' processed by Fayed's staff. Like his colleagues, Hencke claims that Fayed had made all these allegations originally, and that he & John Mullin asked Hamilton about 'cash in brown envelopes' when they interviewed him in 1993.

The evidence shows that Hencke's claim that either he, or Mullin, asked Hamilton about 'cash for questions' in 1993 is a lie. The evidence supports overwhelmingly the contention that the 'cash for questions' allegations against Hamilton were not made until September 1994, by which time Fayed had developed a huge grudge against Hamilton for not helping him on becoming a DTI minister, and that the 'cash in brown envelopes' allegation was not invented until 1996.

The evidence supports overwhelmingly further contentions that Hencke lied throughout the Downey Inquiry on a whole range of issues.

Michael HESELTINE

Tory MP and the President of the Board of Trade during the period that Neil Hamilton was a DTI minister from 1992–1994. Heseltine was also the Deputy Prime Minister when the 'cash for questions' scandal blew up.

He pressurised Hamilton into resigning his ministerial post after the *Guardian* published Fayed's original allegations in October '94.

Though Sir Gordon Downey concurred with the *Guardian*'s interpretation of a note by Cabinet Secretary Sir Robin Butler (which recorded what Butler understood had been said during a telephone conversation between Heseltine and Hamilton), which the *Guardian* claimed showed Hamilton had wilfully deceived Heseltine, Heseltine's letter to Downey instead concurred with Neil Hamilton's version of what had been said between the two.

Despite this, Downey did not release a copy of Heseltine's letter nor did Downey seek further clarification from Heseltine as to whether he considered himself to have been wilfully deceived.

Brian HITCHEN

Former Editor of the *Sunday Express* and, like many of Britain's newspaper editors, a friend of Mohamed Fayed.

He was Fayed's emissary to Prime Minister John Major, visiting him in September and October 1994 to relay Fayed's demands that Major revoke the damning 1990 DTI report into Fayed's 1985 takeover of House of Fraser and give him a British passport. Days after Major's final refusal to do either, Fayed went public on his allegations against lobbyist Ian Greer and Tory ministers: Tim Smith; Jonathan Aitken; Neil Hamilton; and Michael Howard.

Sir Peter HORDERN

Former Tory MP. He was also the registered Parliamentary Consultant for House of Fraser between 1982 and 1991 and a close friend and supporter of Mohamed Fayed. Between 1985 and 1989 he enjoyed Fayed's hospitality and organised meetings and led delegations to ministers of Fayed's Parliamentary sympathisers. These became the subject of a number of allegations made by the *Guardian*, but which had not been made by Fayed. The *Guardian* later dropped all allegations against Hordern, and Downey deemed that Hordern's minor, technical breaches of the rules were 'otiose'.

Michael HOWARD

Tory MP, former Minister for Corporate Affairs, and former Home Secretary. He is also a distant cousin of Francesca Pollard and a distant relative of Lonrho director Harry Landy.

In April 1987, as Corporate Affairs minister, Howard appointed two independent Inspectors to investigate Fayed's acquisition of House of Fraser.

In 1989 Fayed requested Francesca Pollard to parade with a placard alleging that Howard had been bribed with £5 million by Tiny Rowland to appoint the DTI Inspectors. Pollard refused. In February 1990, when publication of the DTI report was imminent, Fayed's staff produced a defamatory pamphlet titled '20 things you ought to know about Michael Howard MP'. Subsequently, acting on Fayed's instructions, Francesca Pollard distributed these widely in Howard's constituency during the weekends of 10/11 and 23/24 February 1990.

Shortly after Fayed lost his appeal in the European Court of Human Rights in September 1994 to have the DTI report quashed, Fayed cited Howard's distant kinship with Landy to allege that Tiny Rowland had bribed Howard, when he was Corporate Affairs Minister in 1987, to appoint Inspectors to investigate Fayed's takeover of House of Fraser. Fayed alleged that Tiny Rowland had paid Howard, via Landy, between £½–1½ million.

When Howard later became Home Secretary, Fayed then accused him of blocking his passport application, though Charles Wardle MP was the Home Office minister who blocked Fayed's passport and Howard had pressed for it to be granted.

Downey investigated Fayed's allegations against Howard prior to investigating Fayed's allegations against Tim Smith and Neil Hamilton. Downey cleared Howard after dismissing the evidence of Fayed employee John MacNamara.

Sir Geoffrey JOHNSON – SMITH

Conservative MP and former chairman of the 1989 and the 1994 all-party Select Committees on Members' Interests, which monitored MPs' probity.

In 1990 the Committee carried out an investigation into Ian Greer's commission payments to Conservative MP Sir Michael Grylls, after being persuaded by Labour Committee Member Dale Campbell-Savours MP. After investigating the matter, the Committee cleared Grylls and concluded: 'It may not be readily apparent from the description of each category contained in the introduction of the annual Register, that commission payments of a minor or casual kind should be registered, or where they should be registered.'

In 1994 the Committee investigated Neil Hamilton's failure to register his stay at the Paris Ritz hotel seven years previously in 1987, leaving Fayed's 'cash for questions' allegations to be dealt with by Sir Gordon Downey once Hamilton's libel trial had ended. After concluding that Hamilton should have registered his stay, the Committee nevertheless recommended no action, on the basis that MPs' attitudes to registering private hospitality seven years earlier was far more relaxed.

In 1995 the Committee investigated a complaint against Labour MP Tony Blair for his failure to register being part of a 1986 all-party delegation to the USA supporting British business interests, which had been organised and paid for by lobbyist Ian Greer on behalf of a consortium of British companies. After concluding that Blair should have technically registered his visit, the committee recommended no action, on the basis that its registrability was not readily apparent.

In 1995 the Committee also investigated a complaint against Labour MP John Prescott for not registering a 'free weekend' at the Gleneagles Hotel in 1994, paid for by Conoco Oil. The Committee concluded that Prescott should have registered his stay, especially as the rules had been made more rigorous the previous year. However, the Committee recommended no action, on the grounds that many Members had still not appreciated the significance of the 1993 rule changes.

Graham JONES

Mohamed Fayed's former Director of Finance. He became subject to an unfounded vendetta by Fayed, which led to him being investigated on criminal charges, after Fayed falsely accused him of fraud. His experience was related to Downey in correspondence from Norman Lawrence. Downey did not publish this.

Charles KENNEDY

Long-standing Liberal MP who sat on the 1997 Select Committee on Standards and Privileges, which deliberated Sir Gordon Downey's report on the 'cash for questions' affair. He endorsed the Committee's report on the Downey Inquiry, which Robert Sheldon sought to represent as an endorsement of Downey's Report. However, during the Commons debate on the Downey report, Kennedy made a point of stating that, as far as he was concerned, Fayed's cash allegations were not proven.

Michael LAND (not to be confused with Harry Landy – see other list)

A former Lonrho employee whom was introduced to Fayed's legal adviser Royston Webb by Sir Andrew Bowden, and who was recruited to help Fayed in his propaganda war against Tiny Rowland. He withdrew after becoming disillusioned with Webb's ethics.

He wrote to Downey and offered to testify before his Inquiry regarding his relationship with Webb. Downey did not call Land to testify.

Norman LAWRENCE (deceased 7/1/1998)

A friend of Graham Jones. Jones was a former Harrods executive, who, like Christoph Bettermann, became subject of Fayed's invented allegations and an amazing vendetta.

When Jones' settlement terms with Fayed prevented him from disclosing the details of his case, Lawrence wrote to Downey and gave details. Downey did not call Lawrence or Jones to testify, nor did he publish Lawrence's material.

David LEIGH

Award-winning journalist on the *Observer*, and a friend of Labour MP Dale Campbell-Savours. He wrote the *Guardian*'s book on the 'cash for questions' affair: *Sleaze: the corruption of Parliament,* along with fellow *Guardian* journalist Ed Vulliamy.

Leigh is also a friend of Andrew Roth, who developed the discredited theory that Ian Greer's commission payments were covert means of rewarding MPs for parliamentary services, which Leigh adopted as the basis for his book *Sleaze*.

In the summer of 1989 Leigh left the *Observer* to work for Granada TV's *World in Action* programme, returning to the *Observer* after Lonrho sold it to the *Guardian* in 1993.

In 1995 *World in Action*'s chief, Steve Boulton (who is also a close friend of *Guardian* editor Alan Rusbridger) commissioned Leigh to produce a documentary based on Fayed's allegations against the minister for Defence Procurement, Jonathan Aitken. Fayed/Granada/ the *Guardian* alleged that Aitken had procured prostitutes for prominent Saudis; was involved in arms dealings with Saudis; and had had his hotel bill discharged by a Saudi national, Said Ayas, when Aitken stayed at the Ritz following a meeting with Ayas there in September 1993. When Aitken issued libel proceedings against Granada TV and the *Guardian*, both companies dropped many of these allegations prior to Court proceedings, but his case collapsed when Granada and the *Guardian* produced evidence showing that Aitken had lied about who paid his hotel bill. None of Fayed's other allegations proffered by the *Guardian*/Granada have been supported by worthy evidence.

David Leigh's account of the late emergence of the three Fayed employees Bond, Bozek and Bromfield does not accord at all with that of Fayed's U.S. lawyer, Doug Marvin, in Marvin's letter to Sir Gordon Downey. This, together with Leigh's totally misleading portrayal of events in *Sleaze* shows him to be heavily involved at the heart of the *Guardian*'s cover-up, along with Alan Rusbridger; David Hencke; Peter Preston and Ed Vulliamy.

Following Martin Bell's inability to justify standing as an anti-corruption candidate during his election-campaign confrontation with Neil and Christine Hamilton on 8 April 1997, David Leigh & Ed Vulliamy travelled from London to Knutsford to prompt Martin Bell on Hamilton's 'admitted wrongdoing'. These 'wrongdoings' had been trumped-up by the *Guardian* mainly from information that Ian Greer and Neil Hamilton had given freely, in preparation for their libel trial.

Thereafter Bell cited Hamilton's 'admitted wrongdoing' in his campaign.

Tom LEVITT

Labour MP, elected in the general election of 1 May 1997. He was immediately seconded by Labour whips onto the 1997 Select Committee on Standards and Privileges, which deliberated Sir Gordon Downey's report on the 'cash for questions' affair. He endorsed Downey's report.

During the Commons debate on the Downey Inquiry, Levitt praised Downey for his thoroughness, citing Downey's conclusion that the evidence against Neil Hamilton was 'compelling'. After the debate,

Jonathan Hunt asked Levitt to list the evidence that, in his view, was 'compelling'. Levitt declined to answer, turned on his heels and walked away.

Terry LEWIS

Labour MP from the extreme Left of the party, known for his animus toward Right-wing Conservatives. He is also a Member of the 1997 Select Committee on Standards and Privileges, which deliberated Sir Gordon Downey's report on the 'cash for questions' affair. He endorsed Downey's report.

Bob LOFTUS

Harrod's former Director of Security. Along with his deputy, Eamon Coyle, Bob Loftus broke ranks with Fayed after becoming at odds with John MacNamara. Loftus then provided Tiny Rowland with information on how Fayed and John MacNamara had broken into Rowland's safety deposit box at Harrods. Loftus also provided ITV's *'The Big Story'* with a whole dossier of information about Fayed's phone-tapping and other surveillance methods used on his staff and others.

On 20 October 1994, Tiny Rowland visited Fayed at Harrods at Fayed's request. On Fayed's instruction, Loftus covertly video-taped the meeting between the two, in a failed attempt to capture Rowland admitting on tape that he had bribed Michael Howard to appoint the DTI Inspectors. Loftus's secretary made a transcript of the tape, which shows that Fayed contradicted his allegations against Neil Hamilton and Ian Greer that appeared in that morning's *Guardian* and every single 'cash for questions' allegation that he and the *Guardian* made subsequently against Hamilton in the three years that followed.

Loftus supplied a copy to Downey via his father in law and Quentin Davies. Though this transcript destroyed Fayed's allegations, Downey cited it in his summing-up as being evidence against Hamilton. When Hamilton asked for a copy Downey refused. Furthermore, though Downey had been made well aware of the source of this evidence, he declined to call Loftus to testify before the Inquiry. Having since read the transcripts of the oral examinations of Mohamed Fayed; Alison Bozek, Iris Bond and Philip Bromfield, Loftus rejects completely their testimonies against Ian Greer and Neil Hamilton on a number of crucial points.

John MACNAMARA

Former detective chief superintendent of Scotland Yard's Fraud Squad, and Fayed's head of security. His responsibilities included organising the bugging the private conversations of Harrods staff, pursuing Fayed's vendettas against former House of Fraser executives etc.

He claimed that former Deputy Chairman of Harrods, Christoph Bettermann, who became the subject of an amazing vendetta based on Fayed's invented allegations of fraud, and who had written to Downey in support of Hamilton, had won all the court cases brought against him by Fayed either on technicalities or by lying. Downey accepted MacNamara's evidence and dismissed Bettermann's accordingly. In Downey's earlier Inquiry into Fayed's allegations against Michael Howard, Downey rejected all of MacNamara's evidence.

Shona McISAAC

Labour MP who was elected in the general election of 1 May 1997. She was immediately seconded by Labour whips onto the 1997 Select Committee on Standards and Privileges, which deliberated Sir Gordon Downey's report on the cash for questions affair. The MP she unseated was Michael Brown, who was also investigated by the Downey Inquiry.

Though McIsaac stood aside from adjudicating on Brown, she adjudicated on Sir Michael Grylls and Neil Hamilton, who had each been accused of an exactly similar alleged offence to Brown, namely the non-registration of a commission fee granted by lobbyist Ian Greer for the introduction of business. She endorsed Downey's report.

John MAJOR

Tory MP and the Prime Minister at time of 'cash for questions' scandal. He received two visits from Fayed's emissary, *Sunday Express* editor Brian Hitchen, relating Fayed's demands for the withdrawal of the DTI report and the granting of his passport. Major refused to give in to Fayed's demands to intervene in either. He appointed Sir Gordon Downey to investigate Fayed's subsequent allegations.

Melvyn MARCKUS

City editor on Tiny Rowland's *Observer* who, along with Michael Gillard and Lorana Sullivan, uncovered the Fayed brothers' true past.

Doug MARVIN

Fayed's long-serving American, Washington-based lawyer. He sent to Downey his signed statement claiming that, a few days before the libel trial was due to begin in September 1996, he happened to be in London on business concerning Harrods. Marvin stated that, whilst he was discussing the libel case with *Guardian* lawyers Geraldine Proudler and Geoffrey Robertson QC, it occurred to him that Fayed's employees might have been involved in paying Neil Hamilton 'cash in brown envelopes'. Marvin then claimed to have had his theory confirmed when he subsequently interviewed Iris Bond, Alison Bozek and Philip Bromfield.

Marvin's explanation for Fayed's employees' late emergence is fundamentally different to the accounts given by Alan Rusbridger in his oral evidence before Downey, and David Leigh & Ed Vulliamy in *Sleaze*.

Despite this, Downey accepted Marvin's explanation uncritically, though he did not call him to give evidence before his Inquiry.

John MULLIN

Guardian journalist who, in July 1993, along with David Hencke, spent a few days investigating Andrew Roth's theory that lobbyist Ian Greer's commission payments were covert payments to three MPs on the Conservative back-bench Trade and Industry Committee, to reward them for parliamentary services rendered.

Despite being one of the two journalists who questioned Neil Hamilton during the crucial interview on July 22 1993, Mullin did not make a witness statement for the 1996 libel trial, nor did he make a written statement for the Downey Inquiry, nor did Downey call Mullin to testify before the Inquiry.

The only document put forward by the *Guardian* to support its contention that the 'cash in brown envelopes' allegation against Neil Hamilton existed in 1993, is a computer note made by Mullin from his shorthand notes. This bears six strong hallmarks of forged amendment, made subsequently, to show that a 'cash in brown envelope' allegation had been put to Hamilton during the interview. In fact, this document is the only document, including Hencke's and Preston's 1995 witness statements, that records that a 'cash in brown envelopes' allegation existed before September 1996, which was when the allegation was first made. It first emerged when Alan Rusbridger presented it to Downey on 19 February 1997, over halfway through his Inquiry.

Alan Rusbridger put forward another false document in Mullin's name, this time an 'affidavit', in which Mullin purportedly states that he asked Neil Hamilton about 'cash for questions' during the 1993 interview. This too first emerged when Rusbridger submitted it over half-way through the Inquiry. Acting at the request of Hunt & Keith-Hill, Hamilton wrote to Downey to have the veracity of this 'affidavit' checked. Downey's reply confirmed that it had not been sworn, nor dated, nor signed, nor even written by John Mullin, but that it had been prepared by someone else in Mullin's name. A few weeks later Downey claimed to have received Mullin's authentication of this document, after being forced by Hamilton to require Rusbridger to supply it. However, John Mullin's position remains unclear.

Despite Rusbridger's late submission of these two documents; despite the fact that they were both submitted in Mullin's name though Mullin gave no evidence to the Inquiry; despite the fact that Mullin did not authenticate them for the Inquiry as being his own unadulterated work; and despite the fact that both are false, Downey accepted at face value Rusbridger's endorsement of their authenticity, and then Downey cited them in his summing up.

Richard NEW
Private investigator who was employed by Mohamed Fayed to facilitate his personal feud with Tiny Rowland.

In June 1986 New 'enrolled' Francesca Pollard to act on Mohamed Fayed's behalf as a disseminator of false and defamatory allegations, in letters that New and Michael Cole had written and then addressed and copied widely to Fayed's actual and perceived critics in Parliament and elsewhere. Many of these letters carried Pollard's signature, which had been forged by New without Pollard's knowledge or consent.

Richard New also researched and produced a document titled 'Fair cop Fuhrhop' [Fuhrhop was Tiny Rowland's original German family name], which contained a highly defamatory account of Rowland's family background and alleged activities. Pollard was instructed by New and Fayed to distribute this document at all opportunities.

Timothy O'SULLIVAN
Friend of Neil Hamilton. He was present during one of only two occasions when Mohamed Fayed alleged that he had paid Neil Hamilton £1,000 in gift vouchers. O'Sullivan signed a statement refuting that such a transaction had taken place, and made plain his preparedness to give evidence on oath in the libel action. Hamilton produced this in his submission to the Inquiry, but Downey did not call O'Sullivan to testify.

Nigel PLEMING QC
Counsel for the Downey Inquiry, responsible for oral examination of witnesses. He exposed a multitude of discrepancies in the testimonies of: Mohamed Fayed and his staff Alison Bozek, Iris Bond, Philip Bromfield, and *Guardian* staff Alan Rusbridger, Peter Preston, and David Hencke.

Downey did not allude to any of these discrepancies in his report.

Francesca POLLARD
Distant relative of both Michael Howard and Harry Landy.

Pollard had stood to inherit £8 million from the business that her grandfather founded, the Israel British Bank. The bank collapsed in the early 1970s after being subjected to a massive fraud which Harry Landy was convicted of perpetrating. Landy had his conviction quashed on appeal, on a technicality, and later became a senior executive in a company owned by Tiny Rowland's Lonrho.

Pollard subsequently allied herself in early 1987 with Mohamed Fayed against Rowland in a pact to recover her inheritance. This involved disseminating highly defamatory letters and propaganda against, and harassment of, Tiny Rowland and other of Fayed's perceived enemies and critics in Parliament and elsewhere.

She alleges that almost all of the letters and other material that Fayed sent out in her name were written by Fayed's private detective Richard New and Fayed's PR man Michael Cole, overseen by Fayed's legal adviser, Royston Webb. Many of these letters carried her forged signature and were sent out without her knowledge.

She split from Fayed in June 1991 after refusing Fayed's orders to harass Robin Maxwell-Hyslop MP; refusing to put her name to a book about Tiny Rowland that Richard New had written; and after refusing Fayed's other demands. She recanted all her allegations against Tiny Rowland in an affidavit dated 28 June 1991. This contains references to MPs whom Fayed considered to be his friends or potential sympathisers, including: Tim Smith, Sir Peter Hordern, Dale Campbell-Savours, Leon Britten, Norman Tebbit, Bryan Gould, Neil Kinnock, Austin Mitchell, Dennis Skinner, Peter Robinson, Sir Edward Heath, and an adviser to Margaret Thatcher, Sir Gordon Reece. Pollard made no reference to Neil Hamilton.

In support of Hamilton, Pollard wrote to Downey and offered to testify before his Inquiry, but Downey did not call her nor did he reveal that she had offered to testify. Pollard also alleges that Alison Bozek lied on crucial points in her testimony before the Downey Inquiry.

Peter PRESTON

Editor of the *Guardian* since 1975, replaced by Alan Rusbridger on 1 January 1995, two months after David Hencke's original article was published. He is a former Chairman of the Association of British Editors and World Chairman of the International Press Institute.

After being contacted by Mohamed Fayed in June 1993, he instigated and oversaw the *Guardian*'s investigation into Ian Greer's lobbying company IGA; Greer's convention of giving commission payments to people who introduced business to his company; and Greer's relationship with Fayed's Tory sympathisers on the Conservative back-bench Trade and Industry Committee.

Preston claims that Fayed made his cash and gift voucher allegations against Neil Hamilton in July 1993, when Fayed first contacted the *Guardian*. The evidence supports overwhelmingly the contention that he lied on this and on other issues before the Downey Inquiry.

Geraldine PROUDLER

Formerly a partner in the *Guardian*'s long-standing solicitors Lovell

White Durrant, and an expert in libel actions. She moved to another law firm, Olswangs, on 31 July 1995, after working a year's notice.

Between October 1994 and October 1996, under Alan Rusbridger's direction, she prepared the *Guardian*'s defence to Ian Greer and Neil Hamilton's consolidated (i.e.joint) libel actions. She also prepared the *Guardian*'s submissions to the Downey Inquiry that followed.

Her role in the late emergence of Fayed's employees Alison Bozek, Iris Bond and Philip Bromfield, as told by Alan Rusbridger before the Downey Inquiry and David Leigh & Ed Vulliamy in the *Guardian*'s book: *Sleaze: the corruption of Parliament*, does not accord with the explanation given by Fayed's U.S. lawyer, Doug Marvin, in Marvin's letter to Downey.

Graham RIDDICK

Former Tory MP who, along with David Tredinnick, was named by the *Sunday Times* as having agreed to take £1,000 to put down a written Parliamentary question in a *Sunday Times* 'sting' operation. This was published in July 1994, three months ahead of the *Guardian*'s 'cash for questions' article.

(Unlike Tredinnick, Riddick insists that he had agreed only in principle to becoming a consultant. However, Riddick decided against this and returned the *Sunday Times* cheque within 24 hours of receiving it. Riddick claimed that the *Sunday Times* falsely reported the arrangement that their undercover reporters proposed. Although the *Sunday Times* reporters admitted tape-recording their conversations with Riddick, they 'lost' the tape that would have shown who was telling the truth.)

Professor Barry RIDER

Adviser to the 1989 Trade and Industry Select Committee, which studied the powers and procedures of DTI investigations. He became subject of a smear campaign by Fayed, including the leaking of false allegations to the Press. Fayed also intended that Francesca Pollard should send him defamatory letters written by Richard New. After writing to Hamilton in support, Rider wrote to Downey and gave information about Fayed's vendetta against him. Downey reprinted this, but he did not allude to Rider's comments in his report.

Rider is now Director of the Institute for Advanced Legal Studies and a fellow of Jesus College, Cambridge.

Andrew ROTH

Journalist, *New Statesman* columnist, former *Manchester Evening News* lobby corespondent and an occasional *Guardian* contributor. He is also a long-standing friend of *Guardian* journalist David Leigh, who is the principal author of the *Guardian*'s 1997 book on the 'cash for questions' affair: *Sleaze: the corruption of Parliament.*

In 1989, Roth published a book on MPs' parliamentary and business interests, *Parliamentary Profiles*, in which he publicised luridly lobbyist Ian Greer's commission payments to the chairman of the Conservative back-bench Trade and Industry Committee, Sir Michael Grylls, which Grylls had been granted for introducing clients to Greer's company, IGA. Roth implied that Grylls commissions were linked to the parliamentary support he gave to certain of Greer's clients, implying that they were really covert payments for his support. The publication of his book led to a private meeting between Roth and Dale Campbell-Savours MP, which, in turn, led to Campbell-Savours persuading his colleagues on the Members' Interests Committee to investigate Greer's commissions to Grylls. Ian Greer later appeared before the Committee. Without naming them, he disclosed that three MPs in total had received his commissions. Roth believed this strengthened his theory that they were corrupt payments to MPs, for delivering parliamentary services to the lobbyist.

Roth's theory was adopted by the *Guardian* three years later when, in July 1993, Mohamed Fayed alleged to *Guardian* editor Peter Preston that his own lobbyist, Ian Greer, had paid the secretary of the back-bench Trade and Industry Committee, Tim Smith, to put down sympathetic questions in Parliament. Fayed also alleged that Greer had organised a visit by the committee's vice-chairman, Neil Hamilton, to the Paris Ritz, which Fayed owned. This led Roth and the *Guardian* to speculate that the three unidentified MPs to receive commissions, which they believed were disguised illicit payments, were three of Fayed's sympathisers who sat on the Conservative back-bench Trade and Industry Committee namely: Sir Michael Grylls, Tim Smith, and Neil Hamilton.

When Tim Smith resigned after the *Guardian*'s original article came out on 20 October 1994, Roth wrote in the *New Statesman* that Smith's resignation proved that Smith was one of the three unnamed MPs to whom Greer, in 1990, revealed he had granted commission payments. But Smith was **not** one of the three MPs to receive a commission payment from Greer. Smith resigned because he had been paid by Fayed himself, thus destroying Roth's and the *Guardian*'s theory. The three MPs to receive commission payments from Greer were actually: Sir Michael Grylls, Neil Hamilton, and **Michael Brown**. However, Smith gave an unclear statement to accompany his resignation, which gave the impression to Roth, the *Guardian*, and the rest of the media, that the *Guardian*'s allegation that Greer had paid Smith was true.

Though Roth's and the *Guardian*'s theory were totally discredited by the fact that Smith had never received a commission payment from Ian

Greer and by the fact that Michael Brown had never given any support to Fayed, Roth nevertheless appeared on a *Guardian* co-produced *"Dispatches"* TV documentary to expound on his other dark theories about Ian Greer and his lobbying methods.

It seems probable that Roth, being the originator of the *Guardian*'s failed theory and also a close friend of David Leigh, is well aware of the *Guardian*'s cover-up.

Geoffrey **ROBERTSON** QC

The *Guardian*'s Leading Counsel. He worked closely with Geraldine Proudler in preparing the *Guardian*'s defence to Ian Greer and Neil Hamilton's libel action and the *Guardian*'s submissions to the Downey Inquiry.

The role of Robertson in the late emergence of Fayed's employees, two years after the original allegations, as told by David Leigh & Ed Vulliamy in their book: *Sleaze: the corruption of Parliament*, does not accord with the explanation given by Fayed's American lawyer Doug Marvin, in Marvin's letter to Sir Gordon Downey.

Roland 'Tiny' **ROWLAND** (deceased 25.7.98)

Born of a German father and English mother in India, he was formerly the Chief Executive of Lonrho – the controversial London-based conglomerate with large trading interests in Africa, including Libya.

Lonrho was investigated in the mid 1970s by the Department of Trade and Industry under the Conservative government of Edward Heath, after Heath branded the company the 'unacceptable face of capitalism'. The DTI report was a devastating indictment of Lonrho and of Rowland's stewardship of the company. Rowland rejected vehemently the DTI investigation and bore a grudge against the Tories ever since.

Rowland/Lonrho acquired the world's oldest Sunday newspaper, the *Observer* in 1981. When his plan to buy Harrods was thwarted by Mohamed Fayed in 1985, he dispatched journalists from the *Observer* to investigate Fayed's background. Their investigations coupled to overt attacks in the *Observer* on Margaret Thatcher persuaded the Tory government to undertake a DTI investigation, which subsequently vindicated the *Observer* journalists' findings.

Mounting losses, coupled to Parliamentary criticism led by Dale Campbell-Savours over Rowland's editorial interference, pressed Lonrho into selling the *Observer* to the *Guardian* for £27 million on 1 June 1993. The *Guardian* had wanted to buy the *Observer* for years.

In December 1995, Rowland's safe-deposit box in Harrods' basement was broken into by Mohamed Fayed and John MacNamara. Rowland filed theft charges against a host of Fayed employees, including Fayed and MacNamara. The Metropolitan Police subsequently arrested Fayed, MacNamara and other Fayed employees on 2 and 3 March 1998 on suspicion of theft. On 20 July 1998 the police dropped the charges on the grounds that it was Fayed's word against Rowland's whether any of his box's contents were actually stolen.

Less than a week later in the London Clinic, Tiny Rowland died of skin cancer aged 80, having failed to see Fayed brought to justice for any of his misdemeanours.

Alan RUSBRIDGER

He replaced Peter Preston as editor of the *Guardian* on 1 January 1995, after being appointed by Guardian Media Group's owners, the secretive Scott Trust. He was nominated twice for *Editor of the Year*, in his first year in the post.

Rusbridger subsequently oversaw the *Guardian*'s defence to Ian Greer and Neil Hamilton's joint libel action, and also the *Guardian*'s submissions to Sir Gordon Downey's investigation into Fayed's 'cash for questions' allegations.

Rusbridger's heavy involvement shows him to be the ringmaster of the cover-up to create the false impression that Fayed made his cash and gift voucher allegations against Hamilton in 1993, when Fayed's false allegations that Ian Greer had paid Tim Smith led the paper to try and substantiate its theory about Greer's commission payments. However, exhaustive scrutiny of the evidence shows that Fayed actually related his cash and gift voucher allegations against Hamilton in September 1994, when the European Court ruling had built Fayed's resentment up to the point that he was prepared to make false allegations against the two Corporate Affairs ministers connected with the DTI report Michael Howard and Neil Hamilton plus two other ministers.

In this regard Rusbridger personally submitted false documents to the Downey Inquiry. The evidence suggests overwhelmingly that he also gave false testimony and knowingly allowed false testimony to be given by his staff to the Inquiry.

Regarding the late emergence of Fayed employees Bond, Bozek and Bromfield, Rusbridger claimed that the *Guardian*'s lawyers had requested interviews with Fayed's employees for some time, but that it took the persuasion of Fayed's American lawyer, Doug Marvin, to make Fayed change his mind and grant access.

This is fundamentally different to the explanation given by Doug Marvin in Marvin's letter to Sir Gordon Downey.

The evidence supports overwhelmingly the contention that Alan Rusbridger lied on this and a host of other issues throughout the Downey Inquiry.

Richard **RYDER**

John Major's Chief Whip at the height of Fayed's war against the Tories. After Brian Hitchen had communicated Fayed's allegations to Major, Ryder informed Hamilton that Fayed claimed to have evidence to support his allegations, and he warned that this could include tape-recordings of their private meetings. Hamilton denied that he had done anything which, if recorded, could be incriminating.

When the *Guardian* printed Fayed's allegations the next day, Hamilton issued libel writs against the *Guardian* and Fayed in full knowledge of Ryder's warning. No evidence has been produced yet of the kind that Ryder feared.

Robert **SHELDON**

Veteran Labour MP, and Chairman of the 1997 Select Committee on Standards, which considered Sir Gordon Downey's report on the 'cash for questions' affair.

He is also a personal friend of Sir Gordon Downey, from the period they worked closely together when Sheldon was Chairman of the Public Accounts Committee and Downey was Chairman of the National Audit Office.

Sheldon fought hard to obtain unanimity among the members of the Committee, but Tory members Quentin Davies and Ann Widdecombe steadfastly refused to endorse Downey's report. Nevertheless, Sheldon was reported in the *Guardian* as having said that the Committee voted "9–0, he took the cash". Ann Widdecombe resigned subsequently in protest at Sheldon's misrepresentation of her vote.

Following the Committee's rejection of Hamilton's address, which Hamilton had given on oath, during which he denied all the central allegations, Sheldon agreed with a proposition put by BBC journalist Jim Hancock, that this amounted to charging Hamilton with lying on oath. In the Commons debate that followed, Sheldon stated: "*He* [Hamilton] *accuses of lying Mr Al Fayed, Mr MacNamara, Mr Webb, Mr Cole, Ms Bond, Ms Bozek, Mr Bromfield, Mr Preston, Mr Hencke and Mr Mullin. Mr Hamilton says that all these people are liars and he is not*".

However, Sir Gordon Downey rejected the evidence and the offers to testify from eight witnesses who supported Hamilton and who questioned the evidence of Fayed, MacNamara, Webb, Cole, Bond, Bozek, and Bromfield. Downey also discounted the evidence of another witness who questioned the evidence of David Hencke.

Furthermore, Sheldon himself rejected the explicit offer from Jonathan Hunt and Malcolm Keith-Hill to appear before the committee to present evidence showing that Peter Preston and David Hencke had lied before the Inquiry and that Alan Rusbridger had put forward evidence in John Mullin's name that was false and which had not been authenticated by Mullin as being his own unadulterated work.

Professor Sir Roland SMITH

Former Chief Executive of House of Fraser, prior to and during its acquisition by Ali and Mohamed Fayed. He recommended the Fayed brothers' offer for House of Fraser.

Shortly after the Fayed brothers acquired House of Fraser, he resigned his post with a severance settlement.

Tim SMITH

Tory MP up to May 1 1997; a former officer of the Conservative Back-Bench Trade and Industry Committee; and a former junior Northern Ireland minister up to October 1994. After Labour MP Dale Campbell-Savours, Smith was Fayed's most active sympathiser in Parliament, having initiated an adjournment debate and having put down 25 written Parliamentary questions and one Parliamentary motion; asked one oral question; and joined all four of Sir Peter Horden's delegations to ministers. He resigned his ministerial post after the *Guardian* published Mohamed Fayed's allegations that he had been paid to ask questions in Parliament by Fayed's lobbyist Ian Greer. But Smith did not resign because he had been paid by Greer. Smith resigned because he had been paid by Fayed himself face-to-face which had not been alleged by Fayed nor the *Guardian*. However, Smith only admitted this allegation privately to John Major, thus creating the impression that the *Guardian*'s allegations against Ian Greer and Neil Hamilton were true.

Lorana SULLIVAN

American journalist on Tiny Rowland's *Observer* who, with colleagues Michael Gillard and Melvyn Marckus, and freelance journalist Peter Wickman, uncovered the Fayed brothers' true past. Sullivan's and her colleagues' research was vindicated by the DTI Inspectors' report, which was published in March 1990.

John SWEENEY

Journalist on the *Observer*; Neil Hamilton's most dogged critic; and a close friend of Martin Bell. Sweeney's animus towards Hamilton appears to stem from Hamilton's lampooning of Fascist dictators during his student days at Aberystwyth, and from a comic two-fingered-moustache gesture that Hamilton made during a visit of MPs to the German Reichstag in 1983. Though Sweeney was scathing in his criticism of Hamilton's role in the 'cash for questions' affair, Sweeney's own lack of involvement in the *Guardian*'s campaign was demonstrated when Jonathan Hunt asked him if he could remember how many oral questions that Hamilton had asked in the House, in support of Fayed. Sweeney confessed that he couldn't remember the exact number (the answer is nil).

Elizabeth SWINDIN
Ian Greer's former secretary. Fayed employee Iris Bond testified that she had, on occasion, dispatched, by courier, packages containing cash to Ian Greer's offices. Bond also testified that Elizabeth Swindin had telephoned on occasion requesting Ian Greer's cash payments. Swindin sent Downey her statement making clear that she dealt with all incoming mail and packages and had never received a package containing cash from anyone. Swindin also denied that she had ever made telephone calls to Bond requesting cash for Ian Greer. Downey did not call Swindin to testify before the Inquiry.

David TREDINNICK
Tory MP who was induced into agreeing to take £1,000 to put down a written Parliamentary question, in a *Sunday Times* 'sting' operation published in July 1994, three months ahead of the *Guardian*'s 'cash for questions' story.

Baroness TURNER (of Camden)
Labour Peeress. Former trade unionist and a director of Ian Greer's lobbying company, Ian Greer Associates, at the time that the *Guardian*'s 'cash for questions' allegations against Ian Greer were published in October 1994. She was Tony Blair's front-bench employment spokesman in the House of Lords, until Blair made her stand down following the *Guardian*'s allegations against Greer.

Subsequently, she became victim of an anonymous hate-mail campaign, and was also subjected to a torrent of unsolicited mail-order goods. She remains a staunch supporter of Ian Greer. Though she is a strong advocate of Press freedom, she campaigns vigorously for the appointment of a Press Ombudsman, independent of the Press, to whom aggrieved parties can complain.

Ed VULLIAMY
Guardian journalist and co-author, along with colleague David Leigh, of *Sleaze: the corruption of Parliament*. This book gives a wholly misleading account of the 'cash for questions' affair and contains a false story to explain the late emergence of the three Fayed employees: Bond, Bozek and Bromfield.

Vulliamy is also a friend of Martin Bell from their time together in

Bosnia, and was sent by Alan Rusbridger, along with Leigh, to Tatton to advise Martin Bell during the election campaign.

Vulliamy did not make any statement for the libel trial nor did Downey require him to appear before his Inquiry. It is rumoured he has become ill at ease about the *Guardian*'s reporting of the 'cash for questions' affair, and his role therein.

Royston **WEBB**

Fayed's legal advisor from 1985 30 September 1996. According to Francesca Pollard, he oversaw the drafting of intimidating and defamatory letters against Fayed's critics in Parliament and elsewhere, which had been written by Richard New or Michael Cole and disseminated as if they were from Pollard.

Webb also provided drafts of Parliamentary questions and Parliamentary motions (Early Day Motions or EDMs) to Ian Greer to present to Fayed's Tory sympathisers to adopt. He also met Fayed's most active sympathiser, Labour MP Dale Campbell-Savours, in private, regularly, and drafted many of the eleven pro-Fayed/anti-Lonrho questions and fifty-eight motions that Campbell-Savours put down.

After leaving Fayed's employ, Fayed retained Webb up to September 2001 for an undisclosed fee, reported to be £1 million payable at £200,000 per annum.

In 1994 Webb expressed no knowledge of Fayed paying Hamilton anything. In 1997 he claimed before the Downey Inquiry that he knew all along that Hamilton was paid. Downey did not question Webb's change in testimony and instead accepted his evidence. Downey also accepted Webb as a character reference for Fayed employees Alison Bozek and Iris Bond.

Ann **WIDDECOMBE**

One of three Tory MPs who sat on the 1997 Select Committee on Standards and Privileges, which deliberated Sir Gordon Downey's report on the 'cash for questions' affair. Known for her independent mind, she once famously savaged Conservative Home Secretary Michael Howard over the sacking of a civil servant. Along with fellow Tory Committee member Quentin Davies, Widdecombe refused to endorse Downey's report. She resigned from the Select Committee, in protest, after Chairman Robert Sheldon reneged on his earlier undertaking not to represent her stance as being an endorsement of Downey's report.

Yet, though she was one of only two highly-vocal dissenters on the Committee, Speaker Betty Boothroyd did not call her to speak during the Commons debate on Downey's report, November 17 1997.

Alan WILLIAMS

Long-standing Labour MP (for Swansea West), and a long-standing associate and friend of *Guardian* journalist, David Hencke. Williams has a track record of close liaison with Hencke, including putting down motions in Parliament based on Hencke's information, thus giving support to Hencke's articles in the *Guardian*. Williams also persuaded Neil Hamilton's opposite number, Labour MP Stuart Bell, to quote from Hencke's original article in the House on the eve of its appearance in the following morning's edition of the *Guardian,* on 20 Oct 1994.

Despite his close relationship with the very journalist at the heart of the *Guardian*'s campaign, whose testimony and evidence Neil Hamilton strenuously denied, Williams nevertheless sat on the 1997 Select Committee on Standards and Privileges, which deliberated Sir Gordon Downey's report.

Jamie WILSON

Guardian journalist whom Alan Rusbridger seconded to assist in the production of the Fulcrum Productions/*Guardian* co-produced documentary on the 'cash for questions' affair. This was broadcast by Channel 4's *"Dispatches"* on 16. 1. 97, less than a week before Downey started oral examination of witnesses. It replicated exactly the *Guardian*'s final story, and replicated exactly the *Guardian*'s style of journalism. Alan Rusbridger denied having any involvement at all with the production of the programme.